SOCIETY
TODAY

Based on
a series from
NEW SOCIETY

D1150836

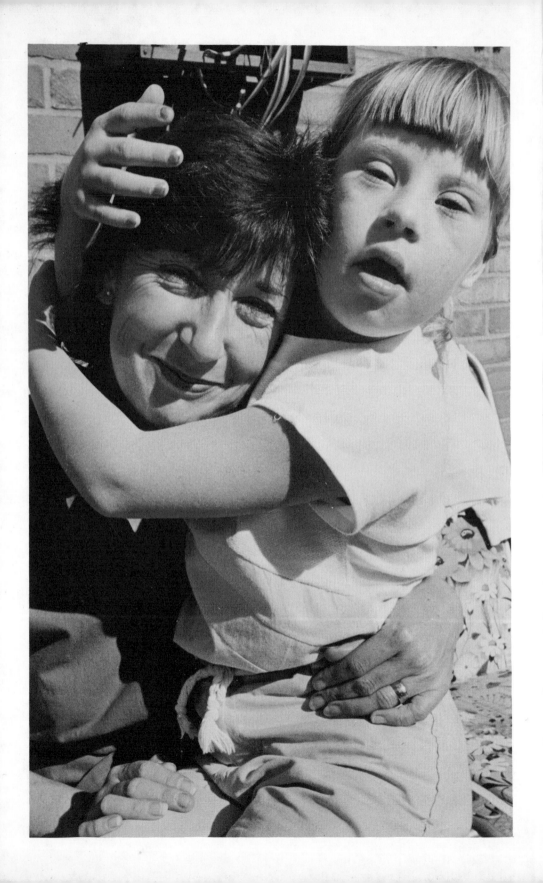

SOCIETY TODAY

Based on a series from NEW SOCIETY

Macmillan Education

ACKNOWLEDGEMENTS

The author and publishers wish to acknowledge the
following photograph sources:

British Tourist Board p. 89
Jim Brownbill p. 251
Central Office of Information (Crown copyright) pp. 19,
169
Ron Chapman pp. 67, 70, 115
Colorsport p.201
The Guardian p. 5
John and Penny Hubley p. 104
Imperial War Museum p. 229
Sheelah Latham cover, pp. 23, 153
By courtesy of the Metropolitan Police p. 127
Ministry of Defence p. 238
Swiss National Tourist Office p. 93
Dave Thomas p. 49
Viewpoint p. 2

The publishers have made every effort to trace the
copyright holders, but where they have failed to do so
they will be pleased to make the necessary arrangements
at the first opportunity.

First published 1986

Published by
MACMILLAN EDUCATION LTD
Houndmills, Basingstoke, Hampshire RG21 2XS
and London
Companies and representatives
throughout the world

Designed by Tony Garrett

Printed in Hong Kong

British Library Cataloguing in Publication Data
Williams, Michael
Society today.
1. Great Britain—Social conditions—1945–
I. Title
301'.0941   HN385.5

ISBN 0-333-42046-2

CONTENTS

INTRODUCTION

It's a fair while now since sociology has been politically fashionable, yet, paradoxically, the eighties have been a decade which has cried out for the special wisdom that social scientists can provide. The collapse of work, riots in the cities, famine in the Third World, the retreat of the unions, the changing structure of the family – all these things have made an important difference to the way in which we interpret the world.

There have been other, subtler changes, too. In going through the past six years of *Society Today* for this book, it has been striking how much the British consensus has changed in such a short time. Our expectations about the welfare state, for instance, have been reduced considerably since 1979. Labour relations look very different indeed in the wake of the miners' strike. More subtly still, there was a marked change in the public response to the urban riots of 1985 compared with those of 1981. The first riots evoked widespread concern and led to the enlightened report of Lord Scarman. Four years later, the attitude had hardened – to become very much one of "crime must be punished."

In all this, the aim of *Society Today* has remained the same – to interpret changes in society, set them in context, and to present them in terms that the lay person can easily understand. In some respects technical language in sociology is unavoidable, but sociologists have rarely made it easy for others. The great expansion of sociology as an academic subject in the 1960s brought a wider audience but, paradoxically, an even greater mystification of the subject. Such exclusivity has done nothing to diminish the bad press of recent years.

This is unfortunate, since a good deal of the wisdom of sociologists has been overlooked or ignored. Even the founding fathers of the nineteenth century can tell us a lot about today's society. Marx, though less fashionable in the west, remains undimmed in world politics.

Durkheim would have had some pertinent comments on recent events in Toxteth and Brixton. And Weber would very well have understood the ideology that underpins Mrs Thatcher's Britain or Ronald Reagan's America.

A very important part of *Society Today*'s role, too, has been to project the work of contemporary British sociologists, the best of whose work stands comparison with research in other more favoured disciplines. Among the names that crop up repeatedly in these pages are A. H. Halsey on education, Anthony Giddens on stratification, John Goldthorpe on mobility, Peter Hall on cities, Howard Newby on the countryside, Peter Willmott and Michael Young on communities, Peter Townsend on poverty, the Glasgow University Media Group on television, Ivor Crewe on the changing demography of Britain. And there are many more.

Finally, a word about the book itself. In a sense, it is *Society Today*'s "greatest hits" – fifty of the most important themes of the series, revised and updated. But it does not claim to be an exhaustive insight into society's problems, nor is it a crib for passing sociology exams. Rather, its aim is to serve as an introduction to the key issues in society, as a handbook to help the reader get a little bit deeper under the skin of the way we live now.

I would particularly like to thank the following people for their advice and contributions during the years of my editorship from 1979 to 1985: Martin Slattery of St Augustine of Canterbury School, Knowsley; Pat McNeill, of St Albans College; Professor Denis Lawton, Director of London University Institute of Education; Peter Hamilton, of the Open University; David Walker, Social Policy Correspondent of *The Times*; Martin Kettle, leader writer with *The Guardian*; David White, former staff writer with *New Society*; Tom Forester, former Labour Correspondent of *New Society*; Peter Wilby, Education Correspondent of

The Sunday Times; Roger Gomm, of West Herts College; John Morrison of ITN; Caroline St John-Brooks, Education Correspondent of *New Society*; Marion Giordan, of the Electricity Consumer's Council; Richard Bourne, Deputy Director of the Commonwealth Institute; Joy Melville, former Assistant Editor of *New Society* and Peter Baistow of *The Sunday Times*.

I would also like to thank the hundreds of readers who wrote in or phoned up with ideas. These were all put to good use in the end.

for Stella

ADVERTISING

"The irritator, the deliverer of half-truths, the uninformer, the disrespectors of persons, the social blackmailer . . ."

This is how Robin Wight characterises advertising in his book about the advertising business, *The Day the Pigs Refused to be Driven to Market.* Wight is an advertising man himself, and today runs a successful agency. But in this whistle-blowing book published in 1972, he puts into words what many people in modern society think of advertising.

That is, if they think about advertising at all. Recently the Advertising Association, advertising's corporate "voice," carried out a survey of people's attitudes to advertising. It found that most people hardly bothered about it. Only 2 per cent thought that major changes should be made to advertising (compared with 34 per cent who thought that there should be major changes in the government of the country). Most people are well disposed towards advertising. Three quarters of the sample said they approved of advertising; ten years ago, the proportion was two thirds.

When advertising is attacked, it is usually by an articulate and influential minority of opinion-formers. Advertising's critics have included economists like John Kenneth Galbraith, writers like Raymond Williams and consumerists like Charles Medawar.

Their criticisms fall into three main categories:

● *Economic:* Advertising is costly and wasteful.

● *Cultural:* Advertising is vulgar and materialist.

● *Social:* Advertising is conformist and often reactionary.

Of course, much advertising is entirely uncontroversial. The classified ads in the local paper and the "for sale" card in the shop window are both fairly innocent forms of advertising. Advertising also includes "socially useful" government advertising; public service advertisements like the Central Office of Information's "Clunk Click" campaign to encourage drivers to use seat belts.

The target for criticism is "manufacturers' consumer advertising." That is, the national selling, through television, press

and posters, of mass-produced goods like washing powder, baked beans and lager. Invariably, there is competition between two different brands of the same product. Manufacturers' consumer advertising accounts for between a third and 40 per cent of the total amount spent on advertising. Currently advertising expenditure totals more than £2800 million a year.

Is this a waste of money? It depends how you look at it. For the manufacturer, money is only wasted if it doesn't help sell his product. The soap magnate, Lord Leverhulme, used to say that half of the money he spent on advertising was wasted – only he didn't know which half.

In relative terms, advertising isn't expensive. Cadbury Schweppes have estimated that advertising represents only 4 per cent of the cost of a product. Yet even 4 per cent may be too large if the consumer has to pay for it. Some economists believe that advertising raises the price of goods. This idea got powerful backing from the Monopolies Commission in 1966, when it told the two washing powder giants, Unilever and Procter & Gamble, to reduce the volume of advertising on household detergents.

The advertising industry rejects the charge that advertising raises prices. On the contrary, it says, advertising keeps prices down and may even lower them. The theory is that advertising increases turnover and so reduces unit costs. Broadly, this is what happens. But there is a ceiling to this reduction in costs; above it, advertising is used merely to maintain a manufacturer's share of the market. If Unilever were to reduce advertising spending *unilaterally*, it would lose sales to its rival, Proctor & Gamble.

One way of breaking this deadlock, perhaps, is to make advertising expensive to the manufacturer. The economist and former government adviser, Nicholas Kaldor, suggested a tax on advertising shortly after the war. During the Heath government of 1970 to 1974, an advertising tax actually became Labour party policy. In 1975, the Nobel Prize-winning economist, James Meade, added his voice to the call for an advertising tax.

Meade distinguishes between advertis-ing which informs and advertising which persuades: "Much advertising of an informative nature is desirable and necessary," he says in his book, *The Intelligent Radical's Guide to Economic Policy: the mixed economy*. "But much advertisement is not of this kind. A tax on advertisement would increase the incentive for firms to seek markets by cutting prices rather than persuasive bamboozlement."

A bamboozlement which was aided, its critics said, by pseudo-science. In the late 1950s, Vance Packard "exposed" the work of motivational psychologists in advertising in his bestselling book, *The Hidden Persuaders*. The most notorious was Dr Ernest Dichter. Dichter applied Gestalt theory to advertising. "When a woman buys a bar of soap, she isn't thinking about soap," he said. "She's thinking about bathtime."

This was the extent of Dichter's "manipulation" – discovering people's feelings about manufactured products. Today, motivational research is still used; but it is merely one of a number of tools available to advertisers. And it no longer makes the public's flesh creep.

Yet is there a clear distinction between information and "persuasive bamboozlement"? Most critics of newspapers and news values would emphatically deny it. Patricia Mann, head of external affairs at the advertising agency, J. Walter Thompson, says that "it might be interesting to speculate whether 'WARNING by HM Government: SMOKING CAN SERIOUSLY DAMAGE YOUR HEALTH' is regarded as informative or persuasive."

How much information do people want? The National Federation of Consumer Groups have proposed a system of "consumer information standards" – basic information about goods which allows people to make real choices between different makes; *Which?* magazine already does something like this. But it is obvious that people will want information about some things and not others – for instance, detailed information about washing machines, but not about toilet soap.

Trying to make a distinction between information and persuasion is like distinguishing between "necessary" and "unnecessary" packaging. Who is to say that packaging is "unnecessary" if it helps sell the goods? And what is "necessary" packaging? Cheap packaging? The plain packaging of cheaper brands costs only marginally less than fancy packaging. Its message to the consumer ("this is a sensible buy for a sensible, cost-conscious person") is more important than any saving in packaging costs.

It could be argued that advertising wastes not only money but skills. For advertising is a skilled business. Aldous Huxley said so in 1932: "No one should be allowed to talk about the *mot juste* or the polishing of style who has not tried his hand at writing an advertisement of something which the public does not want."

Surveys suggest that most people think that advertisements on television are entertaining. It has become a cliché to say that they are better than the programmes themselves. Maurice Healy, of the National Consumer Council's consumer policy unit, thinks that they ought to be since so much money and talent had been poured into them. But he argues that we enjoy these ads regardless of what they are selling. "No one, I think would question the enormous visual variety that advertising brings into our lives or the fact that it is very often brilliant," he points out in the book *Marketing and the Consumer Movement* (1978). "People do place a value on this. . . We do this not because we value the message but because we value the expression of it."

Again, the advertising business doubts whether you can make this distinction. A good ad implies a good product. Advertising creates a "warm feeling" towards what is advertised. Robin Wight, for example, suggests that a clever advertisement makes the consumer well-disposed to a product when he or she next encounters it.

A more serious criticism of advertising is that it persuades people to waste their money; to buy things they don't want and don't need. Advertising, it is claimed, wastes scarce resources because it encourages irrational consumption.

This is the substance of Galbraith's attack on advertising in his book, *The Affluent Society*. It was published in 1958, and the advertising industry has been rebutting it ever since.

Galbraith believes that once people have satisfied their minimum needs (like shelter and warmth) they start looking for "false wants." They move from essentials to inessentials. The motivational psychologist, Abraham Maslow, saw this as a "hierarchy of needs."

At the level of minimum needs, Galbraith says, advertising won't affect us. Advertising has little to do with a decision to buy a house. Only at the level of "false wants" does advertising come into play. In short, the more trivial our wants the more likely we are to be manipulated.

Galbraith thinks that this manipulation is wasteful because it persuades us to buy the wrong things. It produces an irrational pattern of consumption. This, say his critics, is what he's really getting at. Galbraith thinks people consume irrationally. But he cannot say so directly. Instead he attacks the process by which, he claims, people are persuaded to consume irrationally.

Understandably, the advertising business denies that it "creates wants" (false or otherwise). But it happily admits that it "adds values" to the goods we buy.

The phrase "added value" was coined by Martin Mayer in his account of American advertising in the late 1960s, *Madison Avenue USA*. According to Mayer, advertising "adds a new value to the existing values of the product."

There may be no difference between two brands of lipstick. But a girl will feel ordinary wearing one, beautiful wearing the other. Advertising has added a value to the second brand.

A margarine may be sold explicitly on its existing values: that it contains polyunsaturated fats, for example. It will also be sold implicitly on its added values: the suggestion, for example, that it is compatible with a jogging and yoghurt lifestyle.

Mayer says that this is the nearest advertising has got to producing a general theory: a model of how advertising actually works. Why will someone pay more for Brand A when it is identical to Brand B, but won't be persuaded to buy Brand A at the same price as Brand B if it is visibly an inferior product? The answer is added value. The added value is enough to make a brand seem worth a little more, but not enough to overcome an observable deficiency in the product.

The theory of "added value" may also explain why advertising is more successful in good times than in bad. Money, too, has a value. In bad times, the value of money saved outweighs the added values. People trade down.

For critics like Raymond Williams, added values are merely debased values. Advertisers contrive a bogus association of human values like love and respect with everyday things like soap and alcohol. They do this by means of "organised fantasy." The Martini advertisements present a good life of social and sexual success which can be acquired by buying a bottle of Martini.

Advertising agencies retort that people are fully aware that this *is* fantasy. Agencies ask consumers about advertisements. They find that they enjoy fantasy and feel they can handle it.

And yet advertising does insist, relentlessly, that the good life is a matter of goods. It is unashamedly materialist. The advertising industry answers that this is its job – to sell goods. Why should it have to defend itself against charges of materialism? Isn't the corner shop materialist?

It deals with charges of vulgarity in the same way. Of course advertising is vulgar, the advertising business says. "Vulgar" means appealing to the maximum number of people; that is what manufacturers pay advertisers to do.

Most magazines and newspapers, television shows, films and paperbacks are vulgar in this sense. The difference is that the person of sensitivity can keep all these out of his life. He cannot keep out advertising. As Martin Mayer points out, "by presenting the intellectual with a more or less true image of the popular culture, advertising earns his enmity and calumny."

The third major objection to advertising is that it is conformist; that far from dealing in fantasy, it holds up a mirror to the world and reflects the *status quo*. The reflection, however, may be slightly distorted. The Britain of the advertisements is a white Britain. Black people appear only in commercials for Caribbean-style soft drinks. Policemen are invariably jovial, slightly comic bobbies. Grannies are grateful old dears.

In short, advertising deals in stereotypes. But it is in its treatment of women that advertising has attracted the greatest opprobrium. Women are sex objects or domestic slaves, the critics say. Most of the complaints the Advertising Standards Authority gets about "indecent" advertising concern nudity. Yet when the ASA did its own survey of nearly 3000 women aged between 18 and 74, it found that they weren't bothered about nudity.

The subordinate role of women in advertisements has been criticised by the women's liberation movement. They say that women are never shown outside the kitchen or the home; never shown in any role other than wife or mother. This is oppressive since it reinforces men's continuing domination.

Advertising is certainly an important part of women's socialisation process. In his study of advertising in women's magazines, *Images of Woman* (1975), Trevor Millum suggests that advertising moulds women's outlook. Advertisements "serve as a legitimation of those roles in which so many women find themselves." Advertising is therefore a form of social control, keeping women in their place.

Yet women themselves seem barely conscious of the process. The ASA survey findings "do not suggest wide support

BOOKS

Some useful additional reading:
Michael Barnes (ed.), *The Three Faces of Advertising,* Advertising Association, 1975
Erving Goffman, *Gender Advertisements,* Macmillan, 1979
Bryan Home, *Advertising,* Heinemann, 1982
Philip Kleinman, *Advertising Inside Out,* W. H. Allen, 1977
Herbert Marcuse, *One Dimensional Man,* Sphere, 1968

among the sample of women for the assertions about the effects of advertising on the status of women, which have become the stock-in-trade of some leaders of the campaign of women's liberation."

Yet the ASA chairman, Lord McGregor, hedges his bets by saying that small groups *can* work major changes in attitudes; the advertising industry should beware.

However, the advertising industry often feels that it is being held responsible for all the sins of modern society. Paperback romances reinforce the subordinate role of women quite as effectively as advertisements. Advertising can be a convenient Aunt Sally for people whose real target is harder to hit.

THE BLACK ECONOMY

Babysitting and bartending. Taxi driving and typing at home. Plumbing and prostitution. What do these widely different activities have in common?

They are jobs which are often done "off the books"; that is, without the Inland Revenue knowing about them. And they are usually done for cash rather than cheque payment.

These are the hallmarks of what has been variously described as the hidden economy, the underground economy, the subterranean economy, the irregular economy and – most commonly – the black economy.

Every country in the developed world, east and west, has its own black economy. In the Soviet Union, the black economy is as much a part of everyday life as queueing. And in Italy, the black economy is so substantial that it props up the official economy. It has been estimated that it adds almost a third to the gross national product.

Black economies are widespread. They also have a long pedigree. James Cornford, the director of the now defunct Outer Circle Policy Unit, suggests that the black economy in Britain is the survival of those patterns of "making out" which Mayhew, Wright and Booth recorded in their nineteenth-century surveys of the working class.

The difference today is that these patterns can be found at every level of society. What are perceived as high rates of personal taxation, and the high cost of living, have made everyone either a producer or a consumer of goods and services within the black economy. Everybody, as the saying goes, knows a plumber.

Is this a good or a bad thing? Society's attitude to the black economy is ambivalent. It condemns, to the extent that tax evasion by some increases the tax burden of others. It applauds, to the extent that a freedom from regulation encourages initiative and enterprise.

In broad terms, the black economy does represent valuable economic activity, whether or not it is legal. And if full employment is unlikely to return, society cannot afford to sniff at this activity. It will have to accommodate the black economy within a "culture of unemployment." In short, it will have to help rather than hinder people's attempts to "make out."

Much will depend on how we look at the black economy. The simplest view is of an alternative, a *shadow* of the official economy. Anything which isn't official is black. The problem with this view is that it lumps together jobs around the house with, say, "moonlighting." It treats father papering the parlour as part of the black economy – which clearly he isn't.

Social anthropologists of the workplace, like Gerald Mars of Middlesex Polytechnic, and Stuart Henry of Trent Polytechnic, have solved this by dividing the economy into six categories:
● Regular
● Informal

- Social
- Criminal
- Hidden
- Black

This scheme is comprehensive but complicated. It is probably easier to see the black economy, as Professor Louis Ferman of Michigan University does, as one of three economies: *regular, black* (irregular) and *social*.

The difference between the social and black economies is the method of payment. In the social economy, payment is in kind. "I'll paper the parlour if you wash the car." In the black economy, payment is in cash.

There is also a difference in the *sorts* of job that are done in the regular, black and social economies. The regular economy is the place for specialised, complex work. The social economy, however is the place for simple tasks. The black economy stands midway between the two.

Car maintenance provides a good illustration of this. The regular economy handles the major tasks like panel-beating or rebuilding after an accident. The black economy does the simpler overhauls, while the social economy is equipped to do only routine servicing.

There are others, like Professor R. E. Pahl of the University of Kent and J. I. Gershuny of Sussex University's Science Policy Research Unit, who see the relationship between the three economies as triangular rather than linear. There is, they say, a constant flow between the three. Goods produced in the regular economy are used in the social (or household) economy, and repaired or maintained in the black economy.

There is also a three-way movement in the demand for labour. For instance, if unemployment forces down the price of "black" construction works, households may prefer to pay for work to be done than to do it themselves. (This in turn depresses the demand for DIY goods produced by the regular sector.)

The definition of the black economy as a "cash-only" economy makes it, in theory, measurable. One way of finding out the size of the black economy is to measure the amount of excess cash in the

The cheats at work

One of the less acceptable features of the black economy is "fiddling." This, in fact, comes close to the borderline of theft. But, as the social anthropologist, Gerald Mars, has pointed out, fiddling is rife in society. Here are some of the commonest fiddles:

The shop fiddle
The most widespread fiddle in shops is under-ringing by cashiers. Cashiers may ring up less money in the till than they are actually taking from customers. The amounts are small, but they mount up over a day. Cashiers will keep a tally of the money they have made for themselves, using a pile of pins, matchsticks, even sweets. Every time a checkout girl pops a sweet in her mouth, she may be keeping a record of her "take." Shop owners also fiddle by under-ringing. They do this so that less money appears on the till roll and thus they are able to hide the full amount of their earnings from the inspector of taxes.

The taxi fiddle
Unscrupulous taxi drivers and cab owners often set their meters at "hired" when unhired so that they can look for profitable customers – wealthy tourists, for example. This is called "stalking." In this way, they can refuse to take anyone who isn't "profitable" – people who want to make short journeys, for example. They can also charge tourists wildly inflated prices, because the meter has already been running.

The garage fiddle
Most people know very little about car mechanics. So it is easy for garages to carry out unnecessary repairs, or charge for work that they haven't done. The commonest garage fiddle is the minimum service; that is, carrying out as little of a service as possible without detection. In this way, garages do half the work but charge for all of it. On top of this, a garage will do easy but unnecessary servicing – like replacing plugs and points. When these are added to the bill, they merely add credibility to the service. It *appears* that the garage has done a thorough service.

The buffet car fiddle
Staff in railway buffet cars bring their own milk, tea, coffee and sandwiches from home and sell them at a lower price than the official British Rail supplies. By selling at a lower price they increase trade and thus, though their action is illegal, they create a measure of goodwill for British Rail among the customers.

system. Peter Gutmann, an American economist, used this method to arrive at the figure of 10 per cent of the United States' gross national product.

One ingenious way of measuring the black economy is to count up the number of high denomination bank notes in circulation. The theory behind this is that only people who are doing cash-only business have any use for £20 and £50 notes. If this is true, then the black economy appears to be flourishing. A count revealed that the circulation of high denomination bank notes had risen disproportionately – three to four times the rate for all bank notes.

A simpler method is to compare what people say they are spending with what they are assumed to be earning. A British study in 1981 which used this method found a mismatch of between 2 to 3 per cent – the size of the black economy.

This is probably too low a figure. The Inland Revenue has an even simpler method. It estimates from its own experience how many people are likely to be evading tax. This produced a figure of 7½ per cent of the GNP in 1980. A percentage of around 8 to 10 squares with the extent to which people use the services of the black economy. Louis Ferman surveyed 284 homes in Detroit in 1977. He found that, of the services which people said they used, 10 per cent were paid for through the black economy. Some 30 per cent were bought through the regular economy, and 60 per cent were not paid for at all but obtained in the social economy (that is, the services were provided by friends or relatives).

But if the cashless transactions are excluded, the black economy's share increases to 25 per cent. Over half the homes in the Detroit survey had bought at least one service through the black economy.

This is hardly surprising. To an extent, the irregular economy mirrors the regular economy. It has the same broad functions of manufacture, distribution and service. But there are differences. The black economy's workforce is heavily skewed towards the service sector. A survey of people with second jobs in Cardiff, car-ried out by Jeremy Alden of UWIST's department of town planning, found that 80 per cent of them had main jobs in the service sector, and 90 per cent had second jobs in the service sector.

Three quarters of the second job holders came from only four occupational groups – sales workers, service organisations, professional and technical workers and teachers. Teachers, like firemen, are renowned for moonlighting.

The nature of the work in the irregular economy also differs from work in the regular economy. Businesses are small, rarely employing more than three people. Trade is intermittent, slotted in when the opportunity arises. Seasonal jobs, like fruit picking, which are mostly "off the books," are by nature irregular.

So why do people choose to work in the black economy? How do black economies grow? Gershuny and Pahl say that the strongest reason is unemployment. In theory, unemployment forces wage rates down, reducing the price of labour-intensive goods. This increases the demand for labour until full employment is reached. But the state and the trade unions intervene to prevent this, with social security payments and minimum wage levels. However, the black economy circumvents state and union bureaucracy. So full employment *is* reached, but in the black economy rather than in the regular economy.

Another reason for the growth of the black economy, Gershuny and Pahl suggest, is the increased availability of cheap tools. The DIY boom has put a range of sophisticated tools in the hands of laymen. Expensive capital equipment, like scaffolding, earthmoving vehicles and removal vans, can be hired. At the same time office equipment has moved from the office into the home. Word processors and home computers encourage the growth of one-person businesses in the living room.

A third, underrated reason for working in the black economy is the desire for personal autonomy. People want to be their own boss, particularly people who work in tightly controlled jobs. The freedom from government regulations and restrictions is important, too. Often these restrictions have forced people to work in the black economy in the first place. As Gershuny and Pahl point out, yesterday's enterprise becomes today's black economy.

The more the state tries to interfere in people's working lives – often for their own good – the more they will seek to avoid its interference. A report by the Outer Circle Policy Unit points out that "what were once perfectly innocent private transactions can be transformed into criminal activities, and the increase in official surveillance increases the temptation of individuals to conceal what they have previously done openly."

But the idea that governments create black economies may be too simple. There are features of society which, as it were, *demand* a black economy. These are, broadly speaking:

Economic: The goods and services the regular economy produces may be too expensive for the poor and the unemployed. So they look to the black economy instead. Mass produced goods, for example, are made to be thrown away when they go wrong. It is cheaper to replace them. This is why much of the black economy, like the informal economies of the Third World, is built round the salvage of goods produced in the regular economy.

Political: A system of licensing and regulation (for example, of taxis) keeps out newcomers. Minicabs were the response of the black economy to licensed taxis.

Social: The black economy is not an open market. It relies on established social networks and rounds. Entry into the black economy depends on personal recommendation: "I know a little man. . ." This "garden fence" promotion is in strong contrast to the impersonal, nationally advertised services of the regular economy.

It may be wrong, though, to see the black economy as simply an alternative; a kind of counter culture. Louis Ferman thinks that working in the black economy may be an apprenticeship for working in the regular economy. People's ultimate aim, he believes, is to work legitimately.

In the meantime, the black economy has some advantage. It is a useful test-bed for new ideas, which would be too risky, too expensive or simply too frivolous-seeming to test in the conventional market. (Some of these new-style enterprises – singing telegrams, dog-walking services – are so distinctive in their frivolity that they have been dubbed the *mauve* economy.)

Working in the black economy may also be a stage in the career of someone who wants to turn a hobby into a business. It allows the entrepreneur to carry on with a full-time job until the hobby-cum-business is a success (or a failure). And it provides an outlet for skills which the full-time job may not use.

This is the key function of the black economy: to provide an outlet for unused skills, and unmet demands. A report to the Council for the European Communities *(Report and Recommendations on Part Time Work,* 1980) points out that "marginal employment acts as a valve. It proves that the social system reacts against the inflexibilities which it imposes upon itself."

Should society try to close this outlet or valve? Some countries, like West Germany and Belgium, have tried. France has taken a notably tough line. All workers must be registered on a job index. Those who are not may be fined or even imprisoned. One future possibility is the confiscation of any state benefits – a loan for house purchase, for instance.

These draconian measures, Gerald Mars suggests, tackle only the "reactive" features of the black economy (tax evasion). They do nothing to encourage its "active" features (personal initiative). As unemployment becomes an unalterable part of the landscape, this is short-sighted. *Any* economic activity represents some

BOOKS

Some useful additional reading:
Jason Ditton, *Part-time Crime,* Macmillan, 1977
Stuart Henry (ed.), *Can I Have it in Cash?* Astragal, 1981
Stuart Henry, *The Hidden Economy,* Martin Robertson, 1978
Gerald Mars, *Cheats at Work,* Allen & Unwin, 1982
Outer Circle Policy Unit, *Policing the Hidden Economy,* 1978

sort of growth. How is it to be harnessed?

Gershuny and Pahl say that society must take a much broader view of what work is. "What is already going on is a spontaneous process whereby working for money in 'formal employment' is replaced by a less formal pattern. . . it requires us to enlarge our notion of work."

In the short term, though, much illegal activity could be legalised if governments treated the black economy as an enterprise zone of the economy. Some gains, such as employment protection legislation, might have to be surrendered. Would the benefits of fuller employment be worth it?

BRITAIN IN DECLINE

In the late 1950s, just a quarter of a century ago, Britain was the richest country in Europe.

Twenty-five years later, our standard of living is between a half and two-thirds of France's and West Germany's. We have become the poor man of Europe, on a par with Italy, Spain and the Republic of Ireland in terms of gross domestic product (the amount of goods and services we produce) per head.

In the world as a whole, Britain is now one of the also-rans. World Bank figures show that we are in the third division of nations in terms of income per head. The top ten include the United Arab Emirates, Kuwait and Qatar, the Scandinavian countries, Switzerland, West Germany, the United States and Canada. Next comes a second group made up of places like France, Austria, Australia, Holland and Japan. Finally, Britain appears in a third group, rubbing shoulders with Hong Kong, Puerto Rico, the Soviet Union and Yugoslavia.

Some argue that such comparisons based on GDP or income figures can be misleading. Insufficient allowance is made for differences in purchasing power, and in the case of Britain in particular, it is important to take into account differences in the "quality of life." But there is little doubt about Britain's rapid relative decline.

In 1900, Great Britain ruled a fifth of the world's land surface and a quarter of the world's population. Our navy was twice as powerful as the next two combined, so Britannia truly did "rule the waves." Britain's merchant fleet was bigger than the rest of the world's put together, the City of London was *the* world centre for finance and trade, and the pound sterling reigned supreme as the major world currency. Britons enjoyed a standard of living 40 per cent higher than their country's next nearest rival, Germany.

Earlier, in 1850, Britain actually made a third of the world's manufactured goods and produced half the world's coal, iron and cotton. Glasgow and the Clyde Valley were known as the "workshop of the world" while Bradford was the "wool capital" of the world.

In the past hundred years, Britain has undergone a spectacular descent from world supremacy. Our share of world trade – 33 per cent in 1900 – is less than 10 per cent today. Our share of world manufacturing output is less than 5 per cent. In recent decades, Britain has consistently notched up the lowest growth rate of all the main western industrialised countries, with both productivity per worker and investment per worker also the lowest.

If anything, the decline has accelerated in the past few years, because of poor competitiveness, the impact of the recession and the process of "de-industrialisation" affecting all advanced countries. Since the early 1970s, a tidal wave of manufactured imports such as cars, motorcycles, dishwashers, televisions and videos has swept away whole industries in Britain. A host of famous names like Triumph motorcycles, Imperial Typewriters and Garrard record decks have disappeared or been used simply as labels on imports.

A classic example is the famous Hornby toy factory in Liverpool, which made the most famous model trains in the world. Management failed to innovate, the business was sold and the factory finally closed at the beginning of the eighties. Scarcely a month goes by without a major industrial closure. On a single day in 1984 British Rail announced it was to run down the world-famous Swindon railway workshops, and Britain's oldest shipping line, Bibby's, hauled down the flag.

As Britain de-industrialises, some say we shall soon reach the point of no return. When traditional manufacturing collapses, this in turn leads to the decline of railways, merchant shipping, mines and so on, in a process economists call the *downward multiplier effect*. As the infrastructure decays, then profitability is further eroded, investors look overseas and whole areas of Britain – like parts of Merseyside and Strathclyde – come to resemble ghost towns.

There is one bright spot, though: the British scrap industry has been going through a boom period recently. With so many factories and foundries being dismantled, exports of scrap have reached new records. Much of it goes to the far east where it is used to make consumer goods which are later imported back into Britain.

What's wrong with British industry?

British industry started falling behind the German and American competition over a hundred years ago. As early as the 1870s, people were complaining about the high price and outdated design of British manufactured goods.

Throughout this century, more and more countries have caught up with and overtaken Britain in industrial expertise. Japan was the success story of the 1960s and 1970s, but now even Japan is being overhauled in some areas by the "New Japans" of the far east – Hong Kong, Taiwan, Singapore and South Korea.

In recent years, a series of reports from such bodies as the National Economic Development Office have pinpointed some of Britain's many industrial woes:
● Britain spends far too little on research and development compared with our competitors. Over 50 per cent of what we do spend goes on the military.
● Too many big British firms have grown fat and lazy on contracts to supply the Ministry of Defence and public corporations like British Telecom.
● British industry as a whole has a poor record of product innovation – despite suggestions to the contrary that we are a "nation of inventors." Too little attention has been paid to design.
● With a few honourable exceptions, the British are not good at selling their goods abroad. Overseas marketing efforts by British firms are notoriously poor. One recent study showed that British executives preferred to stay at home.
● British firms have an appalling reputation for late delivery, especially of major items like ships and drilling rigs. Surveys have shown that this is the most important reason given by foreigners for not buying British.

In addition, two factors work against us now and will do so in the future:
● Despite a fairly good state education system, Britain has the least well-trained workforce in Europe. We have nothing to rival the kind of technical education and vocational training available to youth in, say, West Germany.
● British managers are among the worst in Europe. The education and training of Britain's key front-line managers is inferior to that of our major competitors. In too many British firms, especially old family firms, the "amateur tradition" is still strong.

Finally, British industry over the past two decades has been characterised by missed opportunities. An early lead in robotics technology and biotechnology has now been completely lost. Too many electronics experts and other have gone down the "brain drain" – mostly to North America. Britain now faces the next decade with a totally inadequate stake in the "high tech" industries of the future.

One recurring problem in this respect is the poor status of engineers in Britain compared with competitor nations. The government even set up a special committee of inquiry into the matter, which resulted in the Finniston report (1980).

This found that British engineers are underpaid and not given posts of sufficient importance in British firms, like seats on the board. A new national body was needed to give the profession a better identity. Studies have shown that West German engineers have always been accorded higher social standing and material rewards than their British counterparts.

Another occupational factor in Britain's decline has been the civil service. In an Institute of Directors lecture, Sir John Hoskyns, Mrs Thatcher's former policy adviser, said that an incompetent civil service, with low calibre ministers and senior civil servants lacking in experience of the real world, has played a major role in Britain's rapid decline in the postwar period.

The paradox of plenty

When we speak of "decline," we mean, of course, decline relative to other nations. While some countries like West Germany and Japan have grown very fast and others like France have grown fast enough to maintain their position, Britain has only achieved a modest rate of growth – on average about 1 per cent a year this century – and has therefore slumped in the world league table.

But this also means that most people in Britain have never had it so good – a curious paradox. Most people are better off than their parents, who mostly are better off than their parents, who can remember the days when children ran around with no shoes on. As the government's statistical round-up, *Social Trends*, shows, Britons as a whole are healthier, better paid and are more comfortable in their homes.

In the past decade, there have been dramatic increases in the proportion of homes with telephones (up from 45 to 77 per cent), freezers (up from 32 to 55 per cent) and central heating (up from 39 to 60 per cent). Car ownership is up to 59 per cent and nearly everyone has a fridge, television and vacuum cleaner. Life expectancy has increased, we smoke less and play more sports. Spending on foreign package holidays breaks new records every year.

Another funny thing has happened on the way to the present: 60 years ago, nine out of ten households rented from private landlords. Now 60 per cent are owner-occupiers, 30 per cent are council tenants and only 10 per cent rent in the private sector. Home ownership has created a social revolution, but at a price. Housing takes an increasing proportion of national wealth: ten years ago, the total value of all private dwellings was about equal to the stock market value of all British companies. Now our houses are worth four times the productive sector of the British economy.

With over three million unemployed, seven million below the poverty line and a growing gap between rich and poor, it may seem strange to talk of a "paradox of plenty" amid decay and decline, but that in a sense is what we have in Britain.

The half-timbered economy

In European terms, Britain is a low wage, low benefit economy. Recent European Commission figures show that average wages in Britain are way below those in West Germany, Scandinavia and the Benelux countries. Only Spain, Ireland and Greece have lower wages.

According to the Office of Health Economics, Britain is way down the list in terms of percentage of GDP spent on health and even in the number of doctors and hospital beds per head of population. Again, EEC figures regularly show that public expenditure as a percentage of GDP is lowest in Britain.

We are, however, spending much more on defence and law and order than most European countries, and we appear to be the most heavily administered country in the EEC: we employ 48 per cent more public servants than West Germany and 60 per cent more than France. We even have twice as many bureaucrats as Italy. The British education system employs 717 000 people who do not teach and only 693 000 who do.

Britain is also suffering from its crumbling infrastructure. We appear to be facing the future with a half-timbered economy more suited to the nineteenth than the twentieth century. Our railways and ~s are in need of major renewal. Our

Myth of the lazy workers?

Could it be that Britain has declined because we are lazier than other nations? Plenty of people will tell you that the West Germans and Japanese – even the Americans and the Australians – "work much harder" than the slow-moving, work-shy British. And recent international surveys have confirmed that the work ethic is weaker in Britain than many other countries.

But work attitudes vary greatly from firm to firm, depending on the quality of the management. American and West German firms investing in Britain told the Department of Employment recently that they found British workers no different. A recent study of Japanese firms in Britain (Michael White and Malcolm Trevor, *Under Japanese Management*, 1983) found that the Japanese managers were getting just as good productivity results with so-called "lazy" British workers.

motorway network, never adequate in the first place, is already breaking up. Our telephone system needs urgent modernisation: while British Telecom is spending £18 per head each year, Germany is spending £30, France £51 and Japan £60.

The knock-on effect in terms of reduced productivity, general lack of efficiency, high costs, delays and so on of infrastructure deficiencies is incalculable. And the longer these deficiencies are neglected, the more expensive it will be to get back on the same footing as our competitors.

What the theorists say

Many of Britain's problems today are, of course, common to other nations. All the industrial countries have been affected by the rise in oil prices in 1973, the current world recession and the rise of new technologies like the microchip, which have consigned large numbers of people to the dole queue.

But Britain is very much a special case. In a sense, we still "lead" the world: we were the first to industrialise, and now we seem to be the first to de-industrialise. Yet as Andrew Gamble points out in his book, *Britain In Decline* (1981), the real puzzle is how we have declined so far, so fast.

How is it that the most dynamic and thrusting nation in Europe two hundred years ago, the strongest economy in the world at the turn of the century, a nation renowned for its skills and the continuity of its institutions, could become so incompetent?

The rise and decline of empires is nothing new: for Britain, you could read Rome, Venice, Greece or Spain. The fall of the Roman Empire has attracted much attention from historians, and recently Professor Mancur Olson, author of *The Logic of Collective Action*, has published his general theory (*The Rise and Decline of Nations: economic growth, stagflation, and social rigidities*, 1982).

Olsen's thesis is that the behaviour of individuals and firms in stable societies leads to the establishment of cartels, lobbies and monopolies. The longer a society goes without a major upheaval, the denser the network of vested interests gets. These special interests are harmful to economic growth, innovation and enterprise. Societies in which these interest groups have been destroyed – by war, for example, in the case of West Germany and Japan – get a thorough shake-up, a fresh start and achieve spectacular rates of growth. The rest get "institutional sclerosis."

Chroniclers of Britain's decline usually point out that Britain in the early part of the twentieth century had become "overextended" in that it had to carry extra burdens like an imperial navy and keeping troops east of Suez, apart from the enormous financial and human cost of two world wars. (Much of this "baggage" is still there. Just recently a Commons select committee criticised the lavish houses and way of life still enjoyed by British diplomats abroad.)

But one important theory – associated with the historians Correlli Barnett and Martin J. Wiener – suggests that the rot set in a lot earlier than that, and was even evident while the industrial revolution was going on. Britain's problem, they

How we came down in the world

Growth in gross domestic product (percentages)

	UK	US	West Germ.	France	Italy	Japan
1950-60	2.6	3.2	7.6	4.4	5.9	8.1
1960-70	2.5	3.8	4.1	5.6	5.5	11.1
1970-80	1.8	2.8	2.8	3.7	4.0	5.3

source: OECD

Shares of world exports of manufactures (percentages)

	UK	US	West Germ.	France	Italy	Japan
1960	12.7	17.9	14.8	7.4	3.9	5.3
1970	8.6	15.3	15.8	6.9	5.7	9.3
1980	6.8	11.5	13.9	6.9	5.5	10.4

source: *Cambridge Economic Policy Review*

argue, was that our governing classes never took to business and industry, always preferring the life of country squires.

Such "gentlemen" despised those who dirtied their hands in the worlds of manufacturing and commerce – and this attitude persisted right through the industrial revolution to the present day. Industry was left to the "traders" and "practical men" who were never truly accepted into high society, although some bought their way in by acquiring huge country estates.

"The successful manufacturer," Barnett writes in his book, *The Collapse of British Power* (1972), "could hope to become, in later life, a member of the gentry or even a peer, have a country seat, ride to hounds, and leave the family business to trundle downhill back in the smoke. His sons would do the 'right' thing: a profession, the army or navy, the civil service or politics."

In other words, even then, in terms of values and attitudes, industry had little going for it – a problem analysed with fresh and fascinating detail by Martin J. Wiener. In his book, *English Culture and the Decline of the Industrial Spirit* (1981), Wiener contends that the British ruling class positively tried to contain and cocoon industry, which it saw as an excrescence on the landscape. The British have always been obsessed by the rural ideal – and this goes for the late nineteenth-century radicals like William Morris and Robert Blatchford as well as the gentry.

In 1976, two Oxford economists, Robert Bacon and Walter Eltis, came out with the first edition of their influential book, *Britain's Economic Problem: too few producers*, which argued that the unproductive public sector was growing at a much faster rate than the productive private sector. There were too many consumers of wealth and not enough producers. In the same year, the Labour minister, Anthony Crosland, announced that "The party is over" as far as local government spending was concerned, and the past seven years have seen regular doses of public spending cuts.

In 1980, two new "theories" of Britain's malaise emerged. Richard Caves and Lawrence Krause of Washington's Brookings Institute took a look at Britain (in their book, *Britain's Economic Performance*), and concluded that our key and chronic problem was "low productivity." We also "lack the ability to adjust to external shocks." This was not especially enlightening since we were told that the source of this low productivity "lies buried deep in the social system." True, but not particularly helpful.

Again, the essential complacency and conservatism of British institutions was highlighted in two major articles in *The Sunday Times* in November 1980, by Harold Lever and George Edwards. They argued that the banks had played a major role in Britain's decline by their unwillingness to lend money – long-term and at realistic interest rates – to industry and others trying to make things rather than simply buying and selling things, like property.

What of the future? Mrs Thatcher and her Conservative government have embarked on a radical course of gingering up the economy by cutting back on state control and spending, and letting the market reign. The Labour opposition, by contrast, is committed to a large public programme for rebuilding and restoring Britain's infrastructure. This, it believes, is a requirement for future prosperity.

Whoever is right, it is certain that we shall need to cut free from old attitudes. As the Cambridge economist, John Eatwell, pointed out in his 1982 television series, *Whatever Happened to Britain?*, "A reconstruction of the British economy will require, as much as anything, a change in intellectual perspectives and prejudices. It is the economic ideas of the past which need to be overthrown before any straight thinking can be done."

BOOKS

Some useful additional reading:
James E. Alt, *The Politics of Economic Decline*, Cambridge University Press, 1979
Wilfred Beckerman (ed.), *Slow Growth in Britain*, Clarendon Press, 1979
Ralf Dahrendorf, *On Britain*, BBC Publications, 1982
Keith Pavitt (ed.), *Technical Innovation and British Economic Performance*, Macmillan, 1979
and for the other side of the story:
Bernard D. Nossiter, *Britain: a future that works*, André Deutsch, 1978

THE COUNTRYSIDE

"**W**herever men have tried to imagine a perfect life, they have imagined a life where men plough and sow, not a place where there are great wheels turning and great chimneys vomiting smoke."

Here, the poet W.B. Yeats suggests that the country has always represented a kind of utopia. Life as it should be. In contrast, the town represents the grimy reality. Life as it is. The idea is summed up in the saying that "God made the country and man made the town."

Sociologists have called this sort of thinking "rural romanticism"; a nostalgia for the simple pleasures of country life. Such romanticism is found in every industrial society, but it is particularly strong in Britain. Four fifths of the British population live in towns of over 50000 people. Yet there is a strong interest in all things rural. For example, a large and mainly urban audience listens to the radio serial, *The Archers,* which was until fairly

recently billed as being "an everyday story of country folk."

The country house, not the town house, has always been a symbol of social success in England. There are signs that people still hanker for a place in the country. The major population movement of the last twenty years has been the flight from the cities to the smaller towns and villages.

Why does the countryside have this attraction? What is it that people look for in rural life that they cannot find in towns?

The answer that many of the early sociologists gave was "a sense of community." As traditional societies have given way to modern societies, as rural life has been encroached on by urban life, so there has been a loss of community.

But what do we mean by community? The term is used in three broad ways. A community can mean simply a locality, a place where people live together. The traditional English village is a community in this sense. A community can also mean a local social system, a network of people who all know each other and who live fairly close to each other. The members of a local amateur dramatic society form a community in this sense.

Finally, community can mean "communion" – a sense of shared identity. This need not be local. It can extend worldwide. But it implies a strong feeling of belonging to a particular group. A religion like Catholicism, and its followers, make up a community in this sense of the word.

As we have seen, some meanings are spatial, others spatial and social, and others purely social. A village community extends throughout the world. However, sociologists have tended to run the three meanings together.

By doing this, they have implied that there is a close and direct relationship between *where* people live and *how* they live. In particular, it has led to the idea that a sense of community can be found only in the countryside.

The belief that the good life belongs to the country first gained support from the work of the nineteenth-century German sociologist, Ferdinand Tönnies, who said that the transition from traditional to modern society involved a change in social relationships from *Gemeinschaft* to *Gesellschaft.*

Broadly, *Gemeinschaft* means "community" and *Gesellschaft* "association" or "society." Community relationships are full relationships, in which people interact with each other at many different levels. To put it very crudely, *Gemeinschaft* means that people know a lot about a small number of people.

In contrast, "association" relationships are partial. People interact with each other at only one level. *Gessellschaft* means that people know a little about a large number of people.

To sum up, "community" relationships are personal, while "association" relationships are impersonal. Tönnies thought that personal, "community" relationships were more likely to be found in rural societies, where "everybody knows everything about everybody."

The French sociologist, Emile Durkheim, devised a rather different theory to explain the characteristics of rural and urban life. In his work, *The Division of Labour,* Durkheim suggests that industrialisation has changed the basis of social order and cohesion (which he calls solidarity). He describes it as a change from mechanical to organic solidarity.

● **Mechanical solidarity** means that people belong to a group because they subscribe to certain beliefs or codes of conduct. There is a consensus about the way things are. Durkheim says that this sort of solidarity is found in pre-industrial (rural) societies.

● **Organic solidarity** means that people cooperate to achieve certain material goals. There is a consensus about what needs to be done. This sort of solidarity, Durkheim says, is found in industrial (urban) society.

The key to organic solidarity is interdependence. Each worker relies on the labour of his colleagues, as each cell of the ᵇ needs other cells. In urban society, re specialists. They do one thing

only. In rural society, people are generalists. They can, in theory, turn their hand to anything.

The theory of the two poles of society has been extended by sociologists like Talcott Parsons. Parsons suggested that the way we decide a person's status differs in rural and urban societies.

In rural societies, people have a status which is *ascribed* to them. Rank and family and kinship ties will determine their place in the community. Who you are matters more than what you are.

In urban societies, people have a status which they themselves have *achieved.* Their standing in the community is decided by the sort of job they do and the amount of money they earn. What you are matters more than who you are.

Of course, things are unlikely to be this clear-cut. Who you are often determines what you are, and what you are determines who you are. Societies rarely conform to the "ideal types" of Tönnies, Durkheim and Parsons. They lie somewhere on the axis between the rural and urban poles. Another term for this is the *rural-urban continuum,* a spectrum of societies ranging from primitive rural life to modern urban life.

The *rural-urban continuum* has an attractive simplicity, and it has greatly influenced sociologists. Early community studies were attempts to place communities somewhere within this continuum. The attempts seemed, at first, to be successful.

In the 1930s, the American sociologist, Robert Redfield, published his study of life in Tepoztlan, a village in Mexico. Redfield had found a happy, settled and united community, which seemed to match the ideal of *Gemeinschaft.* However, when Oscar Lewis looked at the same village some 15 years later, he found a divided and discordant community.

There are several explanations for this. Tepoztlan could have changed, influenced by creeping urbanism. Or Redfield's view of Tepoztlan (and Lewis's) could have been coloured by their expectations.

Another explanation is that societies are more complex than sociologists acknowledge. W.M. Williams's study of an agricultural community in Devon, which he called "Ashworthy," showed that there was constant social change in a community which, in theory, should have been stable. And James Littlejohn's study of "Westrigg" in Scotland suggested that class is an increasingly important factor of rural communities. This is not the effect of urbanisation. Rather it mirrors what is happening nationally.

It became clear in the 1950s and the 1960s that the "rural-urban continuum" was too simplistic. It is descriptive rather than analytical. That is to say, it describes what is going on but does not explain why. It ignores the importance of class. And it encourages sociologists to link the spatial and social characteristics of communities too closely.

Ray Pahl, professor of sociology at Kent University, has dismissed the rural-urban continuum bluntly. "Any attempt to tie patterns of social relationships to specific geographic milieux is a singularly fruitless exercise." he says.

Pahl argues that what matters to the sociologist are not communities but *networks*, the full range of contacts that people have with others. He suggests that the higher the social class, or the larger the income, the wider these networks are likely to be. He cites the comfortably-off characters of Jane Austen's novels, whose extensive social networks enable them to live in the country without ever really belonging to it:

"They moved about the country, staying in each other's houses, wintering in London or staying in Bath. The so-called 'rural communities' in which their friends' houses were located were rustic prisons only for those without the means to escape them."

To put it another way, the close-knit life that characterises rural communities is, in Raymond Williams's phrase, no more than "a mutuality of the oppressed." The deprivations and isolation of rural life had forced people to look to each other for support and comfort.

Middle-class people who move from the town into the country want the cosiness of a close-knit community without the isola-tion and poverty that engendered it. They are, Pahl suggests, merely playing at being country people, with the local people as "rustic props."

This sort of play-acting is most likely to occur in "commuter villages." These are rural hybrids which fit most uneasily in any rural-urban continuum, with one section of the population living in the village but working in the town. Pahl studied a commuter village in Hertfordshire, which he called "Dormersdell." He found deep divisions between the middle-class commuters and the working-class locals.

To some extent, this was a reflection of class divisions nationally. But it became deeper when the newcomers took on, or tried to take on, the role of the squire. The conservative working class, Pahl found, felt that the newcomers were no substitute for the real gentry of the past. The radical working class simply resented being bossed around.

What has happened in villages like Dormersdell, Pahl says, is that one sort of social structure has been displaced by another. The hierarchy of the traditional village, in which everyone knew his place, has been replaced by a two-class structure.

Does there always have to be conflict between newcomers and locals? Some surveys of new rural communities suggest that there does not. A study of the Sussex village of Ringmer – *The Quiet Revolution* by Peter Ambrose, a social geographer at Sussex University – shows that newcomers can integrate effortlessly with locals. Two thirds of the villagers said that they felt there were "no signs" of tension and resentment between locals and newcomers, and only one in 20 saw "clear signs." This is broadly in line with the findings of a survey of villages by the Suffolk rural community council in 1969. This showed that four out of five people thought that newcomers fitted into village communities "quite easily."

However, the real division may not be between the locals and the newcomers but between the "haves" and the "have nots." Howard Newby, Britain's foremost sociologist of the countryside, thinks that this kind of polarisation is the most important change in country life in the last thirty years.

Newby argues that the polarisation is the result, not of creeping urbanism, but of changes in the countryside itself; specifically, changes in the rural economy. Intensive farming has destroyed the old occupational community and put a two-class system in its place. Large farms have swallowed up smaller farms. Mechanisation has replaced manpower. The small farmer and the farm worker have both lost their livings.

Others have benefited from the changes. A new kind of farmer, the "agri-businessman," has come into being. He has joined with the commuting stock-broker to form an affluent majority in the countryside. The rump of the agriculture workers, and their families, make up a poorer minority.

The poverty is relative. The lot of country people has improved, as Newby acknowledges. They are better fed, clothed and housed than in the past. But in other ways they are losing out. They do not have the choice of jobs or homes or amenities that people in the towns take for granted.

Chiefly, they lack mobility. When a village shop closes or a bus route is withdrawn, it is the "rural poor" – the people without the use of a car – who suffer most. The "rural rich" can always drive to where they want to get what they want.

What really divides the two rural classes is the amount of choice they have. The affluent majority live in the country because they have chosen to do so. The improverished minority live in the country because they have to. The worrying thing, Newby says, is that the needs of this minority are being increasingly ignored, as the majority gain greater control of the community. This may produce Utopia for some, but not for all.

BOOKS

Some useful additional reading:
Ronald Blythe, *Akenfield,* Penguin, 1969
Ronald Frankenberg, *Communities in Britain,* Pelican, 1969
Howard Newby, *Green and Pleasant Land,* Pelican, 1980
R.E. Pahl, *Urbs in Rure,* Weidenfeld & Nicholson, 1965
Raymond Williams, *The Country and the City,* Chatto & Windus, 1973

CULTURE

Who is Clint Eastwood? If you're interested in films and the lives of film stars and celebrities, you'll know that he made *Dirty Harry*, and is associated with tough-guy parts and spaghetti westerns. Yet if you're a young British black you would probably think immediately of a different Clint Eastwood: the reggae recording artist of the same name. That is sub-cultural, group knowledge. Such knowledge can be a badge of identification, even a defence.

Years before Brixton started the chain of violent events in British cities, observers were talking about a "new revolution of the mind" taking place in the black neighbourhoods of south London. The police, it was noted, were taking on the ~ of aliens confronted by a culture ~ot understand.

The concepts *culture* and *sub-culture* have become vital terms in explaining society's present discontents. Yet few social science ideas are so slippery. The Cambridge don, Raymond Williams, has spent an academic career chasing the word, "culture." He says it is among the two or three most complex words in the English language and devotes to it the longest section of his modern dictionary, *Keywords*.

Sociologists often define culture as the sum total of ways of behaving that a society or group builds up – the pattern it expects its members to live by. This includes the group's ideals and values and, especially, its means of creative expression – its language and its ways of communicating both internally and with the wider world. There is a sense in which there is a

"British culture" – the idea is often trotted out to explain Britain's poor economic performance by reference to the "anti-enterprise" values of, say, the schools or universities. Equally, a group of Teddy boys and girls on the prom at Brighton has a culture (or sub-culture) that includes the boys' winkle-pickers and the girls' flounced skirts.

The concept of culture is different from the concept of society. A society is an independent and comprehensive social grouping. The culture of society consists of the values, meanings and material items shared by its members. A baby born into a particular society, whether an advanced European one, or a primitive Amazonian Indian one, must learn the skills, knowledge and accepted ways of behaving – the culture – of that society in order to survive. And it is largely culture that makes a Cambodian peasant different, say, from a Birmingham car worker.

Culture, in a broad sense, has two essential features:
● It is learned
● It is shared
One writer, Clyde Kluckholm, says culture is a "design for living." Certainly it would be hard for society to function if its members did not acquire a shared understanding of what it was about. Culture sets out defined ways of behaving for people belonging to a particular society. But different societies behave in different ways – and this can lead to misunderstandings. Even advanced western cultures differ radically over basic things like gestures. For instance, making a circle with your thumb and index finger while extending the others means "OK" in Europe and the United States; usually "zero" or "worthless" in France or Belgium; and is an obscene comment in Greece or Turkey. A v-sign is a rude sexual insult only in Britain. Nearly everywhere else in Europe it means victory. In Greece and Turkey it simply means the number two.

Children learn the culture of their society through *socialisation*. Whether you are born in Croydon or the Trobriand Islands, the business of socialisation is similar – children are transformed from

helpless, dependent human animals into social beings. They learn the language of the culture into which they are born, and also the values, skills and knowledge which allows them to function in that society.

The guidelines which we use to direct our behaviour within our particular culture are called *norms*. For instance, most people in west Europèan culture follow norms that prevent murder, robbery or walking about in the nude. Norms are enforced by positive and negative sanctions – or rewards and punishments.

The other guidelines on which our culture is based are called *values*. These are related to norms, but are different in that they are more general – norms are more concrete and specific. Basically, a value is an idea shared by people in society about what is good and bad, right and wrong, desirable and undesirable. Thus, for instance, we approve of bravery, but not of cowardice. Many sociologists argue that without a shared culture based on shared cultural beliefs, norms and values, society would be unable to operate.

When we talk about culture in society today, it often has another, rather more specific meaning – associated with people's leisure, and their mental life in non-work hours. Culture in this sense is often defined through the arts, music and the mass entertainment media. Culture here has a particularly complex meaning – through its use in distinct intellectual disciplines, and in often-incompatible systems of thought, such as literary criticism on the one hand, and sociology on the other.

One of the long-standing arguments about culture in Britain has been whether the pursuits of the mass of people are somehow inferior to the "opera-house" culture of the intellectual minority. For instance, since the nineteenth century, some of the literary intelligentsia have taken the view that there is a kind of "mass culture" – meaning that the mental life of ordinary people was being patterned and stereotyped by the new media of communication, cheap fiction and popular music.

Thus, in an essay of the late 1930s on boys' weekly comics, George Orwell saw a great social malaise. *Magnet* and *Gem* were held to have an artificial and repetitive style that shrank the imaginations of their working-class readers. Girls were getting from their comics only the illusory romance their future employers thought suitable for them. The expressive and fantasy life of the majority of the people was poverty-stricken, Orwell said; their minds were half-closed.

Orwell's strain of cultural pessimism is a strong one in Britain: it goes back to such nineteenth-century figures as Matthew Arnold, and it continues today. Richard Dyer, in a British Film Institute monograph on television entertainment, published in 1973, criticises popular entertainers, like Cilla Black, Val Doonican and Rolf Harris, for lulling their audiences into a false cheerfulness and ~othering them with "telly-bonhomie."

~e writers see this tradition of
~bout mass culture as reflecting a

suspicion of capitalist manipulation, a fear of change and an idealisation of communication by means of books, as against the new twentieth-century forms of cinema and broadcasting. There is a fairly crude social model involved: society is divided into a "feeling" minority (the intellectuals who are doing the criticising) and a majority – the masses who have lost their hearts and minds to commercial newspaper owners, television and pop music. Note how, in the example above, Richard Dyer himself is not corrupted by watching Cilla Black.

In the work of the influential Cambridge critic, F. R. Leavis, and his wife, Q. D. Leavis, between the 1930s and 1950s culture was idealised as the quality of elite life associated with the contemplation of "great" literature. At first the Leavises hoped that the common people could be persuaded to join this contemplation; followers of Leavis such as Richard Hoggart believed that both better education in schools and through such institutions as the BBC would achieve this. But eventually the Leavises decided that the masses were beyond redemption; only a small group of highly educated literary critics could keep alight the flame of culture (meaning society's ideal self).

By the late 1950s and early 1960s the mass culture debate had become a convenient way of expressing fear at the pace of change. Cultural criticism reached a peak in Britain around the time of the birth of rock music, as literary thinkers tried to fathom social changes being brought about by the huge economic growth of the 1950s.

Richard Hoggart came from a working-class background in Leeds, and a major theme of his widely-read description of his home and the culture in which he grew up, *The Uses of Literacy* (published in 1957), was a deep disappointment that the new mass culture was sapping the will of the common people to secure their collective advancement in society. Hoggart's description of families in the back streets of Leeds, wasting away while listening to light comedy on radio, had a typically British tone of pessimism. Hoggart said working people were exchanging their democratic birthright for a mass of pin-ups. He wrote: "The hedonistic but passive barbarian who rides on a fifty horsepower bus for 3d to see a $5 million film for 1s 8d is not a social oddity but a portent."

But Hoggart's passive barbarians never arrived – or rather if they did it was in a rapid succession of different guises: as Mods, greasers, then, in the 1970s, as would-be barbaric punks. Mass culture turned into something that devotees of high culture would pay dearly for: the discovery that commercial art could be hung on gallery walls made the reputation and fortune of "pop" artists like Roy Lichtenstein. The barbarians turned out to have taste both as audiences and as performers.

Nowhere was this truer than popular music. A critique of popular music, written in 1941 by the German social theorist, Theodor Adorno, had complained of the predigested, formula basis of records; Adorno allowed popular music only one use, assuaging the unhappiness of the masses in capitalist society. But the new popular music responded to a host of individual and collective "uses"; the Beatles could have their working-class audience *and* be praised by the music critic of *The Times* as the greatest songwriters since Schubert.

In *New Society's* words (from Paul Barker's introduction to the collection, *Arts in Society*): "The mass arts have become a natural resource. They provide images and feelings and sometimes words which you can take off the peg and try on for fit." And the sociology of popular culture has changed. With the relatively new discipline (in Britain at least) of sociology arose the idea of plural cultures alongside sociological perceptions of society as a mix of sometimes conflicting groups. The notion of sub-cultures became important: in an essay in 1950 the sociologist, David Riesman, had analysed how young people listened to popular music and established that there were "taste" sub-cultures.

What this meant was shown when the youth-culture sociologist, Simon Frith, and others began looking in detail at how teenagers themselves classified popular music – it was a case, as Riesman had pre-dicted, of "an insistence on rigorous standards of judgment and taste in a relativist culture." Thus a fourth-former told Frith: "I don't know what youth culture means. I think it means what you are – skin, grebo or hairie. The groups have different outlooks on sex, drugs and politics. Music is not important to any group, to me music is what I like, not everybody else's opinion."

The idea of sub-cultures has taken on new importance in Britain with the growth of youth unemployment and ethnic divisions. The hard facts of life: class, education, jobs (or joblessness) remain. But in between them, especially in leisure time, young people can put together a style, drawing bits and pieces from the broad popular culture. From such material, the sociologist, Mike Brake, argues, they can construct a personal identity that briefly celebrates being young.

The evolution of the concept of culture is displayed in the transmutation of the influential Centre for Contemporary Cultural Studies at Birmingham University. This began life under Richard Hoggart in 1964 with many of its interests still defined by the Leavises and the mass culture debate. It went on to special studies of local cultures: for example, the Hell's Angels motorbike gangs. But during the 1970s the centre became much more political – shaping ideas about culture within a broad Marxist framework; the connection with arts and leisure was largely lost.

But culture *is* also an important idea for understanding society politically. When the Labour Party took control of the Greater London Council, Tony Banks, its newly-appointed chairman of arts and recreation, caused a great cultural fuss. He announced that the annual subsidy paid by the council to the Royal Opera House, Covent Garden, was to stop. Instead the money would be spent on "community arts" and pop festivals. How many working-class Londoners, the Labour Party asked, ever dressed up to pay £12 or more a head for a ticket to watch highly-stylised performances of opera and ballet?

The answer is very few. When interviewers on the General Household Survey asked men of differing social backgrounds whether they had attended an opera, ballet or theatre performance in the preceding month, only 1 per cent of the semi-skilled or unskilled said they had, whereas 7 per cent of the professionals and those classified as employers or managers had taken part in these cultural events.

The point is not whether Tony Banks is right ("community arts" often don't actually involve the community). The point is that culture, meaning arts and entertainment, has an important social dimension; understanding the arts involves questions about the stratification of audiences.

This division of audiences was explicitly recognised in the formation of the BBC's radio service. Robert Silvey, the founder of the BBC's audience research surveys, looked back at the division into "Home," "Light" and "Third" programmes: "At the top of the pyramid were the high-brows, the few really discriminating listeners; mostly well-educated, they were to be found in congeries in the (ancient) university cities, in Hampstead (but not West Hampstead), Highgate and perhaps Haslemere but definitely not in Bermondsey, Beeston or Bootle.

"The lowbrows, at the base of the pyramid, were the 'mass audience.' You didn't have to look for them, they were everywhere. They mostly listened to the Light Programme, though they would listen to the Home Service if it broadcast *Grand Hotel* from Eastbourne. Few of them had not left school on their fourteenth birthdays and they read the *News of the World*, the *People* and the *Mirror*. Of course, they were splendid chaps who had been marvellous in the blitz, but there was no denying that in terms of worthwhile broadcasting they were a total loss."

Stratification of this kind usually comes about through the educational system. The French sociologist, Pierre Bourdieu, lays emphasis on the way the schools give prior knowledge of the *codes* of high culture. His study of musuem visiting in France showed that on a national sample of visitors, 30 per cent who had studied the classics to approximately A level at school visited a museum or gallery at least once a ~th; only 8 per cent of those without kind of schooling visited with the

same frequency.

Studies of theatre and concert-going suggest a similar pattern: there is a close correlation between income, advanced education and access to "culture." Audiences at the Crucible Theatre in Sheffield, for example – one of Britain's best provincial repertory theatres – have been shown to be almost totally middle-class, and their social characteristics had not altered by the late 1970s.

Such stratification occurs at other levels, too. Simon Frith found that there was a marked difference in the approach made to popular music according to adolescents' educational level. In one Yorkshire school he studied, there was a distinct sixth-form culture: pupils staying on bought albums rather than singles, had "progressive" rather than Top 40 tastes and watched *The Tube* rather than *Top of the Pops*.

Pierre Bourdieu and other social thinkers have worried about this phenomenon: and asked whether the middle class, who already "control" high culture, are not "taking over" mass culture forms such as the cinema and popular music and imposing a new body of standards on them, perhaps eventually shutting bits of them off. The art-house cinema circuit, for example, is attended by audiences similar in their socio-economic characteristics to audiences for classical music concerts and the theatre.

The sociologist's job, Bourdieu says, is to be an iconoclast. Art and music critics may claim a painting, film or composition has universal aesthetic properties. The sociologist will ask how can it be universal

BOOKS

Some useful additional reading:

Paul Barker (ed.), *Arts in Society,* Fontana, 1977
Mike Brake, *The Sociology of Youth Culture and Youth Sub-cultures,* Routledge & Kegan Paul, 1980
Simon Frith, *The Sociology of Rock,* Constable, 1978
Denys Thompson (ed.), *Discrimination and Popular Culture,* Penguin, 1973
Raymond Williams, *Culture,* Fontana, 1981

when only a tiny minority of society has access to it. But the sociologist's analysis can only go so far. Since at least the time of sociology's founding father, Emile Durkheim, it has been difficult to describe where the boundary lies between our individual freedom to act ("acting" includes song-writing) and our membership of culture with its rules and contraints (that song will never get heard unless a music publisher deems it saleable). There is always a danger that sociological thinking about culture is "overdetermined" – it does not leave room for cultural change, for the likes of George Michael or Bruce Springsteen, say, to redefine his listeners' perceptions of themselves and their environment. Here the "literary" idea of artistic freedom to create becomes important.

Writing about film stars, Richard Dyer says: "We should not forget that what we are analysing gains its force and intensity from the way it is experienced. When I see Marilyn Monroe I catch my breath; when I see Montgomery Clift I sigh over how beautiful he is; when I see Barbara Stanwyck I know that women are strong." In other words, there is a limit to what sociology can say: aesthetics has to be allowed some space. No song, picture or novel can be fully understood outside its cultural context; but social analysis will leave a large area of the work untouched.

The cultural context of the arts and literature takes in a range of organisations: from medieval guilds defining the terms and conditions under which Florentine artists could work, to informal groupings such as the Bloomsbury group or the Pre-Raphaelite Brotherhood. A cultural organisation – mental life in the city of Liverpool in the late 1950s – helps to explain the nature of the Beatles' innovations in popular music.

Yet within the organisations, within the cultural context, there has to be space to explain, for example, why and how the Beatles were "better" performers than other Liverpool groups of the same period. Or why Stevie Wonder, say, is "better" than the hundreds of other black singers who emerged from similar social conditions in Detroit. Where sociology ends, aesthetics – artistic or literary criticism – takes over, and where that ends there is enjoyment and emotional response to the music or the words or the picture.

DEVIANCE

"**D**isgusting! Filthy monsters! Beasts!" These are only some of the terms that have been used to describe the members of the Paedophile Information Exchange, the organisation whose members want to legalise sexual activity between adults and children. They have incurred the wrath of almost everyone from the *Sun* to the Prime Minister.

Surely these people are a classic example of deviance in society? Some of their activities have certainly been deemed criminal as far as British law is concerned. But modern sociologists stress that the idea of what is "abnormal" or "unnatural" is not as clearcut as it may appear. What is normal at one time, in one place, may be abnormal or deviant in another time or place.

For example, Philipe Ariès, in his book *Centuries of Childhood* (1962), describes how the infant Louis XIII was introduced to sexual activity and to the private parts of both adults and older children before he was seven, and how he first had sex with his wife, a thirteen-year-old, when he was fourteen. Was this perversion? Or, rather, a different kind of normality?

In fact, it is impossible to generalise about whether any particular action is normal or deviant. What counts as "acceptable" varies from society to society. Drugs are a good example. In Britain, most people accept and approve of alcohol, though the law controls how much and where it is consumed. Marijuana use, by contrast, is illegal, and is officially frowned upon. But in some Islamic countries, exactly the opposite is the case. Nudism is a similar instance. Nobody bothers much about nude sunbathing on Greek beaches. But try it in

Hyde Park and you'd almost certainly get arrested.

Contemporary sociologists, then, have real problems in trying to define deviance. At one time, the matter was regarded as straightforward. Deviants were people who broke the rules of society – criminals, drug addicts, sexual perverts and so on. The purpose of studying them was to find a "cure" for their behaviour. They were assumed to be different from "normal" people, and many researchers tried to identify the causes of their difference.

In studying the causes of crime, for instance, these essentially *positivist* researchers concentrated on studies of convicted criminals, whose personal characteristics and social backgrounds could be measured and analysed. In 1964, for example, Sheldon and Eleanor Glueck concluded that the key difference between delinquents and non-delinquents was their body-type – whether they were tall or short, fat or thin, muscular or not. Other researchers with a more sociological slant studied the effects that delinquent subculture had on the behaviour of its members. Robert Merton argued that it was the discrepancies between the goals that society set for its members and the opportunities for achieving those goals that caused nonconformist behaviour.

What all these explanations have in common is that they identify deviants – usually seen as synonymous with delinquents – as different from the rest of us, and they look for the external causes of that difference.

The development of *interactionism* and particularly *labelling theory* in the 1960s led to a radical change in sociologists' approaches to these questions. A group of American writers, including Howard Becker, Edwin Lemert, and Erving Goffman, transformed the way in which deviance was understood and studied. Sociologists now started to question the taken-for-granted assumptions that there are "rules of society," and that those who break them are different in some identifiable way. The emphasis was now on how social rules are negotiated rather than given, and how they are negotiated differently in different contexts. It was

argued that deviance and normality are relative. People are not *made* deviant by external social pressures; they *become* deviant through social interaction and negotiation with others.

Sociologists also started thinking harder about the relationship between crime and deviance. It used to be argued that deviance refers to any "abnormal" behaviour, while crime is any act of deviance that breaks the criminal law. But it is not that simple. Most "normal" people have committed some criminal act at some time but unless caught cannot be regarded as deviant in the statistical sense. Indeed, certain minor crimes are often regarded as acceptable, even expected. For example, many employees make use of their employer's property for their own purposes. What office worker has never pocketed the odd biro? What mechanic has never "won" a tool or piece of equipment? Such behaviour is normal, but also criminal.

The whole relationship between crime, deviance and normality is very complex. Once we recognise that there is often no clearcut difference, in terms of their actions, between criminals and non-criminals, or even between deviants and non-deviants, then the old positivist approach looks inadequate. There is limited value in looking for the "causes" of criminal behaviour in terms of the way deviants differ from "normals." The difference between deviants and non-deviants can lie as much in the way others react to them as in their own personalities and backgrounds.

There is also a difference between deviant *acts*, which everyone does at some time or another, and deviant *people*, whose lifestyle is perceived as being organised around their deviancy. While most of us commit crimes, only some are regarded as criminals. Although it appears that most men have had homosexual experience at some time in their lives, only a minority are regarded as or see themselves as homosexuals.

The *labelling theorists* developed these ideas, and made an important contribution to the way we see deviance today. They were interested not so much in the causes of deviant acts, but in the reaction that identified certain acts as deviant, and the process whereby only some people who got involved in such acts become labelled as deviant people. What makes someone deviant, they said, is how others react to what they do. Such reactions could have far-reaching consequences for the identity of the person concerned, and thus for their further actions.

Take a petty thief as an example. Suppose he stole a packet of biscuits from a supermarket. The labelling theorists would call this original act of theft *primary deviance*. Many people commit such acts, for all kinds of reasons. Only some are identified, and are then exposed to the risk of being labelled a thief. If this label "sticks" it becomes the *dominant label*, or *master status*, which then overrides all the other labels. All the person's other social characteristics are then interpreted in the light of the dominant one – thief. Others will interpret future behaviour in the light of this deviant label, and in the end the individual concerned will come to accept the label, redefine their own identity, and behave accordingly – continuing to steal. The labelling theorists call this *secondary deviance*, which is the result of the social reaction to the primary deviance.

Labelling theorists reckon that all action is given meaning in terms of what observers "know" about what other people do. If someone is "known" to be a thief, a drug addict, a prostitute or whatever, then actions that might be interpreted differently in a non-deviant person will be seen as further evidence of the correctness of the original deviant label.

In Erving Goffman's words, people become *stigmatised*. This may lead to social isolation and to their being forced into the company of others with the same stigma. In turn, this contributes to a change in their sense of "self," and to their being confirmed in a pattern of behaviour that reinforces their deviant identity. They *become* deviant. Sociologists call this a *deviant career*. In other words, there is a sequence of stages through which people can pass from the status of "normal" to that of "deviant." Their original action is only the first stage in this process.

It is certainly easy to see how deviants can become stereotyped. Few people have any detailed first-hand knowledge of football hooligans, or muggers, or even the mentally ill, but we all think we know what they are like. The images that we have of these deviant groups are largely derived from the media, whose role in creating stereotyped images can hardly be exaggerated, particularly where criminal deviance is concerned. We know all about "granny bashing" from reading the *Sun*, but how many of us have a granny who has been bashed? The statistics tell us that old people are actually *less* likely to be attacked in the street. And far from always being "young thugs," granny bashers might well be harassed middle-aged daughters.

Once we have certain stereotypes incorporated into our world view, we jump to all kinds of conclusions. Women peace protestors have been labelled, for instance, as "smelly," "lesbian" and "promiscuous." Their individuality and the significance of their own world-view is lost beneath the overwhelming stereotype label which tells us "all we need to know." Recognition of this process has led many sociologists to do *participant observation* studies of deviant groups, in an attempt to describe the situation from their point of view.

Attractive though it may be as an idea, labelling theory has had many critics. It has been pointed out, for instance, that many forms of deviance – like suicide and sexual fetishism – are secret and therefore could not possibly be affected by labelling. And labelling theorists have been criticised for concentrating too much on victimless deviance. They have tended to write about drug use, vagrancy, prostitution, petty theft and alcoholism. What about murder, rape and violent robbery? It's easy to take the side of the underdog when he has caused no obvious suffering.

Marxist sociologists have taken rather a different tack, and have concentrated on the role of *power* in defining deviance. The power to define certain acts, and certain people, as deviant, is central to the exercise of social control. Those with the power to define what is normal have immense power. If the police, with the support of the media, can successfully stereotype certain groups as potential troublemakers, they will more easily secure public support for taking action against them.

The Marxists argue that deviant, or indeed criminal, interpretations put on certain acts when performed by certain people are a central element in the structure of class domination. If vandalism can be stereotyped as the activity of lads with big boots and aerosol cans, then property development can be carried on unopposed, even when it involves the desecration of the environment. If the stereotype of serious robbery and theft involves pickaxe handles and shotguns, then large-scale business frauds and price-fixing cartels – the crimes of the powerful – are unlikely to be investigated so vigorously or punished so severely.

Not all deviance, of course, involves crime. Old age, stuttering, childlessness and even political radicalism have all been defined as deviant by sociologists. There is an important distinction between *culpable* and *non-culpable* deviance.

A classic example of non-culpable deviance is physical disablement. The disabled are not usually blamed for their condition, but they often suffer from labelling, stigmatisation and stereotyping. For instance, people who are deaf or dumb are frequently assumed to be dim-witted. The facially disfigured – like the famous Victorian case of the "Elephant Man" – are often assumed to be impaired in other ways. The mentally ill are even worse off, as their condition is often seen as culpable – they could snap out of it if only they tried.

Ethnic differences, particularly when associated with different skin colour, often lead to attributions of deviant behaviour. Colour is, in the jargon, the master status. Black people have frequently been regarded as promiscuous, lazy and criminally inclined, no matter what their country of origin or social background.

The elderly suffer from the same problem. Old people are lumped together into a single social category, all their individual differences overlaid by the shared fact of their age. Their actions are then interpreted, first and foremost, in the light of their age rather than of their many other social characteristics.

Even gender has been considered from the standpoint of deviance theory. Traditionally, men have been the ones who have defined what is normal in sexual terms. Women who do not conform to the gender stereotype – essentially that of carer and domestic provider – have been labelled, stigmatised and set apart as deviant. Of course, certain male "deviations" have been similarly stigmatised, but, again, this stigmatisation has been controlled by men, not by women.

A divorced woman is still more stigmatised than a divorced man. A single mother may be seen as a culpable deviant, where a single father is often seen as non-culpable, and perhaps not even deviant. It may not be exaggerated to suggest, as Dale Spender does, that ever since Genesis, men have been regarded as normal, and women as deviants from that norm.

As long as there are rules, norms and conventions in social groups, there will always be deviance. Some may be very minor, such as nail-biting or pot-smoking, but it can be serious enough to result in the person's whole identity being organised around the fact of their deviance. The important thing for sociologists is not to take a hard and fast line. In a rapidly-changing world, what is deviant today might turn out to be normal tomorrow.

BOOKS

Some useful additional reading:
Howard Becker, *Outsiders*, Free Press, 1963
Steven Box, *Deviance, Reality and Society*, Holt, Reinhart, Winston, 1981 (2nd ed.)
Jack Douglas and Frances Waksler, *The Sociology of Deviance*, Little Brown, 1982
David Downes and Paul Rock, *Understanding Deviance*, Oxford University Press, 1982
Paul Rock and Mary McIntosh, *Deviance and Social Control*, Tavistock, 1974
Ian Taylor *et al*, *Critical Criminology*, Routledge & Kegan Paul, 1975

DIVORCE

Divorce has increased threefold compared with a decade ago. In 1983 there were 162 000 divorces in the United Kingdom. If current trends persist, it is likely that one in four marriages that took place in the 1970s will end in divorce before their twenty-fifth anniversary.

These are the blunt statistics. But the sort of questions that sociologists ask about these facts are nothing to do with any kind of moral appraisal. They do not, for instance, ask if society is somehow deteriorating. This line of inquiry is, perhaps, best left to bishops. Sociologists want to know whether the divorce figures merely reflect a degree of marital breakdown that was always there beneath the surface, or whether society is changing in a way that is less accommodating to successful marriage. Or whether a more permissive attitude to divorce actually *causes* divorce.

There are important practical issues, too. A result of divorce is a breakdown in family life. The number of one-parent families increased by more than a third during the 1970s, and they now amount to about an eighth of all families. The cost in welfare benefits for these families is huge – some £6 million a week is paid out to people who are unsupported after marital breakdown. Jack Dominian, a psychiatrist who is an expert in these problems, reckons that when the cost of absenteeism from work and psychiatric treatment stemming from marital stress are added, the public cost to Britain could be as high as £1000 million a year.

One fact is clear in plotting trends in divorce – whenever the law has been relaxed, divorce has increased. Before 1857, a private act of parliament was needed to get any kind of divorce. This was an expensive business, beyond the means of all but the most wealthy. Listen to Josiah Bounderby in Charles Dickens's *Hard Times* of 1854 telling his employee, Stephen Blackpool, about the only way he can legally end his marriage:

"Why, you'd have to go to the Doctors' Commons with a suit, and you'd have to go to a court of Common law with a suit, and you'd have to go to the House of Lords with a suit and you'd have to get an Act of Parliament to enable you to marry again, and it would cost you (if it was a case of very plain sailing), I suppose from a thousand to fifteen hundred pounds. Perhaps twice the money."

The Matrimonial Causes Act of 1857, which limited the grounds of divorce to the "matrimonial offence" of adultery, made it cheaper. But divorce was still effectively denied to the mass of working class people. The situation was partly changed by the Poor Persons' Rules of 1925, but it was not until 1949, with the Legal Aid Act, that divorce became, in any sense, widely available.

Legislation in 1950 introduced the grounds of cruelty and desertion. Until that time the only ground for divorce was to prove adultery – which often meant hiring a private detective to witness some contrived rendezvous in an hotel. This was beyond the reach of most people. Even so, divorce cases still had to be conducted by "proving" that one party had wronged the other.

The big change came in 1971, when the Divorce Reform Act (1969) came into effect. This abolished the necessity of proving "guilt" in one's partner – it became enough simply to show that a marriage had irretrievably broken down. This is taken to have happened if husband and wife have been living apart for two years, and both of them want a divorce, or where the couple has been living apart for five years and only one of them wants a divorce. Irretrievable breakdown is also assumed to exist where the behaviour of one of the parties is unreasonable, or where "unforgivable" adultery has taken place.

Since 1973 the law has been further simplified, and a divorce can now be granted on the evidence of irretrievable breakdown submitted in writing, without any court hearing. In 1984, the Matrimonial and Family Proceedings Act brought a further liberalisation: it is now possible to petition for divorce after only one year of marriage.

As Denis Lawton points out in *Investigating Society* (1980) it would be misleading to look at a set of divorce figures without weighing them against this changing legal, financial and social scene. But whichever way you look at the statistics, the trend is an upward curve. There has been an increase from a prewar average of 5000–10000 divorces a year to a current total of more than 160000. The British are not alone in this – divorce in all industrial countries is rising steadily. The level is higher in the United States, Sweden and Denmark, but our level is above that in France, Belgium and West Germany. Divorce was only made legal in Italy in 1970, but the figures are already leaping up.

Divorce rates are a more accurate measure of divorce than simply totalling up the number of divorces granted, because they relate divorces to the people who run the risk of being divorced – that is, the married population. But here, too, the trend is up – from 0.7 per 1000 marriages before the war to 12.2 in 1983.

The divorce trend has been smoother and less steep than is implied by annual divorce rates for what are known as marriage "cohorts" – that is, people who have got married in a particular year. Even so, 14 per cent of couples who married in 1962 had divorced by 1976, after 15 years of marriage. This was twice the proportion among members of the 1956 marriage cohort in 1970, with the same duration of marriage.

The boom in divorce in the 1970s has probably been increased by the Divorce Reform Act. Richard Leete, of the Office of Population Censuses and Surveys, points out that the immediate effect of more lenient laws was to increase the rates of divorce for older couples, and those who had been married for a long time.

Leete's analysis shows that many couples used the new provision of five years' separation, suggesting that the marriages had effectively ended years ago, but the couples were unwilling to use the previous legislation. The backlog raised the number of divorces in 1972 by some 50000 over what would have been expected on the pre-1971 trend.

Of course, mere figures are an inadequate way of exploring all the dimensions of marital breakdown. A marriage in which divorce takes place after four years may never have got off the ground at all. Yet the figures would tell us nothing about that. And as Ronald Fletcher points out in *The Family and Marriage in Britain* (1976), the overt statistics of broken marriage "do nothing whatever to indicate the condition of marriages that endure. It is at least arguable that the qualities of life of some of those which endure – in terms of harmful consequences for spouses and children – are more questionable than some of those which are responsibly ended."

But sociologists have identified certain factors that seem to make a marriage less likely to succeed. There are some who, depending on their circumstances, are more prone to divorce than others. The main factors are these:

● Age at marriage. There is an inverse relationship between people's age at marriage and their proneness to divorce. Roughly twice the amount of divorce occurs among people who got married in their teens, compared with those marrying in their late twenties. There are many reasons for this – particularly that people in their teens are still developing, and are mostly surrounded by people who are unmarried. Teenagers, too, are more likely to have married because of pregnancy. They are also more likely to be working class and suffering the strains that lack of money brings.

● Duration of marriage. There is a high incidence of divorce in the first four years of marriage and another big peak among people who have been married for more than twenty years. The four-year period is understandable. The twenty-year period coincides with the departure of children, when married people have to face up to each other as a couple for the first time since the beginning of their marriage.

● Class and social background. More

working class people get divorced. The highest divorce rate of all occurs where husbands are unemployed. There is also an increased likelihood of divorce if partners come from different classes or social backgrounds. In an advanced society like ours, with increased geographical and social mobility, there are more people from different backgrounds marrying. This brings with it an increased likelihood of marital conflict.

● Religion. Jews and Roman Catholics are less likely to get divorced than people of the other main British denominations, though mixed marriages within these faiths are prone to breakdown.

● Marital status of parents. If one or both partners have parents who are divorced, there is an increased chance that their marriage will end in divorce. One reason given for this is that the unstable home background produces instability in the children. It may also be true that parents who have been divorced are less likely to discourage it in their children.

● Occupation. Divorce is high in jobs where one of the partners is away from home for long periods. This lessens the dependence of the spouses upon one another, and also increases the chance of meeting someone else of the opposite sex while away. Jobs in this category include long-distance lorry drivers and sales representatives.

Many of these problems have always existed. But sociologists are keen to know why divorce has increased so much recently, and whether it will go on growing. Is more divorce simply a result of the improved status of marriage, as Ronald Fletcher argues in *The Family and Marriage in Britain*, or are there simply fewer successful marriages because being married is no longer compatible with a changed society?

Fletcher argues that modern marriage is less hedged around with social convention, its partners are more equal, and that it has "come increasingly to be regarded as something worthwhile in and for itself." It is this very enhanced status of marriage that has made it more vulnerable, especially as there are no longer any social inhibitions on dissolving a part-

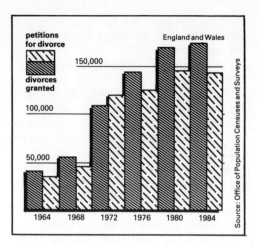

nership that is unsatisfactory.

Other sociologists reckon that marriage fits in less well with the changed nature of social life. Most of us live in a *Gesellschaft* society, a looser association of people than the *Gemeinschaft*, or community, society that went before it. G. F. Ribbens in *Patterns of Behaviour* (1980) comments: "Not only does the community of people around the married couple condition them to the acceptability of divorce, it also determines people's expectations about marriage in the first place."

The one change in society that has had most influence on modern marriage is the improved role of women. It is significant that seven divorces in ten are started by women. Economic independence and relative equality at work mean that women are able, within marriage, to lead more independent and outgoing lives, and also to contemplate divorce more easily. Just how much marriage has been altered by women at work can be seen by the jump in the married female labour force in Britain from 40 to 64 per cent between 1951 and 1971, though this has been slowed recently by rising unemployment.

Emancipation has more or less rid marriage of the "close your eyes and think of England" attitude, and women are much more critical of their relationships. Improved birth control and smaller families mean often that by the time a woman has finished bringing up the children, at the age of, say, 40, she has about half her life ahead of her. In the last century, with lower life expectancy and bigger families, there was often no time for reassessment of marriage.

One writer, Nicky Hart, takes a Marxist view of the changed role of women, in *When Marriage Ends* (1976). In advanced capitalist societies, she says, there is an increasing call for cheap female labour. Both for this reason, and because the capitalist-controlled media have raised her material aspirations, a wife is encouraged to go out to work – to get extra consumer goods for her family. But at the same time the working wife is expected to run the household and look after the children, as well as to play a subservient role to the male head of the household, contradicting her own economic independence. This conflict of roles can cause serious strain on the marriage.

But the view that marriage is somehow redundant in today's society is not borne out by figures which show that growing numbers of divorced people are remarrying. The percentage of marriages involving divorced people rose from 11 per cent in 1965 to 25 per cent in 1974. Currently, a third of all marriages are remarriages of divorced people. It is interesting to compare this with figures for widowed people, who have shown less propensity for remarriage. But in the past fifty years the proportion of people who have been married at some time in their lives has actually grown.

What of the future? Will divorce figures continue to rise? The answer, on past experience, is that they probably will, especially as the law on divorce is likely to be liberalised still further.

We shall never be able to prove scientifically that the proportion of failed marriages now is greater than it was in the days before the church, the law and social convention allowed marriage to be formally ended. But what is most important, perhaps, is that marriage today should be based on mutual respect and affection, not on legal compulsion.

Writing in the nineteenth century, when divorces numbered fewer than 500 a year, Herbert Spencer, one of the "founding fathers" of sociology, said:

"Already, increased facilities for divorce point to the probability that whereas, hitherto, the union by law was regarded as the essential part of marriage and the union by affection as non-essential; and whereas at present the union by law is thought the more important and the union by affection the less important; there will come a time when the union by affection will be held of primary moment."

Spencer's prediction has largely come true, and few would deny that the climate of marriage has been enhanced.

BOOKS

Some useful additional reading:
Robert Chester, *Divorce in Europe*, Martinus Nijhoff, 1977
M. P. Fogarty, R. Rapoport and R. N. Rapoport, *Sex, Career and Family*, Routledge, 1971
Colin Gibson, "Divorce and social class in England and Wales," in *British Journal of Sociology*, March 1974
Oliver McGregor, *Divorce in England*, Heinemann, 1957
B. Thornes and J. Collard, *Who Divorces?*, Routledge & Kegan Paul, 1979

EDUCATIONAL ACHIEVEMENT

"There is a good reason to suppose that substantially higher standards of attainment at age sixteen can be achieved in this country by pupils throughout the ability range." So said Sir Keith Joseph, the Education Secretary, in a major speech outlining ambitious plans to get children to do better in school.

But admirable though the government's aims may be, jacking up educational standards is unlikely to be easy. The factors that make for success at school are complicated, and frequently have their roots far outside the classroom.

What then, about the obvious explanation of success? Isn't it true that the people who do best at school are the "cleverest" or most intelligent? Unfortunately, as is often the case in social science, the "obvious" answer is frequently misleading. There *is* a positive correlation between IQ and achievement at any age level, but it is not very high. So sociologists have looked for other factors to explain why some children (and adults) of more or less the same intelligence are "higher achievers" than others.

The educationist, Brian Simon, has put the problem graphically: "If you happen to have had the luck to have been born a boy in Cardiganshire, your father being in the professional or managerial class, your chance of achieving full-time higher education would almost certainly be about eighty per cent. If, on the other hand, you were born as the daughter of a semi-skilled or unskilled worker living in West Ham, your chance of reaching full-time higher education would probably have been less than 0.5 per cent.

"These figures quantify the extent of differences in opportunity at their extremest point; they show that the Cardiganshire middle-class boy has roughly 180 times as much chance of reaching full-time higher education than the West Ham working-class girl; and this when the country has, in a formal sense, committed itself to a policy of equality."

Simon was writing in 1965, when he claimed that the three most important factors were social class, sex, and where you happened to live. Today, the position has not improved in terms of social class, but sex differences have become a little less important and so has geography. But another aspect would certainly be mentioned today as of very great importance – namely, the ethnic group that you happen to belong to.

If you wanted to make a generalisation about the whole educational process (not just entry to university) you would be safe in picking out three things as important predictors of future "success":
- *Social class* (the middle class still do better than the working class)
- *Gender* (girls are underachievers by the end of compulsory schooling)
- *Ethnic group* (whites do better than blacks).

The pattern is not quite as clear cut as this, however. The relationships are complicated by problems of definition. What, for instance, counts as educational achievement? Sir Keith Joseph sees it as examination success, but teachers are rightly concerned to point out that this is only one aspect of educational achievement.

Another complication is that different patterns emerge at different age levels. At some stages, for example, girls are "better" than boys, but by the end of the educational process this "superiority" has almost entirely disappeared. A better kind of evidence is provided by *longitudinal studies*. This involves studying the same group of children over a number of years and seeing how their performance changes.

One of the best sources of information about children up to the age of eleven is the National Child Development Study.

In the week beginning 3 March 1958, 17000 babies were born in Britain. The study's researchers tried to keep in touch with as many of the 17000 as they could, for as long as possible, and to analyse various aspects of their development. Detailed studies were made when the subjects were aged seven, eleven, sixteen and twenty three.

A major advantage of this kind of longitudinal study is that the *same* children can be compared at various ages. It turned out that there was a good deal of movement up and down during the four years between seven and eleven. The researchers used just three levels of achievement – *high, medium* and *low* – and found that a third of the children who were in the high group at seven had dropped out by the time they were eleven. Meanwhile, a third of the low group had improved and were now included in a higher group.

Those who moved down were most likely to be working-class. By the age of eleven, children of social class I or II (professional, managerial and clerical) were, on average, thirteen months ahead on measures of reading attainment compared with social class V (unskilled manual). At age seven, middle-class children were, on average, already ahead, but by eleven the gap (in both reading and mathematics) had widened.

What are the reasons for this? There are clear indications from the National Child Development Study that poor physical home conditions are associated with declining levels of achievement. Poor housing, overcrowding and even lack of good bathroom facilities appear to be statistically related to behavioural differences such as a tendency to play truant frequently. These are, in turn, related to poor performance on tests of reading and arithmetic.

At the primary school stage, sex differences have an important part to play. At age seven, girls tend to achieve a little better than boys, particularly on any test involving language skills. But by the age of eleven, boys have usually caught up.

It is much more difficult to establish a clear picture of the educational life chances of ethnic minority groups in the primary school. It is often hard to distinguish between what is poor achievement related to ethnic group as such, and what might be poor achievement resulting from the same social class factors that affect whites.

Ethnic minority groups are often clustered in inner city poor housing areas and are sometimes referred to as the "new poor." Although there may be some important *cultural* differences which

The social disadvantages that stick

Various attempts have been made over the years to help children who appear to be achieving less than they could because of sex, race or class. But only the efforts to tackle sex differences have shown good results. The unequal chances of ethnic minorities have been a relatively neglected area of research, and social class differences today are actually widening, even within the state system.

As long ago as 1910, the London County Council paid teachers an extra £7.10s a year if they worked in a school of "exceptional difficulty," and many types of "positive discrimination" for working-class children have been tried since then. The main impetus came in the 1960s, when the Plowden report on primary schools recommended a widespread injection of extra resources into areas of disadvantage, and a number of "Educational Priority Areas" were set up in the inner cities. Though these have now been wound up, inner city schools still get extra cash through the government's Urban Programme.

Other ideas that have been tried include parent involvement and home reading schemes, and courses to raise teachers' expectations. But the combined effect of such programmes has been slight. Some people have argued that the failure is due to inadequate resources, or insensitivity to the feelings of working-class parents. Others have blamed the exam system, saying that as long as pupils in public examinations continue to be marked into fine grades on the basis of timed tests, the gap between the social classes will remain.

The limited efforts that have been made to help ethnic minority children have been equally might affect educational achievement, it is most unlikely that there are any *genetic* differences which would account for poor performance.

Even so, the following generalisations appear to hold:

● Children of West Indian origins are more likely to be allocated to a school for educationally subnormal children than any other group
● In general, pupils from India and Pakistan do better than other immigrants
● West Indian and Turkish Cypriot children do worse than other immigrant groups
● Pupils from most ethnic communities are likely to be over-represented in low streams of primary schools where streaming takes place.

After the transfer to secondary school the patterns of achievement become clearer: social class differences become even more important; boys improve on subjects such as mathematics and science; some ethnic groups, particularly black West Indian boys, lag badly behind. Throughout the secondary period (up to age sixteen) these trends continue: middle-class pupils tend to get into the higher streams, and achieve better results on classroom tests; girls under-achieve in mathematics and science, and children of some ethnic minorities become labelled not only as failures but as deviants.

Why should this be? What accounts for these differences of social class, gender and ethnic group?

Many studies in Britain and the United States have shown that working-class parents and pupils do not value education as highly as middle-class adults or children. They do not "see the point" of education; tend to leave school earlier, and do not view schools as a realistic means to a good job. In other words, working-class children appear to have lower motivation to succeed in school, and this is partly derived from parents' expectations and a lower rate of encouragement.

A lot of studies also point to the fact that working-class families have a less stimulating environment. In recent years, however, this emphasis on home background has been increasingly criticised by sociologists, and more attention has been paid to the school as an institution, the classroom as a socialising agency and the role of the teachers in influencing performance by different kinds of children. These later studies suggest that schools *label* working-class children as less academic, lacking motivation and, in extreme cases, as failures.

The new research suggests that the way pupils are treated in schools is probably as important as any cultural differences the

disappointing. The government-sponsored Rampton report in 1981 showed that black children suffered at school from racism, inappropriate curricula, language difficulties and poor relations with teachers. The various initiatives that have been set up to counter these things – including multi-cultural learning materials, specialist language teaching and supplementary schools – have been bedevilled by disagreement among educational specialists.

Some critics have claimed that special initiatives can easily become racist, while others have argued that multi-racial education is "a misguided liberal strategy to compensate black children for not being white." Even so, in 1983, the Inner London Education Authority announced a wide-ranging set of policies to "eliminate racism" in schools.

The brightest spot in all this comes from efforts to counteract sex differences in school. Encouraged by the Equal Opportunities Commission and the now-defunct Schools Council, many local authorities and individual schools have begun projects which are showing promising results. For instance, in one London mixed secondary school in 1979, only one girl was taking an O-level physics course. A female physics teacher was appointed and the course was modified to remove its "male bias." By 1982 twenty-eight girls had been encouraged on to the course.

In another experiment in Tameside, Greater Manchester, girls in a mixed school were taught maths in single-sex sets. This improved their results considerably. Though they approved of co-education in general, the girls liked single-sex maths teaching because they felt that this was a subject where boys particularly monopolised teachers' attention.

pupils bring with them. There has, therefore, been a move away from crude *deficit theory* explanations of working-class and underachievement to more complex explanations based on *human interaction* in the classroom, including the tendency of teachers to use stereotypes and labels.

Similar arguments have modified sociologists' views about ethnic and sex differences. Clearly, children from some

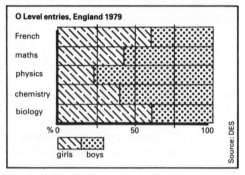

The sex gap

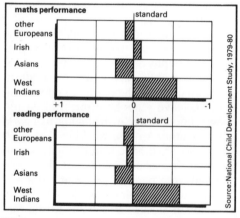

The race gap

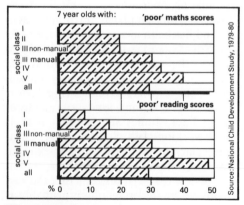

The class gap

ethnic minorities, especially those whose first language is not English, come to school with some disadvantages. But there is also evidence that the system itself causes failure among those children. Their initial disadvantages are made worse by the school system.

Language is another problem. Where English is not the mother tongue, children may have difficulties in trying to master a new language and the school curriculum at the same time. Where the first language is English, but a different dialect (for example, West Indian creole), teachers may underestimate a child's difficulty in speaking both the natural first dialect of the home and also becoming competent in the standard English of the school curriculum. Ironically, this is thought by some to be one of the reasons why Asian children appear to do better. Because their language difficulties are more obvious, they get more help than West Indian children, who may need it as much.

Selection procedures, including tests of "verbal reasoning," are almost certain to discriminate against minority groups with less competence in that kind of "test language." However able ethnic minority children might be, their talents are wasted if they cannot express themselves in terms understandable to examiners.

Sex or gender differences are also sometimes explained by *labelling*. There is evidence to show that teachers tend to see girls as more passive, compliant, polite and non-aggressive. These labels are accompanied by teachers' behaviour, such as expecting girls to talk less in class. By the time girls have reached the middle of their secondary school career they think that it is natural for boys to ask questions, make protests, challenge the teacher and demand explanations. But girls have been socialised to put up with an inferior position, to act in a submissive way towards males, and to under-achieve.

Much of this socialising process will, of course, have begun long before secondary school. At birth, girls are given a sex label in the form of a Christian name; girls will be dressed differently, given different toys, treated differently by their parents. When they reach school the pattern of gender identity will be firmly established, but the school, far from breaking down these gender differences, tends to intensify them. Girls choose arts subjects rather than science at age thirteen or fourteen, so that, for instance, at GCE O-level twice as many boys obtain passes in science subjects as girls.

Class and sex differences also have a major influence on access to higher education. Evidence of this was provided twenty years ago by the Robbins committee report on higher education. The committee found that, of the children born in 1940–41, forty five per cent from professional groups went into higher education compared with only four per cent of the children of skilled manual workers and two per cent of semi-skilled and unskilled manual workers. Even when measured IQ was held constant there were very significant social class differences: of those pupils with very high IQ (130 or more), children from non-manual families were twice as likely to do a degree course as working-class children.

Although the total number of young people going into higher education has expanded considerably since 1963, the *proportion* coming from working-class families has actually declined – during the last ten years there has been a fall of about a third in the proportion of university students coming from working-class homes. It is most unlikely that universities have deliberately become more socially selec-

BOOKS

Some useful additional reading:

Basil Bernstein, "Education cannot compensate for society," *New Society* Social Studies Reader on "Education"
E. Byrne, *Women and Education,* Tavistock, 1978
A. and M. Craft, "The participation of ethnic minorities in further and higher education," *Journal of Educational Research,* vol. 25, No. 2, 1983
A. H. Halsey, A. F. Heath and J. M. Ridge, *Origins and Destinations,* Oxford University Press, 1980
P. Lodge and T. Blackstone, *Educational Policy and Educational Inequality,* Martin Robertson, 1982

tive, so it looks as though middle-class families have been skilful in adapting to a changing situation.

Although the Robbins report was regarded by many as a great reforming document, heralding a major expansion of higher education, it has since been criticised by some sociologists for accepting social demand (that is, mostly middle-class demand) for higher education rather than having a policy of equality of social representation in higher education. In 1980, the Secretary of State for Education stated that "we do not have a policy on the class balance of higher education" – and without a policy, it is almost certain that the social gap will continue to widen during the next few years.

Women are also under-represented in higher education, but, unlike working-class boys, they appear to be catching up. Before the war (1938–39), the proportion was 23 girls to 77 boys; by 1980 it had improved to 40:60. Though this is still a long way from equality, a good deal of progress has been made. One reason for female under-representation is that a number of able girls "choose" not to do A-levels, or take patterns of A-levels less acceptable for university entrance. Of those who do enter higher education, girls are as likely to succeed, although fewer of them take degrees in science and engineering subjects. If girls are to reach equality in higher education, then more positive work will have to be done in primary and secondary schools to encourage them to think of higher education as just as natural for them as for men.

The evidence on ethnic minorities at 18-plus and later is thin, partly because by this time only a tiny minority remain in the system. Recent studies seem to show that the West Indian pupils still at school or in further education at age eighteen have at least as good a chance of getting good A-level passes as native whites – perhaps even slightly better. Those ethnic minority children who have survived the series of hurdles up to the age of eighteen have probably had to demonstrate qualities of perseverance and high motivation well above average for the whole group. But only two per cent of West Indian school leavers gain one or more A-levels, compared with the national average of thirteen per cent.

In 1983 the Association of African, Caribbean and Asian Academics held an inaugural conference in London, and complained about the under-representation of ethnic minorities in higher education, and even more about the fact that this problem was largely ignored by white academics (only one per cent of West Indian pupils enter full-time higher education). Not only are black British under-represented as students in universities and polytechnics, but little is being done to tackle the problem: and there are very few lecturers from ethnic minorities.

Sir Keith Joseph has a major job on his hands with his new initiative. The government is certainly right to suppose that British schoolchildren are not achieving as well as they could. But finding an answer is not easy. It certainly seems that tinkering with the education system alone is not enough. As Professor Basil Bernstein has pointed out, education cannot compensate for society.

EDUCATION AND CLASS

"**M**any of our average and below-average children seem to receive no perceptible benefit from eleven years of compulsory schooling," said Sir Keith Joseph, the Secretary of State for Education, recently.

He puts the proportion at forty per cent of the school population – a figure which can be neither proved nor disproved, but is almost certainly too high. It is true, though, that the achievement of certain groups of school pupils – working-class pupils, girls and children from the ethnic minorities – is lower than it should be. Many of Joseph's forty per cent, for instance, are working-class. Why is it that so many of them do not fulfil their potential in school?

As always in Britain, class is a vexed question. What is meant by a "working-class" family? Usually, it means that the head of the family is in a "blue-collar" (i.e., manual) job, whether skilled, semi-skilled or unskilled. The statisticians call these three manual classes IIIM, IV and V. Advertisers call them C2, D and E. So several different kinds of family are covered by the overall classification. Working-class people are not all unskilled, unemployed, and living in the inner city. They are just as likely to be well-paid skilled workers, buying their own houses in pleasant suburbs.

But sociological research deals in generalisations. One of the most fruitful sources of information on the effect of social class on educational achievement comes from the National Child Development Study, which is examining the progress through life of 5362 English and Welsh children, all of whom were born during a single week in March 1958.

This survey – which sociologists would describe as a *longitudinal* study – shows that achievement in school varies a great deal between the ages of seven and eleven. When the researchers divided the children into high achievers, average achievers and low achievers, they found that a third of the children who were in the top group at seven had dropped out of that group by the time they had turned eleven; on the other hand, a third of the low group had risen to a higher group. And social class was a major factor; those on the way down were most likely to be working-class.

Not surprisingly, such differences have a profound effect on the school careers of children from different social classes, and as they move up the educational ladder these distinctions grow more marked. A. H. Halsey's study, of 8529 boys educated in England and Wales in the mid-1950s and 1960s, shows that a boy from the "service class" (employers, professionals and managers) was four times as likely as a working-class boy to be still at school at sixteen, eight times as likely to be at school at seventeen, ten times as likely to be at school at eighteen, and eleven times as likely to go to university.

Class differences affect who goes to university – and who gets the best jobs – even when people are of equal intelligence. Over twenty years ago, the Robbins committee, looking into higher education, found that, of those pupils with a very high IQ (130 or more), children born into middle-class families in 1940–41 were still twice as likely as working-class children to get on to a degree course. In 1963 the Robbins report recommended a huge expansion in university places.

But expanding the universities benefited the middle class more than the working class. Halsey's research showed that, compared with their parents' generation, the proportion of working-class boys entering university increased by two per cent, and the proportion of boys from the "intermediate class" (clerical workers, small proprietors, foremen) increased by six per cent, but the proportion of boys from the service class increased by nineteen per cent. "Secondary education was made free in order to enable the poor to take advantage of it, but the paradoxical consequence was to increase subsidies to the affluent," Halsey notes wryly.

In fact, working-class participation in university education seems to have fallen since the 1950s. In 1956, nearly a quarter of the new entrants to university were from a working-class home. In 1980, the proportion was only 19.4 per cent. (It should be remembered, though, that the size of the working class is falling all the time, both through social mobility and because its birthrate is dropping faster than the middle-class birthrate.)

The main post-war reforms which were intended to make opportunities in education more equal were, first, the establishment of free secondary education in 1944 and then, during the 1960s and 1970s, the virtual abolition of selective schools in state education. (The top six per cent of the social pyramid, of course, continued to attend selective independent schools.)

The idea of equality of opportunity in education was not just a matter of social justice. Many people felt at the beginning of the century that a lot of talent, especially among working-class people, was being wasted. This meant that Britain was not as economically competitive as it might have been. So the first scholarship schemes were designed to catch bright working-class children and give them a middle-class education.

Ever since state education began, it has been bound up with questions of class.

The ideal system was seen as one which would identify every clever child and provide him or her with appropriate education. When the Education Act, 1944, made secondary education both compulsory and free, the selective model was the one which most local education authorities had in mind.

All children in most local authorities sat the 11-plus. It consisted of English and maths tests and an IQ test, which was thought to show how innately intelligent a child was, regardless of his or her social class or previous education. (Today, it is recognised that it is almost impossible to separate innate ability from learned experience in this way, or to construct a test which is not culturally biased against some social classes or ethnic groups.)

On the basis of their 11-plus results, children were sent to grammar schools, technical schools or secondary modern schools. The grammar schools – for those who were considered academic – only took about one in five children, a fact which is often forgotten by those who now campaign for their return. Technical schools were too expensive for most education authorities, so most children went to secondary modern schools, which were intended to develop a more practical curriculum.

Grammar schools and secondary moderns were supposed to have "parity of esteem" (equal status), because they simply offered different types of education for different types of children. But this turned out to be unrealistic in an unequal society, which values examination success over practical abilities.

But though the 11-plus was merely supposed to sort out clever children from the rest, the grammar schools somehow ended up full of middle-class children. According to J. W. B. Douglas in *The Home and the School* (1967), a child from the upper middle class was five times as likely as a child from the lower working class to get into a grammar school.

There were other objections to the 11-plus. Was it really right to divide children into two groups which more or less fixed their futures at so early an age? About one in ten children were probably sent to the wrong schools anyway, according to A. Yates and D. Pidgeon in *Admission to Grammar Schools* (1958). Although so called "late developers" were supposed to switch to grammar schools later on, few did. Some had had their confidence spoilt by being classified as second-best; others had adopted the unacademic ambience of their secondary modern school.

So comprehensive schools developed as a result of the unpopularity of the 11-plus, and as a way of enabling all children – but especially working-class children – to get more out of their education.

The hope was that by treating all children in the same way, as far as possible, the division into academic sheep and practical goats could be avoided – or at least put off as long as possible. But in spite of the spread of comprehensive schools, and a real increase in opportunities for the child of average ability, middle-class children are still much more likely than working-class children to succeed at school.

Why is this? Three main types of explanation are usually put forward as reasons for working-class underachievement. The first is based on heredity, and the question of innate intelligence; the second is environmental, taking into account the family circumstances of different social classes; the third focuses on how well schools themselves are doing their job.

THE HEREDITY ARGUMENT. This is not usually employed by sociologists. It takes the view that working-class pupils are inherently less intelligent than others; the results of the 11-plus seemed to some people to suggest this. But research has repeatedly shown that when the progress of children who start off with the same IQs is monitored, the working-class children still tend to fall behind over time. An American study published in 1974 showed that, among men with identical IQs, those in the top socio-economic group received nearly five more years of education than those in the bottom group.

It is safe to say that although high IQs and educational achievement are often found together, IQ-based arguments explain very little, if anything, of working-class underachievement. And even if this type of explanation were valid, education planners, teachers and theoreticians would still face the same problem. Hardly anyone denies that many working-class children, whatever their innate intelligence (if there is such a thing), should get a great deal more out of their schooling than they do at present. Their IQs are beside the point.

THE ENVIRONMENT ARGUMENT.
Rather more to the point – and particularly popular during the 1960s – are environmental explanations. The National Child Development Study showed that poor home conditions, such as substandard housing, are related (statistically, at any rate) to behaviour difficulties such as truancy. And these in turn are associated with poor results in reading and maths tests.

And probably just as important as material conditions are cultural conditions. Many studies in Britain and the United States show that working-class pupils and their parents do not value education as highly as the middle classes do.

For working-class children, leaving school and landing a job means adulthood, but staying on at school means prolonging their childhood. And to be interested in schoolwork is associated in their minds with a lack of manliness in boys and femininity in girls.

Paul Willis's book, *Learning to Labour* (1977), shows how working-class "lads" develop their own subculture which runs against that of the school, and despise the more conscientious boys (the "ear 'oles"), who work hard to collect exam passes. Similarly, Linda Measor and Peter Woods in their study of children entering secondary school (*Changing Schools,* 1984) express anxiety about the pressure to conform to a giggly femininity which academic girls experience from their companions.

Conversely, there is, too, a strong cultural link between middle-class homes and schools. The parents often take more interest in their children's schooling, and expect them to do well. They belong to the same social class as the teachers, don't find schools intimidating and "speak the same language."

Language, in fact, is probably a key factor. Basil Bernstein has drawn attention to the possibility that working-class and middle-class people use language differently, and that middle-class children could be more used to an abstract, formal language (or "code") which is easily adapted to the classroom.

During the 1970s, though, this stress on culture and language was criticised as a "deficit model", which implied that working-class pupils do not succeed because they are deficient. Such an approach could be too deterministic, as well, suggesting that children were already so fixed by their backgrounds that schools and teachers could have little effect.

THE SCHOOLS ARGUMENT.
More attention began to be paid to schools as institutions, to how classrooms work, and to the role of teachers. After all, the way pupils are treated in school is probably as important as any differences they bring with them. In 1978, Michael Rutter (a psychiatrist, not a sociologist) and his team found that twelve London comprehensives, all in similar areas with similar types of pupil, had very different results when it came to the achievement and attitudes of their pupils. School "ethos", Rutter decided, was the key. In short, those schools which expected hard work and good behaviour were more likely to get it. Her Majesty's Inspectors, too, agree that "low expectations" are the main problem in comprehensive schools.

Some sociologists have been critical of Rutter's work, and particularly of the notion of ethos, which they see as too vague and simplistic. They have preferred to take as their jumping-off point theories such as those developed by the American sociologist, Erving Goffman. Goffman argues that people are "labelled" by more dominant people or those in authority, and then begin to conform to the descriptions which have been imposed on them.

Perhaps the best-documented examples of this phenomenon are associated with streaming in British schools. David

Hargreaves, in his study of a boys' secondary modern school (1967) and Colin Lacey in his research at "Hightown Grammar" (1970), both found that boys allocated to the lower streams quickly developed an anti-school culture.

Neo-Marxist theories of education, associated with sociologists such as Herbert Bowles and Samuel Gintis in America, and Pierre Bourdieu in France, tend to lead in the same direction, because schools are seen as responsible for selecting and sorting pupils for the job market. Many neo-Marxists would argue that the real role of schools in society is deeply conservative. They reward middle-class children with success, and keep the working classes in their place.

On this analysis, most working-class pupils are bound to fail, because they are inevitably destined for the least desirable jobs society has to offer. The school's function is to teach them obedience, punctuality, and the willingness to work.

Though most approaches to the problem have something to offer, none has the complete answer. Michael Rutter's simple prescription that teachers should expect more of their pupils is probably as near the mark as any. Currently, attention has switched to the curriculum, and there are moves to make it more practical and directed towards the job market.

The idea could work, but many people are worried that it could lead back to the idea of different schooling for the "hewers of wood and the drawers of water."

But one thing is certain: too much has been expected of education. Attempts to achieve equal opportunities in schools which exist within an unequal social system can only have a limited effect.

BOOKS

Some useful additional reading:
S. Bowles and H. Gintis, *Schooling in Capitalist America,* Routledge & Kegan Paul, 1976
A. H. Halsey, A. F. Heath and J. M. Ridge, *Origins and Destinations,* Oxford University Press, 1980
D. Hargreaves, *Social Relations in a Secondary School,* Routledge & Kegan Paul, 1967
M. Rutter, *Fifteen Thousand Hours,* Open Books, 1978
P. Willis, *Learning to Labour,* Routledge & Kegan Paul, 1977

EDUCATION & RACE

Are black people less intelligent than white? Does your race determine how well you will get on in school? Is it true that black pupils are better than whites at passing exams? These are some of the issues that have made the subject of education and race so sensitive and controversial in recent years.

The word "race" is itself a problem. It doesn't mean the same as "nationality", so it is wrong to talk of the German race or the English race. "Race" should only be used to make a distinction between groups of people with very clear genetic differences which make them readily identifiable. Colour of skin is an obvious genetically determined factor, but colour of eyes, texture of hair and shape of nose have also been used to make these distinctions.

Some writers have tried to classify race according to three main types: negro (black), Caucasian (white) and oriental (yellow). Others have developed much more complex theories. Interestingly, Darwin made no attempt to classify races, on the grounds that naturalists should not try to name objects they cannot define. The problem of definition has never been completely solved, and many would prefer to avoid the use of the word "race" and to talk of "ethnic groups", which transfers attention to *culture* rather than race.

In the past, various writers have assumed the superiority of one or other of the racial types – usually their own; the philosopher, David Hume, in his essay, *Of National Characters* (1748), stated that he suspected that negroes might be naturally inferior to whites (although he had no evidence at all to support his view); the Chinese throughout the long period of their civilisation have regarded Europeans as clearly inferior in most respects to themselves.

Throughout the eighteenth and nineteenth centuries various pseudo-scientific theories of race appeared, some of them attempting to reconcile biblical accounts of the origin of man with the Darwinian view of natural selection; some theories of racial superiority appeared including attempts to explain history in terms of racial types. By the end of the nineteenth century, this confusion had been moderated by the work of social anthropologists, many of whom emphasised the importance of cultural differences rather than genetic ones. The point began to be made that race does not determine culture.

Many of the theories of white supremacy were put forward by European intellectuals attempting to equate the development of "civilisation" with white people's behaviour patterns. Most of these theories, however, have been found to be almost totally lacking in convincing evidence. Yet some racist views have survived in the folk memory of some European and American groups, distorting relations between black and white communities in several areas – including education.

One of the most difficult areas surrounds the belief that blacks are less intelligent than whites. This "race and IQ" debate is central to the whole discussion of education and race.

For many years, social scientists have argued about whether intelligence is mainly the result of heredity or mainly the result of environmental conditions (this is also sometimes called the "nature versus nurture" debate). Though few scientists would now claim that intelligence is caused either entirely by heredity or entirely by environment, they do argue about the relative importance of these two factors, and sometimes even try to attach a figure: 80 per cent being due to heredity is one frequently quoted by "hereditarians".

The heredity lobby tends to consist of psychologists. Environmentalists are mainly in the sociology camp, but it is not a straightforward psychology versus sociology conflict; there is also a right-wing/left-wing political association as well. The link with race stems from the fact that some hereditarians reckon that

black children (and working-class children) tend to score lower marks on IQ tests because of heredity rather than environment.

One way of trying to determine the relative importance of heredity and environment is to make studies of identical twins. Identical twins must, by definition, be genetically exactly the same – any differences which appear later in life (including IQ) must be the result of differences in environment – usually because they have been brought up separately.

A number of psychologists, notably the eminent researcher Sir Cyril Burt, have made detailed studies of such separated identical twins, and generally came to the conclusion that heredity was much more important than environment. But in 1974, when Burt had been dead for several years, an American professor, Leon Kamin, scrutinised the data and came to the conclusion (later confirmed by other psychologists) that much of Burt's data was unreliable, and some of it had been invented. An additional problem was that psychologists had frequently underestimated the difficulty of classifying people according to their environment – they often described separated twins as being brought up in *different* environments, where a sociologist might say that the environment was so similar as to prevent "environmental" differences being measured.

Hereditarians, such as H. J. Eysenck in Britain and Arthur Jensen in America, counter with the argument that twin studies form only part of the evidence supporting the heritability of intelligence. The work of A. M. Shuey in America appears to show that the *average* IQ score of white children is about twelve to fifteen points more than the *average* for black children, even where environmental differences appear to be negligible. The hereditarians also argue that if lower IQ scores are reckoned to be due to poor environment, then it is difficult to account for the fact that American Indian children score more highly than blacks, even though their environment is often no better.

Sociologists such as Kamin retort that American blacks have two hundred years of subordination to catch up on, and that IQ tests have been used as a political device for justifying keeping certain nationalities out of the country. They have also helped to maintain the class structure and the unequal distribution of wealth. Some social scientists, in their dislike of racism, are reluctant to acknowledge *any* genetic differences between ethnic groups, particularly those which might be used to designate one group as inferior.

The debate goes on, but the following statements can be reckoned as common ground among all those involved:

● Even where it is correct to say that "whites tend to score more highly than blacks", we are talking of fairly small differences in average marks, and the overlap between the two groups is also very great. So, even if it is correct to say that on average whites are better at IQ tests than blacks, there will still be large numbers of blacks who are better than large numbers of whites.

● All tests are biased in some way: attempts to produce "culture-fair" tests have failed so far.

● The word "intelligence" can be used in at least three ways:

INTELLIGENCE A refers to some innate maximum capacity, genetically determined. (This must exist, but can never be calculated.)

INTELLIGENCE B is what we refer to in commonsense terms as intelligent behaviour – this is a mixture of genetic capacity and opportunity as provided by the environment.

INTELLIGENCE C is what intelligence tests measure – IQ.

If the test is a "good" one, C will be close to B, but not necessarily to A; but if the test is a poor one it may not even give a reasonable indication of B.

So what do IQ tests really measure? Do they really show people's innate capacity or do they mainly reflect the advantages of favourable background circumstances? This difficulty exists in deciding whether working-class children are less intelligent than middle-class children, or simply do not achieve as well on IQ tests; and the same problem exists with racial groups. Black West Indian children, for example, tend to do rather badly on tests compared with white English children and also compared with Asian or Chinese children, but what this "fact" means is a matter of opinion.

However imperfect the tests may be, they *do* correlate to some extent with general achievement at school, and so there are also measurable differences in educational performance between the racial groups within Britain.

These differences in educational achievement are of at least three kinds, but all the data present problems of one kind or another. First, there are measurable differences between native white, Asian and black West Indian children on GCE O-level passes at age sixteen; second, earlier in their school career it is possible to find differences in reading skills between the three groups; third, and much more controversially, black West Indian children tend to be "selected" to attend schools for the so-called "educationally subnormal."

Not only are West Indian children under-represented at the top of the achievement range, they also seem to be over-represented at the bottom. In comparison with white and Asian children they are, as a group, what are known as *under-achievers*. In studying the effects of racial disadvantage at school, researchers have, therefore, concentrated on the problems of West Indian children, though this in no way implies that Asians do not suffer from some of the same problems, notably racism.

Before looking at various explanations for under-achievement, however, it is worth examining the context and making some warning comments about the data.

GCE O-LEVEL RESULTS: In its report on *The West Indian Community* (1977), the House of Commons select committee on race relations and immigration recommended that a committee should be set up to look at the under-achievement of ethnic minorities. This committee (the Rampton committee) made an interim report in June 1981, which included information from the Department of Education and Science about the comparative

age	West Indian average	non- immigrant	expected score
8	88	98	100
10	87	98	100
15	86	98	100

performance at O-level in six local education authorities with a high proportion of West Indian children. (In this report, "West Indian" does not mean "born in the West Indies", but blacks of West Indian descent most of whom were born in Britain.)

The results were sufficiently clear to be disturbing: in English language only nine per cent of West Indian pupils gained an O-level "pass" (grades A, B or C, or CSE grade 1), compared with twenty-six per cent of Asians and twenty-nine per cent of other leavers; in mathematics, only five per cent of West Indians gained passes, compared with nineteen per cent of other leavers. These figures have been challenged on the grounds that they represent only a sample of education authorities, not a national survey, and a biased sample at that. But most observers reacted by accepting that a problem existed, even if part of the problem was that examinations were unfair to ethnic minorities.

Other research has since contradicted the Rampton report figures: a survey of London schools by Professor Michael Rutter showed that where West Indian pupils stayed on at school into the sixth form or beyond the compulsory school leaving age, then their performance improved considerably. This meant that they caught up with and sometimes even surpassed comparable white pupils. Some newspapers misrepresented these findings with such headlines as BLACK PUPILS BEST AT EXAMS. This kind of interpretation was not justified, but Rutter offered a more optimistic picture than the Rampton report.

READING ABILITY: The most important data on West Indian children's reading attainment are in the 1980 literary survey carried out by the Inner London Education Authority. The table above gives the results for children aged 8, 10, and 15. (The expected or average score at each level would be 100 for a "normal" sample – so any score below 100 is "below average".) It appears from this that London children are generally slightly worse than average, but West Indian children not only score considerably below the whites, but the gap widens as the children get older. Once again, the validity of the figures might be questioned, but they probably represent some kind of educational problem.

ESN SCHOOLS: The final source of data is the most controversial. It concerns admission to schools for the educationally sub-normal (ESN). In 1971, Bernard Coard, who was himself a West Indian teacher in an ESN school, showed that the percentage of West Indian children who had been selected as "backward" was considerably higher than what would be regarded as acceptable for white children. The title of his book, *How the West Indian Child is made Educationally Sub-normal in the British School System,* indicated his own view of the problem.

We'll look at some of the arguments to account for this under-achievement in a moment. Unfortunately, it is not clear whether Coard's gloomy view could apply to the whole country, since some local education authorities do not record statistics that make a distinction between black and white pupils. Once again, the data base is inadequate, but the limited evidence available suggests the existence of a problem. But what problem?

Sociologists have put foward several theories to account for under-achievement in school. Here are some of the main ones:

THE ENVIRONMENT FACTOR: West Indian under-achievement, like working-class under-achievement, is associated with a variety of social conditions such as poor-quality housing, over-crowding, working mothers with inadequate child care facilities, one-parent families and so on, all of which tend to be connected with difficulties in coping with school work. This suggests that West Indian children,

like working-class children, are *not* genetically inferior, but have significantly less favourable environmental conditions.

THE MOTIVATION FACTOR: The West Indian child, like many working-class children, tends to lack incentive to learn in school, partly because motivation within the school is geared to "getting a good job". But, in fact, most West Indian school leavers (and working-class pupils) have very poor job expectations. There is, therefore, a mis-match between the ideal of the school and the reality.

THE RACISM FACTOR: Britain, it is argued, is a racist society; teachers are racist either explicitly or without realising their own racism. If true, this theory might have a number of effects:
● If some teachers are overtly racist – that is, thinking that blacks are, or should be treated as, inferior – then this is likely to cause a variety of learning problems for black pupils. For example, the "self-fulfilling prophecy" syndrome would suggest that if a teacher treats a group of pupils as "stupid", they eventually behave in a way that fits in with the teacher's view – they underachieve. This is a variety of what the American sociologist, Erving Goffman, and others have called *labelling theory*.
● A slightly different version of this theory is that West Indian children in Britain (but not in Jamaica) grow up with a *negative self-image* – that is, they lack self-respect and confidence because they themselves believe that they are in some ways inferior to white children.
● If, however, teachers are only unconsciously racist (maybe even thinking themselves as very "liberal" on race) there may be other important unintended consequences of their behaviour towards black pupils. One suggestion is that the "colour-blind" teacher may do the wrong things from perfectly good intentions. An unprejudiced teacher might, for example, say that he or she treats all children alike irrespective of class or colour; but to treat everyone in the same way is not necessarily to treat them *fairly*.

If this is the case, then teachers who ignore such difficulties are not being fair to their black pupils – they could only be truly fair by diagnosing their problems and by making special provisions to cope with them. Many sociologists argue that positive discrimination is sometimes needed to achieve social justice.

Some education authorities have gone for this "positive" approach, arguing, like the Inner London Education Authority, that "more power should be delivered to blacks". But the current "enlightened" consensus is that young black children need better-quality teaching and a curriculum which has been planned for a multicultural society. Maureen Stone, herself a black sociologist from Trinidad, studied the curriculum being offered to young blacks in secondary schools and compared it with what West Indian parents were demanding in their "supplementary" or Saturday morning schools (*The Education of the Black Child in Britain,* Fontana, 1981). In the secondary schools she found well-meaning white teachers of English, attempting to boost the self-image of West Indian pupils by teaching them the West Indian creole dialect (usually very badly) instead of "standard English."

But what West Indian parents wanted was exactly what was offered in their own schools on Saturday mornings – that is, clear English expression of a kind that would help the children to cope with the rest of the curriculum. This is a classic example of what critics of the teaching profession describe as teachers attempting to extend their role too far, and thus neglecting their primary task.

With this problem, as with many others in sociology, there is no single cause and no single theory that would help solve it. But the question of education and race is vitally important for the future of society. If racial disadvantage cannot be sorted out at school, there is little prospect of a racially integrated Britain.

BOOKS

Some useful additional reading:

H. J. Eysenck, *Race, Intelligence and Education,* Temple Smith, 1971
P. Green, *The Pursuit of Inequality,* Martin Robertson, 1981
A. R. Jensen, "Environment, heredity and intelligence," *Harvard Education Review,* 1969
Leon J. Kamin, *The Science and Politics of IQ,* Penguin, 1977
A. M. Shuey, *The Testing of Negro Intelligence,* Social Science Press, 1966

ELECTIONS

All over the world, people have fought and died for the right to vote in free elections. "The vote" is the paramount symbol of citizenship in a democracy and "one person, one vote" one of its core principles.

Yet the universal adult franchise is a remarkably recent achievement. It was not until 1919 that all working-class men in Britain were allowed to vote, and British women did not get the vote until 1928. In the United States, legal obstructions to the enfranchisement of blacks were not removed until 1965, while in Australia the aborigines only got the vote in 1967. Women were not granted the vote on equal terms with men until 1944 in France, 1946 in Italy and Japan, 1948 in Belgium and as recently as 1971 in Switzerland.

There is no such thing as a truly universal adult suffrage. Different democracies exclude certain groups of people from voting, such as criminals and the mentally ill. Foreign nationals like the Turkish and Yugoslav "guest workers" in West Germany are also denied the vote. And electors in western democracies are entitled to vote in a bewildering variety of ways. In Britain, we can vote for local councillors and members of the British and European parliaments. We once had a referendum, in 1975, on membership of the EEC. But we are not as "democratic" as the US, for example, where voters directly elect local authority officials and judges, as well as representatives at town, county, state and national level.

All western democracies hold regular "general elections". These are elections in which most or all elected offices of a

nation's central government are contested. A "democratic general election" such as we have in Britain is one in which six vital conditions are satisfied. There should be:
● Universal adult franchise
● A secret ballot
● A time-limit on office
● Freedom to form parties
● All seats should be contested in the major assembly
● Election campaigns should be governed by strict rules.

"General elections", wrote Sir Lewis Namier in 1952, "are the locks on the stream of British democracy, controlling the flow of the river and its traffic." In a general election campaign, the government defends its record, the opposition seeks to show it could do a better job and then the voters decide.

Of course, one vote is hardly ever likely to make a difference to the result in any election, let alone a general one, so the purely "rational" person would never bother to turn out and vote. In fact, only about three out of four people vote in British general elections and there are signs of a drift down from the high point of 84 per cent in 1950.

Sociologists have distinguished between *instrumental* voters, who hope their vote *will* make a difference to their lives, and *expressive* voters, who turn out more from a sense of duty or civic pride. But sociologists disagree as to whether a low turnout is a *good* sign (Seymour Martin Lipset, 1960), indicating contentment on the part of the populace, or a *bad* sign (Ralph Miliband, 1972), suggesting alienation from the system.

In a detailed study made in 1981 of turnout in twenty-seven countries, Professor Ivor Crewe, of Essex University, found major variations *between* countries but not *within* countries over time. The administrative facility of registering to vote, the organised mobilisation of the parties and the different electoral systems were all relevant factors in creating long-standing national voting traditions.

Karl Marx wrote in 1852 that the universal franchise would lead to the "political supremacy of the working class" and would obviate the need for bloody revolution. Later theorists argued that the universal franchise simply institutionalised class conflict and had functioned to *prevent* revolution and the political supremacy of the working class.

Ivor Crewe, in his turnout study, found that it is the more privileged sections of the community, not the more deprived, who tend to make most use of their vote. He concluded: "Universal suffrage fails to provide the political counterweight to the power of property and wealth in the way that was intended by its more radical proponents."

Farewell to class politics?

In theory, elections are decided by voters listening to the arguments and making up their minds on the issues. But politics are no more about the speeches of prime ministers at election times than history is simply about the comings and goings of kings and queens.

First, opinion polls regularly show that many voters are poorly informed about political issues and find difficulty in describing the policies of major parties. Second, study after study has shown that many voters have a long-standing allegiance to a particular party – though in Britain this is now on the decline. An analytical tradition, chiefly associated with David Butler and Donald Stokes (whose *Political Change in Britain* was first published in 1969), has developed, based on tracing voter "alignments" or "cleavages" – the relationship between voting and such factors as class, sex, age, religion, region, housing tenure, trade union membership and neighbourhood.

Thus a major cleavage of the electorate, like that based on class, is itself overlain by other cleavages, creating a weave of interlocking influences on the voting habits of individuals. Thus a middle-class, church-going pensioner living on the south coast is highly likely to vote Conservative, while an unemployed council tenant on Merseyside is most likely to vote Labour. Researchers like Butler and Stokes also identified *cohorts* or generations of voters who often retain party allegiances throughout their lives. *Psephology* is the name usually given to this type of study.

Thanks to the psephologists, Britain is often cited as a kind of standard model of a party system based on class. Thus Robert Alford in *Party and Society* (1963) wrote that Britain was a class-based system *par excellence,* while Peter Pulzer (1967) was able to claim: "Class is the basis of British party politics: all else is embellishment and detail." The middle class voted Tory and the working class were Labour – anyone who voted the "wrong" way round was dismissed as "deviant".

Unfortunately, this glossed over the fact that a third of the working class continued to vote Conservative, despite the rise of the Labour Party – giving the Tories about half their total votes. The rediscovery of the "working class Tories" in the mid-1960s was marked by the publication of W. G. Runciman's *Relative Deprivation and Social Justice* (1966), Eric Nordlinger's *The Working Class Tories* (1967) and Robert McKenzie and Allan Silver's *Angels in Marble* (1968).

Runciman found that working class electors who *describe* themselves as "middle-class" are more likely to vote Conservative. When asked about their voting habits, Tory manual workers are less likely to mention their occupation or status in society and are more concerned with Queen and Country. Nordlinger concluded that a "sense of economic well-being" led to working-class people identifying with the middle classes and thus voting for the Conservative Party.

McKenzie and Silver isolated two distinctive types. The *deferential* working-class Tories tend to see Conservative leaders as being some kind of natural elite of people "born to rule". The *secular* working-class voters simply backed the Tories on pragmatic grounds – they saw them as more likely to govern competently and deliver the goods – thus making everyone better-off in the long run.

The other group of deviants, the twenty per cent or so of middle-class people who voted Labour, received less attention, apart from a study of CND supporters by Frank Parkin (*Middle Class Radicalism,* 1968). More recently, however, the Oxford Mobility Survey, through the work of A. H. Halsey and John Goldthorpe (1980) has shown how the managerial and professional classes have expanded, drawing in new recruits from the lower middle and working-class – many of whom have kept their allegiance to Labour. In particular, middle-class Labour voters tend to be drawn from groups such as academics and "intellectuals", the sons of active trade unionists and those working in the "caring" professions like social work.

Apart from the issue of the working-class Tories, rising living standards in the 1960s led many to argue that Labour was on the way out because of growing affluence at the bottom of the social scale. This theme was explored by Mark Abrams and Richard Rose in *Must Labour Lose?* (1960), written after Labour lost the 1959 general election. But such fears were seemingly quashed by the famous *Affluent Worker* studies of Luton car workers, by John Goldthorpe and his colleagues (1968). Though they found differences between "instrumental" and "traditional" Labour voters, there was no evidence at that time of a decline in Labour voting – even among the most affluent. Labour went on to win the 1964 and 1966 general elections – but the same fears expressed after 1959 were to return and haunt the party in 1979 and again in 1983.

Despite claiming in 1969 that working-class Conservatism was in decline – pointing to the possibility of permanent Labour rule – Butler and Stokes were forced to concede in the second edition of their book (1975) that social class was losing its hold on the British electorate. They pointed to the weakening of the class "alignment" and growing *volatility* – voters were more likely to switch from one party to another.

Writing in *New Society* in 1974, Ivor Crewe, Bo Särlvik and James Alt of Essex University also pointed out that less than half (forty-four per cent) of all manual workers voted Labour in the February 1974 election, while well under half of all non-manuals (forty-five per cent) voted Conservative. The Liberals did exceptionally well on a specifically class-conciliatory appeal. This implied the very opposite of growing class polarisation.

In 1977, Crewe and his colleagues published an influential article, "Partisan De-alignment 1964–1974", in the *British Journal of Political Science*, which challenged the accepted wisdom that British politics has always been a two-party system based on class. The February 1974 election, they argued, was a "watershed": things would never be the same again.

Likewise, Professor Richard Rose of Strathclyde University published in 1980 a paper called "Class Does Not Equal Party", in which he argued that the relationship between class and voting had been "exaggerated". Britain, he said, now had less of a class-based system than most other European countries and class was fast declining in favour of other factors such as housing tenure. There had been a "loosening-up" of the electorate.

Demographic changes were taking their toll. Old working-class communities had been destroyed by redevelopment schemes and the inner cities were emptying out. Workers moving to new towns and the expanding small towns around London were less likely to vote Labour. Areas of population decline – like northern England and south Wales – had been traditionally Labour, while growth areas – mainly in the south-east – were strongly Conservative. Boundary changes would emphasise this social upheaval.

Writing in the *New Statesman* in October 1981, Peter Kellner said that "the sense of class solidarity which propelled Labour to power in 1945 has all but evaporated". Labour's electoral base had been crumbling away for thirty years. "Even if Tony Benn and Ken Livingstone were blown up by an IRA bomb tomorrow, it is a fact that will not go away."

The social trends that upset Labour's chances

Though the February 1974 or "Liberal revival" election has been described as a "watershed" in British politics, both the 1979 and 1983 elections were remarkable for two reasons.

First, the decline of class-based voting dramatically hastened the decline of the two-party system and the rise of the "third force" in British politics – now the Liberals *and* the Social Democrats. Second, the Conservatives were able under the present electoral system to establish a stranglehold on England, with Labour being pushed right back to its heartlands in the north, in Scotland and in Wales. The 1979 and 1983 elections provided dramatic confirmation of the trends spotted by Crewe and others some years before. They mean that the textbooks will have to be re-written, whether or not the Labour Party under its new leadership manages to pull itself back into lasting popularity.

In 1951, the two major parties obtained 97 per cent of the vote – which meant, in that high turnout year, that 80 per cent of the entire electorate voted Labour or Conservative. Such a command over the electorate was never to be achieved again; a steady decline in the two parties' share of the vote and in turnout meant that by 1964 only 67 per cent of the electorate voted Conservative or Labour.

Then things speeded up: in February and October 1974, the Liberal and Scottish National Party surges meant that the two major parties' share of the vote was down to 75 per cent, representing less than 60 per cent of the electorate. Mid-term by-elections saw increasing volatility among voters, with huge swings against the governments of the day. Despite a fall back to 14 per cent in 1979, the Liberals were steadily increasing their support on a kind of "ratchet" mechanism: three steps forward, two steps back.

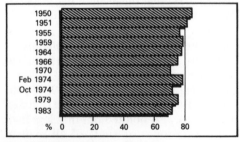

1950
1951
1955
1959
1964
1966
1970
Feb 1974
Oct 1974
1979
1983
% 0   20   40   60   80

Percentage turnout in British general elections

How much does voting matter?

The former Labour Party deputy leader, Denis Healey, recently said that Labour lost the 1983 election in the three years before, not during the three weeks of, the campaign. He might just as well have said the thirty years before, because the roots of election results are buried deep in history and the social structure.

This is not to say that politicians need not bother to campaign at election times or that some electors don't consciously change their voting intention according to the policies on offer. Rather, parties must attune their policies to changing social realities. And though they may seek to emphasise their differences during election campaigns, all politicians face the same realities when they get into office – any government's room for manoeuvre is often quite small, especially in a declining nation like Britain.

Marxists like Ralph Miliband have argued that the election of a Labour or a Tory government makes no difference to the class struggle in the industrialised countries. Elections are merely a device to divert the attention of the masses. This certainly rings true in, say, the Latin American context.

Even in the United States many see election campaigns as an exercise in meaningless razzmatazz, with few evident policy differences between the candidates, many of whom are backed by big business.

In many countries, elections are frequently used by ruling regimes to foster the myth of participation. They can range from being just a meaningless exercise, like those in the Soviet Union, to a downright fraud, like South African elections where the majority of the population has no vote. However, the object – of conferring legitimacy on the government – is the same. In Britain, we may only get a chance to vote for a new government once every four or five years – but at least a genuine opportunity is there for the electorate to throw the existing one out of office.

With the launch of the Social Democratic Party in March 1981, the "third force" in British politics received a further boost, mainly at the expense of Labour. In June 1983, the two parties' share of the vote slumped to 70.6 per cent and the SDP-Liberal Alliance obtained 25.9 per cent (just two per cent behind Labour). The absolute number of votes going to the Liberals had risen from three million in 1964 to six million in 1974 to eight million in conjunction with the Social Democrats in 1983.

The scene for Labour's disastrous performance in 1983 had been set in the 1979 general election, which put Mrs Thatcher into Downing Street with a healthy majority. The socialist *New Statesman* said at the time that Labour had suffered "a serious, and possibly fatal, haemorrhage of support among the people on whom it most depends".

More detailed analyses were provided by Ivor Crewe in Howard Penniman (ed.), *Britain at the Polls* (1981), and

Dennis Kavanagh (ed.), *The Politics of the Labour Party* (1982). Crewe showed, among other things, that a majority of manual workers had not voted Labour. Large sections of the working-class now "regarded Conservative policies and objectives as being more in line with their own interests and values". There had been a "spectacular decline" in support for Labour's traditional policies of public ownership, trade union power and social welfare.

In the months after 1979, there was little evidence of Labour seriously addressing itself to its problems of policy and image. Instead, it plunged into a long round of internal wrangles.

But if the 1979 result was bad for Labour, the 1983 result was a catastrophe, with Labour support falling to its lowest level ever. Despite the Conservative share of the poll actually falling, the split in the opposition meant that the Tories were returned with a landslide 144-seat majority. "The electorate did not embrace the Conservatives," commented the *Guardian,* "it rebuffed Labour and flirted with the Alliance."

The social trends spotted by Abrams and Rose back in the 1959 election and dramatically confirmed in 1979 were even more evident in the 1983 electoral map of Britain: Labour had become the party of declining Britain, forced even farther back into its heartlands. Labour lost forty per cent of its 1979 vote in the south out-

BOOKS

Some useful additional reading:
J. Blondel, *Voters, Parties and Leaders,* Penguin, 1984
Vernon Bogdanor and David Butler (eds.), *Democracy and Elections,* Cambridge, 1983
David Butler, Howard R. Penniman and Austin Ranney (eds.), *Democracy at the Polls: A comparative study of competitive national elections,* American Enterprise Institute, 1981
David Butler and Dennis Kavanagh, *The British General Election of 1979,* Macmillan, 1980
Bo Särlvik and Ivor Crewe, *Decade of Dealignment,* Cambridge, 1983

Last past the post?

There is a bewildering variety of electoral systems in operation in western democracies, many of which involve some kind of proportional representation. Most European countries, including the Irish Republic, now use proportional representation in elections. Britain's first-past-the-post system has become the exception.

The perfect example of the distortions created by the British system is, of course, the 1983 general election result. The Conservatives got 13 million votes and 396 seats, Labour 8.5 million votes and 209 seats, while the Alliance polled nearly as many votes as Labour (7.8 million) but got only 23 seats. It took 33 000 votes to elect a Conservative MP, 40 000 to elect a Labour MP and 339 000 to elect an Alliance MP.

Had the election been carried out on a proportional representation basis, Mrs Thatcher would not have a majority at all, let alone one of 144. The Tories would have got 280 seats, Labour 182, the Alliance 170 and others 18.

side London and won just three non-London seats in the entire south east (Bristol South, Thurrock and Ipswich). Constituencies in growing areas of Britain went Conservative with massive majorities. The Alliance took second place in no less than 311 seats, leaving Labour with 119 lost desposits.

A number of factors were of special help to the Tories, apart from the fact that they were widely perceived as having the best policies. The rapid run-down of British industry and the cuts in public expenditure between 1979 and 1983 had produced a massive decline in manual jobs, especially in manufacturing. This produced a large and sudden fall in trade union membership and reduced the influence of the workplace on millions of (mostly male) voters.

The continuing rise in home ownership, dramatically accelerated by the government's decision to let all council tenants buy their homes, produced a surge of support for the Conservatives, especially in high-sales areas like the new towns.

Working-class home-owners, or the new "midway" class as some have described them, are firmly Tory now. And the further ageing of the electorate continued to benefit the Conservatives – it has long been known that the elderly are more likely to vote Tory.

Curiously, the issue of unemployment seemed to be of little help to Labour. Rising joblessness did not seem to damage the Conservatives – one survey found that forty-seven per cent of unemployed young people stayed in bed on polling day!

More men than women voted Conservative for the first time – thus knocking on the head the accepted wisdom that men are always more strongly Labour. And most of the twenty-three Alliance MPs were elected with the help of substantial "personal" votes – challenging the orthodox view that no individual candidate is worth more than 500–1000 votes.

THE ENVIRONMENT

Back in 1970, the Conservative government of the day created a giant ministry to be called the Department of the Environment. It was meant to be a piece of administrative streamlining, but it was also a measure of how much our consciousness of the environment as an issue had grown. Twenty years earlier, "environment," in the broad sense of the word, would have meant little or nothing to people. Now it is an everyday part of our vocabulary.

There are estimated to be anything between one and three million people involved in the "environmental movement" in Britain today. But environmentalism is not confined to Britain. Disasters like the mercury poisoning episode in Minamata, Japan, and the poisonous gas leaks at Seveso in Italy and Bhopal in India, have encouraged environmental movements in most parts of the world.

What is environmentalism? To say that it means support for the environment is unhelpful, for the environment has no declared enemies. Yet there is now a concern about the impact of man's activities on his natural surroundings. There is opposition to motorways, airports and nuclear power stations because they represent "threats to the environment." There are worries about pollution of the air, the soil and the oceans. There are anxieties about the killing of animals for profit or sport.

The broadest and most generous interpretation of this "environmental awareness" is that it signifies a reconciliation between man and nature. The distinguished scientist, Lord Ashby, who served on the Royal Commission on Environmental Pollution between 1970 and 1973, takes this view. He has argued that, from the book of Genesis onwards, humans have been encouraged to believe that they are superior to every other living thing. This has distanced them from their environment.

Primitive people, however, realised intuitively that man and environment were indivisible. Ashby has suggested that modern man is once again identifying with the environment, not by intuition this time but by the evidence of science. (It is no coincidence that environmental concern has increased at a time when higher education, particularly scientific education, has expanded.)

The idea that Judaeo-Christian beliefs have encouraged people to dominate and exploit their natural surroundings may be too simple, however. Religions have also encouraged the idea of man's "stewardship" of nature, which persists in the modern idea of conservation.

The early social scientists tried to reconcile these two ideas – domination and stewardship. The "social Darwinism" of Herbert Spencer put man at the top of the animal tree. Even Marx and Engels thought in terms of man's "conquest" of nature. Progress demanded such conquest.

But Marx distinguished between progress and capitalist progress. Capitalist progress, with its emphasis on making a fast buck, sacrificed the long-term future of natural resources for short-term gain.

Capitalism was poor stewardship: "All progress in capitalistic agriculture," he wrote, "is a progress in the art not only of robbing the labourer, but of robbing the soil; all progress towards ruining the lasting sources of that fertility."

Engels, too, tempered his belief in human progress with an understanding of the ecological consequences of that progress. "Let us not," he said "flatter ourselves on account of our human victories over nature. For each such victory takes revenge on us. Each victory, it is true, in the first place brings about the results we expected; but in the second and third places it has quite different and unforeseen effects which only too often cancel the first."

This yoking together of a belief in economic progress with a respect for the natural world provides a rationale today for, say, the economic system of the Soviet Union. But in the west, concern for the environment has often been accompanied by a rejection of the idea of progress.

This concern for the environment is no more than a century old. Philip Lowe and a research team at the Bartlett School of Architecture and Planning, University College London, have distinguished four peaks of environmental activity (Lowe calls it "swarming") within the period:

● **From the 1880s to the end of the nineteenth century.** This produced organisations like the Royal Society for the Protection of Birds, the National Trust, and the Garden Cities Association (later to become the Town and Country Planning Association).

● **Between the First and Second World Wars.** This saw the emergence of, among others, the Ramblers' Association, the Pedestrians' Association and the Council for the Preservation of Rural England (since changed to "Protection").

● **The late 1950s.** This period saw the formation of the Civic Trust, the Noise Abatement Society and the Victorian Society.

● **The early 1970s.** This was a time of exponential growth in environmental activity in which many groups appeared, like Friends of the Earth, Save Britain's

Heritage and Transport 2000, the pro-railway lobby. Local groups multiplied. The number of local amenity societies registered with the Civic Trust nearly doubled in six years.

There are differences of emphasis between the four peaks of environmentalism. The Victorian environmentalists saw private individuals as the enemy – private landowners and landlords. They expected the state to curb "individualism" and promote a collective interest in the protection of the environment.

A century later there was quite a different perspective. Environmentalists now saw the state as their opponent, whether it was the transport ministry proposing a motorway or the trade department promoting a third London airport. But the similarities in outlook are striking. The late Victorians, taking their intellectual cue from John Ruskin, John Stuart Mill and William Morris, turned against economic liberalism; the getting of wealth, the constant striving to improve and advance standards of living. In the same way, the environmentalists of the 1970s have adopted a "post-materialist" philosophy. They are opposed to change and growth. They want to retrench and conserve. This philosophy was summed up in the Club of Rome's *The Limits to Growth,* a report by a group of economists in 1969, which predicted ecological disaster if growth was not restrained.

Is growth the problem? Why has the environment, and particularly the pollution of the environment, become an issue? There are several possible explanations.

One theory is that environmental problems have been caused by the sharp rise in the world's population. As the population increases, the theory goes, so does pollution. Yet this cannot be the full answer. The worst pollution occurs in the developed world, where population growth has been lowest.

Another theory is that the environment is threatened by increasing affluence. As people "consume" more goods, so the increasing levels of production cause an increasing amount of pollution. Again this may not be a full explanation. Barry Commoner points out in his book, *The Closing*

Circle (1972), that the production of goods to meet human needs, per head, has not risen significantly since 1945.

Commoner thinks that neither of these explanations is enough. He suggests that technology provides the missing piece of jigsaw.

New technology has certainly caused new problems. The use of plastics and detergents which will not "degrade" biologically and the addition of lead to petrol have all caused environmental problems. But this is a technical rather than an economic or social explanation. It does not tell us why new technologies are necessary.

Here Marx provides an answer. New technologies are necessary to capitalism.

They enable manufacturers to compete profitably. Currently, intensive farming provides a good example of this.

The objection to Marx's theory is that communist as well as capitalist countries suffer from problems of environmental pollution. East Germany's industry, for example, is a major exporter of sulphur dioxide, which is reckoned to be one cause of the "acid rain" phenomenon in Europe.

Overall, though, growth theory is probably the least *un*-satisfactory explanation for pollution. Economic growth has put the environment under pressure.

Pressure on the countryside is an example. In the last thirty years, the number of people in Britain with their own cars has gone up fivefold. The number of people who own their homes has trebled. A growing proportion of these can afford to live in the country. The classic pattern of rural-urban migration has been reversed.

This has coincided with anxieties about threats to the countryside. On the one hand, there are worries about the outward urban migration. Where will the new homes be built? On the other hand, there are worries about the use of the countryside itself. Howard Newby suggests, in his book, *Green and Pleasant Land?* (1979), that newcomers to the country often have utopian, or rather arcadian ideas of what the country should be like. They object to intensive arable farming as it produces a landscape which does not conform to these ideas.

Therefore, the suspicion grows that newcomers to the countryside are interested less in the broader benefits of conservation than in a rather selfish preservation of the status quo.

Environmentalism may thus be a mixture of social concern and simple selfishness. The Bartlett School research team sees environmentalism as an amalgam of two, often conflicting perspectives. In one perspective, human values are seen as more important than materialist values. On this view, the quality of life of people living round Stansted, for example, is rated more important than the earnings from air traffic that Britain would lose if Stansted were not developed as London's third airport.

In the other perspective, change is often seen as unwelcome in itself. Never mind that a development brings jobs to a neighbourhood. If it disturbs the even tenor of people's lives, it is to be resisted. In this sense, environmental concern has become a sort of elitism, with the few protecting what they have from the many.

The charge of elitism is difficult to dismiss. Philip Lowe suggests that the environmental movement, far from widening the base of environmental concern, has concentrated policy-making in the hands of barely one hundred people. Yet this elite has successfully enlisted the backing of up to three million supporters. It has done this, Howard Newby suggests, by appeals to the national interest. Buildings and landscapes need to be preserved, they say, because they are part of a *national* heritage – that is, they belong to us all.

Newby suggests that the nature of the environmental lobby raises a question of political equity. "Does the political mobilisation of environmentalists accentuate the already existing disparities between the favoured environments of the powerful and wealthy and the degraded environments of the deprived?" he asks.

In other words, campaigns on behalf of the environment may allow the haves to hold on to what they have, while doing little or nothing to improve the lot of the have-nots. Anthony Crosland, a former Environment Minister, once complained that environmentalism was a wholly rural phenomenon. It did not concern itself with the towns and cities where 80 per cent of the population spend their lives.

"Part of the conservationist lobby," he argued, "are hostile to growth and indifferent to the needs of ordinary people". He pictured environmentalists as people who had reached the top of the ladder and were determined to prevent anyone climbing up after them. Recent events, however, have shown that the environment is not an exclusively rural concern. The issue of lead in petrol, which has led to a change in public policy, is largely urban. And one of the fiercest battles over the siting of a motorway, the series of Archway road inquiries, took place in London.

There is another less jaundiced view of environmentalism; that it *is* concerned with equity. Pollution is inequitable, because it imposes costs on the rest of society which ought to be borne by the polluter. Economists call these *external costs*. In times of economic expansion, people have the time and resources to query these external costs. This explains the peaks of environmental activity.

Some economists think that in spite of environmental lobbying, pollution is bound to increase. This is because, though the polluter never pays the full cost of his activities, he always reaps the full benefit.

If we are all environmentalists, we tend also all to be polluters. This is because of the so-called "tragedy of the commons". One person's share of the waste he discharges is less than the cost (to him) of purifying that waste before releasing it. So, for the individual, the rational thing to do is to go on polluting. Only society in general benefits from cleaning up.

Yet environmental "awareness" has not always led to awareness of this. Instead, environmentalists tend to cast industry rather than individuals as the enemy, incorrigibly exploitative, a polluter who must be made to pay. Max Nicholson, a former head of the Nature Conservancy, has distinguished between two kinds of environmentalists; the *polarisers* and the *integrators*. Polarisers, like Friends of the Earth, campaign head-on for change in public policy. The integrators work more cautiously, and attempt to change attitudes.

BOOKS

Some useful additional reading:
Eric Ashby, *Reconciling Man with the Environment,* Oxford University Press, 1978
Fred Hirsch, *The Social Limits to Growth,* Routledge & Kegan Paul, 1977
Philip Lowe and Jane Goyder, *Environmental Groups in Politics,* Allen & Unwin, 1983
Max Nicholson, *The Environmental Revolution,* Hodder & Stoughton, 1970
Marion Shoard, *The Theft of the Countryside,* Temple Smith, 1980

The "them" and "us" battles of the polarisers *have* produced victories. Rachel Carson's book, *The Silent Spring* (1962), led to the abandonment of the insecticide, DDT. But in the end perhaps only the integrators can achieve that reconciliation of man and nature Lord Ashby looked for.

THE FAMILY

Everyone knows what a family is: mum, dad, brothers, sisters, uncles, aunts, grandma, grandpa, nephews and nieces. You get to know who is in your family as you grow up: all the people related to you by blood or by marriage. When you look around at your own and your friends' families, it is clear that some are small, some large, some happy, some unhappy. So what else is there to know about the family, and why should sociologists be so interested in it?

It's not only academic social scientists who worry about the family. Politicians of all persuasions have been particularly keen to espouse the cause of the family. Mrs Thatcher, in particular, has warned about the state taking over the functions of the family unit – such as providing care for the children of mothers who want to work. One of the main attractions of royalty in our modern society is that they are seen as a family that sets, ideally, an example to others. This aspect of the Royal Family was emphasised, for example, during the Queen's silver jubilee.

You'll hear it said quite often that the family is threatened, or in decline, or that it must be preserved, as if it were an endangered species, like the grey seal or the whale. The family seems often to be discussed only in terms of social problems that appear to signify its decline: teenage crime, pre-marital sex, loss of parental control, or an increase in the divorce rate, for example.

It is not always easy to make any sense of these grand pronouncements. For example, if the family really is in decline, wouldn't you expect there to be fewer families about than there used to be? Or perhaps what is meant is that although there are still plenty of families – more than ever before, in fact – their quality has somehow fallen off. What is the family supposed to be doing, anyway, if it has begun to fail in its duties?

There is disagreement among social scientists, politicians and other moralists about what is right or wrong with present-day families. But leaving aside for the moment the problem of saying exactly what is meant by "the family", many sociologists agree that it is an absolutely fundamental component or "social institution" in every society.

It is sometimes said that the "nuclear family" – mum, dad and the children – is a universal social institution. This does not mean that the smiling foursome you'll see in a building society advertisement represents an instantly recognisable group which can be found anywhere and is known as "the family." The claim that the "nuclear family" is universal is based on the fact that all children are produced by one man and one woman, and that however societies differ in other ways, there's usually a special link between people related in this way.

This seems to be a pretty obvious and not very useful point to make, though it has been the cause of considerable argument in the social sciences for some time. What is more important from the point of view of the organisation of society is what happens to children when they are born. Who looks after them, clothes them, teaches them?

It is possible to imagine a society in which children are taken away from their mother at birth and brought up in an institution by someone else. The influence of the natural parents over the children would be limited to genetic inheritance. This does happen, of course, when a child is orphaned or abandoned, for example. But it is customary for parents to bring up their own children, and it is chiefly for this one, simple reason that the family is regarded as such an important institution.

Perhaps the easiest way to understand

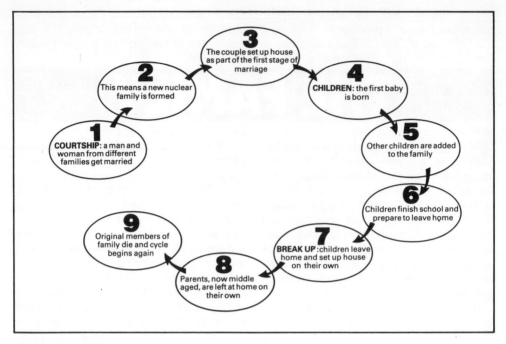

The life-cycle of the family

the significance of this fact is to imagine you want to create a new society with very different values from those held today. It would be very difficult to do so if each new generation of children were raised by their parents who would have their own ideas (probably old-fashioned) on what was right or wrong, good or bad. The simplest solution would be to abolish the family, take the children away at birth, and educate them in special institutions.

This is precisely what a number of utopian theorists proposed in Soviet Russia just after the revolution in 1916. One Commissar of Education wrote of children being educated by "trained pedagogical and medical personnel" and anticipated that the terms "my parents" and "our children" would die out. Children would inherit nothing from their parents: no property, wealth, or values.

By the 1930s, this Soviet dream of a new world had failed to come true, and under Stalin the Soviet Union was extolling the great virtue of a strict family upbringing like the best Victorian moralist. Apart from the emotional problems of separating parents and children, there were few alternative places for the children to go.

There have been other attempts to do away with the family. A less dogmatic and more practical approach was adopted by the Israeli kibbutzniks with the communal rearing of children. Again, they were trying to create a new society, but the experiment has been less successful than some people hoped (see, for example, Bruno Bettelheim's *Children of the Dream,* 1971). The experience of those who have tried to get rid of the family demonstrates that it is a pretty tough institution, and a real stumbling block for revolutionaries.

While, on the surface, the family may appear to represent a simple social arrangement, it is, in fact, quite complicated and woven thoroughly into the fabric of the rest of society. In their attempts to dissect the institution, social scientists often make a list of the things the family is supposed to do.

The family in our society regulates the production of children, and, as long as everyone sticks to the rules, provides the infant with a home, and two adults responsible for looking after it until it is grown up. Again, if all goes well, it provides the mother and father with a stable emotional and sexual relationship.

Future families

From *Future Shock* by Alvin Toffler, 1971.
(Published by the Bodley Head.)
We may expect many among the people of the future to carry the streamlining process a step further by remaining childless, cutting the family down to its most elemental components, a man and a woman. Two people, perhaps with matched careers, will prove more efficient at navigating through educational and social shoals, through job changes and geographic relocations, than the ordinary child-centred family. Indeed, anthropologist Margaret Mead has pointed out that we may already be moving towards a system under which, as she puts it, "parenthood would be limited to a smaller number of families whose principal functions would be child-rearing, leaving the rest of the population free to function for the first time in history as individuals."

A compromise may be the postponement of children, rather than childlessness. Men and women today are often torn in conflict between a commitment to career and a commitment to children. In the future, many couples will sidestep this problem by deferring the entire task by raising children until after retirement. This may strike people of the present as odd. Yet once child-bearing is broken away from its biological base, nothing more than tradition suggests having children at an early age. Thus childlessness is likely to spread among young and middle-aged couples; sexagenarians who raise infants may be far more common. The post-retirement family could become a recognised social institution.

We might also see the gradual relaxation of bars against polygamy. Polygamous families exist now, more widely than is generally believed, in the midst of "normal" society. Writer Ben Merson, after visiting several such families in Utah, where polygamy is still regarded as essential by certain Mormon fundamentalists, estimated that there are some 30 000 people living in underground family units of this type in the United States.

Childless marriage, professional parenthood, post-retirement child-rearing, corporate families, polygamy — these are a few of the family forms and practices with which innovative minorities will experiment in the future.

Under their common roof and shared surname, the family members form an "economic unit" which feeds them, clothes them, tends them when they are sick and keeps them warm in winter. The children are taught to walk and talk, how to eat with a knife and fork, and generally how to behave in the big world outside.

If it were not generally accepted that the family – people related by blood or marriage – ought to perform these tasks, someone else would have to, or the structure of society would fall apart. The constant concern about what is happening to "the family" is therefore understandable.

There are plenty of different ways in which the family can be organised, and still carry out its basic tasks. Although in the modern world, monogamy (the marriage of one man to one woman) is an almost universal pattern enforced by law, there are societies in which a man may take several wives (polygamy) or, more rarely, a woman has several husbands (polyandry). However many wives or husbands each individual may have, there is an enormous range of conventions about how kin (people related to each other) organise themselves and take on responsibilities. Although the study of kinship systems has traditionally been associated with "simple" societies, it is relevant to modern, industrial societies like our own.

A great deal of the work on the family and kinship appears to be motivated by nothing more than curiosity – the collection of strange customs, to be stored away like birds' eggs or butterflies. But from the point of view of social policy, or concern about whether or not our society is falling apart at the seams, there are very practical issues involved in the study of the family. And these are all to do with whether or not, in their day-to-day lives, people are behaving in a way which will cause social problems.

Take, for example, the problem of one-parent families. It is estimated that there are around 730000 in Britain, involving 1.25 million children. Single parents, whether they are divorced or separated women, unmarried mothers, widows, or lone fathers have much lower incomes on average than two-parent families. Their children are likely to be brought up in relative poverty, and perhaps suffer emotionally. This has

What is the point of a family?

There is no "rulebook" for family life. But what are known as the functions of the family can be broadly divided between the biological needs of the individual and the social, cultural and economic needs of society.

A BIOLOGIST would say that sex is an important aspect of the family. It allows the human species to reproduce itself in an organised and broadly acceptable way. The family also provides an outlet for people's emotional needs, such as love and security.

A SOCIOLOGIST would say that the family is an essential part of a stable social system. It allows people to know their position in society and be aware of how they should behave towards others. It is a method of social control, and allows young people to grow up behaving as society wants them to.

The family is also a welfare agency. It looks after the young, the old, the sick and the disabled. In the sense that those earning wages provide for those who don't, it can be a self-contained economic unit, and schools its members into continuing the tradition into the next generation. In fact, the whole of our social culture is transmitted from generation to generation by the family.

been considered a serious enough problem for a government committee report – that of the Finer Committee in 1974.

The break-up of families has accelerated in recent years. There has been a huge increase in the divorce rate since the 1971 Divorce Reform Act. The number of divorces between 1971 and 1983 more than doubled, from 80000 to 162000.

What effect this will have on family life, nobody is certain. Most people who get divorced marry again, and before they do so a large number live with someone else, so a high rate of separation and divorce does not necessarily mean an equivalent increase in the numbers of parents trying to survive on their own. But if the family does disintegrate as an independent economic unit, a greater number of people will have to rely on the state.

In historical terms, sociologists have sometimes seen in the development of the family a gradual "shedding" of its functions, which are handed over to other institutions. Whereas at one time it might have provided all the education, financial support, and welfare an individual was likely to get, these "functions" have been taken over by schools, social services and so on. Part of this process, it is argued, has been the break-up of the bonds between a wide range of relatives (the extended family) and the whittling down of the family to its core – the nuclear family of parents and children living in isolation.

It is important to remember here that an extended family is not the same thing as a big family. The extended family is made up of a series of nuclear families linked by blood, marriage or adoption. The nuclear family contains only two generations (parents and children), whereas the extended family contains three and sometimes four (grandparents, parents and children).

There is no doubt that families are smaller than they used to be, simply because people have fewer children. In late Victorian times the average family would have about six children. In Britain today the average family is just over two.

But it does not necessarily follow that the family of the past was better than the family today. Nor does the evidence demonstrate conclusively that families everywhere used to live in large, happy households, with granny lodged in front of the fire in a rocking chair, whereas today they are isolated in old folks' homes and tidy

BOOKS

Some useful additional reading:
M. Anderson, *Sociology of the Family,* Penguin, 1971
R. Fletcher, *The Family and Marriage in Britain,* Penguin, 1966
A. Oakley, *Sex, Gender and Society,* Temple Smith, 1972
C. Turner, *The Family and Kinship in Modern Britain,* Routledge & Kegan Paul, 1969
M. Young and P. Willmott, *The Symmetrical Family,* Routledge & Kegan Paul, 1973

little nuclear flats and houses. Peter Willmott and Michael Young made a classic study in the 1950s of family life in Bethnal Green (*Family and Kinship in East London,* 1962). They reported: "We were surprised to discover that the wider family, far from having disappeared, was still very much alive in the middle of London."

Historical studies of small areas of the country suggest, too, that the simple idea that extended families are huddled together all over the place is not necessarily supported by the evidence (Peter Laslett, *The World We Have Lost,* 1971).

The argument about exactly what has happened to the family through the last 200 years of industrial upheaval continues to rage. In *The Making of the Modern Family* (1976) Edward Shorter argues that there has been a dramatic change, despite some of the evidence to the contrary. A revolution in sexual behaviour, the nature of romance, the relationship of the family to the wider community, and in ideas about child-rearing have created the modern, conjugal family (as Shorter calls it) hidden away in the privacy of its own comfortable little house.

Shorter's view is that because modern family ties between husband and wife are essentially based on sexual attraction, rather than some pre-arranged property deal, the family is essentially unstable. And because children have little sense of their family past, their parents lack authority. Shorter is not entirely gloomy. This instability, he says, was the price we had to pay for freedom: freedom for people to choose whom they wanted to marry, and from the interference of the community in "private" affairs.

A similar sort of argument was put forward by the anthropologist, Sir Edmund Leach, in his Reith Lectures: "The family with its narrow privacy and tawdry secrets is the source of all our discontents." One solution, he suggested, might be something like an Israeli kibbutz. This kind of criticism of the nuclear family suggests that it has become too closely knit and too isolated. Others are arguing that the spread of women's liberation and the increase in the number of wives going out to work is tearing the family apart.

But for the time being, the family rolls on. Not all investigations about its workings are gloomy: much is to do with the influence of family background on the fortunes of people in education, work and wealth. The occupation of your father is still the accepted sociological shorthand for defining your social class. We really know very little about the intimate life of the family, despite numerous attempts to find a connection between the way people are brought up and the sort of person they become. Even though we have had many generations of children who have spent a large part of their life in school, there is still disagreement about the relative importance of home and educational influences.

As another sociologist, Geoffrey Hawthorn, has put it, "The fact remains that the nuclear family does seem to be the simplest conceivable structure for doing what it has to do, and even if we do not know much about how it does it ... that must be a very powerful restraint on change."

FINDING OUT ABOUT SOCIETY

What is the difference between a sample survey and participant observation? What are quantitative and qualitative data? Why do sociologists carry out research projects? We need to know *how* information about society is arrived at before we can judge whether it is reliable or not.

All research is dependent on theories. The theoretical perspective that the sociologist favours, consciously or otherwise – for example, Marxism, symbolic interactionism, structural functionalism – leads him to ask certain kinds of questions about society. It provides him with a sort of list, or agenda, of problems to solve, and a model of the social world which they relate to. Theories guide sociologists to particular types of "facts" – or *data* – which they use to explain an event, a social relationship, or a social structure.

There are two main reasons for doing research:

1: In order to know more about something – poverty, for example. What are the facts? How many people cannot afford to buy the food they need to live? The reseach into poverty by Charles Booth (1840–1916) and Seebohm Rowntree (1871–1954), and more recently by Peter Townsend, is essentially of this *descriptive* type. It helps us to find out what is "really" out there.

2: In order to *explain* why something happens or has happened – finding the *causes* of something like poverty or racial prejudice, for example. Oscar Lewis's work on the "culture of poverty" is an example of *explanatory* research. He explains the persistence of poverty in terms of the attitudes and beliefs of poor people influencing their behaviour and causing them to remain poor.

Many research studies combine both *descriptive* and *explanatory* research, since knowing in some detail about the subject matter is necessary before we can explain why it is like it is. Put in another way, descriptive research asks *how?* questions; explanatory research asks *why?*

questions. And, generally speaking, *how* questions come before *why* questions.

If we want to explain some aspect of society, then we will need a theory about why it has a certain form – why people with authoritarian personalities tend to be more right-wing in their political views than others, or why a particular sector of the working class tends to vote consistently for the Conservatives. Theories determine the form that research will take. We derive *hypotheses* from our theories. Hypotheses are simple causal propositions about the relationships between events: e.g. "people with authoritarian personalities are likely to be right-wing because their family backgrounds were ones in which rule-following and conformity were stressed"; "skilled working-class voters support the Conservative Party because they believe in the natural rights of upper-class Tories to rule the country."

Both these hypotheses can be tested by conducting an appropriate type of research project. If the hypothesis that has been put forward is supported by the research findings, then we can have some faith in the explanatory power of the theory from which it was drawn. If research does not support the hypothesis then we will have much less confidence in the theory, and may in fact want to change it. If research falsifies the hypothesis, then we must change the theory, or part of it.

In all explanatory research we are interested in the connections between *causes* and their *effects*. Do family relationships of a certain type *cause* schizophrenia? Do the class relationships of capitalist society *cause* alienation? Does the power of psychiatrists to label people as insane *cause* madness? The connections between cause and effect are normally spoken about by sociologists as the relationship between an *independent variable* (the cause), and a *dependent variable* (the effect). A *variable* is something which can vary – i.e. contain at least two categories. Sex is a simple example: there are two possible categories, male or female. The *independent* or *causing* variable is so called because it is independent of, or unchanged by, the dependent or *affected* variable.

When sociologists design explanatory research projects they are careful to identify the variables they are studying, so that they can be sure about the causal relationship between them. But, of course, they also need to know why the independent variable is able to change or vary the dependent variable: why, for example, is the social class background of school students such a good predictor of their ability to get good exam results? In this example the independent variable is "social class of student", which is assumed to *cause* the dependent variable of "exam performance." In other words high class is related to high performance; low class, low performance.

To put it like this does not, in fact, explain the relationship between the two variables. We obviously need to find some mechanism which links them together. This linking is done by what we call the *explanatory variable* or *test factor*. Actually, it is just another sort of independent variable, but its function is to show how the cause operates on its effect. In the case of social class and exam performance the explanatory variable may be something like family attitudes towards school, or perhaps a group of things which can be summarised as "home environment", which act as the bridge between class and exam performance. Most research of this explanatory type, then, will be concerned with isolating the explanatory variable and showing how it connects cause with effect.

Here are some simple rules for making sure that we have identified a *causal relationship* between two variables:

1: The two variables must be *linked together*. In other words a change in the independent variable *must* lead to a change in the dependent variable. To take the example of a school, used above, if the social class background is varied, exam performance must also vary. If this does not happen, then we can only conclude that there is no causal link.

2: The independent variable must occur in time *before* the dependent variable. In other words, social class background must be something which is in existence before exam performance. If it came afterwards, it could not be a *cause* of exam performance.

3: There cannot be a third variable that comes before the independent variable and which will, if held *constant,* make the link between the independent and the dependent variable *disappear.* For example, the causal link between class and exam performance must not be affected by using another variable like *size of school.* If the variation in the size of the dependent variable could be wholly accounted for by a third variable, then for obvious reasons we would have to use it instead of class to explain exam performance.

In all sociological research we are interested in *data* – in selected observations from a world which is infinitely complex. Sociologists generally distinguish between two types of observation or data – *quantitative* and *qualitative.*

Quantitative data is anything that can be put in number form, usually because it is possible to measure it in some way: the amount a person earns; their age; the number of o-levels they have passed; how many cars they own. Alternatively, certain observations can be expressed as numbers: we can, for example, distinguish sex by saying that male is one and female is two. In a more complicated way we can grade socio-economic status from one to seven.

When we give an observation, like "male", or "professional occupation", a number we are *coding* it. But, of course, we can only *code* observations that fall into neat categories: if they were able to overlap or merge into each other it would be silly to give them numbers – one is separate from two and always will be, they can never merge together. If a sociologist wants to use quantitative data he has to make sure that he can either *measure* or *code* his observations numerically.

Once the sociologist is sure that he can collect quantitative data he is also able to do certain things with it that will test the relationships between observations. As long as he has designed his project carefully he can test his *hypotheses* about the links between the independent and

dependent variable in his research, using *statistics.*

Sometimes the sociologist will want to do another sort of research altogether. He may want to *understand* how a particular village community or social group works. He could try and collect a lot of numerical data about the people in the area, but it would not tell him much about their daily life, about why they disciplined their children in a certain way, or looked after their old people in a particular fashion, or why they believed certain things. For this sort of research he would need to collect *qualitative* data – observing what people do, talking to them about their lives, even living among them and sharing their lifestyle. Obviously he could not make hard and fast statements about causal relationships on the basis of this sort of data. But he could use his sociological expertise to "get inside" the social behaviour of those he was studying and understand why they acted as they did.

Qualitative data is usually *verbal* in form – either the interpretations of a sociologist writing notes on his observations, or the direct statements of his subjects. Some sociologists take the view that film can be used in this way, too. One very important reason for using this type of data is to provide a detailed background for the interpretation of causal relationships which may lead to more sophisticated hypotheses. It is true, though, that some sociologists and anthropologists believe in a total reliance on qualitative data.

Although quantitative data and qualitative data are often combined in a research project, they require rather different collection techniques. There are two main forms of quantitative research technique; and two principal types of qualitative research technique.

Quantitative research techniques

(i) *Surveys:* These are of two types: *censuses,* where every member of the population under study is questioned; and *sample surveys,* where a proportion of the population is questioned, and the results generalised from the sample to the whole population. Sociologists almost never use census techniques because of their cost, unless a very small *population* is being studied. In this sense *population* is the term we use to describe the group we want to study – with the national census, for example, the census population is the same as the population of the UK. But a "population" might be only a small social group.

A *sample* is a small section of a population: sociologists usually try to set up *random samples* in order to have a *representative* group to study. If the sample has been drawn properly, and everybody in the study population has an equal (or *random*) chance of being included in the sample, then the sociologist can be reasonably sure that the data collected from that sample will be representative of the wider population. Opinion pollsters use this technique: they use carefully selected samples of voters – probably about 1500 people in all – whom they question about voting intentions. Because their samples are representative ones, they can predict the results of general elections with considerable accuracy.

The critical factors in sampling are the *size* of the sample and the *variability* of the population being studied. In simple terms, the more varied the population the larger the random sample must be to ensure representativeness, up to a point. Once a large enough sample has been drawn, it will be representative of any population: for example, the reliability of a sample of 1000 people of a population of 10000 is very similar to that of ten million.

Surveys and censuses normally use *questionnaires* to collect data: these are simply lists of questions that the researcher wants answered. Questionnaire design is a very important and skilled part of survey research: the questions must both relate directly to the variables in the study and be unambiguous to the *respondents* – the people being questioned. It is normal for many of the questions to be *pre-coded* so the reply may be put in a pre-determined category. A typical example of pre-coding is "How many cars does your family own?" The answer is coded as "nil", "one or two", or "more than two."

Surveys may be either *direct* – where the respondents are read the questions and an interviewer notes down their replies, or *indirect* – where the questionnaires are sent to the respondents by post for *self-completion,* or read out to them over the telephone. Although they cost more to run, direct surveys are better because they give a higher *response rate* (i.e. a greater proportion of the sample answer the questions) and more accurate responses, because the interviewer can explain the questions. It is very hard to get even a 70 per cent response to indirect surveys. If the sociologist gets a low response from his sample – if a lot of people refuse to answer his questions, or answer them badly or in an incomplete way – then the *reliability* of his conclusions is weakened since his sample is no longer representative. Response rates, then, are crucial to the success or failure of a project.

(ii) *Experiments:* In an experiment the objective is to test the relationship between one cause and one effect. Because social phenomena usually have many causes, experiments are difficult to do successfully in sociology. However, let us suppose that we want to design an experiment to test the effect on people's political attitudes of seeing a film about the National Front. We hypothesise that it will make them more left-wing.

It is necessary to have two random samples of the same population: an *experimental* and a *control* group. They must be entirely similar as groups, e.g. with the same average income, or social class background. First, both groups are given a pre-test to determine their political attitudes: both groups should register similar levels. Then, the experimental group are shown the film: the control group are not. A little while later the political attitudes of both groups are monitored. If the experimental group has become more left-wing and the control group remained the same then we might be justified in saying that seeing the film would change attitudes.

Because experiments involve the manipulation of people they pose many ethical problems to sociologists. It is frequently not possible to change social situations in which people live just to test sociological hypotheses.

Qualitative research techniques

(i) *Participant observation* (PO) is so called because the sociologist actually takes part in the society he is observing. It is sometimes called the *ethnographic method* because it is widely used by anthropologists. PO is a technique which allows a detailed examination of small groups in large and complex societies, or of simple and "primitive" societies. The sociologist "lives in" for a period of time with the people he is studying – sometimes for years. He must try to fit in with their way of life and by so doing come to understand why it operates in the way it does. Most of his time will be spent talking to people and observing them, and afterwards writing detailed "field notes." This technique relies upon the sociologist making close relationships with one or more *key informants* and requires him to build up a feeling of sympathy and identification with his subjects.

Problems of over-involvement can arise – several anthropologists have "gone native" over the years, for example. PO calls for a high level of commitment and intensive work over long periods: it also requires the sociologist to constantly refine the problems he is dealing with in order to finish with a manageable account of life in the group or society he has been studying.

Although always fascinating to read, accounts of PO research are difficult to compare, because there is often no common basis of data or analysis. It is, however, an ideal method for uncovering the hidden motivations of behaviour that survey research can never uncover.

(ii) *In-depth interviewing:* This is easier and less time-consuming than PO, and better for some types of study where "living with" respondents would be difficult to arrange. A study of sexuality among teenagers, or of the social dynamics of a rock-group would be best done by *in-depth interviewing* (IDI) rather than PO. Again,

it is the type of technique which only works with small groups or organisations, where specific people are selected for study because of their roles or positions – union leaders, for example, in the study of a strike.

The sociologist begins with a list of areas of general interest that he wants to know about, and produces a list of questions to put to respondents during the interview. What he wants is a full and detailed reply, and he can modify his questions or put new ones, according to what he is getting from his respondent. Since it is difficult to know whether the information being given is accurate, this technique relies upon cross-checking the interviews of several respondents, much as a detective does in assessing the testimony of witnesses to build up a picture of a crime.

In addition to the techniques discussed above, it is also possible to use *pre-collected* or *secondary sources* of data and subject them to quantitative and qualitative analysis: censuses, organisational records, other sociologists' research, government statistics, letters, diaries, even photographs and films. Why don't you try some of these techniques yourself?

BOOKS

Some useful additional reading:

C. Bell and H. Newby, *Doing Sociological Research,* Allen & Unwin, 1977. Accounts of real research – ethical problems, relationships between researchers, difficulties with subjects.
S. Cole, *The Sociological Method,* Rand McNally, 1976. The best short introduction available, very clear and easy to follow.
G. Hoinville and R. Jowell, *Survey Research and Practice,* Heinemann, 1977. Good, practical guide to survey research.
D. Roy, "Quota restriction and goldbricking in a machine shop", *American Journal of Sociology,* vol. 7, 1952, pp427–442.
L. Wylie, *Village in the Vaucluse,* Harvard University Press, 1951. A classic work of participant observation.

GENDER

A natomy is destiny, said Freud, and certainly your sex is a key influence not only on your personal identity, but also on the roles and opportunities you are likely to enjoy in life.

Men and women may be two halves of the same species, but they seem to live in almost separate worlds. Most societies have traditionally regarded men as the "doers" – warriors, hunters, scientists, artists, writers, captains of industry and politics. Women, on the other hand, have been the "carers" – of men and their children. A man's place has been in the jungle, the battlefield or the world of work, while a woman's has been in the home.

This traditional division of labour is still reflected in most of our images of the two sexes today. But are these stereotypes of masculinity and femininity accurate reflections of the real differences between the sexes – ideals to be lived up to if we are to be considered real men and real women? Or are they false notions that prevent us from expressing our true emotions or achieving our full potential?

Evidence about the differences between the sexes is part of the highly controversial debate as to whether "nature" or "nurture" (heredity or environment) is the key influence on human behaviour and intelligence.

The *naturalist* case rests on the assumption that the social differences between the sexes are a direct reflection of innate biological ones. Men are the stronger sex physically, so naturally they dominate. Women produce children, so they have a natural instinct to be caring, passive and dependent. However, despite the vast array of theories about human physiology that have been put forward to "prove" this idea, none have done so conclusively and all have notable exceptions.

For example, the male claim to physical superiority has been challenged by female bricklayers in the Soviet Union, women soldiers in Israel and Vietnam and recent female sporting achievements, notably in long-distance swimming. Moreover, even if men are the "stronger" sex, physical strength is hardly a valid basis for social stratification in advanced technological societies, where brains prevail over brawn and machines do the strenuous and dirty work.

Nurturists, on the other hand, see human behaviour largely as a reflection of the social and cultural environment into which children are born and brought up. According to this view, therefore, gender roles are both "man-made" and variable. The nurturist arguments rests largely on anthropological evidence like Margaret Mead's classic study of three neighbouring tribes in New Guinea (*Male and Female,* 1950).

While she found one of these tribes, the Arapesh, to very sociable, compassionate, loving and passive, the Mundugumor proved to be harsh, violent and quarrelsome. In the Tchambuli tribe there seemed to be almost a reversal of the traditional sex roles, with men doing "women's jobs." Unfortunately, evidence like this is as questionable as that of the naturalists. The accuracy of Mead's work has recently been challenged by other anthropologists, and examples similar to hers are few and far between.

In an attempt to bring some order to the whole debate, two social psychologists, Eleanor Maccoby and Carol Jacklin, published a massive review of scientific research into sex differences (*The Psychology of Sex Differences,* 1974). They concluded that women are as intelligent, creative and imaginative as men, and just as capable of becoming geniuses – or idiots!

What may be different is the way the two sexes think. Girls have a certain superiority in verbal skills, boys in handling numbers and in visual-spatial tests. In fact, girls, on average do better in intelligence tests up to the age of ten or eleven, then they tend to fall behind and stay there, possibly because of what psychologists have labelled "a fear of success."

Girls come to perceive achievement, especially in intellectual and sporting fields, as aggressive and therefore masculine.

Maccoby and Jacklin further found little difference in the personality traits of the two sexes. Boys and girls are equally sociable, emotional and willing to help others – the difference is that girls are much more willing to express their emotions. Men and boys don't like to be seen doing "soft" things like handling babies or cuddly toys. It would spoil the image they have been taught from an early age that "big boys don't cry." One clear and crucial difference does, however, emerge – males are more aggressive. But can aggression alone explain male dominance?

Most research over the past decade has supported Maccoby and Jacklin's conclusions. Moreover, as Professor Denis Stott has concluded (*Issues in the Intelligence Debate,* 1983), the nature-nurture argument can never be settled finally because the interrelationship of genes and environment is just too complex. What does seem to be clear, though, is that whatever natural differences exist between men and women, they do not inevitably lead to social differences of the magnitude seen in most societies. Natural differences become exaggerated to a self-fulfilling degree. Men and women perceive each other as very different and thus become so. But how? What are the key social forces at work?

Obviously, socialisation is crucial. From the moment they are born, children acquire a sexual identity and are subjected to wholesale conditioning into becoming "typical" boys or girls. They are dressed differently, given different toys, treated, spoken to and even touched in a different manner.

This early socialisation is reinforced throughout later life by school, work, the media and various other social institutions, most of which take it for granted that the roles of men and women in society are natural and inevitable.

So natural, in fact, that this most basic of human divisions was for a long time overlooked by sociologists in their obsessive search for the factors that decide social class. It took the advent of feminism in the 1960s and 1970s for sociology to come to grips with the idea of *patriarchy* – a structure of organised power by which, it is argued, men rule women just as firmly as the bourgeoisie rules the proletariat and whites control blacks.

The power of this patriarchy is based not only on male control of all our top social institutions, but on an all-pervasive ideology of male superiority. Children grow up with it, men assume it to be "natural" and most women defer to it both in society at large and in the intimacy of their everyday relationships with men. In contrast to the often-cultivated belief that women today enjoy equal rights with men, feminists have sought to highlight the inequalities that still exist between the sexes:

WORK: Though more than forty per cent of the British workforce is female, women

English as she is spoke ...

What's wrong with the following statement?

"The typical British adult today is likely to be better fed, better clothed and better housed than her mother or grandmother was."

Well, actually there's nothing wrong. As anyone who has done their sociology homework will know, the "typical adult" is more likely to be a woman than a man. But it still *sounds* funny to generalise about people in terms of women.

Part of the problem is to do with English grammar. In most other modern European languages, nouns and pronouns take on masculine and feminine forms usually regardless of sex or its absence. In English, the gender of words is nearly always related to sex, and the danger arises of language being used to reflect patriarchy in society.

In their *Handbook of Non-Sexist Writing* (1981), Casey Miller and Kate Swift say: "Only recently have we become aware that conventional English usage, including the generic use of masculine-gender words, often obscures the actions, the contributions and sometimes the very presence of women. Turning our backs on that insight is an are concentrated in "women's work" – the service and "caring" industries, such as nursing, teaching and typing. They get lower pay and have worse conditions than men. Few women get into top professions and even fewer into top posts, even in their own fields. Fewer than five per cent of architects, engineers, scientists and solicitors are women, and women account for only 2 per cent of university professors and 12 per cent of medical consultants.

THE HOME: Some sociologists, like Hannah Gavron in *The Captive Wife* (1966), see modern marriage as a form of property relationship. Or as Ann Oakley puts it in her book, *Subject Women* (1981): "An institution that ensures women's continued subordination – economically, financially, legally and emotionally."

In another book (*Housewife,* 1974), Oakley has highlighted the frustration,

stress and boredom experienced by women in the home. Advances in household aids have not reduced the amount of time spent on housework because standards of cleanliness now expected are higher. The modern housewife either faces a life of loneliness and lack of reward, or goes to work and so has to face the demands of two jobs.

EDUCATION: Although girls now do better than boys at O-level and almost as well at A-level, their achievements are still primarily in "feminine" subjects – English, languages and the arts. Relatively few girls pursue maths or sciences at a higher level, and though differences in visual-spatial abilities may be part of the answer, it cannot entirely explain why only 10 per cent of physics graduates today are women.

The Equal Opportunities Commission has tried to put this right by advertising science and technical careers in girls' magazines. But as a new study by Michelle Stanworth shows (*Gender and Schooling,* 1983), sexism in schools is often deeply rooted. In the mixed A-level humanities classes she studied, boys demanded and were given greater attention, particularly by male teachers. Girls were under less pressure because of the underlying assumption that even the brightest of them would eventually get married, and so in a way their studies weren't as important as those of the boys.

POLITICS: Though 1979 saw the election of Britain's first woman Prime Minister, it also saw the lowest number of women in parliament since 1951, despite the fact that more women put themselves forward than ever before. The fact is that they were shunted into unwinnable seats. Women form over half the population, yet are represented by just a handful of MPs. Yet women can be notable campaigners on political issues, as the Greenham Common demonstrators have shown.

THE MEDIA: Sex sells papers – both on page 3 of the *Sun* and through "happy housewife" adverts. Young comics, like *Bunty* and *Misty,* encourage girls to be adventurous and independent, but by

option, of course, but it is an option like teaching children the world is flat."

Some people have tried to get round this problem by inventing new words. Some common gender pronouns proposed in recent years to replace he and she have been *co, tey* and *hesh.*

But new words don't solve the problem of writing that disparages the position of women in society. Miller and Swift talk about *gratuitous modifiers,* and quote the following television listing: "Powerful lady barrister and confident young solicitor team up to defend a wealthy contractor accused of murder." The reason that this did not read: "Powerful barrister and her young male colleague" is because in our culture we are not inclined to diminish a man's prestige.

It will probably take time to change this sort of attitude. But there is a precedent. At the beginning of the 1960s we started to become more careful with the words we used about black people. Now it is comparatively rare to come across written usage that demeans them. A similar "consciousness-raising" approach might put an end to what American feminists have labelled BOMFOG – "brotherhood of man, fatherhood of God."

adolescence, magazines tend to offer them only one option in life – boys and eventual marriage.

A survey at Princeton University in 1975 found that 75 per cent of all leading characters on American television were male, and though, more recently, series like *Dallas* and *Dynasty* have had women stars, they are portrayed in highly conventional roles.

But if patriarchy is so obvious and all-pervading, why haven't women been able to break it down? One reason is that feminists are divided in their analysis of the male power structure. Some, like Helen Mayer Hacker (*Women as a Minority Group*, 1972), liken the position of women to that of blacks in America – both are highly visible minorities, both are treated as inferior and child-like, both have a set position in society and both suffer extensive discrimination. Others adopt a Marxist perspective, and see women as oppressed, class-exploited, alienated and suffering false consciousness. Come the socialist revolution, they will be set free alongside the working class and other oppressed groups.

For more radical feminists still – like Shulamith Firestone (*The Dialectic of Sex*, 1972) – even this is not enough since, in her view, the sexual "class" system predates even that of economic oppression. Since this, and men's obsession with power, stem from the fact that it is women alone who bear children, real liberation can only occur when women are freed from their reproductive role by biological engineering.

However, it seems that a true sexual revolution will require more than just women's lib. Men, it can be argued, need liberating, too. As Andrew Tolson points out in *The Limits of Masculinity* (1977), male roles and stereotypes can be just as limiting to men as feminine ones are to women. Men are taught to cultivate a "macho" image of strength and power and to suppress their own emotions and feelings. The historian Sheila Rowbotham, puts it this way: "Men are ashamed of their own sensitivity to suffering and love because they have been taught to regard

these as feminine. They are afraid of becoming feminine because this means that other men will despise them and they will despise themselves."

It could even be that men today have too *few* roles, and women too many. According to a recent Swedish government report on equality, "Many men expressed themselves envious of the emotional rewards that seemed until now to be the prerogative of motherhood." In her book, *Goodbye Father* (1976), Maureen Green calls for a re-evaluation of fatherhood, a rebalancing of the roles in the home and in society in general: "Time should be set aside for family life, for father to be simply a man – not 'he who dominates a woman' nor 'he who provides' but simply 'he, a person who can feel'."

Various attempts have been made to set up "men against sexism" groups – the best-known in Britain is Achilles' Heel. But so far they have had only a limited appeal because though women can feel the anger, frustration and passion of oppression, men tend only to feel guilt. The French writer, Emmanuel Reynaud, puts it eloquently in *La Sainte Virilité* (1981): "When a man finds himself stifled by the meaninglessness of his life and makes an effort to put a final end to his patriarchial power, he will not have far to go to find the enemy. The struggle has to start, above all in himself. To get rid of the 'man' embedded in himself is the first step for any man getting out on the path towards getting rid of power altogether."

But if men and women need liberating, what about the other "genders"? Alongside the protests of blacks and women in the 1960s there grew up the "gay liberation" movement – homosexuals and lesbians determined to escape the oppression, discrimination and stigmatisation of heterosexual society.

As Anthony Smith points out in *The Body* (1976): "No one knows whether [homosexuality] has a genetic cause or not ... but most biologists would put heavy bets on the environment as the main contributor." Hence the extensive delving into the background of homosexuals in search of the cause of their predilections.

But sociologists like Ken Plummer (*Sexual Stigma,* 1975) reject such an individual analysis and point instead to the way our society "creates" homosexuality by labelling certain forms of sexual behaviour deviant. Homosexuals thus have to face public shame, abuse and even physical attacks.

Gay liberation movements have also drawn increasing attention to transsexuals. These are people – usually men – who feel trapped in the body of the opposite sex, and often undergo sex-change operations.

The best-known example of a transsexual is the travel writer and journalist, Jan (James) Morris, whose book, *Conundrum,* eloquently describes the transition from manhood to womanhood. Morris was born male, but experienced, as a grown man with a family, an overwhelming sense of wanting to be a woman. He underwent an operation in Casablanca and took on a new name and new identity.

It is possible, then, to talk, as Morris seems to, of a kind of third gender between male and female? The Xaniths of Oman and the Mohave Indians in North America have been so described. They are biologically men, but take on the behaviour and appearance of women – even acting out the symptoms of menstruation and labour. Most important, these roles are seen as quite normal in their own societies.

Certainly, the sociology of gender, in its broadest sense, forces us to re-examine our traditional assumptions about the "natural" roles and positions of the sexes, and to recognise that many of our stereotypes of masculinity and femininity are social rather than biological creations. They are images we have created of ourselves and of others that form the basis of a structure of power by which one sex has enslaved another. Women and gays are kept down more because of men's fears and anxieties about their own sexuality than because of their innate inferiority or abnormality.

On the other hand, men are continually having to prove their superiority – at work, in the home and in bed. But they are facing not only the growing challenge of women but the changing structure of modern work, where unemployment often means that the wife is the breadwinner, while the husband stays at home. This is often a cause of domestic friction. As Betty Yorburg points out in her book. *Sexual Identity* (1974), "The traditional sex-typed personality traits are poorly suited to the demands of modern life."

So will we have to learn the social roles and sexual traits previously ascribed to the opposite sex, and move towards the kind of androgynous society advocated by Sandra Bem in her essay, "Androgyny versus the tight little lives of fluffy women and chesty men" (1975)? Here, gender would no longer be a primary source of identity and social position, and people would simply treat each other as individuals with both masculine and feminine characteristics. Neither patriarchy nor matriarchy would rule – people would be free of the restraints of sexual stereotypes and the stigmas of abnormality and deviance.

However, such a "human liberation" movement faces a huge task in overcoming the oldest of human divisions, as a recent experiment by the American psychologist, Marcia Guttentag, and her colleagues showed (*Undoing Sex Stereotypes,* 1976). Their attempt to "re-educate" a thousand Boston school-children produced a rise in the self-esteem of girls. Unfortunately most of the boys became even more rigid and stereotyped in their views of women. There's still, it seems, a long way to go.

BOOKS

Some useful additional reading:
Sara Delamont, *The Sociology of Women,* Heinemann, 1980
Irene Frieze *et al, Women and Sex Roles,* Norton, 1978
Barbara Lloyd and John Archer, *Sex and Gender,* Penguin, 1982
John Nicholson, *A Question of Sex,* Fontana, 1979
Carol Tarvis and Carol Offir, *The Longest War,* Harcourt Brace, 1977

HOUSING

Friedrich von Hayek, the apostle of free market economics, once took up the cause of a friend in Austria, a manufacturer with a factory in a small town five hours' journey from Vienna. Why was it, Hayek asked, that the factory-owner could not get fitters, many of them unemployed for years, to leave their tenements in the capital and move into the works accommodation on offer?

For Hayek, and other economists, housing was an obstacle to the workings of the market. The Viennese workers' protected tenancies caused their immobility and prolonged their unemployment. Hayek wanted to treat housing like some kind of "neutral" commodity. Mrs Thatcher and many members of her government currently think he was right, and believe that by removing subsidies on public housing, the markets for labour will be revitalised.

But the economists' generalisations about housing rarely hold because it has too many dimensions other than rents and land values, important though they are. Had Hayek, writing in the 1920s, waited a few years he would have had to explain the passion which those same Viennese fitters displayed when they defended their tenement blocks in 1934 when they were threatened at gunpoint during the government's campaign against the Austrian Socialist Party. Their defence was bitter because those tenements, which were in fact much admired by architects and town planners of the time, were home.

Housing is bricks and mortar, concrete and thatch, but the social meanings people ascribe to their domestic shelter – compare the notions of "home" and "house" – are in constant interplay with the physical forms that housing takes.

Take the English cottage, for example. In a critical book about the spectacular growth of home ownership during the twentieth century (*Home Ownership*, 1978), Martin Pawley, an architect, tells of a cottage in Oxfordshire standing in 1900 at the end of a century when "cottage" was often a synonym for the rural misery produced by the population explosion and the widespread exploitation of agricultural workers. In that same cottage a few years on, just before the First World War, an entire family – an agricultural labourer, his wife and nine children – died of hunger. Fifty years later a Jaguar sat at the cottage door. Cottages had acquired social cachet; thatch meant much to the growing cult of rural nostalgia. This cottage had become an urban dweller's second home, and weekend retreat.

Pawley comments: "Of course the tragic occupants of 1914 had not owned the cottage, but it would have made little difference if they had, for as late as 1950 such dwellings could be bought in pairs for under £150. The difference between then and now lies not so much in the vastly increased demand for ownership as in the change in meaning it has repeatedly undergone in a world the 1914 tenant missed."

Housing is a basic need, like food. Without domestic shelter, social and family life are impossible. In traditional nomadic societies, housing lacks permanence and its social importance is less. Likewise, in some settled societies – the LoDagaba of northern Ghana, for instance – the use of wattle and straw thatch means that housing units are extremely flexible. Bits can be added to accommodate changes in the family unit.

With the use of brick and stone, housing acquires permanence. In developed societies based on private property relations (which usually forbid squatting) this means two things. One is that the owners of housing are potentially agents of power (consider the position of even the most benignly treated lodgers). The other is that housing can have a lifespan that transcends both individuals and generations.

Alison Ravetz (in *Remaking Cities*, 1980) has noted that "in Britain, as probably in most highly industrialised societies, it is exceptional for ordinary private individuals to create or even actively to intervene in their built environments." Often, especially among architects and planners, this regard for the staying power of brick, glass and wood has led to what has been called, in the jargon, *environmental determinism.*

Most often, this belief has taken the form of a conviction that housing, its physical form and location, can change people.

Environmental determinism has generally been the view held by reformers unhappy about the city life that had grown up with the industrial revolution. Some Victorian housing reformers, such as Octavia Hill, were strictly paternalist and laid down tight rules for the occupants of philanthropic dwellings – an attitude which persists today in the lettings policies of some public sector landlords. Some reformers could hardly be said to have contributed much to housing design. Sidney Waterlow's Industrial Dwellings Company used to boast that architects were quite unnecessary.

The urban reform movement, which created the garden cities at Letchworth in Hertfordshire and Port Sunlight, near Liverpool, was often milder in its social views. The conception underlying many twentieth-century housing reforms, notably the new towns, is based on a redemptionist view of people. Uproot them from their East End squalor or Liverpool slums and they will become socially and morally improved in the fresh air of Basildon or Skelmersdale.

But it is now obvious that environment is not a major determining factor. British sociology cut its teeth in the late 1950s with a string of studies showing that the new housing patterns produced social problems rivalling those of the slums that had just been bulldozed.

Such arguments lead some writers to think of housing as what is known in the jargon as a *social epiphenomenon* – a physical object largely governed by social forces. Thus some economists have

emphasised how much housing investment depends on wider movements in the cost of money. Similarly, the physical form of houses often seems relatively unimportant when property markets are booming. One of the most striking and least understood events of the 1970s was the Great Gazumping – the period of six or seven years from about 1971 during which domestic property prices (that is, the cost of shelter) rocketed.

A house bought privately in 1949 for £800 was worth £12000 by the 1960s, and could now be worth £50000. Like all valuations, this figure depends on the operation of a highly imperfect market in which the hyperbole of a "new profession" – estate agents – plays a part. But it illustrates that large shifts in wealth have occurred, sometimes without apparent regard to the age or nature of the structure being bargained over.

There is a *continual interaction* between housing's physical shape and the social structure. There are obviously limits to this: the movement of East Enders to good new housing on the London County Council estate at Dagenham did not emancipate them from their subordinate position as workers at Ford's. But equally, additional bedroom space or more wall points for electrical appliances cannot be written off as not having any social importance.

Three long-term processes have been at work in Britain's housing. The first is on the "micro" level and can only be called "the growth of comfort."

Think again of that rural cottage. A contributor to the *Agricultural Gazette* of 1853 said: "Home has no attractions for the agricultural labourer. When he goes there, tired and chilly, he is in the way amidst domestic discomforts; the cottage is small, the children are troublesome, the fire is diminished, the solitary candle is lighted late and extinguished early . . . He then goes to the public house, where a cheerful fire and jovial society are found and becomes a loose character."

People still go to pubs, where they may or may not become loose, but during the twentieth century there has been a dramatic rise in comfort. At the crudest level

The gap in the welfare state

In 1979, the housing chairman of the west London borough of Hillingdon dramatised the problems of homelessness by having a taxi deposit on the steps of the Foreign Office in Whitehall a Kenyan Asian family with a right to stay in Britain, but nowhere to live.

His protest had much to do with the family's ethnic origin, but also with a new piece of legislation, the Housing (Homeless Persons) Act, 1977. This, for the first time, placed a specific obligation on councils to provide homes for homeless families. Why did it take so long for the welfare state to recognise the problem?

There is a small urban population who live in the streets (the winos and dossers who often choose homelessness as a way of life), but many "homeless" people are living temporarily in someone else's home, and so their numbers are concealed. People, through force of circumstance, have a remarkable facility to "box and cox": but

Why owners are winners

The match between the hierarchy of housing – from wholly owned housing at the top to common lodging houses at the bottom – and society's hierarchy of status is not exact, but is close enough to show that social class is an important determinant of housing quality and location.

The key link is *tenure* – in other words, whether people are owners or renters. In his study of Sparkbrook in Birmingham, the sociologist, John Rex, was so impressed by what tenure could say about social class that he described a series of "housing classes" – social classes redefined on the basis of house ownership or rental characteristics.

But tenure is not wholly aligned with social position. For example, on one estimate, over a fifth of all "poor" households own their own home outright.

Tenure and income are linked. Yet it is widely believed, though figures are sketchy, that a significant proportion of council households have total incomes higher than the median for owner occupiers. (This belief has guided the present government's sale of council houses, though it this can mean overcrowding. According to the *National Dwelling and Housing Survey* there were, in 1977, 253 000 "concealed" households out of the 16.8 million households for England. These were individuals or families living in someone else's flat or house and who wanted to move.

In addition, some 840 000 households are on council waiting lists. Some of these, perhaps living in tension with in-laws or relatives, should be considered homeless, even if the total of families going each year to councils declaring themselves homeless is relatively small.

Recently, some politicians said homelessness no longer existed, since there was a crude surplus of dwellings over households. It is certainly true that the desperate anxiety over housing, represented in the 1960s in a famous TV film, *Cathy Come Home,* has disappeared. But the rate in which households are created seems to be growing. This is due to what sociologists call *fission* – the tendency of families to split up. The rising number of one-parent families is a measure of this.

ignores the fact that working-class incomes fluctuate greatly.) Within the private rented sector, there are considerable numbers of poor people, notably the single old and young; but this sector also takes in wealthy urbanites who can afford to rent in Kensington.

Tenure may not reveal much about housing quality. Most council-provided accommodation is of "high standard", at least according to the definition laid down in the Parker Morris report of the early 1960s.

But it does reveal significant variations in the tax and subsidy system that has grown up in Britain this century. There is little apparent equity in the treatment by the state of owner occupiers with mortgage tax relief and private renters. The balance of subsidy between council tenants and owner occupiers is now shifting to the former group's detriment. According to one recent author, Stewart Lansley (*Housing and Public Policy,* 1979), "there is little doubt that one of the main sources of inequality in housing lies in our system of tenure."

there is more space; there were 5.11 persons per dwelling in 1861 compared with 2.97 by the mid 1960s. "Crowded households", defined officially as those with more than 1.5 people per room, fell in number from 664 000 in 1951 to 150 000 in 1976.

Rooms of course vary in their size; one of the great liberations of owner occupation is often the ability to knock a wall down in a bid to alter the layout of an inherited house that was determined by family patterns that no longer exist. More space can mean children having "a room of their own", with immense consequences for social relations within the family.

When the state began to intervene in the provision of housing, common standards – often based on middle-class models – were decided for working-class housing. One was for a parlour, "to enable", said one First World War offical committee, "the older members of the family to hold social intercourse with their friends without interruption from the children."

Housing design, one of the most conservative of art forms, gradually reflected the comfort revolution, as for some people their house became a sort of envelope for a host of gadgets, of which the most symbolic is the Black & Decker drill.

So, for example, space was found for a fridge; interior colours altered. Externally, a small number of twentieth-century public housing projects – the London County Council's Old Oak Estate or the Byker project in Newcastle – were rated as design achievements and even pleased their tenants.

Hand in hand with the comfort revolution has gone a specifically English and Welsh housing development – suburbanisation. In no other country is the form of a two-storey house and garden so prevalent, or rural nostalgia so potent a force in both architecture and urban planning. In Scotland, as in most European countries, the predominant housing form is the flat, apartment or tenement. Some fifty per cent of Scottish households live in flats; in England and Wales the figure is ten per cent.

But the number of flats has grown since

1945. During the redevelopment of Birmingham in the 1950s, flats were built twelve storeys high – the first "tower blocks." Living in the sky had long been a dream of utopian architects such as Buckminster Fuller, who conjured up a "vertical city" for 300000 families, each unit possessing a "garden box" to catch the sun.

In retrospect, it is easy to mock the architects' lack of social sense, for tower blocks posed many difficulties for families; they did not weld as intended into manufactured communities. Besides, tower blocks have proved more expensive than low-rise forms. A fashion in the 1960s for "system building", using prefabricated materials, ended abruptly with a serious collapse in a tower block called Ronan Point in Newham, east London.

But houses with gardens need space and the growth of many English towns has, as a result, been a kind of decanting over time of populations on the periphery. This has given rise to estates on the edges of towns (Kirkby in Merseyside is a striking example of the process gone wrong) and to satellite towns which still, like Milton Keynes, advertise their urbanity by emphasising their rural qualities.

The third process at work has been the transformation of *tenure,* described in the accompanying article – "the most startling in the western world", one writer has called it. In 1900 less than ten per cent of British dwellings were owned by the people who lived in them; in 1977 it was fifty-four per cent.

"Privatisation" of housing has occurred in two senses. One is the revolution in tenure, a complex process accounted for partly by controls on renting, by a system of tax and other subsidies encouraging owner occupation, and by the peculiar position within British capitalism of the building societies. The other is the great increase in the proportion of time that people allocate to their housing, in parallel with changes in family and community. Examples of this are the expansion of do-it-yourself and the development of the "owner speculator" for whom, especially in recent years, the jump in the value of housing has given sight of unprecedented individual wealth.

Many Conservatives are keen on privatisation because they believe that a "property-owning democracy" is generally a right-wing one. (As a generalisation, this does not help to explain politics in several European countries, where owner-occupation is significantly less than in Britain.) For political reasons, and in the belief that a mixture of tenures will produce a socially mixed community, the Conservative government has recently tried to promote the sale of public sector housing through its "right-to-buy" legislation.

But the government is now discovering a disconcerting example of the interplay between housing's physical form and society's valuations of it. The technology of housing has been such that its "permanence" is roughly of a sixty to seventy-year span. In order to prevent decay, a continuous programme of investment is needed to rehabilitate, modernise and replace old housing. But the government's latest survey of housing conditions shows that in the private sector some households, especially old people, cannot afford to pay for the upkeep of their house.

The current edition of the *General Household Survey* shows that a quarter of Britain's houses were built before 1919. If the housing stock is not replenished through investment, then the next generation will be bequeathed decaying houses with problems that are too large for any enthusiast with a Black & Decker to handle.

BOOKS

Some useful additional reading:
John Burnett, *A Social History of Housing, 1815–1970,* David & Charles, 1978
John English (ed.), *The Future of Council Housing,* Croom Helm, 1982
Frank Schaeffer, *The New Town,* Paladin, 1972
J. R. Mellor, *Urban Sociology in an Urban Society,* Routledge & Kegan Paul, 1977
Stephen Merrett, *State Housing in Britain,* Routledge, 1979

INNER CITIES

Shortly after the Conservative government was returned to power in 1983, the Secretary of State for the Environment, Patrick Jenkin, made the ritual journey for holders of his office anxious to show they care about the inner cities: he visited Merseyside.

Once there, as ministers tend to on such trips, he stepped out of the official Rover to hold a press conference and announce new government measures. He was authorising money under the Inner Urban Areas Act, 1978, to help combat the "severe urban problems" of Knowsley – the main part of which is better known as Huyton, for years the parliamentary constituency of Harold Wilson.

Jenkin's jaunt encapsulates some of the ambiguities both in the concept of inner cities and successive governments' response to the "inner city problem." For instance, the fact that it is the ministry concerned with the *environment* that is in charge illustrates the tendency of policy makers over the decades to think that housing and physical planning can alter social and economic facts. Yet this is now a highly contentious argument.

Even more striking is that "inner cities" money should have been going to Knowsley. Glance at a map of Merseyside and you will see that Knowsley, the metropolitan district between Liverpool and St Helens, is anything but "inner." It is an area of large-scale council estates built by Liverpool corporation in the days when it was fashionable to shift people from congested central districts out to green fields on the periphery.

Yet Knowsley is probably quite as typical of the "inner city problem" as areas like Toxteth, which is geographically in central Liverpool, or Moss Side in Manchester, or Spitalfields in the east London borough of Tower Hamlets. In fact, you can puncture any geographical generalisation about inner areas by pointing out that the City of London is also "inner city", as is Mayfair and middle class districts like Edgbaston in Birmingham and Hillhead in Glasgow.

"Inner city" is more a shorthand social description than a precise geographical reference point. The phrase itself would mean little to people shopping in Huyton or working in Walthamstow – both would point out that their areas include green belt land. What they would agree on, however, is that Huyton's Cantril Farm estate is one of the worst in the country and that Walthamstow's growing number of immigrants have given it race-related problems equivalent to anything in say, central Birmingham.

In other words, "inner city" describes a cluster of variables which are manifested in particular districts. These include:

● Architectural failures
● Long-term shifts in land use and values
● A loss of population and jobs
● Family breakdown
● Non-white immigration and racial discrimination
● Poverty of resources and income
● Poor environment

The common denominator here is *decline*. Knowsley and Haringey and Gateshead and Lambeth, together with the other areas conventionally defined as exhibiting inner city symptoms, are part of conurbations which are on the skids. From the early 1960s to the mid-1970s, the total population in the seven conurbations of England and Scotland declined by nearly 8 per cent. Loss has been concentrated especially in central districts.

For example, Manchester's population fell by 18 per cent between 1971 and 1981 and Glasgow's by 22 per cent. In some areas the shrinkage of numbers has been dramatic. In the 1930s Tower Hamlets had 500 000 people, but only 146 000 by the mid-1970s.

Population decline is inextricably linked to the economic rundown of areas built up during the Industrial Revolution and the period of expansion of Britain's staple industries during the nineteenth century. What has marked the inner cities especially has been a fall in manufacturing jobs. Such jobs have been lost throughout the country, but city districts have suffered particularly from the death of private companies or their decision to transfer to new, often suburban sites. The reasons for this include the high cost of central sites, poor roads and "infrastructure."

Liverpool – the hardest-hit city – has lost jobs with the decline in its role as a commercial port. Its workforce tends to be unskilled and the result has been persistently higher levels of unemployment. Liverpool has suffered especially from being a "branch-plant economy" – that is, an area where multinational corporations have set up subsidiary factories that are managed from, say, Detroit or Milan or London.

Here is one recent view of the city's decline: "Merseyside has been a typical victim of the postwar trend towards bigger and more remote companies, corporations and institutions. The absorption of the family business, the capital gains-orientated tax systems, the centralising sophistication of the Stock Exchange, all pushed ownership into fewer and more remote hands.

"The vital links between those responsible for creating wealth and the communities in which they operated were greatly weakened. There was little concern for the general community because those who exercised ultimate power identified less and less with any local loyalty."

This judgement comes, not from a Marxist economist, but from the former Conservative Environment Secretary, Michael Heseltine. During his time as minister for Merseyside he saw too many multinationals pull out not to be convinced that market capitalism was severely penalising Liverpool people.

Heseltine's concern for the plight of Merseysiders is in a long tradition of special pleading for inner-city communities. Nearly a century and a half earlier, Karl Marx's collaborator, Friedrich Engels, had written a passionate denunciation of life in another Lancashire city, Manchester. In the 1880s Charles Booth produced his huge survey of life in the London slums, the *Life and Labour of the London Poor*.

Yet conditions that were bad in the mid nineteenth century had hardly improved by the mid twentieth in some parts of British cities. In their book, *Inner City Poverty in Paris and London* (1981), Charles Madge, Peter Willmott and Michael Young conjure the feel of urban deprivation that would have been familiar to Engels. This account is of a visit to a flat in Stockwell, south London:

"The woman was on her own, and said she had no man – she's been in England for 13 years and has six children between the ages of twelve and two. The flat, smelling of stale greens and dampness, is in a block that is coming down – out of about 120 flats only six or seven are still inhabited, and the outside passages are dark and littered. Her two small children at home were dirty, clad in knickers and tops, sucking bottles."

A similar sense of hopelessness is conveyed in Paul Harrison's *Inside the Inner City* (1983), an account of life in the east London borough of Hackney, one of the most deprived areas in the country:

"Many slums were cleared by blitz or bulldozers, but the public housing that replaced them was in some respects worse. Local government was poor in resources, with a narrow and declining base on which to levy rates.

"Educational results were spectacularly poor, perpetuating the shortage of qualified labour. Redevelopment, emigration and immigration progressively ate away at the community, the extended family, even the nuclear family. Socialisation and social control of the young began to fail. Crime and vandalism blossomed. Good neighbourliness gave way to apathy."

Yet poverty, deprivation and the breakdown of social control, as the government has discovered with places like Knowsley, are not confined to inner areas or even large towns. This fact makes some sociologists suspicious of separating out "urban problems" from the society-wide effects of economic change or social inequality. Professor Peter Townsend, for instance, has noted that however the boundaries of specific areas of social deprivation are defined, unless half the area of Britain is included, there will be more people living outside them than within.

Townsend was among several writers in the 1960s and 1970s who challenged the sociological orthodoxy that there was a culture specific to city life. This idea was first set out by Louis Wirth (1887–1952), a German-American sociologist and member of the Chicago School. Wirth thought that you could understand the city's problems by looking at what he considered to be its major social characteristics. These included problems of geographical division along class and race lines, and the potential for conflict that arises from high population density and a loss of community.

But some sociologists, notably Marxists influenced by the Spanish writer Manuel Castells, have taken issue with this view. They have argued that Wirth and his followers are describing not the culture of urbanism but the culture of capitalist urbanisation, which is simply made more manifest in cities. Blaming the inner cities is convenient for the ruling economic elite, the Marxists argue, because it allows them to convey the impression that society's problems can be contained in limited geographical areas.

Yet in Britain at least, the inner cities, for all the blurring of the lines with other deprived areas, do seem to have a special dynamism of their own. They have provided an extraordinary crucible of culture – from Charles Dickens to Linton Kwesi Johnson to *The Boys from the Blackstuff*. They have helped to integrate successive generations of immigrants into the wider society. And they have, in places, shown a powerful capacity for self-regeneration – witness the gentrification of Camden Town, or Jesmond or Moseley. It would be unfortunate if a scenario recently outlined by Professor Peter Hall were to come true.

Without major investment, Hall says, "the result will be further decline and decay until increasingly our cities resemble the unfortunate model set by some of the American disaster cases. This will be the all too easy way to go; it will cost very little in the short term (apart from the costs of policing and controlling the remaining inhabitants) while the majority will enjoy satisfactory – if slightly one-dimensional – lives in the suburbs and the smaller towns."

The lessons of the riots

Unless you happened to live there nobody ever thought much about Toxteth or Brixton. But in the summer of 1981 and again in 1985, violent riots put them very much on the map.

The riots in Liverpool, London, Bristol and Birmingham have had ramifications at several levels. On the political right they reawakened old Tory fears of the mob: one response has been the atavistic cry for more "law and order." The left have taken the line that Mrs Thatcher's economic policies have been pushed too far and stirred up social discontent.

They were certainly a dramatic reminder that race and rebellion are two of the many elements in the inner city package. They were also a reminder that "benign neglect" of the cities as a policy leaves the door open, as happened in Brixton and Tottenham in 1985, to a chain reaction sparked by a single incident. It is significant that riots did not occur in, say, Glasgow or Gateshead, where deprivation is arguably as severe. The missing factor was race; more specifically, a local history of tense relations between inner city blacks and the front line agents of social control, the police.

Martin Kettle and Lucy Hodges, two journalists who studied the events of 1981 (*Uprising*, 1983), emphasise that the sparks that ignited the riots fell into the tinder box of inner city policing.

But behind the "failure" of policing lie objective facts about housing and job discrimination. A study of Hackney by the Commission for Racial Equality published in 1984 found that the Labour-controlled council was guilty of racial discrimination in allocating council houses. Black people were getting the worst houses on the "dump" estates. And Professor John Rex found in his studies of inner Birmingham that while blacks and Asians are not necessarily more likely to be unemployed, non-white groups often act as a "buffer" in the labour market – the first to go in recession and the last to be hired.

There have been efforts to repair relations between the black inner-city communities and the police, and enough progress has been made to disappoint those on the extreme left who welcomed the riots as the beginnings of social revolution.

But in policing the inner city, there remains a gulf between the agents of law and order and blacks. A major study of the Metropolitan Police in 1984 by the Policy Studies Institute found substantial evidence of racism in the force. And as Paul Harrison notes in his study of Hackney: "It is an unfortunate fact of cultural diversity that many young Afro-Caribbeans, innocent or otherwise, behave in a way that makes hairs stand up on white policemen's necks."

The medicine that failed to work

There has been no shortage of official ideas about what to do with the inner cities. Indeed, some would argue that there have been too many – and that they have often been contradictory and self-defeating.

Inner-cities policy is a child of the 1960s when enthusiasm for social experiments ran high and for a time there was unbounded faith in the ability of governments to solve problems.

Typical of the decade was the push for "urban renewal." In 1964, Richard Crossman, the newly-appointed Housing Minister in the Wilson government, wrote: "We have to concentrate upon six or seven places: Liverpool, Manchester, Birmingham, Glasgow, London, where the problem of housing is so bad ... there should be large-scale state intervention in those blighted areas of cities where Commonwealth citizens settle and where there are racial problems."

In the event the renewal was half-hearted, and left in its wake massive public building projects that have in their turn contributed to the inner-city malaise of the 1980s. But Crossman's concern with race was widely shared.

Enoch Powell's notorious "rivers of blood" speech about the effects of black immigration is thought to have prompted the Prime Minister, Harold Wilson, to announce in 1968 an Urban Programme – a scheme for grants for projects mounted by local authorities in areas of urban stress. The programme is still in existence, having paid for about 5000 projects. But it is fairly unfocused, with money going on such diverse things as vasectomy facilities in Bristol, and the translation of government pamphlets in Luton.

More ambitiously, in 1969 the Home Office began establishing twelve Community Development Projects to experiment in "action research" on social service provision and community self-help in deprived areas. Inevitably the activists attracted to the scheme were left-wing, and by the mid 1970s the projects had become an embarrassment to politicians and were ended. They have left behind, however, some incisive analyses of the inner-city problem, albeit written from a Marxist standpoint.

The 1970s saw both a diminished faith in governmental solutions and a flood of anxiety about the decay of British cities; there was even, in 1976, a conference funded by the Gulbenkian Foundation entitled "Save Our Cities." In 1974, the Environment Secretary in the Heath government, Peter Walker, set up inter-disciplinary teams to undertake detailed studies of three inner areas, Stockwell in Lambeth, Small Heath in Birmingham and Liverpool 8.

A part consequence of these studies was the enthusiasm of the Labour government in the late 1970s for an inner-urban policy to deal with the multiple problems they revealed. Labour's 1978 Inner Urban Areas Act set up the framework that still exists for cooperation (at least in theory) between central government and inner-city local authorities.

City councils are classed as *partnership* (the worst areas of deprivation), *programme* and *designated* authorities, and the government pays varying amounts for agreed projects. The fatal weakness of the plan – which became apparent when the Conservatives came to power in 1979 – is that it runs entirely outside the framework of rate-support grants to councils. Labour councils, in particular, have claimed it is irrational for the government to pay partnership money with one hand and with the other cut the rate-support grant in the name of economy.

Current urban policy is mainly associated with the ideas of Michael Heseltine, Environment Secretary from 1979 to 1983. Though Heseltine's general philosophy was to encourage the private sector to regenerate the inner areas, he introduced several new state powers. Persuaded by the success of the New Towns' development corporations, he appointed special non-elected public authorities to take over and run sections of London's and Liverpool's docklands.

Liverpool became a special focus of "Heseltinism" – a mixture of brash public relations and genuine concern to arrest inner city decline. On Merseyside, Heseltine experimented with a "task force" made up of civil servants and local business people, and he twisted arms to secure promises of finance from the City of London and building societies.

Generally, though, Conservative policy towards the inner cities puts the emphasis on private business activity. Indeed some of Mrs Thatcher's colleagues are highly sceptical about any government involvement at all. Privately, some Conservatives argue that the decline of the cities is inevitable. Government should accept the market's verdict and merely cushion the social impact – while paying special attention to law and order to minimise the danger of further riots like those in 1981 and 1985.

BOOKS

Some useful additional reading:
Manuel Castells, *The Urban Question*, Edward Arnold, 1977
David Harvey, *Social Justice and the City*, Edward Arnold, 1973
R. E. Pahl, *Whose City?*, Penguin, 1975
C. G. Pickvance (ed.), *Urban Sociology: critical essays*, Tavistock, 1976
John Rex and Robert Moore, *Race, Community and Conflict*, Oxford University Press, 1967

KNOWLEDGE

How do we know what we know? The physical and mental processes of the mind are the province of brain surgeons and psychologists. The ordering of words, ideas and meanings are of particular interest to philosophers. But the relationship between people's knowledge and understanding of the world and the society to which they belong – this is the domain of the sociology of knowledge.

We sometimes talk about optimists as people who look at life "through rose-coloured spectacles" – in other words we believe that people's understanding of events can be modified by the preconceptions that they bring to them. Sociologists of knowledge go further. All of us – individuals, families and whole societies – are wearing such spectacles all the time. What is more they serve purposes which can be defined and analysed – and they can be changed.

We generally acquire our ideas and beliefs through *socialisation* – our outlook is created and shaped by our education, our jobs and the newspapers we read. As a result people's beliefs vary according to the nature of the society they live in. A Moscow office-worker reading *Pravda* will have a different perception of the truth from a London commuter reading the *Daily Telegraph*. It is not the job of the sociologist to decide who is right, but to establish why people believe as they do.

Unfortunately, the process is complicated by the fact that social scientists have long disagreed over the nature of knowledge itself. On one side are the *positivists*, in the tradition of Emile Durkheim (1858–1917), who believe that social knowledge is measurable using the methods of the natural sciences.

Durkheim, and to some extent Marx,

believed that pure "scientific" knowledge was superior to philosophical and religious belief, and that by using the scientific approach to identify, analyse and develop theories about social facts, a complete explanation of human existence could be arrived at.

In contrast, there are the *phenomenologists,* who believe that there are no such things as absolute social facts, since society does not have a reality of its own, independent of its members. Rather, it is socially created by people's interactions, both with other members of society and with the sociologists who are studying them. As a result, sociologists cannot provide "objective" meanings, since the topics they select, the way they conduct their research and analyse data must all be the result of interpretation and value judgments based on their own culture and ideology.

This idea that knowledge is relative is a central concept in the sociology of knowledge.

Relativism in this sense refers to the relationship between a set of ideas and the society that produces them. Thus, the notion held by some South Sea islanders that Prince Philip is a god, should be considered in its own context, which is quite different and separate from the context in which some British MPs regard him as a parasite. Bearing in mind the concept of relativism, the sociologist will not act as arbiter between various views, but try to understand how those beliefs came into being and how they relate to the wider culture of the society in which they are found.

This sort of non-judgmental approach was taken, for example, by Max Weber (1864–1920), in his classic study, *The Protestant Ethic and the Spirit of Capitalism* (1905). He argued that there was an "elective affinity" or a mutual compatibility, between the driving need of early Calvinists to prove that they were in a state of grace by means of their hard work, and the economic forces of sixteenth and seventeenth-century capitalism. But he did not have to demonstrate that Calvinism was "true" or "untrue" – merely that it was related to a specific tide of economic and social change.

Ideology is another very important concept. This means more than just a "governing set of ideas," which is how we generally think of the term today. In the sociology of knowledge it represents a body of ideas which serve to justify the interests of those who hold them, however altruistic they may sound. Thus, an ideology that supports the inequality of wealth is attractive to the rich; while one which stresses equal shares is more appealing to the poor. Sociologists largely follow Marx's definition of ideology as "systematically distorted knowledge" – knowledge which is distorted in the interests of the groups who are producing and consuming it.

KARL MARX: In fact, Marx (who lived from 1818–83) provided the first major impetus for the development of the sociology of knowledge, in relating systems of thought to their social context. For him the "production of consciousness" was directly interwoven with the material activity and economic structure of society at any particular time. This consciousness is altered, however, when economic and social relationships change. "The class which is the ruling material force of society is at the same time its ruling intellectual force," he argued. As a class rules materially, its rule extends to the field of knowledge and culture as well, regulating the production and distribution of the ideas of its age.

Marx believed that all knowledge is tied to ideology – so the prevailing ideas in a capitalist society, for example, are capitalist ones. The only exception to this was "scientific socialism" – the practical application of which would be the eventual creation of a classless society, in which self-interested ideology would be unnecessary.

KARL MANNHEIM: The German sociologist, Karl Mannheim (1893–1947), built on Marx's ideas to provide the first coherent modern theory of a sociology of knowledge. When he published his influential book, *Ideology and Utopia,* in Weimar Germany in 1931, it seemed that a sociology of knowledge might provide the answer to some difficult questions, since the country was split by the competing intellectual and political creeds of fascism, communism, socialism and liberalism. This discord eventually led to war.

Many intellectuals at the time believed, like Mannheim, who was teaching at Frankfurt University, that the solution to the country's problems lay in finding a way of evaluating rationally the competing ideological claims of all the political groupings vying for power. Mannheim did not believe it was possible to determine the "essential" truth or falsity of any particular ideological position – but it was possible to demonstrate that these positions were *related* to the social position of the group involved.

Mannheim adapted Marx, but with an important difference. Where Marx believed that you could penetrate ideology with the "true science" of socialism, Mannheim believed that *all* thought, with the exception of some pure sciences like mathematics, was related to its social context, and could not be freed from that relationship.

According to Mannheim, ideology is not a distortion of the truth, but a complementary aspect of it. Each social position has its own perspective, and it is the sociologist's job to identify that perspective.

Mannheim awarded a special status to sociologists in getting to the bottom of the social origins of ideas. The reason that sociologists could make such independent judgments, he said, was because those who practised the sociology of knowledge – the intellectuals – had a form of education that allowed them to avoid class standpoints, and so to rise above ideology. His view, which seems rather outdated now, was that the intelligentsia was "socially unattached" and therefore uncommitted. Intellectuals could arrive at a "total perspective" by relating all the partial perspectives of various social positions.

THE FRANKFURT SCHOOL: Another reassessment of Marx's ideas about the sociology of knowledge came from the 1930s onwards from sociologists at the Frankfurt Institute for Social Research – notably Max Horkheimer, Theodor Adorno, Herbert Marcuse and Jurgen Habermas. Like Mannheim's, their theories developed in the volatile intellectual climate of Weimar Germany, and their aim was the study of "social life in its totality."

Though their allegiances were basically Marxist, they developed a *critical theory*, which not only opposed all forms of positivism, but all interpretations of Marxism which were excessively scientific and dogmatic – particularly the way in which Marx was being interpreted by Stalin.

According to Horkheimer (who coined the term), critical theory could replace the "traditional" theory used by natural science. The idea was that it would form the basis on which knowledge could be used to *transform* society. In other words, traditional theory simply allows society to be reproduced in its present form, whereas critical theory allows it to change.

For the followers of the Frankfurt School, science became a symbol for an authority system and a structure of social relations which stood in the way of truly rational and free organisation of society. Indeed, where others saw fascism as the triumph of the irrational, Horkheimer and his colleagues saw it as a triumph for a certain kind of technical, manipulative rationality.

Habermas went even further in his search for a "pure" form of knowledge. In his book, *Knowledge and Human Interests,* he talked about a type of knowledge called *self-reflection* – by which an individual could criticise social reality against an "objective" standard of truth which came from within himself, rather than from society. This involved going beyond what is actually "there" in external reality.

If people didn't have this "ideal" standard by which to measure the "truth," Habermas said, what could be the meaning of words like "exploitation" and "cruelty"? He thought that we could only move towards a freer and more truthful society if we say what we "really" mean. Societies often *repress* our ability to do this by making us afraid of what might happen – a form of social control.

Habermas's attempt to solve the problem of how people can escape the social conditioning of their thought was in the tradition of Marx's critic, Max Weber, who took a highly individualistic stance. Weber wrote: "Interpretative sociology considers the individual and his activity as the basic unit, as its 'atom' – if the disputable comparison for once may be permitted. In this approach the individual is also the upper limit and the sole carrier of meaningful conduct ... In general, for sociology, such concepts as 'state', 'association', 'feudalism' and the like, designate certain categories of human interaction. Hence it is the task of sociology to reduce these concepts to 'understandable' action, that is, without exception, to the actions of participating individual men."

For Weber, in contrast to Marx, material factors including the economic organisation of society, have a role secondary to ideas and knowledge in explaining social change. His sociology of knowledge reserved some autonomy, therefore, to a more individualistic world of ideas, and he saw social history in terms of an increasing rationalisation of human activity.

Though it may seem as though its concerns are rather abstract, the sociology of knowledge has important practical applications. It has been brought to bear on research into areas like stereotyping and labelling theory (especially the means by which society describes people and their actions as delinquent) and into media studies (particularly the methods by which the media collectively orchestrate a "hidden agenda" of information and opinion). It also gives an insight into the "hidden curriculum" of the education system (by which society tells its young how knowledge is partitioned, and passes on a variety of unofficial "lessons", which

And now for the bad news ...

If all knowledge is relative, as most sociologists claim, what about, say, the BBC news? Surely, this must be a pretty absolute representation of events as they actually happened?

Not so, say the Glasgow University Media Group, who have made a special study of the way news is presented on television. In their books, *Bad News* (1976), *More Bad News* (1980) and *Really Bad News* (1982), they argue that much of what passes as balanced and factual news-reporting is produced from a highly partial viewpoint. Knowledge, they suggest, is being used in the interests of the powerful – that the media work to "legitimise" the status quo and manipulate information to fit a dominant view.

It's not just what goes into the news that counts, but the way its contents are organised: "We all know that strikes are bad, unless they happen in Poland. The news neglects to tell us that, if British workers acted in the same way as their Polish counterparts, they would be breaking the provisions of the Conservative government's Employment Act. Poland in Britain would very definitely by reported as

MORE VIOLENCE OUTSIDE FACTORIES AS FLYING PICKETS FIGHT POLICE."

The group also points out that different rules apply for describing different sections of society, depending on whether you are powerful or weak, a man or a woman, and black or white: "In 1980 thirteen children died in a terrible fire during a party in Deptford. It is not hard to imagine what the coverage of this event would have been like had the children been white. The tragedy of each victim would have been outlined – their parents, their hopes, their prospects – young lives cut short. But the victims were black, and there were overtones of racial violence."

Other writers have gone further in criticising the way knowledge is "used" by the media. Ralph Miliband writes, in *The State in Capitalist Society* (1973): "It does not seem extravagant to suggest that radio and television in all capitalist countries have been consistently and predominantly agencies of conservative indoctrination and that they have done what they could do to inoculate their listeners and viewers against dissident thought. This does not require that all such dissent should be prevented from getting an airing. It only requires that the overwhelming bias of the media should be on the other side. And that requirement has been amply met."

can be as influential as those which lead to examinations).

The heavy financial commitment to schooling in the advanced and developing countries has made the sociology of educational knowledge particularly important in recent years. The unequal performance in schools of pupils from different ethnic backgrounds, especially first-generation immigrant children, has prompted much research into the relationship between intellectual skills and the cultural needs of different social groups.

Michael F. D. Young (in *Knowledge and Control*, 1971) quotes a study which compared the performance of adults in a tribal group, the Kpelle, with that of American overseas volunteers in estimating how many cups of rice could be filled from a particular bowl. The Kpelle were far superior at this task, but the volunteers were far better than the Kpelle at sorting coloured cards carrying geometrical symbols. It would be hard to say which group was mathematically superior, although a mathematics test geared to western assumptions would always give the advantage to the Americans.

Sociologists who have specialised in educational knowledge have examined it from several angles – from the systematic organisation of schools as such, to the hidden curriculum in the classroom. Samuel Bowles and Herbert Gintis are Marxists who have examined (in *Schooling of Capitalist America,* 1976) the close fit between the organisation of schools and the needs of a hierarchical class society. In Britain, too, a considerable literature grew up to show that the pre-comprehensive system, widespread from 1944 to 1970, matched knowledge with social class needs: a small, wealthy upper middle class sent children to independent public and direct grant schools which reflected conservative, proprietorial and higher bureaucratic values; a more ordinary middle class sent children to grammar schools on passing the 11-plus; and the broad working class used secondary modern schools at which work discipline was important but exam attainment was often irrelevant.

This kind of critique has extended to the way in which exams work as socio-economic rationing systems guarding the entry to more advanced education and the higher-earning professions. The traditional respect attached to the classics and the humanities within English schools, and the lower status attached to practical and scientific studies, related to the literary "gifted amateur" self-image of a governing class, and the disparagement of the "dirty hands" of production, trade and technology.

In France, Pierre Bourdieu has looked at schooling as a means of reproducing social capital, whereby knowledge, the education system and social values are interwoven to maintain the dominance of certain classes. In Britain, Basil Bernstein has considered the language of schooling, and argued that the "elaborated code", in which middle-class children are more comfortable, provides them with an automatic advantage in the classroom over their working class peers who are used to a "restricted code."

One of the most radical attacks on the distribution of knowledge has come from Ivan Illich in his book, *Deschooling Society* (1971). Illich considers that the "dire influence" of the teaching force has extended its tentacles from the developed to the developing countries. According to him, teachers, like other professional groups, have a constant tendency to monopolise their areas of knowledge, to mystify and make dependent the rest of society, and to stand in the way of the sharing of skills which developing countries especially need.

What all these approaches have in common is that they reject the idea that any area, or type of knowledge is *intrinsically* superior to any other. They are concerned not with whether knowledge is correct, but with how what *counts* as knowledge relates to the distribution of power in society.

And, of course, all the various debates about the sociology of knowledge are of crucial importance to sociology as a disci-

pline, for it is itself a form of knowledge. As Pat McNeill points out in *Fundamentals of Sociology* (1981), "If all knowledge is ideological, then society is, too. If all knowledge is socially constructed and therefore relative, then our knowledge that this is the case is itself socially constructed, and we must accept our own relative status."

Nevertheless, the analytic stance of a sociologist of knowledge can be as revealing as that of a philosopher, a psychologist or a social historian. When knowledge is both power and weakness, *how* we know is as crucial as *what* we know.

BOOKS

Some useful additional reading:

C. Cook, "What is knowledge?", in R. Meighan *et al, Perspectives on Society,* Nelson, 1979

J. C. Curtis and J. W. Petras, *The Sociology of Knowledge,* 1970

P. Hamilton, *Knowledge and Social Structure,* 1974

K. Mannheim, *Essays on the Sociology of Knowledge,* 1952

W. Stark, *The Sociology of Knowledge,* 1958

LEISURE

A two-day week; a stimulating job involving decision-making, technical skill and social worth; an income sufficient to indulge your wide recreational and educational interests? Sounds exciting? But what would you do with all this free time?

It seems far-fetched in an age of rising unemployment, but, according to the apostles of the microchip, most boring and repetitive tasks could be eliminated, and we could all have an interesting job *and* more leisure. The chip, some people argue, could bring work of a different kind, rather than simply fewer jobs.

But at the moment its introduction on to production lines and in office work is proceeding fast and with no central control. Recently, the white-collar union,

ASTMS, launched a pungent campaign drawing attention to the chip, with slogans like "One chip can replace 800 white collars", and "Anything you can do, a chip can do better."

The way we handle this new technology is obviously going to influence considerably our pattern of life. Clive Jenkins, general secretary of ASTMS, has called for a programme in Britain to meet what he described as the "collapse of work", citing forecasts of unemployment running as high as five million in both Britain and West Germany by the late 1980s. Meanwhile, a British woman, Kathleen Smith, recently founded the Work and Leisure Society, which is campaigning for a reduction in the working year to about 1000 hours from about twice that amount. This, she argues, is the next step forward in civilisation. A few years ago this might have been regarded as cranky, but now it is a serious matter.

If work is becoming less important, the corollary is that leisure is becoming more so. But are we really prepared for what could be a fundamental change in the human condition? Many writers think not, and the vision of future leisure as a great human problem has been summed up recently by one of the most famous science-fiction writers, Arthur C. Clarke, author of *2001*:

"In the world of the future, the sort of mindless labour that has occupied 99 per cent of mankind for much more than 99 per cent of its existence, will, of course, be largely taken over by machines. Yet most people are bored to death without work – even work that they don't like. In a workless world, therefore, only the highly educated will be able to flourish, or perhaps even to survive. The rest are likely to destroy themselves and their environment out of sheer frustration. This is no vision of the distant future; it is already happening, most of all in the decaying cities. So perhaps we should not despise TV soap operas if, during the turbulent transition period between our culture and real civilisation, they serve as yet another opium for the masses. This drug, at any rate, is cheap and harmless, serving to kill time for those many people who like it

better dead."

Such pessimistic arguments see man as ill-prepared for a life of leisure, and suggest that there may eventually be some kind of social chaos. Before the Industrial Revolution, Britain and other advanced societies were rural communities with people leading much more leisurely lives, geared to the cycles of the agricultural year. Now they are attuned to dynamic production, and, since the war, to full employment. The Protestant ethic has encouraged thrift and hard work in western societies. To move suddenly to a more leisure-based society might be seen as part of our "moral sickness."

Since the industrial organisation of society seemed to require rather more work than the pre-industrial, perhaps this is quite understandable. There were far more holidays in the pre-industrial world. Often, when the weather was bad, people simply could not work at all.

It was in the United States, a country which, paradoxically, was largely built upon a Protestant work ethic, that the study of leisure first attained credibility, and where increasing leisure for industrial man was first seen as a threat. George Barton Cutten wrote his book, *The Threat of Leisure,* in 1926, drawing on work and writings from late nineteenth and early twentieth century America. The latter included Thorstein Veblen's important *Theory of the Leisure Classes* (1912), a

consideration of the leisure lifestyle of the newly very rich in American society.

The basis of all the "threat" arguments is that through the increasing use of technology, man has gradually less work, or what is called obligated activity, and that because he is ill-prepared for the alternative, some sort of social chaos would inevitably result. Such an attitude presupposes that we know what leisure is and something of its place in both individual behaviour and society. But deeper investigation by sociologists has only recently got under way.

Leisure means different things to different people. Probably the most common definition arises from the Latin root of the word itself, *licere,* meaning "to be permitted", which suggests a meaning of "time free from obligation" (hence the use of the phrase "free time" as a common synonym for leisure). But as the American sociologist, Max Kaplan, demonstrated, a number of other interpretations are possible, including leisure as recreation (in preparation for more work). An example of this is an actor who takes exercise to prepare himself for a physically demanding role.

Another interpretation sees a relationship between the activities carried out in leisure time and the economic system. For instance, you might think of do-it-yourself home improvements in this way. Also, leisure may be endowed with specific qualities – i.e., it is *for* something, and does not just exist in isolation. In other words, society might be encouraging certain leisure activities to suit its own purposes, as with athletes in East Germany. This is not just a modern phenomenon: it applied also to participants in the public games of ancient Rome, or medieval archers, whose sport could quickly be applied to military purposes.

It is useful to see leisure as part of a dual concept alongside work, and the two words can be understood fully only in relation to one another. Unfortunately, unlike certain other easily defined double relationships, like husband and wife or parent and child, there is a large middle ground to the work-leisure relationship. This means that many quite normal and frequent activities such as housework, do-it-yourself, gardening and even eating or sleeping, are difficult to classify completely as one or the other. Perhaps it would be useful for you to think of the range of activities carried out during the week by members of your own family, and attempt to classify them as either work or leisure. Take the case of a gardener in a park who comes home and digs his own garden in the evenings. Which is work and which is leisure?

However, there is agreement on the central features of a definition of leisure. First, that it concerns a period of *time*, and second, that there is an element of *choice* about what use is made of that time. One writer, Ray Maw, has proposed that it is possible to allot most daily activities along a sliding scale from essential to leisure. But in any given situation no individual may agree with the placings he has made. Where would you put choosing a birthday card or cooking a meal for friends? Leisure also includes an element of play (which defines it as being other than work) and one of psychological satisfaction (one uses leisure to "feel good"). Leisure can also break down the social hierarchy – so a teacher can play in a school Saturday soccer team, for instance.

The problem of definition is faced by anyone wishing to find out what people are actually doing with their leisure time, as well as being crucial to understanding the role and meaning of leisure in life. Even from the earliest days of group life in man, leisure has had considerable, if sometimes neglected, impact. In producing "bulk leisure" for a small minority the early civilisations created the special conditions necessary for the development of the arts, sciences, games and other products of civilised life.

Cutten remarked that "in fact, civilisations were the product of leisure, and yet they have not always admitted their origin." During the nineteenth century, despite a considerable emphasis on work in industrial society, it was recognised by some that leisure was becoming much more important. Disraeli himself noted that "increased means and increased leisure are the two civilisers of man." Today the core of the philosophical debate about work and leisure concerns the extent to which society has moved from being work-centred to being leisure-centred.

Stanley Parker, who has done much modern research into leisure, has said that "today vestiges of the Protestant work ethic remain, but it has been strongly challenged by a more leisure-based ethic: that work is a means to the end of enjoying oneself in leisure. Earlier, work gave a man his sense of identity. Today, it is claimed, his leisure is more likely to supply it." The extent to which we in Britain are in such a leisure-centred culture is debatable. We still rely on inherited attitudes. But soon the debate about whether or not we become more leisure-centred will be more urgent.

Traditionally leisure has been associated with religious rituals – and many of our holidays are still based round religious festivals. Leisure has also, until recent times, been the prerogative of the rich, who have had more time and money to indulge in such things. But technological change and a wider spread of wealth have brought more leisure time for all social classes. The working week, for example, has shrunk since 1900.

For manual workers normal hours worked (which exclude overtime) dropped from 52–54 hours per week at the beginning of the century to 48 by 1920, 44 in 1948 and to less than 40 by the mid-1970s. However, *actual* hours have dropped less dramatically (and indeed *increased* between 1938 and 1955). Workers have tended to opt for more pay through overtime rather than shorter hours. Add to this increased travelling time to work from many suburban areas and it seems that many later twentieth century Britons do not have a vast amount of extra leisure time in comparison with their grandfathers.

The big exception is paid holiday, which has increased greatly since the war. It has also given working-class people access to places that once were only available to the rich. Although it still tends to be true that manual workers have less holiday than professional people, you are just as likely to find a car factory worker as a bank manager on the beach in Majorca.

Improved affluence and mass-production techniques have made modern leisure activities more diverse and varied. The motor car has given people more choice, and the development of the mass media has changed leisure patterns radically. Fewer people make their own entertainment, but many more read books and magazines. The entertainments industry has led to the professionalisation of football, tennis and golf. Professional footballers can be among the highest-paid people in the country.

There are all sorts of factors that influence people's choice of leisure activities. On the simplest level, men might prefer bowls, while a woman might prefer embroidery. Obviously among young school leavers, who have newly-acquired economic independence, many spend a lot of time out of the home with their

What we do with our leisure time

Some of our popular spare-time activities
(% of people participating)

Listening to records/tapes	63%
Reading books	56
Going out for a drink	54
Gardening	44
Going out for a meal	40
Do-it-yourself	36
Needlework/knitting	27
Dancing	11

Participation in active sports
in Great Britain

Men

Walking	19%
Darts	11
Billiards/snooker	11
Indoor swimming	7
Football	6
Fishing	4
Golf	4
Outdoor swimming	4
Squash	4
Table tennis	2

Women

Walking	17%
Indoor swimming	7
Athletics/keep fit	5
Darts	4
Badminton	2
Outdoor swimming	1

source: General Household Survey 1983

friends. Currently discos, pubs and the cinema are the most popular activities with young people.

When people get married, their leisure activities tend to change. Things like do-it-yourself and home decoration become important. A study by Mark Abrams of the "five ages of leisure" found that a quarter of a group aged between 25 and 34 had not been out of the home for leisure purposes in the preceding week. As people get older, the emphasis on the home increases and television becomes more important, though older people still undertake some of the more traditional private leisure activities like playing cards.

One important factor in a person's choice of leisure activity is his occupation. In a study by Stanley Parker, 200 people in ten occupations were interviewed. Several patterns were found. Bank employees were found to be least involved in their work, tending to see it merely as a means to earning a living. They were not so engrossed in their work that they wanted to take it over into their spare time nor were they so damaged by it that they were hostile to it. Child care officers tended to enjoy their work, and often related it to their leisure. Work and leisure for them were often similar in content, and existed comfortably side by side.

Miners and deep-sea fishermen, on the other hand, had a pattern of opposition between work and leisure. Leisure functioned for them as something totally distinct and separate – something that compensated for dangerous and difficult work. There was what might be described as hostility between work and leisure.

The General Household Survey provides the most recent picture of our leisure-time activities. This, together with surveys by the BBC and the Pilot National Recreation Survey (1967), shows clearly that most of our leisure is spent in the home, and that watching television is by far the major activity. The average weekly viewing of men and women is about 23 hours. Children and old people watch more than young adults and the middle-aged. Disparity also exists between the social classes, with the lower socio-economic groups watching up to a third more than the higher ones.

But television-watching is not undiscriminating, as many people suppose. During recent TV strikes, evidence shows that many people simply switched off their sets. More people listened to the radio and went to public houses and the cinema than previously.

Other important home-based activities include listening to records and tapes, reading books (a higher percentage of the adult UK population claims to read daily than in any other European country), do-it-yourself and gardening. In many ways the home is a leisure-centre, and too often designers and architects fail to appreciate the importance of this in providing for things like sound insulation.

From some viewpoints leisure spent outside the home is more important, certainly in commercial and space-using terms. Here the popularity of the public house remains undiminished, despite a fall in the number of pubs, and perhaps the only major change has been the rapid postwar decline in cinema attendance. Only a small proportion of the population take part in active sports (although a large number watch them). Outdoor pursuits in general have been popularised by the technological products of our society – for example, the lightweight tent.

In reality, choice of leisure-time activity is by no means free. It is dependent upon personal factors (age, car ownership, class, income and education) and by what are described as environmental constraints. This means either lack of facilities, lack of knowledge of what is available or inability to travel there. There has been

BOOKS

Some useful additional reading:
Ian Appleton, *Leisure Research and Policy*, Academic Press, 1975
J. A. Patmore, *Land and Leisure*, Penguin, 1973
S. Parker, *The Sociology of Leisure*, Allen and Unwin, 1976
Ken Roberts, *Contemporary Society and the Growth of Leisure*, Longman, 1979
Ian Simmons, *Rural Recreation in the Industrial World*, Edward Arnold, 1976

much concern over these constraints during the past decade, and the Sports Council and local authorities have tried especially to improve facilities for active sports, for example. Unfortunately many of the large multi-purpose sports centres may actually have created greater inequality of access, because of the difficulty and cost of getting to them by non-car owners.

For the future we face many different leisure problems. At a general level come considerations of exactly how much leisure is going to be available, to whom, and in what proportion, and whether society will be willing to make the necessary readjustments (by job sharing or other means) to enhance the role of leisure in life satisfaction. In contrast, we may ask if it is possible to reduce inequalities in access to recreation facilities, so that better use is made of existing leisure time. Of course, it would be nonsense in a free society to plan people's leisure for them. Rather, we must plan *for* people's leisure-time activities.

MARRIAGE

Why should marriage be any of society's business, you might ask. Isn't falling in love and choosing a partner one of the few individual and intimate matters of choice left to us? A sociologist would probably answer: On the contrary, marriage is an important element in the social fabric and seems likely to stay that way, despite all the predictions of its demise.

As well as providing an orderly way of rearing and socialising children, marriage is connected with all sorts of other aspects of our lives, like economic production and household organisation. Getting married is a binding contract, made very much on society's terms. It not only wins you social approval, but also defines a set of duties and obligations that help to keep society stable. When the Russians tried to abandon marriage in 1917 for a system of complete moral and sexual freedom, there was so much chaos that they had to go back to the old system nineteen years later.

Marriage is hardly a new idea – you have only to look at the number of times it is mentioned in the Bible to see that. Yet it has changed enormously over the centuries. What we expect from marriage in 1980 is very different from the sort of aspirations even our grandparents had. We think of personal happiness as being paramount for a successful marriage. Yet until comparatively recently, other considerations like property and lineage were far more important – and they still are in many other societies.

Marriage in pre-industrial Europe was largely a matter of convenient contract. Edward Shorter, in *The Making of the Modern Family* (1976), even maintains that the eighteenth-century French peasant probably valued his cows more than his wife. Comparing now with then, he says: "Affection and inclination, love and sympathy, came to take the place of 'instrumental' considerations in regulating the dealings of family members with one another. Spouses and children came to be prized for what they were, rather than for what they represented or what they could do."

Of course, these pre-industrial expectations of marriage were set against a social background in which life was shorter and death and disease were part of daily life. In the seventeenth century, the average life expectancy was only 32 years, and the death of a member of the family was so common that no one could afford too much of an emotional investment. Very often the life cycle of a marriage was such that a couple got married, had children, and by the time the children reached marriageable age the parents died.

The prevailing social pattern, where marriages would often be organised according to the wishes of the parents rather than the couple involved, lasted well into this century. This was combined with rigid roles within marriage – authority was expected of the husband

and submission of the wife. The man was generally expected to be head of the family, responsible for all decisions and initiative; the wife's role was limited to childbearing and looking after the home. During the industrial revolution wives often had to work long hours in factories and mills as well.

Marriage has been transformed by improved material well-being and health, contraception and greater equality of the sexes. In Britain, today we can afford to be far more idealistic about marriage – we choose our partners freely, we have mostly equal status with them, expect to have an equal say in making decisions.

We can live independently of family ties and have a right to expect mutual compatibility with our partners. Marriage in the twentieth century has become worthwhile in itself rather than a handy means to some other end. But, as Ronald Fletcher points out in *The Family and Marriage in Britain* (1973), that brings its own dangers: "We have so improved the marital relationship that it depends entirely upon free choice and personal responsibility; we have made it at one and the same time more rewarding and potentially more unstable."

The other important way in which modern marriage has changed is that it has lost much of its religious importance. More than a half of all marriages now take place in a register office, whereas as recently as 1966 the proportion was only a third. Whether this has led to some kind of decline in the quality of marriage is hard to measure. In any case, a church wedding does not necessarily mean a religious commitment to marriage. As the sociologist, Bryan Wilson, has pointed out, church ceremony is often no more than a way of marking an important personal turning point – a *rite de passage*.

Certainly, the Christian idea that sexual relationships should be confined to marriage has no great historical tradition. As Edward Westermarck points out in *The History of Human Marriage* (1921), "among many peoples true married life does not begin . . . until a child is born, or there are signs of pregnancy."

The extent of marriage in a monoga-

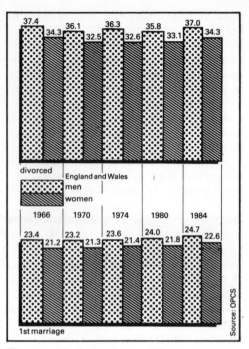

The most likely age for marriage

mous society like our own depends very much on whether there are equal numbers of men and women. In societies where polygamy (taking more than one wife) or polyandry (taking more than one husband) is allowed, any imbalance can to some extent be remedied. The problem in Britain for a long time has been that there were more women than men, but in the past twenty years this trend has been reversed.

The impact of the change is summed up in the 1971 Finer report on one-parent families: "The distinctiveness of today's situation, with a surplus of men in all age groups up to 44 may be appreciated by recalling how, in mid-Victorian England, almost a third of the women aged 20 – 44 had to remain spinsters because differential mortality and large-scale emigration so depleted the reservoir of men that there were not enough to go round." A similar imbalance occurred after the First World War. The first sign of a reversal came in the 1960s when for the first time there was a surplus of men. This surplus has continued to grow, and is now starting to be reflected in the marriage figures.

For most of this century, however, the

improved ratio between the sexes has been accompanied by the increasing popularity of marriage. The annual total of first marriages for both partners rose in the United Kingdom with the growth of the population, from about 250 000 at the turn of the century to 369 000 in 1971. Since then, though, the number of first marriages has fallen every year, to 255 000 in 1982.

One reason for this seeming drop in the popularity of marriage, put forward by the Office of Population Censuses and Surveys, is that people are getting married later. There has been quite a big decline in the marriage rates of people aged 25 or less, and particularly among teenagers. There has been a much smaller decline in the first marriages of those between 25 and 29, and hardly any change at all in the over-30s.

From 1980 to the late 1960s the "median" age of marriage (the age that divides the group so that half are younger and half are older) fell fairly consistently. But the median age of first marriages has now gone up for men from 23.3 in 1971 to 24.2 in 1982, with a slightly smaller rise for women.

Alongside this trend towards postponement of marriage is a decline in shotgun weddings. Between 1964 and 1976 the number of brides who were pregnant dropped from 22 per cent to 12 per cent. Obviously, improved contraception accounts largely for this, as it does for the increase in the number of people who choose to live together before marriage.

The General Household Survey shows that the number of people who live together before marriage is increasing. The proportions of women aged 16 to 34 at the time of marriage in 1979–82 who had cohabited with their husband before marriage were 25 per cent in the case of first marriages and 65 per cent for remarriages.

In other countries in the west the proportion may be even higher. A French survey in 1977 estimated that about a third of young married people had cohabited with their partner, postponing marriage by more than six months.

How do we choose our marriage part-ner? After all, as Edward Shorter points out, it is only recently that we have had much choice at all. We no longer have to consider land settlements, dowries or even our parents' wishes. We are free from an early age to mix with the opposite sex, and are no longer restricted to choosing someone from our own "village." The kind of attitudes that said a woman should be a virgin on marriage have largely disappeared.

Shorter's view is that "romantic love" is the foundation of modern marriage. It would be banal to ask what is love – Plato, Shakespeare and a thousand pop music lyricists have all had a go at defining it. It would be equally wrong to disparage it and say that it's somehow an invention of advertisers and the media – that it doesn't really exist. Even so, it's true to say that we are socialised into falling in love from an early age – not just by our families, but by pop songs, television, films, magazines and people who want to sell us engagement rings. Teenage magazines with titles like *True Romance* sell in their hundreds of thousands; pop songs without the word love in their lyrics are fewer than those with it; novelists like Barbara Cartland have made fortunes writing books about love.

But the kind of love that the media presents to us – that mixture of sexual excitement, intense emotion and idealisation of one's partner – may not be the best foundation for a lasting marriage. People feel cheated when the passion fails to survive the domestic routine. Many sociologists have found, rather, that sharing common interests is one of the most important factors in marital stability.

In fact, most people in this country broadly marry within their own groups. The technical name for this is *endogamy,* and at its most extreme is found in South Africa's race laws, or among orthodox Jews, who traditionally mourn children as though they were dead when they marry a non-Jew. In this country it means that people tend to marry within their own racial, ethnic, class and age grouping.

The opposite of this is *exogamy,* which is the obligation to marry outside one's own social group. This most often applies in small societies, where most people are already related by blood or marriage. In modern British society exogamy is expressed through the incest taboo – the only legal restriction we make on choice of partner. The incest taboo (against sexual relations with close relatives) applies almost universally throughout all societies. The most common reason advanced by sociologists and anthropologists to explain it is that hostility and rivalries within the kin group could disrupt stability. This is certainly the reason the Church of England gives for opposing marriage between non-blood relatives. There are also biological reasons against intermarriage, though this has not prevented certain royal families from practising it in the past.

Apart from our own close relatives, we are free to marry anyone. But we tend not to – there are distinct patterns in the way we make our choice. We tend overall to marry people who are familiar to us. Though Britain is a multi-racial society, inter-racial marriage is still comparatively rare, and people tend to marry others of their own religion. This is especially true of Jews and Roman Catholics. Similarity of age is also important, partly because those in the same age group tend to have common interests. This is also true of social class and education, where surveys have shown that more than three-quarters of the population marry within their own class. All the computer-dating agencies that have sprung up in the past few years trade precisely on this like-marries-like principle.

Though the 1980s couple go into marriage on technically equal footing, true equality within marriage is still something of an ideal. The idea of the "househusband" is still fairly rare, as Ann Oakley found when she looked at the domestic division of labour in *The Sociology of Housework* (1974). She asked 20 working-class and 20 middle-class housewives how far their husbands helped out with the housework and looking after the children. Fewer than a quarter of the husbands gave the kind of help that could be described as doing an equal share of the work – and these tended to be middle-class, as Peter

Willmott and Michael Young discovered in an earlier study, of the London district of Woodford (*Family and Class in a London Suburb,* 1960).

Oakley also found that joint decision-making and leisure pursuits were more likely to be found among the middle classes. She called this kind of sharing a "joint" marriage, and one where husbands and wives differed in these matters, a "segregated" marriage. But "jointness" in decision-making and leisure activities did not necessarily mean that the husbands helped out with the housework – "'joint' marriages are still frequently those in which the husband's domesticity is low and the wife's high." Even so, wives with joint marriages were, on the whole, happier with their marriages than those with segregated ones.

There is some evidence that roles within marriage are connected with the wider social networks of friends and relatives outside. Elizabeth Bott did some research into family life in London (*Family and Social Network,* 1971) and found, broadly, that if the social network of friends and relations is close-knit, that is the friends and relatives know each other socially, then the conjugal roles tend to be "segregated." But if the friends and relatives do not know each other socially (a loose-knit social network) then the roles tend to be "integrated."

The theory is that where the social network is close-knit the couple probably come from the same community and remain there after their marriage. The influence of the friends and relatives tends to encourage the couple to follow more traditional segregated roles, and at the same time provides an independent means of emotional support. Where there is no such external network, then the couple are more likely to look towards each other in a closer emotional relationship and a more integrated marriage.

All this, of course, relates to western, monogamous marriage – the pattern which is the norm today. It was not always so. The anthropologist, George Murdock, studied 238 mostly pre-modern societies and found that 195 practised polygamy and only 43 monogamy. Polygamy can still be found among some African tribes and among many Moslems.

Some sociologists argue that we already have a form of polygamy in our own society – the "serial polygamy" that comes from a high rate of divorce and remarriage. Jessie Bernard, the American sociologist of the family, writes: "Plural marriage is more extensive in our society today than it is in societies that permit polygamy – the chief difference being that we have institutionalised plural marriage serially or sequentially rather than contemporaneously."

Bernard's view is shared by the anthropologist, Lionel Tiger, who says: "Our society, once based on the principle of solid monogamy until death do us part, has shifted towards a pattern of serial polygamy, in which people experience more than one spouse, if only one at a time. Thus we appear to be moving to a new and imprecise system we might call omnigamy, in which each will be married to all."

But there are two sets of hard statistics that are likely to confound the cynics for a while to come. Our increase in life expectancy means that most marriages are lasting longer than ever before – the majority of people can reasonably expect their marriage to last between 40 and 50 years. And the number of people who have been married at some time in their lives shows no sign of waning from the current figure of more than 90 per cent. Although the prophets may have it in for marriage, people don't seem to want to give it up.

BOOKS

Some useful additional reading:
Michael Anderson, *The Sociology of the Family,* Penguin, 1980
David Cooper, *The Death of the Family*, Penguin, 1971
Jack Dominian, *Marriage in Britain, 1945–80,* Study Commission on the Family, 1980
Robin Fox, *Kinship and Marriage,* Penguin, 1970
Office of Population Censuses and Surveys, *Changing Patterns of Family Formation and Dissolution in England and Wales,* 1979

MEDICINE

The medical establishment has become a major threat to health. The pain, dysfunction, disability, and anguish resulting from technical medical intervention now rival the morbidity due to traffic and industrial accidents and even war-related activity, and make the impact of medicine one of the most rapidly spreading epidemics of our time.
Ivan Illich, *The Limits to Medicine* (1977)

How could anyone write so damning an indictment of modern medicine? Can it *really* cause pain? Is it right to talk about it as a sort of epidemic? Surely, under our National Health Service, we are all equal in health?

In fact, Illich's criticisms, though extreme, are among the many reassessments that have been made of the power of medicine and the direction it is taking. Medical sociologists, and even some doctors, are seriously questioning the orthodox medical view that:
● illness is solely biological;
● medicine is a science;
● medicine is necessarily good.

The question of defining illness seems simple, on the face of it. You feel unwell, the doctor diagnoses you and provides a cure if he can. But sociologists would point out that things aren't quite as neat as this. Where a doctor talks of sickness, a sociologist might well talk about *illness behaviour.* You would assume, for instance, that feeling ill is abnormal, but according to morbidity (sickness) surveys, most of us feel sick most of the time. The General Household Survey found that "overall, 56 per cent of men and 70 per cent of women reported that they had a health problem all the time, or one that kept recurring. Yet only 9 per cent of men and 12 per cent of women questioned had seen their GP or family doctor in the preceding 14 days."

Sociologists make the distinction between disease as a biological state – a virus or broken arm – and disease as a subjective feeling of ill-health. Such feelings are greatly influenced by cultural factors. For example, women in the advanced western world expect morning sickness as a natural part of pregnancy, but the anthropologist, Margaret Mead, found none among the Arapesh women in Polynesia. She thought this could be due to their belief that no child exists until immediately before the birth.

One of the reasons why the biological basis of illness has come under question is the fact that modern medicine has failed to defeat today's major killers – cancer and heart disease. These currently kill more than 100000 and 300000 people respectively in Britain. Medicine's failure to find a cure has led to an increased interest in *epidemiology*, the study of the social causes of disease. For example, America has one of the highest rates of heart disease in the world, Japan one of the lowest. Why? No one knows for certain, but epidemiological studies have highlighted certain key risk-factors:

SOCIAL CLASS: The class you are born into not only has a major influence on your health, but on the type of disease you are likely to suffer, or even die from. This was dramatically summed up in the 1980 report by Sir Douglas Black, president of the Royal College of Physicians, which looked at the regional and social incidence of disease. Black showed that for every male baby in social class I who dies in the first year after birth, four die in social class V.

WORK: The 1972 Robens report on safety and health at work pointed out that "every year about half a million people suffer injuries in varying degrees of severity. A total of 23 million working days are lost annually on account of industrial injury and disease." Patrick Kinnersly in his book, *Hazards at Work* (1974), thinks these figures are a serious underestimate, and would double most of them. The millions of days lost annually through strikes

are widely publicised and considered preventable. Why not the total of 300 million or more working days lost annually through all kinds of sickness?

UNEMPLOYMENT: One person in eight is now unemployed in Britain, and there are signs that more joblessness means more illness. Harvey Brenner, an American medical sociologist, recently estimated that a rise in unemployment of a million spread over five years would bring:
● 50000 extra deaths;
● 700 extra suicides;
● 600000 extra cases of mental illness.

LIFESTYLES: Cancer and heart disease are often described as diseases of civilisation, caused by the way we live, with smoking and our fatty diet as two key factors. The government's chief medical officer has estimated that nearly 100000 people die prematurely in Britain each year because of smoking – more than all the civilian casualties in Britain in the Second World War.

INDIVIDUAL PSYCHOLOGY: Not everyone who smokes heavily or eats a poor diet dies of cancer or heart disease. Emotional factors also seem to have an influence, and there may be some truth in the old saying that a happy man does not get cancer. The unhappiness following a bereavement, a financial crisis or an accident seems sometimes to be followed by an onset of physical illness.

This *multi-causal* approach to disease contrasts with the traditional medical approach. Like an engineer, the doctor diagnoses the faulty part or blocked system in the human body, and our hospitals repair or replace it with the latest drug or spare part – a heart or a kidney or limb.

We tend to look with awe at such technological feats. Certainly, it is on this "scientific" basis that medicine has risen from the world of quacks and herbal remedies to its present pre-eminence. Using the laboratory techniques of the natural sciences, pioneers like Pasteur and Fleming made major advances in the analysis and cure of disease. On these grounds, medi-

Expectation of life: the number of further years we might expect to live

United Kingdom, years

	males: year of birth				females: year of birth			
	1901	1931	1951	1981	1901	1931	1951	1981
Expectation of life from birth	48.0	58.4	66.2	69.8	51.6	62.4	71.2	76.2
from age								
1 year	55.0	62.1	67.5	69.6	57.4	65.1	72.1	76.1
10 years	51.4	55.6	59.1	60.8	53.9	58.6	63.6	67.2
20 years	42.7	46.7	49.5	51.2	45.2	49.6	53.9	57.4
30 years	34.6	38.1	40.2	41.6	36.9	41.0	44.4	47.6
40 years	26.8	29.5	30.9	32.0	29.1	32.4	35.1	38.0
45 years	23.2	25.5	26.4	27.5	25.3	28.2	30.6	33.3
50 years	19.7	21.6	22.2	23.1	21.6	24.1	26.2	29.0
60 years	13.4	14.4	14.8	15.6	14.9	16.4	17.9	20.6
65 years	10.8	11.3	11.7	12.4	11.9	13.0	14.2	16.7
70 years	8.4	8.6	9.0	9.5	9.2	10.0	10.9	13.2
75 years	6.4	6.4	6.7	7.4	7.1	7.4	8.0	10.0
80 years	4.9	4.8	4.8	5.5	5.4	5.4	5.8	7.3

source: Government Actuary's Department

cine has always claimed responsibility for the dramatic falls in mortality rates in the second half of the nineteenth century, and for the doubling of our life expectancy ever since.

However, according to Professor Thomas McKeown in *The Role of Medicine* (1976), such claims are, at least, dubious. It was, he says, improvements in our environment – better food, water, hygiene – that had the most impact. In fact, he says, the death rate began to fall *before* the medical advances against diseases like tuberculosis, measles and polio ever began.

Our modern National Health Service – still described as the envy of the world – is very much based on traditional medicine. Its services are used by a million people every day, and in many ways it is very successful – particularly in making treatment available to everybody, without qualification, and removing the fear of being ill. Yet it has come under some serious criticisms:

MEDICAL: It has failed effectively to reduce the infant mortality rate and perinatal deaths. We are well down the European league table in what is considered to be a major indicator of the effectiveness of a society's health services. In the words of the 1976 Court report: "Infant mortality is a holocaust equal to all the deaths in the succeeding 24 years of life ... children still die in our lifetimes for nineteenth-century reasons."

DISTRIBUTION: How true is it that treatment under the NHS is allocated solely according to need? There is increasing evidence that social class is a key influence – a view summed up by Richard Titmuss in *Commitment to Welfare* (1968): "We know from 15 years' experience of the health service that the higher income groups know how to make better use of the service, they tend to receive more specialist attention, occupy more of the beds in the better-equipped and staffed hospitals, receive more selective surgery; have better maternity care and are more likely to get psychiatric help and psychotherapy than the lower income groups – particularly the unskilled."

Wealthier still means healthier, and such bias is further compounded by geographical inequalities – working-class

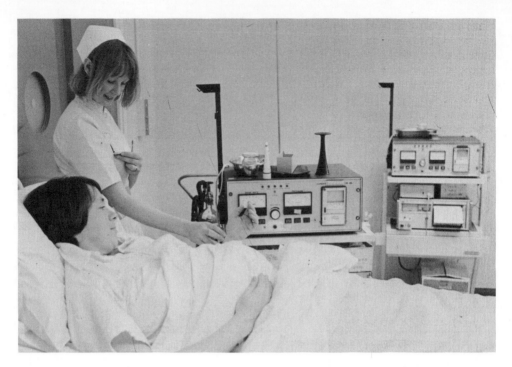

areas tend to attract fewer qualified doctors and poorer medical resources than middle-class ones. Though the NHS has helped to raise the standard of health of the whole population, it has failed to lessen the relative gap between the social classes.

COST: "Contrary to popular opinion, our NHS is health on the cheap," the doctor and writer, David Widgery, said in a recent analysis. As a proportion of our gross national product, British health spending is below such comparable European countries as France and West Germany.

Such criticisms have led medical sociologists, like Ian Kennedy in his recent Reith Lectures, to ask: "In whose interest is the NHS really run?" Some see it as being dominated by a medical elite. Victor Navarro, in his Marxist analysis, *Medicine under Capitalism* (1976), comments that Nye Bevan had to "choke the consultants' mouths with gold" to get their cooperation in setting up the NHS. This included a secret system of awards and the right to private practice, a perk that included the use of some NHS facilities and beds.

Another group that dominates the NHS is the drugs industry. The 1977 NHS drugs bill amounted to £1.8 billion. The profits are huge, and are gained largely by developing further brands of a successful drug, rather than new ones. Up to £50 million a year is spent on drugs promotion and sales in Britain. "On average," David Widgery points out, "a doctor can expect to have £30 000 a year spent on his 'education' by the drugs companies." However, there is considerable evidence that drugs are not only ineffective, in many cases, but can be dangerous – as the thalidomide affair demonstrated.

Many sociologists see medicine as a major agent of social control, as Talcott Parsons termed it, with doctors possessing a considerable degree of power over our lives. Indeed, *Your Life in their Hands* was the title of a well known television series. Such power derives from:
● Medicine's ability to label and to judge not only our bodily symptoms but, as the Reith lectures argued, our very ethics. It is doctors who decide what is illness and what is health – not us. They dominate such ethical decisions as abortion and euthanasia. It is they who decide who is

mad. As Irving Zola said in *Cultures and Symptoms* (1966), modern societies have become "medicalised." "The medical profession has first claim to jurisdiction over the label 'illness' and anything to which it may be attached, irrespective of its capacity to deal with it effectively."

● Medicine's control of treatment. Once they are officially labelled, the sick are expected to enter what Talcott Parsons called the *sick role* and defer to the doctor's authority completely. Often the sick are put into institutions, hospitals and even asylums, where medical control is total.

● Medicine's professional status, backed up not only by the state, but by what E. Freidson in *The Profession of Medicine* (1972) called "legitimately organised autonomy." The medical profession has successfully resisted all attempts to monitor its effectiveness from outside. Doctors have traditionally demanded the right to "police" themselves.

● Doctors' domination of the doctor-patient relationship. It is difficult to question the expert – even when it's your body. It is difficult to change doctors, as permission of both the old and the new GP are required – and the patients who do change tend to be labelled trouble-makers. It is also extremely difficult to sue a doctor – as evidence from another doctor is required.

However, certain groups are seeking to resist such power. Feminists, for example, believe that it would be a major step in women's liberation if they could regain control over their own bodies and take away from doctors, who are predominantly male, the right to decide such questions as abortion, birth control and even childbirth (95 per cent of all births in Britain take place in hospital). Similarly, many Third World countries are resisting the seductions of western-style medicine and wonder drugs as being far too expensive, and irrelevant to the health of the mass of their people. The World Health Organisation estimates that the burden of sickness in the world would be reduced by 80 per cent if everyone had access to clean drinking water.

Though we, in the west, continue to be mesmerised by the wonders of heart surgery and limb transplants, it seems likely that plain lack of money will force us in the future to look more closely at prevention rather than miracle cures. Campaigns in the United States and Scandinavia have shown considerable success in getting people to smoke less, exercise more and to alter their diets.

Such "ecological" approaches to illness are often resisted by the medical profession and the drug companies. But it seems likely that economic necessity, if nothing else, will force us all to take more responsibility for our own health and lifestyles. And the NHS could become a real health service, instead of the sickness one we have at present.

BOOKS

Some useful additional reading:

C. Cox and A. Mead, *A Sociology of Medical Practice,* Collier-Macmillan, 1975
Bernard Dixon, *Beyond the Magic Bullet,* Allen & Unwin, 1979
Roger Gomm, "Social science and medicine" in Meighan *et al, Perspectives on Society,* Nelson, 1979
D. Tuckett and J. M. Kanfort, *Basic Readings in Medical Sociology,* Tavistock, 1978
David Widgery, *Health in Danger,* Macmillan, 1979

MENTAL ILLNESS

"**W**e are all born mad. Some remain so." So said one of the characters in Samuel Beckett's play, *Waiting for Godot*. This is not so absurd as it seems in a society in which one in three of us suffers at some time from mental disorder.

In fact, if you look at the statistics, you could argue that we are becoming madder. In 1900, ninety people for every 100000 of the English population were admitted to psychiatric institutions; by the late 1970s this figure had risen to 380 per 100000.

It's important to say, of course, that mental illness and madness are not necessarily the same thing, though the actual definition of mental illness, its causes and treatment, have long been the subject of argument among doctors and sociologists. Traditionally, doctors divide mental illness into two groups: the psychoses and the neuroses.

THE NEUROSES are emotional disturbances which, though severe at times, do not usually require a person to be admitted to a psychiatric hospital. The minor mental disorders classified under neurosis fall into four general categories:
● Anxiety states (anxiety, fear)
● Reactive depression (i.e. depression as a reaction to an event)
● Hysteria (symptoms like a physical disability, produced to help solve a conflict or crisis)
● Obsessional neurosis (persistent thoughts or compulsive actions)

THE PSYCHOSES usually distort the whole personality, and a psychotic can rarely distinguish between his or her delusion or hallucinations and reality. Psychoses fall into four categories:
● Schizophrenia
● The affective psychoses (i.e. severe mood disorders, like mania or severe depression)
● Paranoia
● Psychosis associated with other physical conditions (e.g. hallucinations after a surgical operation)

A sociologist would probably prefer to classify the mentally ill in a rather different way – according to such criteria as social class, sex, culture, ethnic group and environment.

SOCIAL CLASS: Most studies of mental illness and class have come to the conclusion that the lower the social status, the higher the risk of psychological problems. But psychologists and sociologists differ in their reasons for this. Some believe in the *social causation* theory – that the social factors experienced by lower social groups, like low pay and poor living conditions, lead to more stress. Others have favoured the *drift hypothesis,* which argues that those with mental problems cannot maintain their position in society, and tend to drift down the social scale.

SEX: Each year, some forty per cent more women than men in England are admitted to mental hospitals. Women do not outnumber men in all categories of mental illness, however. There are, for instance, just as many male as female schizophrenics. But the biggest difference between the sexes is that far more women than men suffer from depressive illnesses.

The traditional explanation for this is that women are biologically more prone to emotion than men, more susceptible to "nerves." But early this century, more men than women were admitted to mental hospitals, and the sharp rise in the number of women patients has only taken place since the last war.

A more likely explanation lies in the social role of women. Women have, in general, less control over their lives. Once married, motherhood may mean giving up their job; they may also have to move if their husband has a change of employment; and they may be expected, more than a man, to devote their spare time to an aged parent. Holding down a job and running a home can increase stress. Housework itself – accepted a century ago as a fulfilling, demanding job – has been downgraded. All these factors are likely to play a part in the increase in the number of women patients since the war.

Traditionally, too, while men are seen as "coping", women are seen as more passive. It is more socially acceptable for women to admit to emotional distress. The medical magazines reinforce these stereotypes. And by invariably portraying a woman when promoting pills for depression and anxiety, they confirm male GPS' attitudes towards women patients. Women also actually visit the doctor more frequently, because of caring for young children and aged parents, and so are more likely to be in a position to ask for help over depression or anxiety.

A 1978 study of the psychosocial influences in depression in women (G. W. Brown and T. Harris, *Social Origins of Depression: a study of psychiatric disorder in women)* found four factors that made women vulnerable to mental disorder: the loss of a mother before the age of 11; three or more children in the family under 14 years; the lack of a confiding partner; and the lack of paid employment. Working-class women were four times more likely to be depressed than middle-class women, owing to the likelihood of their experiencing one or more of these conditions.

CULTURE: It is estimated that one person in three in the United States and Europe suffers at some time from some form of mental disorder. But, contrary to general belief, it is not true that there is always a higher incidence of mental illness in advanced societies. Rather, many sociologists go along with Emile Durkheim's view that the more socially integrated the society, the less likely its members are to experience social problems like mental illness.

ETHNIC GROUPS: According to the Community Relations Commission, in *Aspects of Mental Health in a Multi-cultural Society* (1976), minority ethnic groups in Britain are much more liable to be mentally ill than the native British.

Migrants, it says, suffer from stress partly because of having to adapt to a different land and lifestyle but also because they encounter so much racial hostility in their daily life.

But not all surveys come to the same conclusions. In a study of mental hospital statistics for immigrants in Britain, the psychologist, Raymond Cochrane, found that only the Irish-born and to a much lesser extent the West Indian-born communities had more than their share of mental patients. Those born in India and Pakistan had conspicuously lower rates of admission to mental hospitals than those born in Britain.

Cochrane suggests that the groups most isolated from the host community, both because of prejudice and an attempt to maintain separate traditions (like the Pakistanis) are the least vulnerable to psychological disorders. The West Indians, who perhaps sought integration only to have it denied them, are at more risk of psychological disorder.

ENVIRONMENT: While it's true that rats in a crowded cage tend to behave in a disturbed manner, sociologists are wary of drawing parallels with the human environment. High-rise flats and crowded housing conditions can be associated with a high incidence of stresses such as poverty, unemployment and loneliness. People in Britain's inner cities have often found it hard to live in the large blocks of flats built in the 1950s and 1960s, and many have had to be demolished. Such blocks have, however, proved perfectly satisfactory for the more privileged inhabitants of Manhattan or Mayfair.

Because certain mental illnesses have a physical cause (like dementia, caused by brain disease), the predominant medical view over the years has been that all mental illness is physically based, caused by a chemical imbalance of some kind. But the "medical model" of mental illness has come under attack – particularly in the past twenty years or so.

The psychoanalytic schools have long argued that childhood events figure largely as the cause of neuroses. The British psychiatrist, John Bowlby, has been a leading proponent of this view with his work on maternal deprivation. But the movement against the medical model of mental illness really gained ground in the 1960s under the banners of the Scottish psychiatrist, R. D. Laing, and the American, Thomas Szasz. Laing argued that the cause of schizophrenia was not a chemical imbalance, but a way in which people escaped from the reality of personal, often family-based, problems. Szasz went further and rejected the whole idea of mental illness.

The notion that mental illness can somehow be socially constructed is still a very fashionable one today. Psychologists and sociologists have pointed out that mental illness is often *culturally relative* – that is, it is perceived differently by different societies and in different periods of history. Szasz quotes the example of an article written by a doctor in a New Orleans medical journal in 1871 to account for slaves running away. This, he said, was because of a mental affliction called *drapetomania* (from the Greek, *drapetes,* meaning runaway slave), and recounted a long explanation of how to cure it.

Very often, people who deviate from society's norms are classified as mentally ill. In this sense it is a means of social control. Thus, Victorian women who deviated from that society's chaste norms were "nymphomaniacs"; those schoolchildren who do not defer to their teachers are "hyperactive"; Soviet citizens who are not unreservedly devoted to the ideals of the Marxist-Leninist system are described as "schizophrenics."

What is happening here, sociologists

BOOKS

Some useful additional reading:
Anthony Clare, *Psychiatry in Dissent,* Tavistock, 1976
Raymond Cochrane, *The Social Creation of Mental Illness,* Longman, 1983
Michel Foucault, *Madness and Civilisation: a history of insanity in the Age of Reason,* Random House, 1965
Thomas Szasz, *The Manufacture of Madness,* Harper & Row, 1970

say, is that people are becoming *labelled* – a social process that can have a devastating effect on an individual. Once a Soviet dissident, say, has been labelled as mentally ill, then everything he subsequently does can be seen in that light. Despite his denials, he begins to feel uncertain, not least because his perception of himself is affected by the way other people see him. It may not be long before he really does start to suffer from mental illness, which is exactly what the authorities want.

The same can happen even to an ordinary person who suffers from a minor neurosis. Once the label "mental illness" is applied, then an entire self-fulfilling prophecy can get to work. In a celebrated experiment to show how easily this can happen, the American psychologist, D. L. Rosenhan, asked twelve collaborators to go to a mental hospital and complain of hearing noises in their heads. All were admitted, and most were diagnosed as schizophrenic.

As Ian Kennedy argued in his recent series of Reith lectures, great caution should be exercised in conferring the status of mentally ill on anyone: "Once he is diagnosed or fixed with the label of mentally ill, then his liberty and future life become something for others to dispose of."

Treatment of the mentally ill varies according to how the illness is perceived. If schizophrenia, for example, is seen as being caused solely by organic factors, it is treated with drugs. If it is reckoned to be caused solely by conflict in family relationships, then psychotherapy will be used. Depression likewise. Neurotic disturbance may be attributed to past childhood trauma (requiring analysis, psychotherapy), or to "learned" behaviour (in which case, behaviour therapists will help patients "unlearn" it).

Not only are the patients confused; so are the psychologists and psychiatrists. The treatment of mental illness has become confused with debates about the politics of psychiatry and the health service. In his book, *The Future of Psychiatry* (1932), Hans Eysenck called for a "divorce", in which the neurotics are looked after by psychologists and the

From madness to Valium

Both physical and mental disorders were originally attributed to possession by the spirits – and the cure was exorcism. Hippocrates (460–367 BC) taught that madness was caused by a disturbance of elements in the brain. These elements, which he called humours, influenced the four passions – sanguine, choleric, melancholic and phlegmatic. As mental illness was therefore attributed to either an unbalanced humour or to spirit possession, no stigma was attached to it.

People's view of the mentally ill changed in Europe during the Middle Ages, when paranoia about heretics extended from witches to the mentally ill, because of their assumed possession by the Devil. The mentally ill were locked up in madhouses: the public would visit them as entertainment. This attitude lasted for several centuries, and even minor ailments were seen as symptoms of madness.

Attitudes changed again in Victorian times in Britain, when mental illness was often put down to people's own wrongdoing. "Moral treatment" was tried: so were purging, blood-letting and whirling chairs. The mentally ill were socially stigmatised: they remained locked up, out of sight, in bleak institutions.

The First World War radically changed society's attitudes, as many soldiers developed traumatic neurosis. This was regarded with sympathy – an illness to be treated and not regarded as incurable. Psychotherapy was practised more widely. Until the 1950s, however, admission to a mental hospital was often a life sentence (whereas nowadays the average stay is some two months).

The dramatic drop occurred in the mid-1950s, after the introduction of anti-psychotic drugs (used for mania, schizophrenia, depression). Benzodiazepines (tranquillisers, sedatives) came on the market in the early 1960s. Latest figures show that 21 million benzodiazepines are prescribed annually in Britain. The treatment of both major and minor illness is now by drugs, though many of these have addictive side effects that were not originally known about. Instead of being locked into asylums, some people are now locked into an unwanted addiction to drugs like Librium and Valium.

psychotics by psychiatrists. At the other end of the spectrum, R. D. Laing has questioned the whole system of value judgment about what is mental illness and what is "normality."

Although the number of people in England admitted to psychiatric institutions is still rising, current government policy is to reduce the number of large institutions, and rehabilitate the mental patients through a system of "community care." But the results of this policy have not so far been very successful. Though big institutions have been discharging patients – one London hospital has reduced its inmates from 3000 to 850 – community resources are still minimal.

The psychiatric hospitals that remain receive a relatively minor slice of the available medical resources. This is despite the fact that there are more psychiatric patients than any other kind. Although psychiatric patients take forty five per cent of hospital beds, only eleven per cent of all consultants are psychiatrists. Some sixty five per cent of England's mental hospitals were built before 1891.

Certainly, many psychologists and psychiatrists believe that they are a bad thing. Thomas Szasz, for instance, has declared that mental patients, having been "created" and stigmatised, are unnecessarily incarcerated, in the way witches once were. This point was also made by Erving Goffman, in his book, *Asylums* (1968): "Stigmatisation as mentally ill and involuntary hospitalisation are the means by which we answer . . . offences against propriety."

Asylums, based on research carried out in 1955–56 in a Washington hospital, is the best known study of the personal and psychological effects on patients of being in a mental institution. It shows patients' general reactions – including initial mortification, then adjustment, withdrawal and sometimes rebellion. (The film, *One Flew Over the Cuckoo's Nest,* based on Ken Kesey's book, is an example of a rebellious mental patient, ultimately subdued by a lobotomy – a controversial treatment which involves destroying parts of the brain.)

But the currently fashionable view about mental hospitals and community care may be changing again. Most countries have been going through the process of "deinstitutionalisation." This has had the twin advantage of pleasing both the radical critics of mental hospitals *and* those who want to cut social welfare budgets.

In 1978, Italy passed the world's most radical legislation relating to the mentally ill. It prohibited new admissions to mental hospitals and stopped the readmission of old patients after 1982. But the national network of out-patient clinics did not materialise, and the situation in Rome, with hundreds of uncared-for mental patients on the streets, was described as "chaotic." The fact is that even "civilised" nations have found it difficult to deal with their mentally ill people in a civilised way.

THE MIDDLE CLASS

Friedrich Engels described England as "the most bourgeois of all nations"; George Orwell as "the most class-ridden country under the sun." Both statements still hold good today.

Nowhere else is there quite the same fascination with the small subtleties of accent and education which define people's precise social position nor the same admiration for middle-class attitudes and values. The nation's favourite radio serial, *The Archers*, is not so much "an everyday story of country folk" as a chronicle of the quintessentially middle-class lives of the church-going, horse-riding, grammar-school-educated family in the title.

Who exactly are the middle classes? In the old days it was a simple enough matter defining them. As Angus Maude and Roy Lewis remarked at the beginning of their classic study, *The English Middle Classes* (1949):

"Before the war, when textile supplies and laundry facilities were more ample, it might perhaps have been held that the middle classes were composed of all those who used napkin rings (on the grounds that the working class did not use table napkins at all, while members of the upper class used a clean napkin at each meal), and that the dividing line between the upper-middle and lower-middle classes was the point at which a napkin became a serviette."

Nowadays the mass of data regularly collected by government departments, market researchers and sociologists has greatly widened the range of possible definitions for membership of the middle class. We know, for example, that they are twice as likely as members of the working class to use contraceptives and retain all their own teeth, and less likely to watch football, die of lung cancer or marry in their teens. They have smaller families, longer holidays, thinner figures and higher wages than the national average.

People's perceptions of the size and composition of the middle classes vary considerably. Some see them at the top of the social pyramid, some as the broad middle of a diamond and others as a narrow compressed stratum squeezed from both above and below. One school of sociologists emphasises the extent of social mobility in Britain, and the ease of moving into the middle classes from below, while another emphasises their closed, caste-like nature. The middle classes can be defined narrowly as those in the professions and management or broadly to include all who own their own homes and work in white-collar jobs.

On one important point, however, there seems to be general agreement. Opinion polls show that the great majority of the population continue to recognise the existence of different social classes in Britain. The classless society heralded by some sociologists in the 1950s has not arrived, at least in the eyes of the general public.

It also seems that most people see only two basic classes, middle and working. All but a tiny handful readily assign themselves to one of these two basic groups when asked their social class. Not surprisingly, perhaps, the results of such polls produce a rather higher figure for the total proportion of the middle classes in the population than the more objective findings of social scientists and researchers.

The most authoritative and comprehensive picture of the size and composition of the different social classes in Britain is produced by the government's Office of Population Censuses and Surveys under the direction of the Registrar General, on the basis of data collected in the national census carried out every ten years. It is a sign of the national obsession with class that Britain was the first country in the world to introduce social classification as one of the main forms in which the information derived from its census was presented. Social classes were first defined in 1911 for use in analysing statistics on fertility and infant mortality.

Since 1921 the Registrar General has recognised five basic classes based entirely on the occupation of heads of household. Class 1 comprises those in professional occupations which require a high level of training; Class II, managers, administrators, those in less highly trained professions, and certain intermediate occupations like farmers; Class III, those in skilled occupations; Class IV, those in partly-skilled manual occupations; and Class V, those in unskilled occupations. An important new feature was introduced in 1971 when Class III was divided into IIINM, covering skilled non-manual occupations, and IIIM covering skilled manual occupations. Those in and above Class IIINM are generally seen as middle-class, those in IIIM and below as working-class.

Market research organisations use a similar class scale, based primarily on occupation, to present the results of their surveys of public opinion. Their scale, which runs from A to E, broadly conforms to the Registrar General's (the division between IIINM and IIIM is mirrored by a split between c1 and c2). There are some differences, however, as the market researchers take more account of income and spending power. Their bottom class E, for example, is composed of those people with no earning capacity, such as pensioners and the unemployed, regardless of

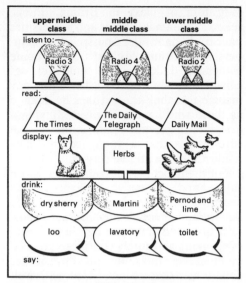

Where are you on the social scale?

their previous jobs.

There are several clear advantages in taking occupation as the main criterion for establishing social class. It is probably the most common single factor on which people base judgments of class. The non-manual/manual distinction in particular has often been used as a simple way of establishing the dividing line between the middle and working classes. In 1948 the Labour politician, Herbert Morrison, rhetorically asked: "What is the middle class? Perhaps the best generalisation is that varied section of the community that works with its brain rather than its hands." A correspondent to *The Times* in 1975 defined the middle classes as those "having to do with people rather than with things."

In general, income follows occupation and provides another good criterion for establishing social class. For a long time, indeed, the middle classes could be defined as those who paid income tax. They remain broadly the better-off section of society, although there are, of course, anomalies. Clergymen, members of a profession which most people would unhesitantly identify as middle-class, have stipends which are well below the earnings of many manual workers.

Education and housing are also clear

indicators of class in Britain. Public schools, grammar schools and universities have traditionally been passports to membership of the middle classes. So has home ownership. Indeed, if the middle classes can no longer be defined as those who pay income tax, they can perhaps be defined as those who have mortgages. Buying a house on a private estate is one of the surest signs that a young couple have made it into the middle classes.

For many people, of course, it is more subtle and subjective indicators, like accent, manners and dress, which really determine someone's class. Bernard Shaw once observed that "an Englishman's way of speaking absolutely classifies him. The moment he talks he makes another Englishman despise him." George Orwell noted that "the great majority of the people can still be 'placed' in an instant by their manners, clothes and general appearance." These matters are particularly important in determining which part of the middle classes someone comes from: upper middle, middle middle, or lower middle.

It is, indeed, much more accurate to talk about the middle classes rather than about one single middle class. There is an enormous difference in income, status and life-style between the stockbroker at the upper end of the upper-middles and the shorthand typist hovering uncomfortably between the ranks of the lower-middle classes and the skilled manual workers. The middle classes have always resembled the crowds on a department store escalator, with some going up to the top floor and others descending towards the bargain basement.

One thing that can be said with certainty is that the crowds have got steadily bigger. With the general rise in living standards, the spread of higher education, and the transformation of Britain from an industrial to a service economy, the middle classes, however defined, have made up an increasingly large proportion of the population.

In the 1950s, indeed, there was a widely-held view that the whole population was becoming middle class. The *embourgeoisement theory*, as it became

If "middle-class values" include the encouragement of varied and individual choice, the provision of fair incentives and rewards for skill and hard work, the maintenance of effective barriers against the excessive power of the state and a belief in the wide distribution of individual private property, then they are certainly what I am trying to defend.
—Margaret Thatcher (1975)

Sir,
There have been a series of rather complicated formulae put forward recently to define "class."
    But surely "class" in human beings derives from the same factor that determines "class" in race horses and pedigree dogs, namely good breeding over two or three generations.
—Letter to *The Times* (1980)

The Rich arrived in pairs
And also in Rolls Royces
They talked of their affairs
In loud and strident voices
The poor arrived in Fords
Whose features they resembled;
They laughed to see so many Lords
And Ladies all assembled
The People in Between
Looked underdone and harassed,
And out of place and mean
And horribly embarrassed.
—Hilaire Belloc (1938)

Howard and Eileen Weybridge – middle-middle class
"Howard Weybridge lives in Surrey or some smart dormitory town. He works as an accountant, stockbroker, surveyor or higher technician. He probably went to a minor public school or a grammar school. He never misses the nine o'clock news and says 'Cheerio.' He wears paisley scarves with scarf rings and has no bottoms to his spectacles."

Bryan and Jen Teale – lower-middle class
"The most pushy, the most frugal and the most respectable of all the classes, because they are so anxious to escape from the working class. The successful ones iron out their accents and become middle like Mr Heath and Mrs Thatcher. The rest stay put as bank and insurance clerks, door-to-door salesmen, toast-masters and lower management."
(From *Class* by Jilly Cooper, Corgi, 1981.)

known, was stated most clearly by Ferdinand Zweig in a book called *The Worker in an Affluent Society,* published in 1961. Zweig argued that because of general economic and educational advance, the working classes were becoming more middle-class in their lifestyles and values. He predicted that they would abandon their traditional collectivism and class consciousness. Already, he pointed out, many had given up their traditional loyalty to the Labour Party and were voting for their "class enemies", the Conservatives.

Zweig's theory was, however, knocked down by an important study carried out in 1964 by a team of sociologists led by John Goldthorpe, and published five years later under the title *The Affluent Worker.* Goldthorpe carried out his investigations among car-workers and others in Luton. They were among the most highly-paid manual workers in Britain and therefore could be expected to show signs of embourgeoisement if Zweig's theory was correct.

In fact, the survey found that they retained their proletarian attitudes and lifestyle. They continued to hold the traditional working-class view of their jobs simply as a means of making money. They also saw their increased earnings as something to be spent quickly rather than saved and put towards a house or private education for their children. The great majority of them had also continued to vote Labour.

The results of a much wider social study carried out under the direction of Goldthorpe and Professor A.H. Halsey was published in 1980 in a book entitled *Social Mobility and Class Structure in Modern Britain.* The Nuffield Social Mobility Survey was based on interviews carried out in 1972 with more than 10 000 men aged between 20 and 64. Its main finding was that while there has been considerable upward social mobility in Britain in the last 60 years, with more people reaching the middle classes from below because of general economic progress and changes in the occupational structure, there has been no change at all in the relative chances of those born into different social classes reaching the top.

Goldthorpe found that the middle classes have grown and the working classes have shrunk during the present century. Although the "service class", as he prefers to call those in professional, managerial and administrative occupations, still contains a preponderance of those who were born into it, there has also been a large injection of people from other classes. This widening of its recruiting base, he argues, has made the traditional middle class far less coherent and far more heterogeneous than it used to be. It is, in his words, a "class of low classness."

Goldthorpe's findings on social mobility are confirmed by Professor A. H. Halsey's detailed work on educational oportunities *(Origins and Destinations: Family, class and education in modern Britain,* 1980). This showed that the net effect of all the measures taken to increase the opportunities of the working classes, from the 1944 Education Act to the expansion of the new universities after the Robbins report, has in fact been to increase the proportion of middle-class children going on to higher education.

Both Goldthorpe and Halsey agree that the message of their survey is a depressing one for all those, like them, who have believed that the welfare state and the policies of social democracy would bring about a greater equality of opportunity in Britain. The fact is that the middle classes have consistently kept one jump ahead and have remained better-off, better-fed, better-educated and healthier than the working classes. They have even proved adept at taking advantage of institutions which were set up specifically to benefit the working classes like the National Health Service and the Workers' Educational Association.

Another institution originally set up to help the working classes has also been taken over with considerable enthusiasm in recent years by the middle classes. Trade unionism is no longer just for manual workers. The growth of white-collar unions, and the increasing militancy of professional and administrative workers in pursuit of pay claims, has been one of the most striking features of British society in the last ten years.

In his book, *White-Collar Unionism; the rebellious salariat* (1979), Clive Jenkins, who lists among his hobbies in *Who's Who* "organising the middle classes" writes that "there is nothing startling in the growth of middle-class trade unionism. It was historically inevitable." He argues that many middle-class jobs have, in fact, become proletarianised and made as dull and repetitive as those on the factory production line as a result of the introduction of computer technology into offices.

The espousal of militant trade unionism by many in the middle classes has, of course, been regarded with horror by others, particularly the small businessmen who traditionally make up the *petite bourgeoisie*. Their response to the rapidly rising inflation and what they saw as the increasing socialism of the 1970s was to form defence groups and call for a return to the principles of free enterprise and individualism. They even briefly formed a Middle Class Association to fight for the preservation of the species.

The rise of Mrs Thatcher, herself the daughter of a grocer and in many ways the personification of the traditional virtues of the bourgeoisie, seemed to indicate salvation for the middle classes who had felt themselves trampled over, discriminated against and generally unloved in the 1960s and early 1970s. However, seizure of power from Labour in 1979 was, in fact, made possible by a swing to the Conservatives by skilled manual workers in the c2 group. In social classes A and B there was actually a swing to Labour. Although Mrs Thatcher as Prime Minister has continued to preach the traditional bourgeois values of hard work, thrift and standing on your own two feet, there is little evidence that the lot of the small businessman or shopkeeper has, in fact, got much better under her government.

The fact is that the middle classes have always been a very heterogeneous body and, as Goldthorpe says, they are becoming more so. There has probably never been any such thing as middle-class consciousness.

In their book, *The Fragmentary Class Structure* (1977), Kenneth Roberts and a team of sociologists examined the attitudes of 243 male white-collar workers and found a number of different images of the middle class:

● 27 per cent held a *middle mass* image of society. They saw themselves as part of a massive group in between a small, powerful upper class and a small, poverty-stricken lower class

● 19 per cent of the sample saw themselves as part of a *compressed middle class* – sandwiched between increasingly powerful working and upper classes

● 15 per cent had no class loyalty, and often rejected the idea of class

● 14 per cent saw themselves as working-class, and at the bottom of the class ladder.

Roberts and his colleagues conclude that: "The days when it was realistic to talk about the middle-class are gone." But the middle *classes* shouldn't be written off as a force in society. As the writer, Ian Bradley, points out: "If there is one lesson for the future which a study of the history of the English middle classes teaches, it is surely that any obituary of them is decidedly premature. The species may evolve but it will not disappear. Its resilience and capacity for survival are considerable, as the experiences of the last 30 years in particular have shown, and there seems no reason to doubt that at the dawning of the next millennium the British bourgeoisie will not only still be around, but also be bigger and probably better-off than they are today."

BOOKS

Some useful additional reading:
Colin Bell, *Middle Class Families*, Routledge & Kegan Paul, 1968
Ian Bradley, *The English Middle Classes are Alive and Kicking*, Collins, 1982
Patrick Hutber, *The Decline and Fall of the English Middle Class and How it Can Fight Back*, Penguin, 1980
Roger King and John Raynor, *The Middle Class*, Longman 1981
Roger King and John Raynor, *Respectable Rebels: Middle-class campaigns in Britain in the 1970s*, Hodder and Stoughton, 1979

OLD AGE

"If a Renaissance or Georgian man could return, he would be as much astonished by the sight of two or three thousand septuagenarians and octogenarians lining a south coast resort on a summer's day as he would by a television set. Astonished and maybe shocked. His was a world where it was the exception to go grey, to retire, to become senile and to acquire that subtle blend of voice, skin and behavioural changes which features so largely in our long-lived times."

So writes Ronald Blythe in his book, *A View in Winter* (1979). In fact, our average lifespan has shot up from an average of 40 years to 70 years within the experience of many old people alive at the moment. We accept old age as being a normal part of the life cycle. Yet before the twentieth century, poverty, hardship and disease meant that very few people "saw out their time." Most people didn't get involved in the process of ageing, and lived without any thought or preparation for it.

Today, far from being exceptional, old people are a major group in society, having grown hugely over this century. The number of people aged 65 or over is nearly five times greater now than it was in 1901, and in 1983 represented over 15 per cent of the population compared with 5 per cent in 1901. It is important to remember, though, that this growth has little to do with advances in medical science keeping *old* people alive longer. It is mainly due to a dramatic reduction in infant and child mortality, which has allowed a much higher proportion of young people to reach old age. The average life expectancy of a person aged 70 has increased by only four years between 1901 and the present day.

The increase in the number of people over 65 will slacken off between now and the end of the century. But during this time the elderly population will itself be ageing. The biggest change will be among those aged 85 or over, who are projected to make up 12 per cent of the elderly in 2001, compared with less than 8 per cent in 1983. These very elderly people will be the survivors of the first generation to benefit from the dramatic fall in the child mortality rate in the first half of this century.

This may have important consequences for British society. The explosion in the elderly population has come at a time when the extended family is in decline. The trend towards greater geographical mobility, women at work and small nuclear families means that there simply may not be enough people at home to look after the elderly. Already a third of elderly people live alone, and the fact that the fastest-growing group of old people is the least independent means a growing burden on the health service and social services. As things stand, the elderly take up a third of the budget of the main social welfare programmes and occupy a half of all National Health Service beds.

One of the side effects of old people becoming more numerous in society is that they have suffered a drop in status – and some sociologists suggest that their status will continue to fall. In many societies in the past old people occupied the most exalted positions. The Roman writer, Cicero, wrote an essay in praise of old age, titled De Senectate, in which he said: "If there were no old men there would be no civilised states. States have always been ruined by young men and restored by old." The word "senate" comes from the Latin word senex, meaning old man, and the gerusia, the name of the governing body of Sparta came from the Greek word meaning old. In some societies – gerontocracies – people did not have the right to rule unless they were old.

In Britain, and most industrialised societies today, the low status of most elderly people is underlined by the fact that they are prevented from working, and consequently their income and power is reduced. Some social historians infer

from this that the change in status of the old came with the industrial revolution – that before this time there was some kind of golden age for the elderly, when they were universally respected for being all-wise.

While it is certainly true that the industrial revolution brought about institutionalised retirement, many social historians doubt whether this was a chief reason for the changed position of the old. The Cambridge historian, Peter Laslett, argues particularly strongly against the "golden age" idea in his book, The World We Have Lost (1968).

The American writer, David Hackett Fischer, in Growing Old in America (1977), says that the period between 1770 and 1820 was the time of transition from high to low status for old people in the United States. But in Britain, there seem to have been several factors over a longer period of history. The rarity factor certainly brought prestige (only 3 per cent of people in the nineteenth century lived to 70), but more important was the role of the old in passing on traditional knowledge of crafts, farming techniques and so on. This was devalued first by the advent of printing and then by technological development. As the anthropologist, Margaret Mead, has pointed out, in a future-orientated society the skills of the old become quickly dated.

There have been other factors, too. The English obsession with witchcraft in the sixteenth and seventeenth centuries was, as the historian, Alan Macfarlane, shows in Witchcraft in Tudor and Stuart England (1970), related to increasingly hostile attitudes to poor, old people. The Reformation, in the sixteenth century, resulted in children often having a different religion from their parents. And in the eighteenth century, the Age of Enlightenment brought a further split between young and old by throwing out many established ideas associated with the older generation.

Paradoxically, despite their status having gone down in society's eyes, the material welfare of the old has improved enormously. When the first legal provision for poor people was made with the

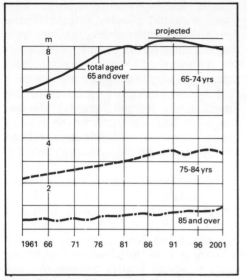

m
8

total aged
65 and over

projected

65-74 yrs

6

4

75-84 yrs

2

85 and over

1961 66   71   76   81   86   91   96   2001

**How the very elderly are increasing
in numbers**

Poor Laws of 1601, there was no separate provision for the old – they were simply lumped in with the general poor. By the nineteenth century, this meant that most old people ended up in the workhouse.

A Royal Commission on the Aged Poor in the 1890s gained them better accommodation in the workhouse. But apart from the reduction in the pension age to 65 in 1928, it wasn't until the advent of the welfare state in 1948 that anything serious was done to improve their lot. Now, all old people get a state pension and have access to the National Health Service, though many argue that society could do much more to help them.

In particular, it is suggested that material well-being is not enough – that we may have a social conscience about the elderly, but are somehow uninterested in them as people. As Ronald Blythe puts it: "Staring at the new bureaucracy, which is taking more and more charge of his expanding needs (the average cost of a 75-year-old is seven times that of the state treatment for a worker), fixing his unfooled eye on the professionally kind rest home entrepreneur, the aged man or woman can repeat, with Jean-Jacques Rousseau: 'These people do not love me'."

Robert Butler, who won a Pulitzer prize for his book, *Why Survive? Being Old in America* (1975), puts it even more pungently: "Our attitudes towards the old are contradictory. We pay lip service to the idealised images of beloved and tranquil grandparents, wise elders, white-haired patriarchs and matriarchs. But the opposite image disparages the elderly, seeing age as decay, decrepitude, a disgusting and undignified dependency. Childhood is romanticised, youth is idolised, middle age does the work, wields the power and pays the bills, and old age, its days empty of purpose, gets little or nothing for what it has already done. The old are in the way – an ironic example of public health progress and medical technology creating a huge group of people for whom survival is possible but satisfaction in living elusive."

Why do we view the old in this way? One clue lies in what the American sociologist, Talcott Parsons, called the *sickness role*. According to our conception of sickness, Parsons says, we take the view that people are not responsible for their illness, and not responsible for fulfilling the duties of a healthy person. On the other hand, the sick person *is* responsible for getting well, and for seeking the advice of a "competent" person such as a doctor. If people don't do this, then their behaviour is seen as somehow abnormal or deviant.

Because old age is generally beyond the ability of medicine to cure, and in a sense is resistant to the power of doctors, old people are somehow forced to feel "wrong" about ageing. While serious illnesses are seen as "legitimate" the progressive decline of old age is often seen as "unjustified", particularly when nothing can be done to reverse it.

It shouldn't be assumed from this, however, that we in any sense victimise the elderly in Britain – despite some newspaper headlines that imply the contrary. For instance, it is often claimed that we are in the midst of a wave of "granny-bashing." While it is certainly true that there is some physical abuse of old people, there is little evidence that it has increased, or is increasing. (Simone de-

Beauvoir in *Old Age,* 1977, shows how many societies act harshly towards the old on occasions. When the Eskimoes were short of food, for instance, they would simply abandon their elderly on ice floes.) The truth about granny-bashing is probably that there is a greater public awareness of assaults, rather than an increase in the number of assaults themselves.

A similarly widespread belief is that families increasingly "dump" their elderly relatives in institutions or old people's homes. This isn't borne out by the facts, either. A survey by Mark Abrams for Age Concern *(Profiles of the Elderly,* 1977) showed that the majority of old people live either with their spouse or their children. Just 5 per cent of old people live in institutions – a proportion that has hardly changed this century.

Despite their difficulties, old people seem, on the face of it, to be generally satisfied with their lot. A survey, done by the Office of Population Censuses and Surveys *(The Elderly at Home,* 1978), asked people to rate their satisfaction with various aspects of their lives on a scale from nought to ten. When asked about their housing conditions, people over 60 scored an average of 8.5, compared with 7.4 for younger people, despite that fact that the old live in worse housing on the whole. They were also generally more satisfied with their standard of living and leisure facilities than younger people, despite their owning fewer consumer goods and being less mobile.

Why should this be so? One reason is that the elderly today were brought up in an era when common men and women had much less power than they have now. As Muir Gray and Gordon Wilcock put it in *Our Elders* (1981): "Young people who have never had to live through hard times base their expectations on the assumption that things could be better than they are. Elderly people, on the other hand, often view their position on the supposition that things could be worse."

It is rather more difficult to capture in a survey the attitudes of old people to the business of ageing itself. In books written by elderly people one of the most powerful feelings is one of "separateness."

In *A View in Winter*, a series of interviews with old people, Ronald Blythe found that another strong feeling was a fear of ending up like the mythical character, Tithonus. (Tithonus was a beautiful young man who so delighted in being alive that he asked Aurora, goddess of the morning, to make him immortal. She did, but as it had not occurred to him to request perpetual youthfulness as well, he simply became an old man who could not die.)

Other anxieties about old age have been expressed by writers through the centuries. Shakespeare's King Lear had ungrateful children; Chaucer's hero in *The Merchant's Tale* had his wife stolen by a younger man; Swift wrote one of the most powerful tirades against old age ever; Samuel Beckett, author of *Waiting for Godot,* sees the impotence of old age as half comic and half appalling.

There is nothing, of course, that society can do to reverse the problems of ageing, but there are some specific social problems of old age that *are* potentially within our power to put right:

RETIREMENT: In Britain, men retire at 65 and women at 60. This is broadly the pattern in most industrial countries, whether capitalist or communist. But there is no biological reason for forcing people to give up work at this age. The ageing process obviously has something to do with it – a man of 65 will not be as fit as one of 20, but this does not mean that he'll be any worse at doing his job. There is probably a good reason for a scaffolder to give up at 65, but should the same apply to a shop worker?

We compel people to retire for social and economic, and not, on the whole, personal reasons. In fact we set the age at its present level to ensure that sufficient numbers of people retire to create vacancies for unemployed people and school-leavers, and to allow for promotion within organisations.

The sociologist, Peter Townsend, says that retirement today is a euphemism for unemployment: "The phenomenon has been enforced and is being enforced in a number of countries at earlier ages and yet is, paradoxically, being represented as a social achievement in both capitalist and state socialist countries alike." The spread of retirement, Townsend says, is interpreted as reflecting the success of campaigns on behalf of the rights of workers when they have "earned a rest", and is associated with the rights of old people to peace and dignity. But the abrupt termination of economic activity causes serious problems for many people.

One major problem arises, for instance, from the way we tend to fuse people's identities with their occupations – we say that someone *is* a journalist rather than does journalism. Not only does this identity disappear with retirement, but all the social networks and friendships connected with the job go also.

Other difficulties arise from a vast increase in leisure time in a society that is still highly work-orientated, the lack of money to pursue that leisure to the full, and the problems in personal relationships that can arise from couples spending long periods of time together.

POVERTY: It is reckoned that some two million old people live at or below the poverty line in Britain today. Nearly 20 per cent of pensioners get supplementary benefits, and the Department of Health and Social Security estimates that a further 600 000 pensioners are eligible, but don't claim. A recent Age Concern survey found that one pensioner in 14 couldn't make ends meet.

The main problem is that successive state pension policies have failed to provide an adequate level of benefit, and inflation has made things worse. When the welfare state was set up in 1948, it was thought that pensions would have to be increased every five years to keep up with inflation. By the early 1970s they were having to be increased every year, and in 1974 the Labour government made a law that pensions should rise in line with prices or incomes, whichever was the higher. This was scrapped by the present Conservative government on the grounds that it was too expensive.

The other welfare state ideal – that pensions should be 50 per cent of the average industrial wage – has never been achieved. (They currently stand at about 37 per cent.)

Low pensions continue to be at the root of several problems among the old.

HOUSING: Some 94 per cent of old people live in ordinary houses, but these houses tend to be in poorer condition than those of younger people. For instance, one household in every seven with people over 85 lacks an inside toilet. Housing for the elderly is generally worse because the houses themselves tend to be older. Elderly owner-occupiers may not have the money or incentive to improve them. The other problem is that a far greater proportion of elderly people (about a fifth) live in private rented accommodation, which is acknowledged to be worse than other types of housing.

COLD: A survey done by the National Institute of Medical Research and the Centre for Environmental Studies in 1972 measured the room temperatures of 1000 elderly people and compared them with the government-recommended minimum temperatures. A total of 91 per cent had morning living-room temperatures below the minimum, and a tenth had body temperatures below a safe level.

ISOLATION: About a third of elderly people live alone – 80 per cent of them are women and 44 per cent are women and men over 75. The number of old people living alone increased by nearly 60 per cent between the early 1960s and late 1970s. This was largely due to the increasing longevity of women and is a trend that will increase.

If our welfare state cannot cope with these problems now, how will we manage by the end of the century, when there will be more old people around, but fewer workers to support them? The answer is that society might have to rethink its ideas about the role of the elderly. In any case, even if we were to improve social welfare in its present form, might that necessarily be the best thing? Peter Townsend argues, in *The Structured Dependency of the Elderly* (1981), that we are in danger of creating a class of passive, dependent citizens, more reliant on institutionalised welfare than they need or want to be.

One way of getting round this might be to give the elderly more economic independence through a flexible retirement age. The Americans have led the way already by making it illegal to discriminate in jobs against people under 70. They have set the pace in other respects, too. Pressure groups like the Gray Panthers have made old people a political force to be reckoned with. They swelled the conservative tide that put the 70-year-old Ronald Reagan into the White House. And "ageism" (discrimination against the old) has become a dirty word, in United States, just like racism.

There is little sign of political consciousness among the old in Britain so far, but it's a fairly safe bet that it will develop in years to come. If anything is certain about the next generation of the elderly, it is that they will not be as tolerant and accepting as the present one.

The theories of ageing

With the large increase in the elderly population since the war, sociologists have become increasingly interested in old age as an area for study. This is particularly so in the United States, where the elderly are a powerful lobby. Several main theories have been put forward to account for the social processes of getting old:

Disengagement theory: This has been one of the most widely held theories of ageing, and has been adopted mostly by *functionalist* sociologists. It maintains that people entering old age must be phased out of important roles for society to function. By phasing out the old in this way, their deaths are not disruptive to the functioning of society. Disengagement theorists say that happiness in old age consists of individual's recognising that they are no longer young, and that there are more competent people to take their places. In the past few years, there has been a lot of criticism of this theory for being too simplistic, and it is now discounted by many experts.

Activity theory is the opposite of disengagement theory. It claims that to be happy in old age, people need to keep active. Happiness is achieved by denying the onset of old age and by maintaining a middle aged way of life, values and beliefs for as long as possible. Activity theorists take the view that if existing roles or relationships are lost, it is important to replace them, or there will be a drop in the level of life satisfaction. One of the main criticisms of this theory is that people need a high morale to keep up an active lifestyle, and that it takes little account of people who are ill or demoralised.

Subculture theory: The American gerontologist, Arnold Rose, has suggested that old people form a subculture which shapes and forms their behaviour (a *subculture* is a group within a general society that has many of the cultural aspects of the general society, but has several characteristics that are unique to it alone). Supporters of this theory believe that old people are a legitimate subculture because (a) they form a very large group in society, (b) they are separated from the rest of society by retirement, emphasis on youth and so on, and (c) because old people have an "age consciousness" – they recognise that they are "different" from the rest of society.

Personality theory maintains that activity and disengagement theories are wrong in focusing on the amount of *activity* people get involved in. It is personality types that are important in determining life satisfaction. The American gerontologist, R.J. Havighurst, defines two main types of old people – the "reorganisers", who are happy keeping their middle aged lifestyle, and the "disengaged", who are equally happy with the rocking chair approach to life.

Labelling theory: This is based partly on the

BOOKS

Some useful additional reading:
Mark Abrams, *Beyond Three Score and Ten*, vols 1 and 2, Age Concern, 1978 and 1980
D.B. Bromley, *The Psychology of Human Ageing*, Penguin, 1966
Alex Comfort, *A Good Age*, Mitchell Beazley, 1977
Richard Crandall, *Gerontology*, Addison Wesley, 1980
Muir Gray and Gordon Wilcock, *Our Elders*, Oxford University Press, 1981
Anthea Tinker, *The Elderly in Modern Society*, 1981

ideas of Erving Goffman, and suggests that, through the process of labelling, people are forced into acting out specific roles. Once somebody has been labelled "senile", for instance, this label has a major impact on the way they will be perceived and treated by others. It is difficult then for that person to change the label, because all subsequent behaviour will be interpreted in the light of the new identity. Someone who has been labelled old, senile, dependent or sick will experience a marked reduction in the number, types and options of roles available.

ORGANISATIONS

Organisations are not a new invention. The armies, governments and guilds of ancient and medieval societies were often highly organised. What is new is their size and power: "If General Motors were a nation, its 'economy' would be the 23rd largest in the world, with Standard Oil (New Jersey) and Ford not far behind", a recent United States Senate study concluded.

There are organisations to control organisations, such as the Monopolies Commission; supranational organisations such as the EEC and United Nations, and even countries where the major organisation is not part of society, it *is* society. This is the case in the centrally-planned economies of communist eastern Europe.

Organisations of every possible type have provided us with a tremendous range of goods and services, but they have also left many people with the sense of frustration, powerlessness and alienation so vividly described in the works of Franz Kafka and Arthur Koestler. It often seems that organisations control us rather than we them – indeed, the sociologist, W. H. Whyte, dubbed the American white-collar worker the *Organisation Man* (1956), because he has "taken the vows of organisational life."

This conflict between organisations'

need for order and efficiency and the individual's need for freedom is at the centre of any discussion about modern organisations. Unfortunately, the picture provided by the sociology of organisations is as bewildering and cloudy as any of Kafka's novels.

The most obvious way to define and analyse the *formal* organisation would seem to be in terms of its goals. Schools, for example, exist to educate, hospitals to heal, and such goals apparently explain why schools and hospitals are organised as they are. But do they? Are an organisation's formal goals necessarily its *real* ones? In terms of health care, for instance, the American medical system is relatively inefficient, but in terms of making profits it is highly effective.

It is controversies like this that sociologists have sought to explain, and certain broad approaches can be identified.

THE BUREAUCRATIC TRADITION: The study of the administrative side of organisations stems largely from the work of the German sociologist, Max Weber (1864–1920). He considered bureaucracy to be the type of organisational structure best suited to the needs and values of industrial societies – whether capitalist or communist – and he outlined its "ideal" features as follows:
● A specialisation of administrative tasks
● A hierarchy of authority
● A system of rules to ensure that officials act in an entirely fair and impartial manner.
Most large-scale organisations today are based on these principles because, as Weber argued, "the decisive reason for the advance of bureaucratic organisation has always been its technical superiority over any other form of organisation."

But is bureaucracy always efficient? Is it the only way to organise? Isn't bureaucracy noted more for its obsession with "red tape" and the lack of consideration summed up in a recent report by the National Consumer Council: "Modern British officialdom induces hopelessness, frustration and the sense of being cast away in limbo?"

The American sociologist, Peter Blau,

The most boring job

"It's the most boring job in the world. If I had a chance to move I'd leave right away. It's the conditions here. Ford class you more as machines than men. They're on top of you all the time. They expect you to work every minute of the day. The atmosphere you get here is so completely false. Everyone is fed up. You can't even talk about football. You end up doing stupid things. Childish things – playing tricks on each other." A Ford car worker, quoted in *Working for Ford* by Huw Beynon (1973)

has sought to show that an organisation's formal structure may not be the only, or the most efficient, way to get things done. In *The Dynamics of Bureaucracy* (1963) he made a study of a state employment agency and compared two sets of job placement interviewers who worked with different organisational methods. He showed that those interviewers using fairly informal techniques were often more successful in placing clients than those who went through the supervisor. In Blau's view, rules and regulations are merely a framework. Real efficiency can often depend on workers developing their own informal methods and relationships.

Alvin Gouldner's research into industrial relations at an American gypsum plant *(Patterns of Industrial Bureaucracy,* 1954) came to similar conclusions, and also showed that there can be "degrees of bureaucracy", depending on particular situations. The factory section of the plant, dealing with the routine production of wallboards, functioned very effectively under a bureaucratic structure, but down the gypsum mine, where conditions were dangerous and uncertain, it was felt to be vital that miners were given the freedom to organise themselves.

The other chief criticism of bureaucracy has been its power – the misuse and abuse of its authority. Weber was well aware of such dangers: "The trained official is more likely to get his own way in the long run than his nominal supervisor, the cabinet minister, who is not a specialist" – but he put his faith in the ability of parliaments to control the bureaucratic machine. Weber's contemporary, Robert Michels (1876–1936), was not so optimistic. His analysis of European trade unions and socialist parties – organisations deliberately constructed to promote democracy and radical change – led him to develop his *Iron Law of Oligarchy*.

Even in organisations as idealistic as these, he argued, oligarchy will eventually emerge and the organisation be run more in the interests of the leaders and officials than those of the rank and file. The German Socialist Party, for example, in time became part of the German establishment rather than its critic.

No study since has disproved Michels's thesis, and many modern sociologists and politicians have written about how government bureaucracy can obstruct radical change and defend the interests of the rich and powerful. The Labour cabinet minister, Richard Crossman, complains in his diaries about how the Wilson government of 1964–70 was thwarted by civil servants, and another Labour politician, Brian Sedgemore, writes more trenchantly still, describing the power of the civil service as *The Secret Constitution* (1980). Even Mrs Thatcher's setting-up of a Cabinet Office "efficiency unit" has not been enough to inflict more than a scratch on the "body bureaucratic." A major part of the problem, as Weber explained, and Lenin discovered, is the difficulty of replacing existing officials, because often only they have the necessary knowledge. In the United States, not noted for its bureaucracy, President Roosevelt was forced to assemble almost a whole new set of officials to carry out his New Deal reforms in the 1930s.

THE MANAGERIAL TRADITION: The study of "efficiency" in organisations stemmed initially from the work of another contemporary of Weber's, Frederick W. Taylor (1856–1915). His *Principles of Scientific Management* (1911) – or time and motion studies, as we know them today – became the basis for the early mass-production factories like Ford's, and the bible for a generation of managers. Every stage of the production process was analysed in minute detail to ensure that workers did their jobs as fast as was possible to ensure efficiency, mostly with piecework or other financial incentives.

However, despite the "rationality" of such schemes, the factories of the 1920s began to suffer from high rates of absenteeism, apathy and labour turnover, and one study into this – ironically using Taylor's own techniques – led to a fundamental re-examination of the basic principles of scientific management. A study by Elton Mayo in 1924 of workers producing telephone relay equipment at the Hawthorne plant of the Western Electric Company in Chicago found, contrary to expectations, that it was not the pay, the length of rest periods or any other structural factor that was encouraging the workers to increase production, but just the fact that they were being studied. The "Hawthorne Effect", as it became known, meant, simply, that someone had taken an interest in them.

In contrast to *scientific management's* belief that people's main motivation for working is financial, the Hawthorne studies showed that workers have emotional and psychological needs as well. These conclusions became the basis of the *human relations* approach to management, stimulating the growth of personnel departments, management schemes and things like sports facilities and subsidised canteens.

The Peter Principle

"In a hierarchy every employee tends to rise to his level of incompetence. The competence of an employee is determined not by outsiders but by his superior in the hierarchy. If the superior is still at a level of competence, he may evaluate his subordinates in terms of the performance of useful work ... But if the superior has reached his level of incompetence, he will probably rate his subordinates in terms of institutional values: he will see competence as the behaviour that supports the rules, rituals, and forms of the status quo." From *The Peter Principle: why things always go wrong* by Laurence J. Peter and Raymond Hull (1969)

THE FUNCTIONALIST PERSPEC-TIVE: After the war, various American economists, sociologists and business studies experts tried to put organisation studies on a more "scientific" basis. Following the *functionalist* ideas of the sociologist, Talcott Parsons (1902–79), they concentrated particularly on the ways business organisations should change and adapt themselves to survive amid the cut and thrust of commercial life.

According to the functionalist view, an organisation is like a living thing – which is much greater than the sum of the individuals it is made up of. So, if something goes wrong with one "part" of the organisation – say, the productivity of the workforce – then tinkering with another "part" – say, the technology – could put it right.

But this rather deterministic outlook assumed, on the whole, that organisations were basically harmonious structures, with goals shared by all the workforce. It tended to overlook the human angle – particularly conflicts between management and workers. Put simply, it is a bit like British Leyland concentrating on a car factory because of its suitable size, and not studying the labour relations record.

THE SOCIAL ACTION APPROACH: In the late 1960s, many sociologists reacted against the deterministic views of *functionalism,* which, they felt, saw society as controlling people, rather than people society. The *social action approach* is based on a *phenomenological* view of man and society – a perspective that sees human action as a result not simply of external forces, but an individual's interpretation of a given situation. People are not puppets manipulated by outside forces, but conscious, thinking beings who act on their environment rather than merely reacting to it. The size of an organisation, its rules and technology are simply the framework, the "theatre" within which individuals perform their organisational roles and interact with others.

The social action approach is a highly individualistic and subjective view of life in an organisation. It seeks to understand *why* its members act as they do – their motivations and meanings, whether they are managers or workers.

The most vivid example of this way of looking at things is the work of Erving Goffman. In his book, *Asylums* (1968), he analysed *total institutions,* and sought to show not only the power that organisations like prisons, mental hospitals and barracks have, but also the strategies the inmates adopt as they struggle to preserve their identities by resisting the system. The film, *One Flew Over the Cuckoo's Nest,* illustrated Goffman's point about how mental hospital patients can resist such total control.

THE MARXIST PERSPECTIVE: Though Marx himself said little about organisations as such – beyond seeing the state as an instrument of class rule – there has been a considerable revival of Marxist interest in this topic in recent years.

From a Marxist perspective, capitalism represents a particular epoch in our his-

BOOKS

Some useful additional reading:
For a general overview of the subject, David Dunkerley's *The Study of Organisations* (Routledge & Kegan Paul, 1972), and John Child's *Organisation* (Harper and Row, 1977) are both clear and thorough. Charles Perrow's *Organisational analysis – a sociological view* (Tavistock, 1970), is good, unpretentious and full of detailed examples taken from the American business magazine, *Fortune.*

The different sociological perspectives on organisations are well presented in the following:
Structural functionalism: W. R. Scott, *Organisations: rational, natural and open systems* (Prentice Hall, 1981); A. Etzioni, *Modern Organisations* (Prentice Hall, 1964)
Marxism: Graeme Salaman, *Class and the Corporation* (Fontana, 1981); Stewart Clegg and David Dunkerley, *Organisation, Class and Control* (Routledge & Kegan Paul, 1980)
Social Action: David Silverman, *The Theory of Organisations* (Heinemann, 1970)

Paralysed by bureaucracy

"The story has been told of a Soviet citizen taking a rifle into Red Square and firing a number of shots at President Mikoyan's car. Red Square at that time was saturated with security guards but they did not dare act immediately without orders because they could not be sure that the attempted assassination was not sanctioned by an even higher authority than Mikoyan. The guards were effectively paralysed until higher 'clearance' was obtained to shoot the offender." From *The Concept of Organisations* by David Bradley and Roy Wilkie (1974)

torical and economic development in which the means of production are owned by a tiny minority, the bourgeoisie – a ruling class that uses its power to control and exploit the rest of society in the pursuit of profit. Marxists see all major social organisations as instruments of class rule – politically (the government), physically (the army and police), and ideologically (the media, the judiciary, the educational and religious systems). The mass of the population thus come to see the "values" of capitalism (inequality, privilege, materialism, competition) not only as inevitable but just, and are thus distracted from organising to defend their own true interests.

Power within organisations is, therefore, related to the distribution of power and wealth in society at large. The division of labour and the hierarchy of authority within most modern organisations is seen by Marxists not as a means to efficiency ("efficiency for whom and for what?" asks Graeme Salaman, in *Class and the Corporation*, 1981), but a means of control.

The division of labour, Marxists say, fragments the workforce and ensures the ablest "workers" are on the side of capital. Hierarchies of authority are even more effective, not only because their control is impersonal and difficult to challenge, but also because they help to justify inequality. They make it seem that those at the top of our organisational hierarchies are there through merit, and so deserve

rich rewards. Yet, as many studies have shown (J. Stanworth and A. Giddens, *Elites and Power in British Society*, 1974, for example), such elites are there as much through social background and privileged education as through ability.

However, the real power of capitalism is economic, and its chief representatives today are the multinationals, those giant octopus-like companies that dominate not only British commercial life, but the world economy. Ford, for example, is the third largest company in the world. It employs half a million people and a further two million people depend on it for their jobs. "But its ruler, Henry Ford", say Counter Information Services in *Ford* (1977), "is accountable to no electorate, least of all to those whose livelihoods are affected by his decisions." The company's products extend across five continents and its management operates according to a "global strategy", of which the manufacture of the Ford Fiesta in several different countries is a classic example.

Such strategies allow firms to influence national governments, and, if necessary, to bring them down – as the telecommunications firm, ITT, helped do to the Marxist Allende government in Chile.

Power to the people?

Modern organisations "dominate our lives, our fortunes and our honour. To restore the liberty of men we must free them from the domination of powerful organisations", wrote Peter Blau and Richard Schoenherr in *The Structure of Organisations* (1971). But how?

The most obvious organisation to control other organisations is the government. But many people feel that the government itself is not accountable enough. Repeated attempts to introduce a Freedom of Information Act, in Britain, along the lines of those in Sweden and the United States, have been rejected by Parliament.

At the grassroots level, the obvious solution is greater control and participation by citizens, consumers and especially workers. Unfortunately, experience to date is not hopeful. The Bullock Report, recommending greater participation by workers in management of their companies, was presented to the last Labour government but was not acted upon. And where "worker-participation" exists, sociologists have found that managements have developed a whole battery of tactics to ensure they retain control of decision-making – not convening meetings, sending along management representatives of low authority and so on.

Attempts at workers' control have, on the whole, been even less successful. Many of the big cooperative experiments in Britain, such as those at KME in Kirkby and the *Scottish Daily News,* collapsed. The world picture is not particularly bright, either. According to G. Hunnius (*Workers' Control,* 1973) even in socialist countries like Yugoslavia, workers' control is more symbolic than real. As an alternative, the economist, E. F. Schumacher (*Small is Beautiful,* 1974), has suggested that we not only move away from large organisations altogether, but also try to establish smallness within those that already exist, since small organisations tend to be less bureaucratic and more open.

But this approach still leaves real control in the hands of management. So should we go to the extremes advocated by Ivan Illich – to deorganise society altogether and return to the simple life? In his view (*Deschooling Society,* 1973), our educational, health and welfare systems exploit and control us because we have come to depend on them, instead of learning how to look after ourselves. But the problem here is: how to find a single organisation with the power to destructure all the others?

Even so, attempts to establish popular control continue unabated. The best recent example is the struggle in Poland between the people's organisation, Solidarity, and the ultimate in organisational power, the totalitarian state.

THE POLICE

The British police are the best in the world – or so the saying runs. This may still be true. But in the past few years the police and their actions have become increasingly controversial.

Urban riots, sieges, gun battles, terrorism, corruption and arguments over police powers have ensured that the cosy old image of *Dixon of Dock Green* has gone for ever. During the miners' strike, it was widely suggested that Britain had become a police state.

While this is undoubtedly an overstatement, police powers, organisation and priorities have been coming under a good deal of scrutiny from all quarters of society. Even some Conservative MPs have been forced to raise questions about such issues as police tactics in the miners' strike, or some of the policing that led up to the riots in Tottenham and Brixton in 1985.

The main worry among the critics of the police over the past few years has been that tendencies towards centralisation, high technology, violence and surveillance are combining to place them beyond control by democratic processes. Far from being servants of the public, the police, the critics say, are becoming autonomous from the rest of society.

To their credit, the police have responded to these criticisms, though in a contradictory way. Some have said that these developments are more or less inevitable responses to rising crime, to increased disorder and to more sophisticated challenges and outdated policing methods. This approach has been dubbed the *fire brigade* style of policing, in which the car, the radio and the computer dominate, and in which police officers are basically responders to reported incidents.

Other elements in the police have tried to revive what is commonly seen as a more traditional approach. Here the aim is on prevention rather than response, on greater personal contact between locally based police and their neighbourhood, and on coordination of police aims with those of social workers and teachers. This approach is dubbed *community policing.*

In reality, most policing in Britain draws on a combination of both approaches. At present, the initiative is with the advocates of community policing. This is the approach favoured by the current head of London's Metropolitan Police, Sir Kenneth Newman. But even his influential approach makes extensive use of computers, riot technology, surveillance and the other paraphernalia of "reactive" policing.

Newman and his colleagues have followed the proposals of Lord Scarman in his report on the 1981 Brixton riots, in which police relations with the public, particularly young black people, were found to be poor and, in some cases, based on hostility and aggression. The emphasis now is on good police-community relations and good police training. But here, even the most enlightened police planner faces a big problem – police culture.

During the past twenty years, the social status of the police has changed. Repeated calls for better "law and order" have led to huge increases in police wages. The recruitment of graduates has blossomed. Large injections of capital investment have been put into new technology.

As police work has shifted away from the streets and to the desk and the visual display unit, so police social expectations have risen and an ethos of "professionalisation" has emerged. Police have become more middle-class, and indeed earn more than many middle-class occupations such as teachers or architects. In urban areas, many police can now afford to live in pleasant suburbs, commuting into the inner cities where they work. Just as crime has become more white-collar, so have the police.

Nevertheless, the overriding image of the police is still that of the crime fighter. For more than a century, fictional works, like the novels of Georges Simenon and Raymond Chandler, and television series like *The Sweeney,* have depicted police work as exciting, active, physical and dan-

gerous. The aims of policing are clear-cut – suppressing crime and trying to pin down criminals.

This mythology still dominates police culture and public expectations of the police. It is vigorously sustained by the public, the media and the police alike.

The public, it is argued, needs the myth to sustain the confidence that, when you are in trouble, the police will bring swift and effective aid. And the police also symbolise something larger for many people – the prospect of an ordered society, the power of the state to preserve that order and the maintenance of common moral values through the law.

The media feeds the myth through its depiction of fictional police work and its reporting of actual police work. In both cases, the treatment is highly selective, concentrating on certain crimes (murder, rape, armed robbery, mugging) while largely ignoring others (fraud, traffic offences, theft and most burglaries). And only the most dramatic examples of even selected types of crime are normally depicted, thus painting an extremely misleading and fear-inducing picture of crime.

The police themselves help to sustain the mythology through the value-system

The local bobby still rules

In spite of increasing levels of administrative and technological coordination, Britain still has a local police system. There is no national police force. There are 51 different local forces (two in London, 37 in the rest of England, 4 in Wales and 8 in Scotland). Northern Ireland, by contrast, has only one force, the Royal Ulster Constabulary.

In England and Wales (except London), police forces are managed by police authorities, two-thirds of whose members are elected local councillors and one-third of whom are magistrates. In Scotland, police authorities consist only of elected councillors. In London, the Metropolitan Police is under the direct control of the Home Office (there is a small separate force in the City of London).

Police authorities are responsible, under the Police Act, 1964, for "the maintenance of an adequate and efficient police force." They have no direct control over "operational" matters, which are the sole responsibility of each force's chief constable. In recent years this has led to several sharp local disagreements between councillors and chief constables.

The police are funded half by the police authority, through the rates, and half by central government (the Home Office and the Home and Health Departments of the Scottish Office are the departments responsible). Expenditure on police in England and Wales in 1981–82 was £2392 million, of which 84 per cent was spent on wages and salaries. Police pay is decided nationally each year on the basis of an index of public-sector pay settlements over the preceeding year.

At the end of 1982, Britain had 134 103 police of whom 26 303 were in the "Met", the country's largest force. Just under 9 per cent of Britain's police are women.

The police are forbidden by law from joining a trade union or going on strike. However, all police are members of statutory police representative organisations, which act in the same way as trade unions. The great majority of police, up to and including chief inspector rank, are members of the Police Federation. Above them there is the Police Superintendents' Association and, for the highest ranks, the Association of Chief Police Officers.

of police culture. Several studies, of which the most important was the study of the Metropolitan Police by the Policy Studies Institute in 1983, have drawn attention to the importance of this point.

These studies have shown that police highlight the violent, exciting and competitive nature of their work – all of which is characteristic of a male-dominated culture. Police look upon making arrests – "feeling collars" – as the best test of achievement. Other aspects of police work, which in fact make up the bulk of the job, are seen, at best, as marginal to and, at worst, as getting in the way of "real policing."

A study by a Hampshire policeman, Mervyn Jones, has shown that while police *talk* as though beat officers are the

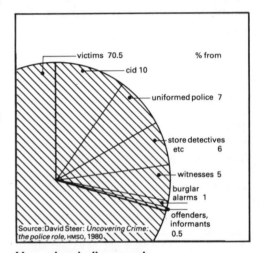

victims 70.5
% from
cid 10
uniformed police 7
store detectives etc 6
witnesses 5
burglar alarms 1
offenders, informants 0.5

Source: David Steer: *Uncovering Crime: the police role*, HMSO, 1980

How crime is discovered

Most crimes are reported by victims themselves. But in some instances, the police can influence the amount and type of crime that is reported. (It is important to note that an increase in *reported* crime does not necessarily mean an increase in crime itself.)

For instance, if police efficiency improves, then crimes may be uncovered that would otherwise have gone unrecorded. A police drive against some particular problem area like vice or mugging can also lead to an increase in cases reported. But a headline like BIG RISE IN MUGGINGS may reflect no more than the fact that the police have taken a special interest in the subject.

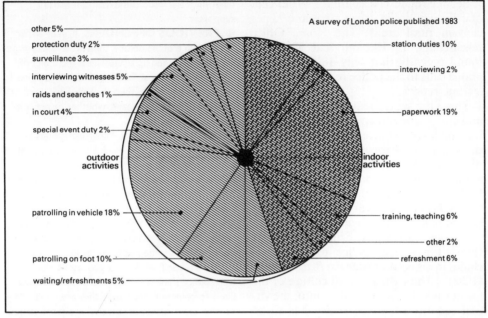

A survey of London police published 1983

other 5%
protection duty 2%
surveillance 3%
interviewing witnesses 5%
raids and searches 1%
in court 4%
special event duty 2%

outdoor activities

patrolling in vehicle 18%

patrolling on foot 10%

waiting/refreshments 5%

station duties 10%
interviewing 2%
paperwork 19%

indoor activities

training, teaching 6%
other 2%
refreshment 6%

What do the police do all day?

crucial section of the force, in *fact* the force is geared towards promotion. As a result, little notice is taken of beat officers and they are looked down on for their lack of motivation.

This exposes one of the major problems in the recent re-emphasis on getting police back on the beat, on foot patrol. The problem is that the police don't like doing it. As the Policy Studies Institute puts it: "For a police officer, patrolling tends to be boring, not only because it is uneventful but also because it is rather aimless. A considerable amount of police behaviour can best be understood as a search for some interest, excitement or sensation."

Most police performance is still judged almost exclusively acccording to statistical yardsticks of crime. Rises in the crime figures or outbreaks of particular crimes – whether they are real or not – are interpreted as requiring ever-tougher crime-fighting solutions of the traditional kind. All the emphasis is placed on increased police powers, increased police numbers, and more and better weapons and technology of every kind, regardless of whether they are effective or not.

In fact, according to two Home Office criminologists, R. Clarke and J. M.

Hough, it is probably beyond the power of police to have a direct effect on most crime. Many recent studies now agree that it doesn't matter what tactics the police actually employ – whether they have stronger technical support or stronger legal powers – the amount of actual crime committed will not be greatly affected.

All this is naturally disturbing to the police's self-image. However, if the police saw themselves in a less exclusively crime-fighting role, things might be different. But they receive little public or political encouragement to do so.

In reality, most policework is already not to do with crime. A number of sociological studies have shown that only about a third of police time is concerned with crime matters. And most policework on crime is done by the CID, themselves a mere 15 per cent of the force.

This is a reflection of the actual demands placed upon police by the public. In 1973, M. Punch and M. Naylor found that most calls to the police are classifiable as "service requests", which they divided into seven main groups: domestic occurrences, highway incidents, property (lost, found and abandoned); people (lost and found); errands; health; and animals.

Service requests account for 49 per cent of calls to police in urban areas and 73 per cent in rural areas. The Home Office researchers, P. Ekblom and K. Heal, found recently that only 18 per cent of phone calls to the police required filling in a crime report.

There are signs today that some policy-makers, police and civil servants, are paying much greater attention to these questions of public expectation and the limits of police effectiveness. A new bill tightening up some police powers is currently in Parliament, but another important question is: how can ordinary police officers be helped to see their job differently?

As one sociologist, Simon Holdaway (himself a former police officer), concludes in his book, *Inside the British Police* (1983): "The tightly bound culture of the lower ranks has to be broken into; the virtual sanctity of police policy has to be demystified, not just to denounce but also to check power and to gain a wider appreciation of the possibilities and limitations of policing. Whatever reforms might be effected, more attention has to be paid to the lower ranks as they work from day to day. The occupational culture remains the final testing ground of sociological analysis and policy intervention."

Police attention

One of the main areas of complaint about the police in recent years has been over the way they appear to pick on some people and not on others.

Obviously, it would be unreasonable to expect the police to arrest everyone they came across who had committed an offence. But sociologists have noted how certain groups in society appear to get more police attention than others.

Researchers have distinguished several factors which appear to influence police decisions on whether people should be arrested:

● **TYPE OF OFFENCE.** If the offence is serious then the police will probably make an arrest regardless of the circumstances. But most offences are not serious, and the police have wide powers of discretion. For instance, an elderly down-and-out who insults a policeman will probably not get arrested, simply because the police realise that an arrest would have little deterrent effect. The story would probably be different if the insult came from a football supporter.

● **PREVIOUS OFFENDERS.** If an offender has been in trouble before, then he or she is more likely to be picked up again. This is the effect of what sociologists call *labelling theory*. If you give someone a bad name, then they are henceforth seen in terms of that image, whether or not it is subsequently justified.

● **SOCIAL GROUPS.** Particular groups in society – young people, black people, people of unusual appearance – are often seen by the police as especially prone to trouble. Lord Scarman, in his report on the 1981 riots, showed how much more likely young black people were to come under suspicion. And the 1983 Policy Studies Institute report found the attitudes of some Metropolitan Police officers to be positively racist.

There is a self-reinforcing process at work here. If the police think some types of people are more likely to commit crimes, then they are more likely to stop and question or search them in the street. If this happens frequently, then the people who are stopped will become hostile and defiant to the police. This, in turn, will make them more likely to get arrested.

Furthermore, the labelling process can come into play. If someone is continually harassed or arrested for something they did not do, then their image of themselves may change. If they are perceived for long enough to be some kind of criminal, then they may eventually come to behave like a criminal.

● **"CRIMINAL DISTRICTS."** The same reinforcing process applies to geographical areas. If the police think a particular area – like, say, Toxteth or Brixton – is full of people who are likely to break the law, then the traditional approach has been to put more officers on the

BOOKS

Some useful additional reading:
Robert Baldwin and Richard Kinsey, *Police Powers and Politics,* Quartet, 1982
Crime Control and the Police (Home Office Research Study No. 67), HMSO, 1981
T. A. Critchley, *A History of Police in England and Wales* (2nd ed.), Constable, 1978
Robert Roshier, *Crime and Punishment,* Longman, 1976
The Brixton Disorders: the report of an inquiry by Lord Scarman, HMSO, 1981

streets. As a result, people from that area who *do* commit crimes are more likely to get caught than offenders from other areas. Official statistics will then appear to show that the area *is* more heavily populated with criminals.

This "vicious spiral" is sometimes called *amplification* by sociologists. It shows particularly that more police do not always mean less crime.

POPULATION

A total of 1806 million people in the world today live in cities. By the end of the century that number will be 3208 million. If you live in Sweden you can expect to live to be 75 years old. But someone in Nigeria can expect to live to only 37 – half that age. These sort of figures are one reason why the study of population matters. It is more than just the business of counting heads.

The population of any region or state is the product of four factors: births, deaths, migration in and migration out. None of these rates stays the same. Even in a developed society like Britain with 56 million people, which is unlikely to suffer from a sudden killer disease, birth and migration rates can vary from year to year. Hence population forecasts – which we rely on for providing school places, housing or hospital beds for old people – can never be certain. They rest on a mix of variable factors, which is why demographers (people who study population) usually present a range of possible population levels which grows wider the further they look into the future.

The birth rate in Britain has been going down steadily since about 1871 – well before the use of the most primitive artificial contraceptives, let alone the pill. Demographers talk about the birth rate in numbers of live births per 1000 of the population. This is usually referred to as the crude birth rate. It has fallen from over 35 per 1000 in 1871 to 13 per 1000 in 1983, with the only significant hiccup being an upturn to around 19 in the late 1950s and early 1960s. Many reasons have been advanced for this overall decline. Among them are improved standards of health, which mean that parents can assume that most babies will survive; better old age pensions, which mean that elderly people do not have to rely on the earnings of numerous children; an association between greater family prosperity and a smaller number of offspring; and the increasing desire of women to go out to work, particularly since the Second World War. We also now have much better *means* of contraception. The pill is generally more reliable than the condom.

By 1983 the birth rate in this country had fallen below the level at which it would be necessary for the population to replace itself (i.e. when the death rate exceeds the birth rate). It was down to about 60 births per 1000 women of child-bearing age.

All developed societies have seen a similar decline – including Roman Catholic countries like Italy, where there have been religious obstacles to most forms of contraception. Slow population growth in Europe means that the European Community share of the total world population is expected to decline from 6 per cent in 1982 to under 5 per cent by the year 2000.

As for the United Kingdom, births are projected to rise until the mid-1990s, resulting in moderate growth in the population from 56.3 million in 1983 to 57.2 million in 2001. This is an improvement on the situation in 1976–77 when the population actually decreased for the first time this century in peacetime.

Just as there is a crude birth rate measured in births per 1000, so there is a crude death rate. For Britain this was about 11.8 per 1000 in 1982. But this crude death rate is, of course, an average across age groups, sexes and classes. There has been a particularly rapid decline in the death rate of children since the 1940s, but the life expectancy for men in Britain has scarcely improved since 1960. Over the last 140 years, however, there has been a steady decline in the death rate and an increase in life expectancy for both boys and girls.

The reasons for the fall in the death rate are not so different from those which have led historically to a fall in the birth rate: wider prosperity and better nutrition; improved drugs and medical care. These things are associated in Britain with better housing and hygiene; and the introduction of the National Health Service. In 1841, when mortality statistics were first collected in England and Wales, a 15-year-old boy could expect to live a further 43.4 years, and a girl 44.1 years. By 1960 a boy could expect to live a further 55.3 years, about the same as his present life expectancy, while a girl's expectancy had increased much more – to 60.9 years. She has again pulled ahead by more than a year in the last two decades.

The disparities in life expectancy and death rate are not only between the sexes. Death rates among unskilled workers and their families in all age groups have been around twice those for the professional classes, ever since comparisons began in this country in 1911. Money, nutrition and different ways of life help to account for this. Manual workers are more at risk of occupational diseases (particularly miners and chemical workers). Ways of life which involve more smoking and alcohol and less physical exercise, particularly in middle age, lead to higher death rates. Major causes of death have changed with the elimination of former killers like tuberculosis. Accidents and violence have become relatively more common causes of death in the young, while relatively more middle-aged and old people now die from heart attacks and cancer.

The crude death rate varies between countries according to life expectancy and the structure of the population. That is to say it will be lower both when people live longer, and when there is a large proportion of children in the population, as there is in most developing countries. Nevertheless the crude death rate in the United Kingdom in 1982 (11.8 per 1000) was higher than in several comparable countries – Denmark (10.8), France (10) and the Netherlands (8.2).

If birth rate and death rate make one pair of variables, the two others which are naturally compared are migration in and migration out. There has been so much attention focused on immigrants to Britain over the past 20 years that it is easy to forget that this country, like Ireland, has been one of the major exporters of people over the last 150 years. Were it not for arrivals from Britain over this period, the population of the United States, Australia

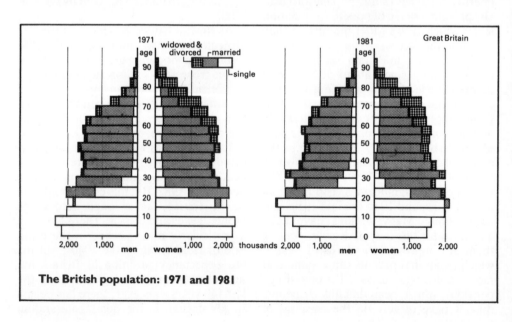

The British population: 1971 and 1981

and many other countries would be a great deal smaller today.

Between 1881 and 1921, for instance, this country experienced a net loss of population of between 2 and 3 per cent a year. The total loss by emigration between 1911 and 1921, covering a period when the male population had been drastically reduced by deaths in the First World War, was 919 000. This net export of people has continued to the present. The only major exception was between 1931 and 1951 when there was a net import of 462 000 people, many of them European refugees. Since then net inflows (more people coming in than going out) have only been recorded in a few years and they may usually be explained by special circumstances. There was a net inflow in 1961–62, caused largely by Commonwealth immigrants wishing to beat the deadline for the first major Immigration Act which would control their arrival. There was another net inflow in 1972–73, caused largely by Uganda's expulsion of Asians holding British passports. But in the period from 1967 to 1975, when immigration to Britain was at its height of political controversy (and Enoch Powell was making his most famous speeches), there was actually a net loss of 410 000 people from this country. Though this does not, of course, mean that we ended up with fewer *coloured* people.

Except where they have actually been expelled – like the Jewish refugees from pre-war Germany, or Asians from Uganda – the reasons why people leave a country like Britain are no different from those which bring others here: hopes of making a better living, family ties, and a feeling of restlessness and dissatisfaction in their own societies. Black or brown

BOOKS

Some useful additional reading:
A. H. Halsey (ed.), *Trends in British Society since 1900,* Macmillan, 1972
R. K. Kelsall, *Population,* Longman, 1975
J. H. Lowry, *World Population and Food Supply,* Edward Arnold, 1976
C. W. Park, *The Population Explosion,* Heinemann, 1965

migrants to this country are, of course, more visible than others. This does not necessarily mean that they outnumber white immigrants to any particular neighbourhood. In 1983, about 94 per cent of the population in Great Britain were of white ethnic origin. About half of the rest were known to be of West Indian, Guyanese, Indian or Pakistani ethnic origin.

Within the coloured section of the community the Asians – both those who have come directly from the Indian subcontinent and those who have come via Africa – are steadily outdistancing those of West Indian descent. In the five years from 1971–76 there was a small net emigration to the West Indies from Britain, and the main inflow was from the Indian subcontinent. In 1983 there were half a million people of West Indian origin here, compared with rather more from the Indian subcontinent.

For both government and commercial purposes much use is made of the population forecasts which demographers make. But with four variables to work from (and the birth rate and emigration figures are particularly hard to predict) it is inevitable that the projections of population change quite rapidly.

Recently the government has had to cut back more sharply than it expected on teacher training and new schools. Furthermore, the demographers really only have secure figures to work from once every ten years, at the time of the census, when everybody is counted up. (The next is due in 1991.) Between censuses they must rely on samples, estimates, registered births and deaths and the slightly less trustworthy migration statistics. Recently, the Irish Republic discovered from a fresh census that it had 100 000 more inhabitants than it had supposed on the basis of the annually adjusted estimates.

If national projections have an element of risk, this is even more true for regions within a country. Recent projections for England suggest that only three regions will grow much in population by 1991: East Anglia, the south west and the east midlands. A small gain in the south east as a whole conceals the fact that Greater London is expected to lose 10 per cent of its population.

In theory, world population figures and projections ought to be simpler to ascertain, because demographers do not have to worry about the figures for migration, which can be so difficult at a national level. In practice, because so many governments do not collect regular or adequate census statistics, it is only possible to estimate the world population. The best estimates are that the world total was 2501 million in 1950 and 4800 million in 1984, a growth of about 100 per cent in a quarter of a century. Although world population growth seems to be slowing down, with deaths and births expected to be in rough balance by the year 2100, by then the population is expected to have risen to about 10.2 billion.

Whereas we in the rich world (where the average number of children per family is two) think of extra children as an expense, people in poor countries (where the average number of children is five) think of them as an economic asset. If you live in a country where there is no unemployment or sickness benefit then a big family can bring security. The more children that work, the more wages are brought in. And, of course, the birth rate is closely linked to the death rate. A peasant family in rural India, for example, has to have an average of 6.5 children to be 95 per cent certain of one surviving son. This kind of consideration is almost unheard of in Britain.

POWER & AUTHORITY

Why do people do what they are told? Why do we stand on the right on escalators or stop our cars when the police flash their lights? What would happen if a lot of people decided not to obey those in positions of authority over them?

These are questions of vital interest to anyone concerned with the functioning of society. Indeed, the whole idea of social relationships involves the notion of power. Questions of obedience and disobedience arise in families, in classrooms, in playgrounds, on sports fields, between couples, on the streets, and at work. Whenever two or more people are engaged in some activity, potential conflicts will arise, and will have to be resolved.

Sometimes the conflict manifests itself in physical force: wives get battered, soccer fans are stabbed. Much of the time, though, the potential for conflict is scarcely apparent, even to the participants. In school, for instance, the fact that most pupils are doing what their teacher wants most of the time, without the teacher having to exercise obvious authority, does not alter the fact that the authority is there.

These days, curiously, power has become almost a dirty word. It tends to be something that we attribute to people, organisations or governments that we disapprove of. We often talk about the power of President Gorbachev in the Soviet Union or General Jaruzelski in Poland in a way that implies it is in some respect being abused.

In our own system of government, which we regard as democratic, power is usually invisible. But, as with personal relationships, this does not mean that it is not there. Indeed, prolonged conflicts such as the miners' strike, have brought issues of power rather nakedly into the open. What has upset many people is the way the strike has revealed the power of the state in its least attractive guise, that of physical force.

The concept of power has always been a central part of the thinking of the major sociologists. It is a key element in the sociology of Max Weber (1864–1920) and of Karl Marx (1818–83), and important in the structural-functionalist ideas of Talcott Parsons (1902–79).

Weber's is the best known definition of power, but his ideas, expressed in his native language, German, do not often translate very elegantly. Power, according to Weber, is "the probability that one actor within a social relationship will be in a position to carry out his own will despite resistance, regardless of the basis on which this probability rests." In other words, power is something that people exercise over each other in face-to-face relationships. On this view, what is good for the powerful may not be good (or even will not be good) for the powerless, with resulting conflicts of interest. Power, on this reckoning, involves restrictions and limitations being imposed on the powerless in the interests of the powerful.

Other writers have preferred to see power deriving from the overall structure of society rather than what individual people do within it. For example, in a school, relationships are usually hierarchical, with teachers, pupils, and other staff ranked above each other in a system rather like the rungs on a ladder. The power that teachers exercise over pupils is not personal to them, but a result of their position. They have little choice in the matter, once they are part of the system. They can, of course, abuse the power they have, but they cannot discard it as a matter of personal choice, other than by resigning and leaving the hierarchy altogether. This view of power as part of the social structure has been associated with the very different ideas of Karl Marx and Talcott Parsons.

For Marx, the origins of all power can be found in the ownership of the means of production. Power is used by the minority to exploit the majority. It is also used to prevent the majority from bringing about any change that might reduce the power of the minority. A Marxist might see the present government's revision of the trade union laws as an example of such an approach. This will often involve resistance, with strikes and, Marx thought hopefully, revolution.

After a revolution, power is taken over by another group, who then exercise it in their own favour. This view sees power as being in finite supply, so that an increase in the power of one group necessarily involves its loss for another group, who will resist that loss. Parsons has referred to this as a *constant-sum* (or *zero-sum*) notion of power.

Parsons prefers a *variable sum* notion of power. He sees society as an interdependent system, in which power helps to maintain the equilibrium and the balance between groups by making it possible to effect change and to get things done. Parsons makes a comparison with money, which circulates through the system as a lubricant to assist collective action. There is not necessarily a fixed amount of it available, but rather the system generates what is required and distributes it to those who are most able to make a contribution to the smooth running of the system. The important aspect of this view of power is that it makes almost no reference to the possibility of resistance and conflict. In Parsons's *consensus* model of society, such challenges are limited to disputes within the overall framework, which can be resolved without basic structural change. Essentially, all power is acceptable to those subject to it.

It is important to distinguish between different kinds of power. The nature of power varies according to whether the people over whom it is exercised think it justified.

COERCION refers to power which is used without the consent of the subject individual or group. It must therefore be backed up by the threatened or actual use of force. (This is not, however, the same thing as doing something that you do not want to do. The school bully may be able to force his victims to carry out some action against their will, but this is different from a teacher making a pupil do homework, when the pupil recognises, however unwillingly, the teacher's right to set the homework.)

Exercising power through coercion usually requires great resources of physical, political or economic power. For a colonial power to rule a subject people through coercion, an occupying army will usually have to be provided, as the Russians have done in Afghanistan. Sooner or later, the power will either become accepted by the subject people, or their resistance will build up to a point where they can no longer be held under, as happened with a number of European colonies in Africa during the 1950s and 1960s, and some people believe will eventually happen in Northern Ireland.

Power exercised as coercion is of Marx's *constant-sum* variety; that is, if one group gains more of it, the other loses some. There are winners and losers in the conflict.

AUTHORITY, however, is a different version of power. The ideas of Max Weber have provided the most useful insights here. The key thing about authority is that the people who are subject to it perceive the power being exercised as justified, or, in Weber's term, *legitimate*. This is usually the case when those under orders believe that there is some common good to be served by obedience. Weber identified three kinds of authority: *charismatic*, *traditional*, and *rational-legal*.

● **Charismatic authority** rests on the personal qualities of a particular leader. Such a leader tends to appear at times of crisis, and to make promises that involve overturning the authority of the established society. Whatever we may think of their moral standing, people like Hitler, Lenin, Joan of Arc, Castro, Christ and even Arthur Scargill, have all demonstrated authority of this kind.

● **Traditional authority** rests on a belief in the sanctity of old traditions. Those who exercise power are obeyed, not because of their personal qualities, but because they continue tradition. Where charismatic authority appeals to those who wish to make fundamental changes, traditional authority appeals to conservatives and those who support existing social ties. The British royal family is a classic example of traditional authority.

● **Rational-legal authority** rests on subordinates' believing that the rules being enforced are legal, that those giving orders are entitled to do so because of the office that they hold, and that the order given is more or less sensible. This is the type of authority that we are most familiar with in our society. It is the authority of the official in the tax office, of the boss at work, and of the school headmaster. The rules may be changed, but the new ones will continue to be enforced because of their *rational-legal* basis.

It is important to remember that these three categories are *ideal types* rather than descriptions of the real world. Any real-life ruling figure may base their power on a combination of any of these types of authority. The Ayatollah Khomeini, for instance, has taken and held power by combining charisma with an appeal to ancient tradition, and is certainly not averse to the use of coercion if it is needed.

Just as important as the *nature* of power is the way it is distributed in society. In general, sociological theories about this fall into three main groups:

RULING CLASS THEORY. Followers of this line take their inspiration from Karl Marx, believing that in a capitalist society, those who own the factories, the land, and the financial institutions thereby control all the other institutions. Their economic power, concentrated into relatively few hands, enables them to rule politically. Their power is ultimately coercive, though mainly invisible, and the institutions of the state (the courts, the civil service, the legislature and so on) are all under their control. Their real power is their ability to get others to have the desires that they want them to have. This is the power that the Italian communist writer, Antonio Gramsci, called "hegemony."

BOOKS

Some useful additional reading:
Tom Bottomore, *Elites and Society*, Penguin, 1966
Stephen Lukes, *Power, a radical view*, Macmillan, 1974
Phil Stanworth and Anthony Giddens, *Elites and Power in British Society*, Cambridge University Press, 1974
John Urry and John Wakeford, *Power in Britain*, Heinemann, 1973

ELITE THEORY was first developed as a conservative reaction to Marxism. Writers like Gaetano Mosca (1858–1941), Robert Michels (1876–1936) and Vilfredo Pareto (1848–1923) maintained that every society necessarily includes a political elite, who are in that position by virtue of their superior qualities. Any suggestion that some other arrangement might work is a nonsense. Beneath this elite is a disorganised mass, which needs to be led and organised.

Socialism, for followers of this theory, is an impossible dream, since every social group generates a small group at the top, an oligarchy. Pareto believed that the sort of people who made up the elite changed regularly in a pattern which he described as the *circulation of elites*, but that there was nevertheless always an elite. There would always be a sub-elite, placed between the elite and the mass, who would carry out the instructions of the elite.

The radical sociologist, C. Wright Mills (1916–62), developed a model of American society which rests rather uncomfortably between the *ruling class* and the *elite* models. He described a "power elite", made up of the military, economic and political elites together. These were separate elites, whose power came from various sources, but they were linked by intermarriage, by social ties, and by the ease with which individuals could move from one elite to another. The British Marxist writer, Ralph Miliband (*The State in Capitalist Society*, 1969) made a similar case, but identified this group clearly as a ruling class.

PLURALIST THEORY. Both the *ruling class* and the *elite* models tend to favour a *constant-sum* idea of power (the more power one group has, the less is available to others). A *pluralist* model of power rests more on the *variable-sum* view associated with Talcott Parsons. On this line of thinking, power is distributed among various groups, none of which is supreme. These elite groups can be found in business, in the trade unions, among consumers, voters, educationists, journalists, and so on. The state is regarded as having the role of mediator, or "honest broker" among these competing groups.

Policy emerges from the free interplay of debate and influence among the groups, and power is decentralised. Checks and balances make it impossible for any particular group to grasp complete control, and every group has the opportunity to be heard. This view of power is very close to the commonsense one held by many people in Britain today. It is certainly a widely-held view of how British democracy operates.

Critics of this idea, who take a more conflict-oriented view of society, whether from a ruling class or an elite perspective, maintain that it is an ideology of control. If people can be made to believe that society is democratic, they will perceive the system as fair and just, and will not attempt radical change. This is clearly in the interests of the rulers.

So, which model most closely fits Britain today? Is there a group of people, in whose hands economic power is concentrated, who are able to control the state in accordance with their own broad interests? This is the general view of the leading British sociologist, Anthony Giddens. Or is there a variety of elites, in every walk of life, no single one of which is able to dominate the political process?

Or are these elites so interlocked with each other that they amount to a power elite? And, if there is such a group, how open is it to outsiders to enter through their own efforts?

Perhaps the best check we have against the abuse of power in British society today is that it would be hard to get agreement on the answer.

THE PRESS

"ELSIE QUITS THE STREET", said the headline across the front page of the *Sun* not long ago. The *Daily Mirror* simply said: "ELSIE QUITS".

A visitor from overseas might have been confused. Which politician, captain of industry or foreign potentate was called Elsie? But the 4.2 million people who bought *The Sun*, the 3.3 million who bought the *Daily Mirror*, and the 1.3 million buyers of the *Daily Star* would have known immediately. "Elsie" was the actress, Pat Phoenix, who was leaving the cast of the Granada television serial, *Coronation Street*, bringing an end to the character, Elsie Tanner.

The fact that the editors of these papers decided to lead on this rather than President Reagan's offer to cut the numbers of cruise missiles, or the 21 IRA prisoners who happened to be on the loose that day, is a measure of the way in which newspapers have come to terms with their rivals in an increasingly competitive media age.

With *News at Ten* scooping what used to be the following morning's headlines and rivalry from new forms of media (the Sony Walkman is more portable than *The Sunday Times*), newspapers have had to adapt to survive. They have done this remarkably successfully, despite all the prophesies of their decline.

We may be living in the "television age", but TV has not made the inroads into newspaper consumption that many commentators predicted. Instead, it has vastly increased the amount of time we spend on the media as a whole. The amount of "audience time" spent on the press has declined relatively little since the early 1960s, when TV first became popular.

Circulations *have* gone down – by about 30 per cent since 1945. Yet compared with other western countries Britain remains a nation of news hawks, with a remarkably high "penetration" by newspapers of households. Some 77 per cent of individuals in the social class A (professional) category read a morning national paper; the figure is above 70 per cent for all groups except group E (unskilled workers) where 62 per cent read a paper each day.

Some 38.3 million people read a daily paper, according to newspaper industry estimates. Of these, three million read one of the "qualities" and 35.3 million read one of the "popular" papers. Local newspapers are well perused, too. Take two evening papers at random: the *Gloucestershire Echo* is bought by, or delivered to, 68 per cent of households in Cheltenham; the *Leicester Mercury* claims to be seen in 74 per cent of Leicester's homes.

The press has several factors on its side, compared with other media. It takes by far the bulk of advertising revenue spent in Britain – some two thirds of the total – compared with just over a quarter for television. The prestige national papers like *The Times* and *The Financial Times* are by far the most influential of the mass media. And newspapers are still the only media that all sections of the population actually carry round with them for most of the day. A survey by the *Daily Mirror*, for instance, showed that much reading of the paper is done at work, before work, and in the evening before going to bed.

The most crucial factor that differentiates newspapers from other media, though, is social class. Whereas TV has a largely homogeneous audience (ITV is slightly more working-class than BBC), the British national press is the most socially polarised in the western world – a fact seized on by marketing staff at *The Times* when they launched it as the "top people's paper." There is an advertising agent's joke that lists the papers: *The Times* is read by the people who run the country, *The Financial Times* by the people who own it and *The Guardian* by the people who would like to run it.

Table 1 shows the social profiles of *The Sun* and *The Times* to be almost symmetrical; the *Daily Mail* alone among the titles has a spread between all the social groups. Such divisions are seen in the provincial press, where the city evenings are akin to the popular national dailies while the morning papers, like the *Yorkshire Post*, have a more "upmarket" flavour. The two nations of newspaper readers are paralleled in the magazine world (Table 2). *Woman's Own* is mainly working-class; *Time Out* and the *Economist* are scarcely read by the non-affluent. The papers are stratified on sex lines, too, as Table 3 shows. *The Sun* is much more of a "man's paper" than the *Daily Mail*.

Some sociologists have blamed television for this polarisation of the press. Jeremy Tunstall, of the City University, says, for instance, that "television influences have played a large part in destroying the middle-brow, middle-market sector of the British press." But there have been other, economic factors that have forced newspapers to seek readers at opposite poles of the socio-economic spectrum.

One factor is the way they get their revenue. Prestige papers like *The Times* and *The Guardian* cannot make enough money from the numbers of copies they sell, so they depend on advertising rates for their money. This exaggerates their upmarket inclinations, since the highest rates can be charged for delivering the richest readers to advertisers. For popular papers like *The Sun*, the reverse is true: advertising income is small and they depend on mass sales – which encourages circulation wars to the death, like the recent bingo and "Be a Millionaire" campaigns.

Of course, people don't read newspapers just for bingo or for ads for Porsches in *The Sunday Times*. So why do they read them? One survey found that 69 per cent gave the obvious reason of "keeping up with the events of the day." But 42 per cent cited "human interest", and 25 per cent said they read in order to "be able to discuss things with other people." In other words, newspaper reading is a distinctly social activity.

Some sociologists have pointed out the role of newspapers in "ethicising" social norms. They play a part in stimulating public outrage against breaches of social convention: the "construction" of outrage against the seaside antics of groups of Mods and Rockers in the 1960s has been well studied. Similarly, any group that steps outside society's broad consensus – whether the Paedophile Information Exchange or the IRA – incurs the press's censure. It is a unique form of social control.

The British popular press has made a speciality of images of crime. The Yorkshire Ripper was "tried" and found guilty by some newspapers before he ever got to the Old Bailey. Similarly, *The Sun* and the *News of the World* have sustained outrage over a single crime – the Moors Murders – by keeping tabs on the perpetrators in prison. At no time have British broadcasters (trammelled by statutes and conventions) been as explicit as newspapers in expressing atavistic feelings on issues such as hanging and imprisonment.

The quality papers are not exempt from this socially integrative process. For instance, the phrase "*Guardian* woman" connotes not just a reader of the *Guardian* women's page but a set of attitudes that might be described as middle-class, feminist, liberal. Similarly the letters page of *The Times* has often been seen as a kind of tribal notice board for the establishment. E.P. Thompson once singled out a letter written in 1973 during a power worker's dispute which began, "Dear Sir, May I, writing by candlelight, express my total support for the government." It was an exercise, he said, in the newspaper helping define the normative contours of society.

This emphasis on the integrative function of newspapers would probably make many journalists on them unhappy. Newspaper journalists like to emphasise the non-routine, contingent aspects of their life. For some journalists, some of the time, this is appropriate. No less a source than the eminent sociologist, Max Weber – who was a regular freelance contributor to the *Frankfurter Zeitung* – said "the journalist's life is an absolute gamble."

With this goes the competition between journalists for the "scoop" – getting the story first – and the "exclusive" – getting a story no other paper has. Competition at its worst was shown when *The Sun* and the *Mirror* battled over the words of the widow of the Falklands VC, Sergeant Mackay. According to the Press Council (a largely ineffective guardian of press ethics), *The Sun* fabricated a statement in order to appear to have the story and so devalue the *Mirror*'s "exclusive."

The reality of the newspaper journalist's life is often prosaic. Professor Tunstall found that most lead stable, suburban lives. Much of the work is routine. Most journalists, especially on the popular papers, work at processing information according to what sociologists call institutional criteria, or journalists prefer to call news values.

The difference in wording here is important. Journalists maintain that their special expertise, acquired through training and experience, gives them a "nose for news" – in other words, they are able to recognise events of interest to a wide public, and process stories about them into an accessible and interesting form. They are, they say, giving the readers what they want.

Sociologists have often taken rather a different view. They have suggested that journalists emphasise certain events at the expense of others: they pick on "bad news" or items that are quirky or titillating, or which can be talked about in terms of personalities. In other words, sociologists say, journalists set their own agenda which excludes whole areas of society – often those relating to the poor and the powerless. As Professor Stuart Hall has pointed out: "The media do not simply and transparently report events which are 'naturally' news-worthy in themselves. News is the end-product of a complex process which begins with a systematic sorting of events and topics according to a socially constructed set of categories."

This criticism has been taken up most notably in recent years by senior Labour politicians like Tony Benn and Ken Livingstone, who say that the press has consistently ignored the party's policies because of its obsession with person-

Table 1: Social profiles of three daily newspapers

	Times	Daily Mail	Sun
AB	59	24	6
C1	32	32	17
C2	11	6	40
DE	4	18	37

Table 2: Social profiles of selected provincial newspapers and magazines

Provincial papers

	Birmingham Evening Mail	Manchester Evening News
AB	14	9
C1	23	24
C2	32	35
DE	31	32

Magazines

	Time Out	Woman's Own	Economist
AB	32	15	58
C1	31	27	27
C2	20	34	8
DE	17	24	7

These social categories, used by such bodies as the Audit Bureau of Circulations and the Joint Industry Committee for Newspaper Research, divide up the population as follows:

A	Upper middle-class households (forming 2½% of all households)
B	Middle-class households (10%)
C1	Lower middle-class, e.g. white-collar workers (23%)
C2	Skilled manual and clerical workers (33%)
D	Unskilled manual working-class (22%)
E	Families living on the subsistence level; pensioner households (9½%)

Table 3: Daily newspaper circulations, 1983

Popular papers	average net sales (millions)	% of adult readers males	% of adult readers females
Daily Express	1.8	16	13
Daily Mail	1.8	13	11
Daily Mirror	3.3	27	22
Daily Star	1.3	13	8
Sun	4.2	31	23
Quality papers	**(thousands)**		
Daily Telegraph	1266	9	7
Financial Times (UK)	165	2	1
Guardian	437	4	2
Times	336	3	2

alities. There have even been suggestions of conspiracy. But as the sociologists, Peter Golding and Philip Elliott, have pointed out (in the context of broadcasting, but with equal relevance to newspapers), "The content of the news portrays a very particular view of the world that we can label ideological. This is not the result of a conspiracy within the newsrooms or of the inadequacies, professional or political, of journalists. It is a necessary result of the structure of newsgathering and production."

It would, of course, be surprising if the press as a whole *did* align itself with the views of Benn or Livingstone, since most newspapers are owned by, or linked to some of the largest capitalist enterprises in society.

The degree of concentration among newspaper owners is striking. Some 85 per cent of all Sunday and daily newspapers printed for the national market are owned by only seven firms. More than half the total national circulation is currently controlled by three giants. One is United Newspapers, publishers of the *Daily Express* and *Daily Star*, who own a large empire of provincial newspapers and magazines. News International, controlled by Rupert Murdoch, owns *The Times* and *The Sun*, as well as newspapers in three continents, television interests and an airline. The third group, which owns the *Mirror, Sunday Mirror* and *People*, belongs to

Robert Maxwell's printing corporation, BPCC.

But do these powerful groups actually influence the content? Sociologists have spent a lot of time studying the power and influence of newspaper owners, and it is perhaps a tribute to the strength of the British press that they have come to such widely differing conclusions about newspaper content.

Take, for example, the front page of the *Daily Express* for 15 June 1982, which was entirely taken up by a huge v, enclosing a photo of Mrs Thatcher in a warrior's pose. This was the day after British troops entered Port Stanley at the end of the Falklands war. A *Marxist* sociologist might argue that this was a crude attempt by a business conglomerate which had an interest in the war through its subsidiary, Cunard, to manufacture patriotic sentiment on behalf of Mrs Thatcher and the Conservative Party. Even if the chief executive of Trafalgar House, the paper's owner at that time, did not dictate the presentation personally, his editor would know what was expected of him. What's more, the Marxists might argue, the same newspaper's "Be a Millionaire" contest is both an example of the manufacture of a "false consciousness" and part of a sales war illustrative of the self-destructive tendencies of British capitalism.

Functionalist sociologists, on the other hand, might take an opposite view of the ownership of the press by large business conglomerates. They would point out that papers are bought by such companies not for propaganda but for prestige. The obvious potential for corrupt self-interest is more likely to lead to exaggerated probity, and a high degree of autonomy for journalists.

Nevertheless, the press in Britain does have a distinctly right-wing flavour, emphasised by the fact that two of the major newspaper collapses since the war have involved centrist and left-wing publications (the *News Chronicle* and the *Daily Herald*). Only two mainstream daily papers could be broadly described as non-Conservative: these are *The Guardian*, which, though liberal, supports no particular party on the left, and the *Daily Mirror,* which supports the Labour Party.

There have been attempts from within the unions to get a left-wing national newspaper off the ground, and there have been plans for a new union-backed Sunday paper, the *News on Sunday*. Its ultimate success, though, will depend not on its editorial slant but on whether people actually read it. The editor will ignore the stars of *Coronation Street* at his peril.

Why we don't always read all about it

A fascinating exercise on any Friday morning when Parliament is sitting is to collect together all the national newspapers to compare the stories written under the "by-line" of their political correspondents and editors. The chances are that some phrase, some idea, will crop up several times; and there will be noticeable recurring code words such as "sources close to the Prime Minister", "it is said in Whitehall", "a senior government source said. . ."

The reason for this is simple. On Thursdays at 4.15 pm in a room in the Palace of Westminster, the existence of which is supposed to be a secret, an organisation called the Parliamentary Lobby gathers to be briefed, first by the Prime Minister's press secretary, then by the Leader of the House, then, after a decent interval, by

News from the right

British daily papers are overwhelmingly Conservative. On the two days before the general election in June 1983, *The Times,* the *Daily Mail,* the *Daily Express,* the *Daily Telegraph, The Sun,* and the *Daily Star* all explicitly urged their readers to vote for the Conservative Party. *The Guardian* spoke of denying Mrs Thatcher a landslide and urged votes for Alliance candidates or, selectively, Labour. The *Financial Times* was not printed because of an industrial dispute with printers. The *Daily Mirror* alone of the national dailies urged, albeit with some misgivings, a Labour vote.

the Leader of the Opposition. Their words, by convention, are "not for attribution." This means the Prime Minister can float ideas, and denigrate her colleagues, but all through the mouth of her press officer and all in a form which is totally deniable.

The Parliamentary Lobby – a 140-strong group of political specialists mostly based at Westminster – is an information cartel, useful to journalists and useful to the government. It represents one of the many little-known ways in which the "news" that appears in the papers is, in fact, structured and far from random.

Superficially the news can appear diverse. Look at the front pages of one

BOOKS

Some useful additional reading:
Jeremy Tunstall, *The Media in Britain,* Constable, 1983
Brian Whitaker, *News Limited: Why you can't read all about it,* Minority Press Group, 1982
Harry Christian *The Sociology of Journalism and the Press,* Sociological Review Monographs, University of Keele, 1981
Annabelle May and Kathryn Rowan (eds), *Inside Information: British government and the media,* Constable, 1982
Simon Jenkins, *Newspapers: the power and the money,* Faber, 1980

typical day. Front page news of the *Daily Star* is "CAR TRAGEDY. Mum kills her son as he runs from his school bus." For *The Times:* "Thatcher ignores pressure to reveal 'battle plan'." For the *Daily Telegraph:* "Brake on EEC prices by Britain." For *The Sun*: "I STAY! TV-am boss begged me, says Parky."

But underneath this, the core of news can be quite similar, despite the differences of space (dictated by paging and advertising) and presentational style. One reason is the reliance of all newspapers on material from press agencies, notably the Press Association, a cooperative of the major publishers. International news is largely in the hands of a small number of agencies, British (Reuters), French (Agence France Presse) and American (Associated Press, United Press International).

In addition, as Brian Whitaker pointed out in his book, *News Limited* (1982), all papers routinely monitor the same sources, from Parliament to the police, the courts, councils and the royal family. A single news agency, Brennans, supplies all Fleet Street with stories from Heathrow airport about the arrival and departure of celebrities.

Much of what ostensibly ought to be news falls between the cracks: institutions dealing with difficult things (e.g. the science departments of universities) and institutions dealing with secret things (all government departments) are often missed. David Murphy, in a study of the local press *(The Silent Watchdog,* 1980), shows how the "little people" of society get little space, unless they can get themselves organised.

During the 1960s, efforts were made to establish an "alternative press" to present events and people missed by the national newspapers. A few papers, including the successful *West Highland Free Press,* survive; but apart from *Private Eye* (which has an oddly incestuous relationship with the establishment) readership is small.

Journalists and editors like to recall a celebrated leading article written for *The Times* in 1852 when it was edited by John Delane. It said: "The first duty of the press is to obtain the earliest and most correct intelligence of the events of the time and instantly by disclosing them to make them common property of the nation." It remains a fine principle, but of little relevance to the processes by which news is gathered and shaped in modern newspapers.

THE PROFESSIONS

Recently, a private member's bill to remove the long-standing legal monopoly solicitors enjoy over house conveyancing was introduced in the House of Commons. The House Buyers Bill was designed to enable building society officials and others to carry out conveyancing work, and would have dramatically cut the cost of moving for home-owners.

The bill reflected a growing concern in society about the power and the high financial rewards of those occupations known as "the professions." Predictably, it was vigorously opposed by the solicitors' body, the Law Society, which claimed that it was "protecting the interests of the established legal profession."

The bill was rejected.

But what exactly *are* the professions and what does the term "professional" really mean? Army recruitment posters urge us to "Join the Professionals" while on TV *The Professionals* are a team of detectives. Prostitution is sometimes referred to as "the oldest profession." We also talk about professional footballers and other sportsmen who "turn professional" and sell their skills full-time. Moreover, bankers, accountants, valuers and estate agents proffer "professional" advice, and a whole range of occupations, from engineering to teaching, are referred to loosely as "professions." It can be a bit confusing.

As John Raynor remarks in *The Middle*

Class (1969), "The concept of a profession is not very precise ... and it has a curiously old-fashioned air about it." "Modern" professions have little in common with the idealised, olde worlde portrayal of the traditional practitioner of medicine or the law. Nowadays many professional scientists, planners and social workers work in large bureaucracies and are servants of the state rather than independent business people with their own clientele.

The term "profession", however, still denotes high status of the kind associated with the "older" professions like the church and the academic world. The French sociologist, Emile Durkheim, saw "professional" occupations as moral communities, with their members dedicated to a life of altruism and service. This rather lofty view accords with the nineteenth-century ideology of the gentlemanly pursuit of knowledge and the tradition of public service.

But the twentieth-century saw a rapid growth in many more kinds of white-collar jobs, many of them "professional" in character. One group consisted of scientists, engineers and technologists as manufacturing and industry became more sophisticated. Another group, associated with education, health and the social services, multiplied rapidly with the growth of higher education and the welfare state during the 1950s and 1960s.

The result, as can be seen in the table, was that while manual workers declined from 79 per cent to 58 per cent of the workforce between the beginning of the century and the 1970s, the "professions" rose from 4 to 11 per cent of the total. Over the same period the church slumped from 11 per cent to only 1.5 per cent of all professional jobs, while engineers, technologists and scientists shot up from 8 per cent to 37 per cent.

In trying to make sense of this fast-changing reality, sociologists have tried – largely in vain – to isolate the special characteristics or *traits* of "true" professions. One such attempt was made by G. Millerson in his book, *The Qualifying Associations: A study of professionalism* (1964). Millerson bundled all the characteristics of a profession most frequently mentioned in sociological literature into a "model" profession. The six "traits" he identified were:
● A skill based on theoretical knowledge
● An extensive period of education and training
● The testing of competence before admission to the profession
● The existence of a code of conduct
● A theme of public service and altruism
● The freedom of the profession to regulate itself.

However, other sociologists have found it difficult to apply this model both to the existing "professions", like teaching, and to occupations aspiring to professional status, like undertakers or "funeral directors." It has, therefore, become necessary to distinguish between the "higher" professions (largely doctors and lawyers) and

The changing class pattern

	professional	employers & managers	clerical workers	foremen	manual workers
	%	%	%	%	%
1911	4.05	10.14	4.84	1.29	79.67
1921	4.52	10.46	6.72	1.44	76.85
1931	4.60	10.36	6.97	1.54	76.53
1951	6.63	10.50	10.68	2.62	69.58
1971	11.07	12.49	13.90	3.87	58.23

source: Guy Routh, *Occupation and Pay in Great Britain*, 1980 the "lower" professions (for example, librarians and social workers) and between established, marginal and new professions, such as "information technologists."

The six traits also present a rather idealised view of the professions. In his book, *Professions and Power* (1972), Terence Johnson questions the whole notion of a "true" profession, arguing that this is too uncritical of the claims made by the older professions to superior wisdom – claims made, he says, to help justify their privileged position in society. He also doubts whether altruism plays much of a role in the motivation of many professionals – it is, he says, an image used to justify high status and income in the public mind.

Certainly, the traditional view of the role of the professions in society is a rather narrow one. Back in the 1950s, for instance, American sociologists like Talcott Parsons argued that the high rewards received by professionals reflected the value of their contribution to society and the high regard in which they were held by people at large. Professionals, they said, worked in the best interests of the whole community and not just a small section. Their primary motivation was public service, rather than a desire to make money. Their behaviour was strictly controlled by a rigid code of conduct. In short, the professions – particularly those involving health, justice and education – were upholding the "central values" of society.

These assumptions have been seriously challenged in recent years. For example, Professor John Griffith in *The Politics of the Judiciary* (1977) showed that the legal profession is primarily used by the rich and powerful in order to protect their own interests. Far from representing "central values", in society, they represent the values of a wealthy elite. The high fees that lawyers have come to expect means that most people are unable to afford their services, despite legal aid schemes.

Doctors were similarly "unmasked" by Ian Kennedy in his 1980 Reith lectures, in which he challenged the status accorded to doctors in society and asked why people were willing to give up so much power to them. He quoted the case of Christiaan Barnard, the South African heart surgeon, who "filled the massive football stadium in Rio twice when he talked of how he performed the world's first heart transplant, yet the majority of his audience could not afford the simple medicine to rid themselves of their intestinal worms."

Some sociologists now take the view that professionalism is essentially a "market strategy" – a method by which certain occupational groups use their position to try to improve their market situation and thus their income. Rather like trade unions, in fact. This has been outlined in a book by Noel and José Parry (*The Rise of the Medical Profession*, 1976), in which it is argued that professionalism is "collective social mobility." Professionalism involves the restriction of entry into an occupation, the formation of an association to control the conduct of members and a monopoly in the provision of particular services. In the case of doctors and lawyers, this monopoly is backed by law.

The Parrys illustrate their argument with an historical analysis of the differing experiences of the medical profession (through the formation of the British Medical Association in 1832) and the teaching profession. To this day, the General Medical Council (founded in 1858), a self-governing body, controls the medical profession, making medicine a "classic" profession. In contrast, teachers were less successful in their attempts at professionalism and they failed to achieve the same status and rewards as doctors. Once state education became established after about 1850, teachers became relegated to a fairly lowly status: they missed their chance at becoming "professional" and their future market strategy become unionisation, hence today's National *Union* of Teachers.

Big earners in a class of their own

Professional people not only have the highest status in society, they also have the fattest pay packets.

Data on the precise incomes of doctors is notoriously hard to come by, but government and British Medical Association figures suggest the average GP earns more than £25 000 a year. This is an *average* figure, and there are big variations between regions, practices and individual doctors. An energetic doctor can earn a great deal more by taking extra surgeries and doing private work on the side. Top consultants and surgeons in hospitals often have earnings in excess of £100 000 a year.

Very few solicitors earn less than £18 000 a year, while barristers probably average £40 000 a year. Again there are big variations depending upon length of service, qualifications and type of business undertaken. A senior partner in even a local firm of solicitors might earn £50 000, while highly-specialised solicitors and company lawyers in the City of London might well be in the millionaire bracket.

Access to this big money is limited by the fact that the professions tend to be "self-recruiting." Malcolm Johnson, in *The Sociology of the Professions* (eds, Robert Dingwall and Philip Lewis, 1983), studied 497 doctors who graduated from five medical schools in London, Leeds, Liverpool and Bristol (not the top ones by any means). Some 30 per cent had been to public school, 15 per cent to direct grant schools and 48 per cent had attended grammar schools. 18 per cent had at least one parent who was a doctor and 30 per cent of those with doctor fathers went to the same medical school. Entry to medical school and the choice of medicine as a career, says Johnson, is largely determined by family and thus class influences.

Class bias is also evident in the legal profession and especially among judges. In 1977 John Griffith surveyed all the studies made of the social background of judges and found that they all came up with similar results. About 80 per cent of the judiciary came from public schools, about 80 per cent went to Oxbridge and about 80 per cent came from the upper middle-classes. In the case of high court judges, the figures are closer to 90 per cent. These proportions have held steady for a hundred years.

Griffith writes that judges are selected from practising barristers and it is very difficult for anyone without a private income to survive the first years of practice. Occasionally "the brilliant lower middle-class or working-class boy" wins through, he says, but the vast majority of successful barristers have been born into a "reasonably well-to-do family" – which has sent them to public school and Oxbridge and provided the financial backing that is vital for success.

Professionals or proles?

Several of the occupations that we would now automatically regard as middle-class and "professional" were once of lower status.

In the eighteenth century, clergymen, solicitors and surgeons were regarded as little better than tradesmen. Being a member of a "profession" was largely an arbitrary matter of, say, whether you happened to have a knowledge of Latin or a connection with the aristocracy. It wasn't until the nineteenth century – when bodies like the Royal College of Surgeons and the Institution of Civil Engineers were founded – that the professions took on the form they have today. But now, in the final quarter of the twentieth century, things may be changing again. Some sociologists have been pointing recently to the "proletarianisation" of professional workers.

This view is most closely associated with the American Marxist, Harry Braverman, whose *Labour and Monopoly Capital: The degradation of work in the twentieth century* (1974) has been very influential. Braverman's basic argument is that the professions are not only the agents of capitalism, they have also become the trained

BOOKS

Some useful additional reading:
Ian Bradley, *The English Middle Classes are Alive and Kicking,* Collins, 1982
Ian Kennedy, *The Unmasking of Medicine,* Granada, 1983
J. Westergaard & H. Resler, *Class in a Capitalist Society,* Penguin, 1976
C. Wright Mills, *White Collar,* Oxford University Press, 1951

servants of capitalism. The necessity of working for corporations in which they undertake "alienated" labour "bears the mark of the proletarian condition". The massed ranks of draughtsmen, technicians and medical ancillary staff are the new proletariat, he says.

Braverman's thesis has received a boost from the arrival of the microchip and the introduction of new technology, which has allegedly led to a further "degradation of work" in the form of de-skilling. This has affected all sorts of groups from airline pilots to draughtsmen.

Some professions have been hit by other changes in society – notably the recession. Thousands of architects are on the dole because the public building projects that burgeoned in the 1960s and 1970s have largely been brought to a halt. Compared with twenty years ago, their pay and status has slumped.

Meanwhile, white-collar unions have been quietly getting on with the job of unionising higher and higher up the occupational ladder. The 1960s and 1970s success story in trade unions was, of course, Clive Jenkin's Association of Supervisory, Technical and Managerial Staffs (ASTMS), which grew from 40000 members in 1961 to around 400000 today. Others, like APEX (clerical, computers), have also put on impressive growth.

Quite high-ranking bank staffs are joining unions in increasing numbers, while in local government, membership of NALGO includes accountants, solicitors and even chief executives. The university lecturer's union showed its teeth recently during the battle over staff cuts. Even top civil servants have their own union – the appropriately named First Division Association.

Illich – the professional scourge

By far the greatest critic of the power and prestige of the professions is the Austrian-born writer, Ivan Illich.

In a series of books over the last decade or so, including *Deschooling Society* (1971), *Celebration of Awareness* (1971), *Tools for Conviviality* (1973) and *Limits to Medicine* (1976), Illich has launched a veritable onslaught on the professions and established institutions, including the education system, health services, the church, the police and the military. He has railed against self-styled "experts" and the pretensions of those who possess "professionalised knowledge."

In *Deschooling Society,* Illich says that people learn, *despite* being forced to attend school. Pupils are "schooled" to confuse teaching with learning, examination success with education, diplomas and certificates with competence, and fluency with the ability to say something new. Self-education and education through work in the community are the best education, he says, and pouring money into the established education industry is a waste of time. Schools, he says, do nothing to correct social injustices, and they actually damage home life by supposedly relieving parents of their educational responsibilities.

After tackling the education profession, Illich broadened out his attack to all "welfare bureaucracies claiming a professional, political and financial monopoly over the social imagination, setting standards of what is valuable and what is feasible." For example, dying and death – once dealt with in the community – had now come under the institutionalised management of professionals and "looking after oneself" had come to be looked upon as irresponsible, unreliable and even subversive. "Basic needs have been translated by society into demands for scientifically-produced commodities."

In *Limits to Medicine,* subtitled *Medical Nemesis: the expropriation of health,* the medical establishment is denounced as "a major threat to health." A profession-based health care system, Illich says, is "sickening" because it actually damages people's health by the prescribing of unnecessary drugs. It obscures the political and environmental conditions that render society unhealthy and it takes out of the hands of individuals the power to heal themselves and shape their own lives. "Such medicine", he writes, "is but a device to convince those who are sick and tired of society that it is they who are ill, impotent, and in need of technical repair."

Illich believes that there is a clear need to challenge professional power and the status quo, not only in medicine, but across the wider spectrum of society. We should realise that professionalisation is tied up with the "industrial mode of production" and a "cultural revolution" is needed to free us from its grip.

RACE AND PREJUDICE

There have been black people in Britain for centuries. Today, there are 1.7 million black and Asian people in this country (more than the whole population of Northern Ireland), most of whom are immigrants. But an increasing proportion – now more than 40 per cent – were born in the United Kingdom.

The original immigrants came here to work. They came to take low-paid and low-status jobs which native white workers were reluctant to do, but which were nevertheless so indispensible to the maintenance of the economy that they had to be done. But they also came to better themselves economically.

Large-scale migration of labour in Britain was not a new phonomenon in the 1950s. The Irish had formed a substantial part of the workforce in trades such as construction from the middle of the nineteenth century onwards. What was new was that the post-war migrants were black. They faced hostility and prejudice from whites for that reason above all others.

This prejudice eventually led the British government to impose immigration controls, starting in 1962. Successive tightening of these controls ensured that, for at least twenty years, British race relations were dominated by the immigration question. It was widely argued by whites that good race relations were only possible if immigration was strictly limited. Thus the victims of racism were blamed for being the cause of it.

Modest moves to combat racial discrimination through the law began in 1965, with the passing of the first Race Relations Act. They were only partially successful. In 1968 and again in 1976, Parliament was compelled to strengthen the law. The law now outlaws "indirect" as well as "direct" discrimination; victims have rights to take their cases to industrial tribunals; and there is a government-funded enforcement body, the Commission for Racial Equality, which has powers to investigate discriminatory practices.

Nobody, though, can pretend that the law has been thoroughly successful either in eliminating discrimination or in establishing good race relations. In spite of the slowing-up of immigration, race relations have not prospered. Discrimination and disadvantage are still widely prevalent and racism has many direct and indirect manifestations in everyday life. This has led some critics to argue that there is something called "institutionalised racism" at work – either consciously or unconsciously – in many areas of British life.

In particular, attention in recent years has focused on the problem of eradicating "racial disadvantage" – the proven fact

"As long as the black man has a strong white government and a numerous white population to control him, he is capable of living as a respectable member of society" (Editorial, *The Times*, 13 November 1865).

"Tolerance does not require that every Englishman should have a black man for his neighbour" (Editorial, *The Times*, 10 July 1981).

that black people are not equal with whites in their opportunities and rewards in society. Compare blacks with whites in terms of jobs, housing, education, access to services, and the evidence shows that blacks suffer what the House of Commons Home Affairs Committee called in 1981: "a complete fabric of social and economic disadvantage."

Race and jobs: When they can get them, black people have "worse" jobs than whites and earn less, too, and the situation has not improved in recent years, while in some respects it has worsened, because of the unequal impact of the economic recession.

Black workers suffer higher unemployment than whites. They are more likely to work in the unskilled or semi-skilled sector. They are much less likely to work in non-manual jobs and to get the best managerial posts. They have to rely on shift work more than whites, and more black and Asian women are looking for work than white women.

The latest major study of race in Britain by the Policy Studies Institute attributes this to many factors: different educational backgrounds, poor command of English among some Asian workers, concentration of black and Asian workers in particular economic sectors and, not least, to racial discrimination.

The result, concludes the PSI, is that it is extremely difficult for black workers to break into new areas of employment, especially in manufacturing industry. Job expectations (rather than job aspirations) therefore become self-fulfilling, aggravating the problem of low status and low pay. "The British job market has changed little in its hostility to black workers, except that it now excludes more of them from work altogether", the report concludes. "We are left with a rigid pattern that not only has survived through the 1970s, but also shows no signs of breaking down in the near future."

Housing: All studies agree on the importance of housing conditions in reflecting and determining the pattern of race relations.

The black and Asian populations in Britain are concentrated in towns and also in particular towns and parts of towns. Moreover, Asians and West Indians have housing tenure patterns which are quite distinct from one another, as well as from white people.

Asians are more commonly found in owner-occupied housing than whites, while West Indians live more commonly in council and housing association property. Overall, though, whites live in better housing than either group. Blacks are more likely to live in flats, in worse flats and in overcrowded conditions. These differences are explained in part by differences in disposable income, but also by other factors, including discrimination.

Education: Education is one of the most crucial aspects of racial disadvantage, not least because the black population is disproportionately young.

Early concern about the failure of the education system to solve the problems of equality centred on the high numbers of West Indians who were being held back either through being classified as educationally sub-normal (which meant they

The British ethnic population

thousands

birthplace:	United Kingdom	outside United Kingdom	not stated
ethnic origin			
White	48728	1792	254
West Indian or Guyanese	248	257	4
Indian	263	513	14
Pakistani	139	210	4
Bangladeshi	26	55	1
Chinese	21	83	–
African	32	58	2
Arab	10	58	1
Mixed	149	47	1
Other	24	86	–
Not stated	656	34	261
All origins	50297	3196	541

source: Labour Force Survey, 1983.

were taken out of the mainstream) or through general "underachievement" (which meant they were diverted away from academic parts of the curriculum).

Today, though underachievement remains a major problem (and not just for West Indians), attention has shifted to providing what is seen as a more appropriate multicultural programme of teaching. Nevertheless, the report of the Swann committee on ethnic minority education concluded that racial discrimination in society at large continues to cause underachievement, and that racism within schools, both direct and indirect, is part of the explanation, too. In spite of this, all ethnic minorities retain high expectations that the education system will provide an important means of improving their status.

Civil rights: Of all the issues which sharpen the sense of unequal treatment, relations with the police are the most dramatic, particularly for young people.

Home Office research has shown that young blacks are more likely than any other group to be stopped and searched by the police. Blacks are more likely to be arrested and are more likely to be treated harshly by the courts than their white counterparts.

Black communities face other special problems from the police. Their community events – like the Notting Hill carnivals – are more heavily policed. So are their demonstrations. And Asian communities have special complaints about the role of the police in enforcing immigration law.

These grievances about what the police do are compounded by what the police are alleged not to do. In particular, they are accused of indifference towards racially-motivated crime against blacks, especially in the form of racial attacks.

A Home Office study in 1981 concluded: "The anxieties about racial attacks are justified. Racially-motivated attacks, particularly on Asians, are more common than we had supposed; and there are indications that they may be on the increase." The PSI study found "an alarmingly low level of confidence in the support from the police against racial attacks." Recent waves of such attacks suggest that this is still true.

Future trends: In spite of many efforts to roll back the tide of disadvantage and discrimination, ethnic minorities continue to suffer a worse deal than whites.

The evidence suggests that this is likely to continue. The PSI study found not only that disadvantage had increased since the 1970s, but also that expectations of improvement had fallen. In a separate PSI report, published in 1985, the authors also concluded that discrimination continues to be widespread, with "tens of thousands of acts of racial discrimination in job recruitment every year."

Part of the problem is that, by comparison with, say, the United States, the ethnic minorities form only a small part of the population. In America, several cities, including Washington DC, are majority black cities. Many other cities have extremely large black minorities which have enabled blacks to break through into high-status jobs and to win important elective offices.

Britain's blacks and Asians have no comparable strength. No single parliamentary constituency yet has a majority black electorate. The black middle class is tiny. One of the greatest problems facing the ethnic minorities' attempts to gain equality is that there are so few of them. This means that calls for positive discrimination have little leverage and that the

BOOKS

Some useful additional reading:
Colin Brown, *Black and White Britain: the third PSI survey,* Heinemann, 1984
Colin Brown and Pat Gay, *Racial Discrimination: 17 years after the Act,* Policy Studies Institute, 1985
A. Pilkington, *Race Relations in Britain,* University Tutorial Press, 1984
Martin Kettle and Lucy Hodges, *Uprising: the police, the people and the riots in Britain's cities,* Pan, 1982
Paul Gordon and Francesca Klug, *British Immigration Control: a brief guide,* Runnymede Trust, 1985

prospects for eliminating entrenched disadvantage are likely to remain poor for some time to come.

Getting the terms right

Race: The belief that human beings can be clearly catagorised on the basis of their skin colour and physiognomy has a long history. It was once widely believed, mainly by whites, that there were important mental, physical, moral and intellectual differences between black, white, brown and yellow-skinned people. This idea of race was extremely common in the nineteenth century, and many attempts were made to dignify it scientifically. It still persists to some extent, but modern genetics has destroyed such simplistic theories.

Today, few trained people use the idea of race, partly because it is so emotive. Social scientists prefer to use the more limited idea of ethnicity. But the term "race" is still popularly used in the sense of common descent, independent of language, territory or beliefs, based largely on skin colour and associated physical characteristics.

Ethnicity: The Greek word *ethnos* means a tribe. Today the term ethnic group is used to describe people who, through longstanding association of kinship, culture and, often, religion – as well as skin colour – share a common sense of identity. An ethnic group may or may not share a common territory.

The effect of the modern emphasis on ethnicity rather than race is to make the study of relations between such groups more complex, because it involves more and smaller categories. Thus, for instance, a list of Britain's racial groups would be much shorter than a list of Britain's ethnic groups, which would include Cypriots, Italians, Irish, Vietnamese and even, arguably, Welsh, Scots and English.

Racialism/Racism: These two terms are sometimes used interchangeably. However, the difference is reasonably clear. Racialism means the belief that there are significant differences between races or ethnic groups, whether these are differences of physique, intellect, morals or culture. Racism is the belief that such differences exist and that they provide grounds for treating the different groups in more and less advantageous ways. Racism is always, and racialism is sometimes, accompanied by the theory or assumption that one race or group is superior to others.

Racial disadvantage: This term is used to define the special nature of the economic and cultural deprivation suffered by members of the ethnic minorities as distinct from the deprivations of other groups within the ethnic majority. It acknowledges that there are other forms of disadvantage within society, created by, for example, class, sex and age, but recognises that there are special degrees of disadvantage which affect people because they are members of ethnic or racial groups.

Racial discrimination: This term is used to describe unequal treatment on the basis of race or ethnicity. Racial discrimination has been explicitly illegal in Britain since 1965.

According to the law, there are two types of racial discrimination. *Direct* discrimination is when a person treats a person less favourably on racial grounds. *Indirect* discrimination is when a person imposes conditions which in practice amount to treating people less favourably on racial grounds. Thus a "no blacks" rule is direct discrimination. And a "no people whose grandparents were born outside Britain" rule is indirect discrimination.

Racial prejudice: This term is used to describe the belief, without reasoned support, that members of other racial groups are different and inferior. It is therefore an important constituent of racism.

The prejudiced British

Race prejudice is alive and well and living in Britain today. So say the British people in answer to questions from opinion pollsters. What's more, prejudice is on the up.

The 1984 British Social Attitudes survey found a near-unanimity of view – among 90 per cent of the people – that there is prejudice against both black and Asian people in Britain today. Half the population thinks there is "a lot" of such prejudice.

The situation is getting worse, according to the public. Only one in six people think there is less prejudice today than there was five years ago. Only one in six thinks there will be less in five years' time.

Overall, 35 per cent of people think that they are racially prejudiced themselves. The figure is highest – 46 per cent – among Conservative voters. For both Labour and Alliance voters the figure is 28 per cent. People in England are more prejudiced than people in Scotland and Wales. White-collar workers are more prejudiced than blue-collar.

Asked whether they would mind if a close relative married a black or Asian, 54 per cent said that they would and 78 per cent said that most white people would, too. But among the 18–34 age group, there was a two-to-one majority who would not mind.

Not all surveys are pessimistic about race relations, though. A September 1985 Audience Selection poll asked: "Would Britain be a better place to live if only white people lived here?" The overwhelming majority – 80 per cent – said no; only 15 per cent said yes.

The immigration issue: Race is not an issue in Britain alone. Third World migration to the richer countries of the industrialised north is a European-wide phenomenon. France and West Germany, among others, have also encouraged an influx of immigrant labour to take low-paid and low-skill jobs.

Race is today a much bigger issue in France, for instance, than in Britain. There are four million immigrants in France, a third of them from North Africa, forming 7 per cent of the overall population. The racist National Front party polled 11 per cent of the votes in the 1984 European elections in France – far more than the similarly-named party in this country.

A recent poll of French attitudes showed that 71 per cent thought the French were racists, 65 per cent believe immigrants are an important factor in crime and 82 per cent want imprisoned immigrants to be expelled. Nearly half want unemployed immigrants expelled, too.

RELIGION

A religious revolution in Iran changes the face of Middle East politics. A Catholic-backed uprising in Poland shakes the Marxist-Leninist world. The Church of England hits the headlines when the Bishop of Durham disputes the Virgin Birth. Despite all the prophecies of its decline, religion seems very much on the agenda these days.

But what has religion got to do with sociology? Isn't belief in God a personal, spiritual matter that, by its nature, cannot be understood by science or social science? Though religion does often seem to run counter to scientific ideas, religious beliefs do not exist in a vacuum. Believers are part of society. Beliefs are acquired through contact with other members of society and have a powerful influence on people's behaviour.

Take Islam, for example. Though religion in Britain is mostly a "Sundays only" affair practised by a minority of people, Islamic countries like Saudi Arabia are suffused with it. Civil law and religious law are the same thing, and all areas of private and public life are governed by its "bible", the *Koran*. Whereas we think of religion as something "other-wordly" the Islamic code makes it very much part of this world, with its prohibition of alcohol and justification of horrendous punishments for adultery and petty theft.

Emile Durkheim, one of the first

sociologists to write about religion, goes so far as to argue that the myths and "imaginary forces" that religion inspires are, in fact, created by the collective sentiment and shared morality of people in society. In other words, when we worship God, we are really worshipping the moral order of society. Durkheim's book, *The Elementary Forms of the Religious Life* (1912), was important in showing how people are bound to society through religion.

Durkheim made a particular study of Australian aborigines and their beliefs, and argued that the earliest forms of religion began when primitive hunters got together into tribes. Their friendship and collective feelings developed into rituals, which eventually came to be regarded as holy. These rites created what he called *social solidarity*: society was held together in a shared moral order, a kind of "collective conscience."

In other words, religion is the "cement" that holds society together. This idea has been developed by later writers, notably the British anthropologist, Bronislaw Malinowski, who showed the importance of religious ritual in helping people to cope with "life crises" – situations of emotional stress that threaten the stability of society (*Magic, Science and Religion*, 1948).

Malinowski went to live among the Trobriand islanders in the South Seas and noted how religion was invoked at all the stages of life that caused anxiety – birth, adolescence, marriage and death. "The existence of strong personal attachments," he said, "and the fact of death, which of all human events is the most upsetting and disorganising to men's calculations, are perhaps the main sources of religious beliefs." Like Durkheim, he saw religion as oiling the wheels of society.

The founder of modern communism, Karl Marx, took this view as well – but with a crucial difference. Where Durkheim thought religion was necessary, Marx believed it was a kind of confidence trick. Marx agreed that the "super-natural" had no reality, that mankind had created God, and that religion somehow smoothed over people's difficulties. But he also called it "the opium of the masses." Religion, he believed, served to cover up the real injustices of social life by encouraging people to focus on the "hereafter", instead of their present condition.

Religious belief helped to keep the dominant class in control by promoting the idea that society was divinely ordered – "the rich man in his castle, the poor man at the gate." In the view of Marx and his collaborator, Frederick Engels, "the parson goes hand in hand with the landlord."

This idea still has a lot of currency in modern society. In India, the Hindu caste system has been responsible for much poverty and inequality, and in Britain, the history of the Methodist church is a good example of Marx's idea of religion as social control. One reason why John Wesley and the early Methodists were so successful was because the working classes were dissatisfied with the Church of England. Wesley brought them hope, opportunity and respectability. But though Methodism seemed to be challenging the status quo, its values in fact were those of the religious establishment. It provided an outlet for protest, while at the same time preaching the same old gospel of inequality.

The early sociologists, including Marx, were particularly interested in the development of the Protestant churches and the growth of capitalism. It was noted that from the sixteenth-century onwards, the merchant classes preferred Protestantism to Catholicism. Marx thought that the bourgeoisie "adopted" Protestantism because the rules were rather more in its own favour. Whereas the Catholic church frowned on money-lending and the accumulation of wealth, the Protestants were lax about both, and this suited business life better.

Marx's contemporary, Max Weber, was much taken by this idea, but stood it on its head. Rather than Protestantism being a creation of capitalism, it was the other way round. Weber thought that religious values could influence economic ideas. He argued that Calvinism (a type of Protestantism) had created a cultural climate which was favourable to the growth of capitalism. Calvinism preached the *Protestant ethic* of thrift and hard work, which was exactly what businessmen wanted to hear.

In *The Protestant Ethic and the Spirit of Capitalism* (1905), Weber showed that whereas the religious life of Catholics was based on prayer and devotion, the Calvinist ideal was to work hard and live simply. Hard work and success in this life meant that you would have a secure place in the next.

There is plenty of the Protestant ethic around today – indeed, it could be said to underpin Mrs Thatcher's entire political philosophy. However, in no sense could Britain be described as a religious society. The Oxford sociologist, Bryan Wilson, has talked about religion being an "optional extra", and almost everywhere the picture is of loss of interest and decline.

According to the 1851 census of religion, about forty per cent of adults in England and Wales went to church each Sunday; by 1900 this had dropped to thirty-five per cent, by 1950 to twenty per cent, while today the total is eleven per cent. In 1950, a third of all children went to Sunday school; today less than fifteen per cent do. The number of Christian churches in England has dropped by a thousand over the past decade.

The main British denominations lost an average of five per cent of churchgoers during the second half of the 1970s, with the biggest drop (of eight per cent) among Roman Catholics. Previously, this had been the only denomination showing any growth – partly because of immigration from Ireland and high birth rates. Today, the only exceptions to the general Christian decline are the small African and West Indian and Pentecostal churches.

The name sociologists give to this general loss of interest in religion is *secularisation*. But the problem with measuring secularisation and deciding how far it has gone is defining religion in the first place. Though sociologists are broadly agreed that religion is in decline, they don't agree as to what religion actually *is*. As a result, there are several different approaches to the idea of secularisation:

DECLINE IN CHURCHGOING: Smaller congregations imply that there is less interest in religion, but they don't *prove* we are less religious. In the last century, churchgoing was a convention expected by society – it wasn't necessarily any proof of deep religious conviction. Even today certain public dignitaries – such as the prime minister and the Queen – attend church regularly because they need to be seen to do so.

RELIGION AND THE STATE: In England in the Middle Ages, the state and the church were almost inseparable. The king was literally "defender of the faith", and the law of the land was God's law. Shakespeare's history plays provide a vivid picture of how bishops were as powerful as barons.

Things are very different today. Bishops still have their place in the House of Lords, but their voice is little heeded in public debate. Even forty years ago, the church had a major say in the abdication crises; recently, there have been occasions when the prime minister has been "too busy" to see the Archbishop of Canterbury. The recent row about the Church's report on the inner cities was exceptional in the amount of attention it received. As Bryan Wilson says: "To invoke God in political dispute would today be regarded as, at best, bad taste." There wasn't much mention of God during the recent Falklands war – even by church leaders themselves.

SECULARISATION OF THE CHURCHES: Another indicator of secularisation, according to some sociologists, is the way religious organisations have become more "this-worldly", rather than "other-worldly." This is also an explanation of the curious fact that religion in the United States has been relatively insulated from decline, compared with every other country in the western world. (Four out of ten Americans today are still regular churchgoers). As the American sociologist, Will Herberg, has pointed out, religion has survived because beliefs have been adapted to fit in with those of the wider society. Unlike the situation in Britain, religious values are broadly "American values".

Two other American sociologists, Peter Berger and Thomas Luckmann, have shown how this has happened. Religious leaders have gone out and sold their "product", adapting it to the demands of the consumer. If that meant "diluting" religion for a more secular society, then they were prepared to do so. In contrast, European churches have stuck more rigidly to their values and have been largely left behind by a changing society.

ECUMENISM: Bryan Wilson has suggested that the desire for church unity is a symptom of secularisation. In the summer of 1982, the Pope preached alongside the Archbishop of Canterbury in Canterbury cathedral – something that would have been unthinkable twenty-five years ago. Wilson interprets this sort of thing as a sign of weakness – ecumenism is not popular when churches themselves are strong.

DE-SACRILISATION: According to Weber, one of the by-products of the neat dovetailing of the Calvinist religion with the practical worldly concerns of its adherents, was that people were becoming more *rational*. The rise of the rational religious ethic meant that the world was becoming a less "enchanted", mystical or sacred place. Our actions are guided less and less by "sacred" considerations.

The development of modern science has aided this *de-sacrilisation process*. Darwin shattered the creation myth, and Freud laid bare areas of human psychology, showing that God wasn't the only influence on the human psyche. Society today no longer seems to be dependent on divine will, but on social planning. We can create babies in test-tubes, make rain in the desert, bring the "dead" to life with heart transplants, or destroy the entire human race with the push of a button. None of these things is thought of any longer as a "miracle", or "God's work".

But could it be that sociologists have been taking too narrow a view of what religion is? One of the broadest modern definitions is by Peter Berger and Thomas Luckmann, who see religion simply as the manifestation of identity, meaning and purpose in people's lives. Luckmann has suggested that what we are experiencing is not necessarily *less* religion, but a shift from a narrow, institutional religion to a wider, private one.

There is certainly plenty of evidence of people's yearning for spiritual fulfilment. Though some of the new quasi-religious groups may be oddballs, like the Hare Krishna movement, or involve dubious activities, like the Moonies or the Scientologists, there is no shortage of recruits. Nor have people given up believing in God. A recent Gallup survey into the religious beliefs of the British found that seventy-three per cent believed in God and fifty-three per cent in heaven. More than one person in four believed in reincarnation.

Even more significantly, David Hay, of the Religious Experiences Research Unit at Nottingham University, says that "at a minimum, well over a third of all women and just under a third of all men in Great Britain claim to have had some sort of religious experience".

In their research, Hay and his colleagues used a scale for the measurement of "psychological well-being" and found that "religious experiencers" were more likely to be balanced and personally happy than other people. There have been similar findings in the United States. Robert Wuthnow, of Princeton University, reported that among a large sample of residents in the San Francisco Bay area of California, people claiming contact with the sacred were less materialistic, less status-conscious, showed more social concern and found life had more meaning than others.

It could be that religion in the western world today is a more positive influence than we think.

Who goes to church, anyway?

Though Britain can't be described as a religious society, there is a certain pattern to religion in terms of age, sex, class and geography:

AGE: On the whole, older people are more religious than younger. In terms of actually going to church, the pattern shows a peak period up to the age of fifteen, then a general loss of interest up to the age of thirty. During the thirties and forties, enthusiasm picks up again, and there is another peak between forty-five and sixty-five.

Attendance rates drop again for retired people, but this is more to do with decreased mobility than loss of faith. It is perhaps significant that more young people under fifteen are involved in church activities than might be expected from their share of the total population. Young people account for twenty-six per cent of total church attendance in England, compared with only twenty-one per cent of the total population.

SEX: Women are more likely to be involved in religion than men. In Anglican churches, this is only marginally the case, but among Christian Science churches, women outnumber men by four to one. One social psychologist, Michael Argyle, has suggested that women are more likely than men to have feelings of guilt, and are thus attracted to churches that offer salvation. Another suggestion has been that women's religious interest has to do with their social roles – working women, for instance, are less likely to become involved in religion.

CLASS: In general, church attendance and professed religious belief is higher among the middle class than the working class. The Church of England has been called "the Tory Party at prayer," and there is some truth in this. Sociologists have also found that the more established and "mainstream" a religion is, the more likely it is to attract the middle classes. Fringe churches and sects are more likely to draw working-class congregations. But there are exceptions: Roman Catholics are more likely to be working-class and Quakers to be middle-class.

This class orientation is reflected in voting patterns. Thus, Anglicans tend to vote Tory and Catholics to vote Labour, as do many Methodists, because of the church's links with the rise of the Labour Party.

GEOGRAPHY: Religious participation varies widely according to where people live. For instance, thirty-five per cent of adults in Merseyside and thirty-two per-cent in Lancashire are church members, compared with only nine per cent in Humberside and eleven per cent in Nottinghamshire. One obvious reason for this is immigration: Liverpool has a big population of Irish Catholics, just as north London has its Jews, and Bradford its Moslems and Sikhs.

But internal migration plays a part, too. When the Scottish steel firm, Stewarts and Lloyds, moved to the east midlands town of Corby at the beginning of the century, they brought with them a skilled Scottish workforce. These people set up their own Presbyterian churches, establishing a free church tradition that has lasted to this day.

Denomination, sect or cult?

Why are some religious organisations called churches while others are best described as denominations, sects or cults? The sorts of definitions that sociologists might use are as follows:

A CHURCH is a stable and formal organisation of religious believers. It is generally integrated with other social institutions – the state, the schools and the family – and has an organised clerical hierarchy and a fixed body of doctrine and dogma that ties in with the accepted beliefs of society. In Britain, the most obvious example of this is the Anglican church, which is formally aligned with the state, and has the Queen as its head.

A DENOMINATION is one of a number of minority religious organisations that are broadly considered acceptable by society. Unlike a church, a denomination generally avoids any formal connection with the state, though its members usually come from a representative cross-section of society.

Protestant denominations in Britain range in size from the Methodists, with 477 000 regular churchgoers, to the United Reformed Church, with 139 000.

A SECT is smaller and less formally organised than a church or denomination. It is often insular in outlook and sometimes at odds with the beliefs of society as a whole. It is common for sects to have few or no officials, with organisation left to members themselves, who tend to come from the lower occupational classes.

Sects are usually formed by people protesting about established religion straying from the "correct" teaching and are often very puritanical in outlook, such as the Jehovah's Witnesses, the Mormons and the Plymouth Brethren.

CULTS are similar to sects, except that they are more concerned with finding new ways to salvation rather than returning to old ones. They are often based around the discovery of a new "prophet", such as the Rev. Sun Myung Moon of the "Moonies", or the Rev. Jim Jones of the People's Temple, who encouraged 900 people to commit suicide in a Guyanan jungle.

BOOKS

Some useful additional reading:
M. Argyle and B. Beit Hallahmi, *The Social Psychology of Religion*, Routledge & Kegan Paul, 1975
P. Glasner, *The Sociology of Secularisation*, Routledge & Kegan Paul, 1976
T. Luckmann, *The Invisible Religion*, Macmillan, 1967
R. Robertson (ed.), *The Sociology of Religion*, Penguin, 1969
B. Wilson, *Contemporary Transformations of Religion*, Oxford University Press, 1976

THE RICH

One of the most potent images associated with Mrs Thatcher in the popular imagination is that of the humble grocer's daughter, brought up thriftily above a small-town corner shop. So different from the usual kind of wealthy Tory with interests in big business or land.

But, much as the Prime Minister enjoys fostering this image, it is not entirely accurate. Mrs Thatcher and her husband are, in fact, millionaires. In 1965, Denis Thatcher sold his family firm to Burmah Oil for a price equivalent to about £3 million today. Quite apart from any other wealth they might have, this puts the Thatchers (along with other millionaire members of the government, including the deputy prime minister, Viscount Whitelaw) very firmly among the rich elite in Britain today.

Not that the Labour Party has been much truer to *its* image as champion of the poor and powerless. In 1952, the social historian, R. H. Tawney, wrote that the political programme of social democratic reform introduced by Labour in the post-war period had produced distinct advances "towards the conversion of a class-ridden society into a community in fact as well as name." As events turned out, nothing of the kind has happened.

In 1979, at the end of the last Labour government, the Royal Commission on the Distribution of Income and Wealth (the Diamond Commission) reported that the share of wealth owned by the bottom 50 per cent of the population had hardly changed in thirty years. Apart from some adjustments at the top end of the scale, the gap between rich and poor was as wide as ever.

Not surprisingly, perhaps, information on the rich is hard to come by, and not very reliable. The most sustained attempt to fill the gap was the Diamond Commission, but this was wound up by Mrs Thatcher in 1979 on the grounds that it encouraged "the politics of envy." Investigations of wealth now are limited to the Inland Revenue's statistics of estates, which give an idea of how much people possess when they die, or looking at people's income from investments, and then trying to work out the assets on the basis of the income.

Whatever system of calculation is used, the ownership of wealth in Britain today remains chronically unequal. This is the picture, based on the Inland Revenue's 1982 figures:
● The top 1 per cent of individuals own 21 per cent of marketable wealth (i.e. things that can be bought and sold – housing, land, stocks and shares, etc.).
● The top 5 per cent own 41 per cent of marketable wealth.
● The bottom fifty per cent own just four per cent of marketable wealth.

Though this may seem surprising in a democratic society, the shareout is, on the face of it, less unequal than in the quite recent past. In 1950, for instance, the top 1 per cent owned 47 per cent of wealth. In 1923 this top 1 per cent had 60 per cent of the wealth. But the redistribution is not quite all it seems. If you look at the table, you can see that although the share of the top 1 per cent has fallen drastically, the top 2–5 per cent have more or less retained their slice of the cake since the 1920s. As A. B. Atkinson remarks in his book, *Unequal Shares* (1974): "It seems that what redistribution there has been is not between the rich and the poor, but between the rich and the rich."

Another factor that misleadingly affects the redistribution picture is the increase in home ownership. Owner-occupiers – up from 30 per cent of the population in 1951 to 60 per cent today – form an increasing proportion of wealth-owners. Not only that, but house prices have done rather better against inflation in recent years than stocks and shares. Consequently, houses now form a much bigger proportion of total wealth than shares. But here it is important to distinguish between different forms of ownership.

Tawney talked about two kinds of control which wealth confers:

● Property for use
● Property for power.

In the first category come owner-occupied houses and things like cars, freezers and dishwashers. Even if you own a house worth £250000 with a dream kitchen, it's not much use as a source of personal income or profit unless you choose to sell it and live in a tent. As for consumer goods, they decline in value from the moment they leave the shop. But property in the second category is different, for it includes factories, farming and building land, and stocks and shares. This *productive* property can provide massive unearned income and is overwhelmingly still concentrated among the very rich. For instance, the top 10 per cent own 37 per cent of the housing but 90 per cent of the privately-owned shares and 85 per cent of the land. By contrast, the bottom 90 per cent, who own 63 per cent of the houses, own only 10 per cent of shares and 15 per cent of the land.

While it's hard to provide accurate statistics about the rich as a group, it's even more difficult to pin down precise information about them individually. It's not much use looking at income alone, since this isn't necessarily related to how rich you are. For instance, the former Beatle, Paul McCartney, is reckoned to be Britain's top earner – his £25 million-a-year income works out at £68493 a day. But he is very much less wealthy than, say, the Prince of Wales, whose personal income is a fraction of McCartney's but who has vast landholdings in Cornwall and London. Compared with their 21 per cent of wealth, the top 1 per cent have only 5 per cent of total income, even before tax.

Research by historians does show, though, that the rich are *not* on the whole, self-made men like, say, the publisher Robert Maxwell, or the computer tycoon, Sir Clive Sinclair.

This has been demonstrated by Professor C. D. Harbury, who compared the wills of men leaving large sums in selected years from the 1950s to the 1970s with those of their fathers, traced through probate and birth registration records at Somerset House. Harbury found that 60 per cent of men leaving £100000 or more

since the 1950s had rich fathers. And some three-quarters of these had fathers whose fortunes were ten times the amount that would have included them among the richest 10 per cent of the population.

The Cambridge sociologist, Anthony Giddens, believes that there are three main categories of rich people in Britain today. These might be loosely termed the "jet set" rich, who made their money out of the media, sport and entertainment, the land-owning rich and the "entrepreneurial rich", whose money resides in companies and stocks and shares. (In all, this is not a great body of people. The top 1 per cent, for instance, is roughly equivalent to the crowd at Epsom on a fine Derby Day.)

THE JET SET. Rock singers like Simon le Bon and Mick Jagger, or writers like Frederick Forsyth, form by far the smallest category of the rich. There seem to be a lot of them about only because they get the most exposure in the press. But such fortunes can be precarious: George Best and John Conteh are both once-rich sportsmen who went bankrupt.

THE LANDOWNERS are typified perhaps by this news item from the *Daily Mail* of 12 August 1983: "The Duke of Roxburgh, 28, will be up at the crack of dawn today, potting the defenceless birds that become fair game on the Glorious Twelfth. Those shot on his 60000-acre grouse moor at Lammermuirs will be available for breakfast at his hotel near Floors Castle . . ."

Though the "landed gentry" seem often to be something of an anachronism and a joke, and though many aristocratic estates have been broken up because of economic pressures, they still include some very rich individuals indeed. Altogether, the landed aristocracy owns some 40 per cent of Britain's land, compared with 19 per cent owned by government and local authorities, and 1 per cent owned by the church and crown.

The fortune of the richest man in Britain, Gerald Grosvenor, sixth Duke of Westminster, derives from his landholdings. Grosvenor, who is 33 and has two

O-levels, owns 138000 of the world's most exclusive acres, including 300 acres of Belgravia, Mayfair and Westminster, 13000 acres at his ancestral home in Cheshire, and 100000 acres in Scotland. These riches are almost entirely a combination of inheritance and luck. The sixth duke inherited from his father, who inherited down the line from his ancestor, Sir Thomas Grosvenor. In 1677 Sir Thomas married one Mary Davies, who provided as her dowry some soggy acres of farmland in Mayfair. This was to become one of the most expensive slices of real estate in the world.

THE ENTREPRENEURIAL RICH. Even though the real value of stocks and shares has declined in recent years, especially in relation of housing and land, they still represent the most important kind of wealth and the most unevenly distributed of any kind of property. The share capital of companies is important because, in addition to their surrender value and the dividends they produce, they also confer control over the main productive resources of society. It is this entrepreneurial group of the rich about which least is known, and who are least in the public eye.

If you exclude the recent floating-off of British Telecom, only 7 per cent of British adults own shares, and within this small group, there is an even greater concentration. Just 1 per cent of shareholders own over 80 per cent of privately-held shares, while 5 per cent own 98 per cent of the total.

Despite the image of large companies as "faceless corporations", many major British firms are controlled by directors with very large personal shareholdings. This is particularly true where there is a "family" connection. Some of Britain's richest families are directly associated with some of the most prosperous firms. These include the Guinness family (brewing), the Cadbury family (confectionery), the Cowdray family (banking and publishing), the Pilkington family (glass), the Sieff family (Marks and Spencer), the Vestey family (meat) and the Forte family (hotels and catering).

Of course, the landowning aristocracy and the entrepreneurial rich are not completely separate groups in society: Lord Sainsbury is not so different from Lord Salisbury. One of the key features in the perpetuation of a wealthy elite in Britain has been the merging of a new bourgeoisie with the traditional aristocracy. This process, maintained through marriage and attendance at select public schools and universities, has helped to ensure that wealth is transmitted successfully across the generations. It is even possible for the newly rich to buy their way into traditional respectability. Lord Nuffield (former motor mechanic), Lord Wolfson (former retailer) and David Robinson (former television rentals man) have all endowed Oxbridge colleges. "The old money", as Giddens says, "absorbs the new".

So why, amid the many social democratic reforms that have taken place since the war, have attempts at the redistribution of wealth failed so markedly? There have been promises enough. In 1974, Denis Healey said: "We will squeeze the rich until the pips squeak". Later, when the last Labour government introduced the "social contract" with the unions, it promised to "bring about a fundamental shift in the balance of power and wealth in favour of working people and their families".

But none of it materialised. The director of the Low Pay Unit, Chris Pond, has suggested that this is partly because the size and scale of wealth "defies comprehension", thus making it difficult to organise a political campaign against it. Another explanation is given by John Westergaard and Henrietta Resler in *Class in a Capitalist Society* (1976): "Taxation and public welfare provision have done little to alter the broad pattern of material inequality, because the objectives and effects of public policy are limited by the needs and influence of business in an economy where private enterprise continues to play the predominant role".

Certainly, Labour governments have brought in only very limited reforms, and these have been vigorously opposed by organisations like the CBI. Little has been done to change, for instance, the "unprogressive" nature of our tax system.

What the British are worth

Distribution of personal wealth

In 1982, the total of marketable wealth in the UK amounted to £602 billion. This is how it was divided up (with earlier years for comparison):

% of wealth owned by:	England and Wales			United Kingdom			
	1923	1938	1950	1966	1971	1978	1982
	%	%	%	%	%	%	%
most wealthy 1 per cent	60.9	55.0	47.2	33.0	30.5	23	21
most wealthy 5 per cent	82.0	76.9	74.3	55.7	51.8	44	41
most wealthy 10 per cent	89.1	85.0	—	68.7	65.1	58	56
most wealthy 25 per cent	—	—	—	86.9	86.5	83	81
most wealthy 50 per cent	—	—	—	96.5	97.2	95	96
least wealthy 50 per cent	—	—	—	3.5	2.8	5	4

source: Trevor Noble, *Structure and Change in Modern Britain* (1981), and Inland Revenue

(A progressive tax system is one where the tax rates increase with the sums taxed.) Between 1959 and 1975, the average tax value paid by 90 per cent of the population more than doubled, while the richest 10 per cent faced increases of 25 per cent and the richest 1 per cent increases of only 10 per cent. Nothing was done, either, to alter the large proportion of taxes that are flat-rate.

Perhaps the most potentially radical Labour reform was the introduction of Capital Transfer Tax – in effect, a tax to be paid when wealth was transferred. But the law was riddled with loopholes. By the time of the 1979 election, it was producing only 2 per cent of tax revenue – less than the old estate duty which it replaced.

No wealth tax – one that taxes people on what they own rather than what they acquire or pass on – has ever been introduced in Britain (probably the nearest thing we have to it is local authority rates). Most EEC countries have one, though, and, indeed, it is the oldest kind of tax, dating from the days when a man was assessed on the number of fields and cattle he owned. But it's very hard to make a wealth tax work effectively. You can't, for instance, hide stocks and shares from the taxman, but diamonds and Krugerrands can be slipped into the attic. Such a tax might, therefore, make people pull out of industrial investments.

And what would happen to forestry plantations and agricultural land, which would probably have to be exempted from such a tax? The result would most likely be that wealthy tax-avoiders would buy into farms. Farmers who already owned land would make a windfall gain, which could only be realised by selling out to tax-dodging tycoons and giving up their jobs.

A sensible alternative might be a "gift tax", which, unlike Capital Transfer Tax, would be levied on the recipients rather than the donors of wealth. This could be made progressive, so that the more gifts a person received over, say ten years, the higher the rate of tax. This might encourage the very rich who are trying to reduce their tax burden to give away their money to people who are not already wealthy.

But there is almost no chance of such a reform being introduced in Britain today. The overall effect of the taxation measures introduced since the Conservatives came to power in 1979 has been that the rich have got richer and the poor poorer. (You can argue that cutting taxes provides the incentives that encourage more people to try to get rich, but that's a different story.) Over the lifetime of the 1979–83 Conservative government, it has been estimated that £2030 million was taken from the poor through cost-saving measures, like abolishing earnings-related unemployment benefit. On the other hand, the rich benefited to the tune of £2405 million through tax concessions.

Mrs Thatcher has defended the principle of individual wealth by citing the case of the Good Samaritan. "No one would remember the Good Samaritan," she said, "if he'd only had good intentions. He had money as well." But according to psychologists, having money isn't always good for you. In his book, *The Privileged Ones* (1981), the child psychologist, Robert Coles, talks about the confusion, restlessness and insecurity experienced by children of wealthy parents: "Obviously, there are certain advantages to being rich, such as better health, education and future work prospects. But most important is the quality of family life. Money can't buy love."

It can't, by all accounts, buy happiness, either. According to an Opinion Research Centre poll for *The Times* in 1980, only 4 per cent of people in Britain wanted to have £1 million or more. And 24 per cent said they were happy with their lot.

If the "politics of envy" ever existed in Britain, they do not appear to be a very powerful force today. In a recent poll, *The Sunday Times* asked people whether they thought property and possessions worth more than £150000 should be subject to a wealth tax. Only 32 per cent said yes. Chesterton's remark about the oligarchic character of the British is still true: "It does not rest on the cruelty of the rich to the poor. It does not even rest on the kindness of the rich to the poor. It rests on the perennial and unfailing kindness of the poor to the rich."

BOOKS

Some useful additional reading:
Counter Information Services, *The Wealthy*, 1980
William Davies, *The Rich*, Sidgwick & Jackson, 1982
Frank Field, *The Wealth Report*, Routledge & Kegan Paul, 1983

The wealthy pensioners?

Some economists, when looking at redistribution, count in people's pension rights as part of their "wealth". This certainly changes the figures dramatically. If you include state and occupational pension rights, the top 1 per cent own 11 per cent, instead of 21 per cent of the wealth. And the bottom 50 per cent of people own as much as 22 per cent of the total, instead of 4 per cent.

But there is a lot of argument about how comparable pension rights are to other forms of wealth. How far, for instance, are pension funds "owned" by people who contribute to them? Certainly, the vast assets that are controlled by the funds – including over half the shares of quoted British companies – do not appear in the statistics as belonging to any individual. In this sense, they belong to ordinary working people. Yet these people have little say in how their "wealth" is controlled and invested – certainly not in the way Tiny Rowland might buy and sell companies or the Duke of Devonshire farmland.

For a start, most pension funds are controlled by the merchant banks and insurance companies, and not by representatives of the eleven million people who finance them. Though employee representatives are becoming more common, they usually have little power or expertise, as Tom Schuller and Jeff Hyman found out in a recent survey. One employee-representative they interviewed was quoted as saying: "There I was, supposed to be making a £2 million investment decision, and me wondering if I had 20p for the bus fare home."

Partly for this reason, the funds have been criticised for not using the "wealth" of ordinary working people in their best long-term interests. For instance, pension funds poured money into the ailing property boom at the beginning of the 1970s, helping to keep property values artificially high. In 1977, believing that interest rates were about to rise, the funds got together and refused to buy government securities. In effect, they forced interest rates up and this in turn forced the government to pay more to service its borrowing, leaving less to spend on socially useful projects.

ROCK MUSIC

Frankie says Relax. And the advice of the 1984 super-group is worth heeding when applying the concepts and methods of sociology to rock music.

Frankie's catchphrase reminds us (in the words of the sociologist, Simon Frith) that "the essence of rock is fun." Much is ephemeral. Heard in snatches on badly-tuned radios or at disco decibel, socially meaningful lyrics can pass by unnoticed.

The conceptual heavy artillery of class, culture and capitalism may miss the fact that rock is sound and rhythm to dance to, drive to, make love to. Musical taste is fickle. Who can satisfactorily explain why, for example, the 1978 melodic dirge, *Mull of Kintyre,* appealed simultaneously to so many people (and became the biggest selling single ever released in Britain)?

Paul McCartney, who actually wrote and performed it, certainly can't. In a radio interview he said, "Music isn't words. If you can talk about it, then it wouldn't be music." This "subjective" view of rock music is often expressed in the musical weeklies, like *New Musical Express* or the *Melody Maker,* and the fanzines where rock performers and composers are often talked about as "artists" in language borrowed from nineteenth-century romanticism. This way of looking at rock music allows no social influences (like money or the availability of Musicians' Union-approved session men) to colour the purity of the work.

The same note is frequently struck by rock musicians themselves. Frank Zappa, the self-consciously innovative founder of the 1960s group, Mothers of Invention, contrasted his "creative action" with "a commercial pile of shit thrown together by business people who think they know what John Doe and Mrs Jones really want."

But it's not always enough to take music at its face value. The example of Frankie Goes To Hollywood is instructive. Their hit single, *Relax,* was released in October 1983; but it was not a certified hit till February 1984, by which time there had been significant spending on promotion and the unfailing guarantee of a ban on BBC Radio One. Frankie don't play live: their sound is made only in a studio. Their producer, Paul Morley, is credited with thinking up the gimmicks, the T-shirts and slogans and the image of overt sexuality (hetero- and homosexual).

The "creation" of rock groups is, of course, not new. One of the most famous examples of this was the Monkees – an "instant" pop group formed in the United States in the mid-1960s as a kind of ersatz Beatles. Taken to an extreme, this line of thought sees rock music as what sociologists would call an *epiphenomenon* – a spin-off from the social forces within capitalist society that own and control business, including the record business, and manipulate taste in the name of profit. An important influence here has been the German sociologist, Theodor Adorno, a leading light of the Frankfurt School. From his continental Marxist perspective, Adorno saw all mass popular music as "banality, relentlessly controlled in order to make it saleable."

Rock music, according to this perspective, may provide its youthful customers with the illusion of freedom from the dominant culture, but examined from the balance sheets of EMI or CBS, it dovetails neatly with the interests of British or American capital.

It was inevitable, sociologists of this school would argue, that sooner or later Johnny Rotten – for all the apparent anti-establishment nihilism of the Sex Pistols – would concede: "Yeah, you have to put yourself down as a company or else they'll fucking fleece you for every halfpenny you've got."

What appear to be autonomous cultural choices by young people, in clothes and in music, are, on this view, a sham. Ian Taylor and David Wall (in *Working-Class Youth Culture,* edited by Geoff Mungham and Geoff Pearson, 1976) argue that "the sense of classlessness conveyed by much contemporary pop music and youth cultural style is merely a reflection of the creation in a consumer-capitalist society of a one-dimensional economic product for universal consumption."

But is this really true? If Bob Siner, for instance, could manipulate public taste that easily he would be a wealthier man than he is. Siner is president of MCA Records, part of the Universal Studios films conglomerate. On one famous occasion, he announced that he had counted the factors that determine the success of a single record. "On reaching 4200," he said, "I gave up."

Give or take a few hundred, Siner was right. Similarly, the rise in the 1970s of punk music was not ordered by some clever record executive: it resulted from a spontaneous expression of taste. Making a record requires innumerable choices, governed by money, musicians' abilities and record company strategy as well as artistic inspiration.

The sociology of rock, in other words, needs to be pluralist. It has to marry economics (in 1979 the American record industry proudly announced that it had achieved a dollar turnover greater than the gross national product of Burma) and culture.

Sociologists also have had to wed such disparate things as:
● Individual creativity and mass consumption
● Demography (the birth of rock coincided with the postwar baby boom) and ethnic identity
● British exports (35 per cent of singles now selling in the US market are British) with American exports (rhythm and blues)
● The influence of society on music and the effect of a song – for example The Who's *My Generation* – on society.

Adorno's "mass communications" perspective is correct insofar as rock music is generally a product manufactured by large companies for a mass audience. But the industry differs from other capitalistic enterprises in important respects.

In 1979, for instance, the rock industry suffered its equivalent of the great stock market crash of 1929. The EMI conglomerate (responsible for about a fifth of the albums sold in the United Kingdom) saw profits slump from £32 million in 1977 to only £1.8 million, through a combination of high costs and a sharp fall in sales.

Sales fell because of the recession and the failure of most of the industry to come up with products as attractive as *Saturday Night Fever* – the multi-media (film, album, singles) package, which made the fortune of the German-American firm, Polygram.

In a sense, the history of the rock business since 1980 has been the search by the major firms (EMI, CBS, WEA and Phonogram together have over 50 per cent of the British market for albums) for artists that can be packaged as successfully as the Bee Gees. Michael Jackson with *Thriller,* and new artists such as Boy George and Madonna, have been hailed as the industry's salvation. But no one can ever be sure whether the momentum can be maintained.

The problem is that, though the record companies have great economic power, it is limited by the way the market operates. Of the 3000 or so singles released each year, 400 at most can be expected to reach the Top 40 charts. Promotion by advertising has grown in importance, but outlets for "new product" are still narrow: BBC radio disc jockeys can be bought lunch and dinner by record promoters, but the rules strictly govern any other influences.

The "big business" side of rock music also sits uneasily with the fact that its social identity is still predominantly working-class. Among the performers, Roger Daltrey of The Who (skilled manual; metal-working apprentice before full-time musician) is more typical than Mick Jagger (father a schoolteacher, himself a college student). Some writers have detected a parallel between the musical roots of rock among American blacks and its appeal to modern, white, working-class young people. Simon Frith argues that rock music has been a vehicle for feelings of liberation from the drudgery of work, yet, he says, those feelings tend to give rise to a sense of rootlessness and estrangement from the wider community. "This paradox – leisure as an experience of freedom so intense that it became, simultaneously, an experience of loneliness – is rooted in the working-class experience of work, in alienation", Frith writes.

To compensate for its deficiencies in other respects, the record industry tries its best to package the consumer. For instance, record executives haven't missed the fact that the baby-boom generation who fuelled the pop music explosion of the 1950s are still busy buying records, so the search is on for a "sound" that will best appeal to ageing rockers. The industry relies on the continuing productivity of such artists as the Rolling Stones and the Kinks, the promotion of new/old rockers such as Bruce Springsteen, and has devised new categories such as "soft rock".

Simon Frith argues that the "industrial power structure" tries to freeze consumer choice in order to manage it better. "Record companies, radio programmers, music papers, deejays, writers, all attempt to define and categorise musical demands and so ease the processes of meeting them."

But this argument, which is an extension of what Adorno was saying, assumes that audiences for rock music are always somehow passive. An important corrective to this way of thinking comes from the "subculture school", which looks at such leisure groupings as punks, Teddy Boys, Rastas and skinheads and describes the way in which particular kinds of music are chosen as the badge of the group. For example, the variants on reggae in recent years – rapping or the music for break-dancing and so on – were not dreamed up by the record industry; they emerged from the black communities themselves.

Dick Hebdige writes that "subcultures are expressive forms [and] what they express is a fundamental tension between those in power and those condemned to subordinate positions and second-class lives."

But this doesn't mean that the music of subcultures cannot be rich and various. Subcultures may, as Hebdige argues, serve as points of reference for resistance to the "symbolic order" of society. But they are also looser arrangements for lei-

Talkin' 'bout my generation

Traditionally, popular music has used three modes of expression – sentimental, melodramatic, and trivial-novelty. Although the majority of popular songs have nominally been about love, rarely have they attempted to confront either the emotional or the physical reality of love relationships: *love, adore, care, need, want* were used as substitutes for expressing feeling, with dramatic overstatement or narcissistic simplification. *Charms* was the universal descriptive term, which simultaneously invoked the loved one's physical attractiveness and his or her personality. Singers were not concerned with real relationships, and their songs did not seem to be located in any real physical context.

Only by determined resistance to this fare did the audience of the mid-fifties force the music industry to provide something else: rock 'n' roll. Drawn in varying proportions from the music of southern country singers and northern city singers, rock 'n' roll was an improbable cultural mixture that had magical effects on those who heard it, whether in the form of Chuck Berry chiding, "Maybellene, why can't you be true", or Gene Vincent wailing in tortured delight, "Well, Be-Bop-A-Lula, She's My Baby."

Cars, streets, suede shoes, alleys, hotels, motels, freeways, juke boxes, stations, parties, and parents provided the context in which singers began to consider love that not only had physical aspects but also was not inevitably eternal.
– Charlie Gillett, *The Sound of the City*, Souvenir Press, 1983

sure enjoyment. Instead of a single national chart of favourite records, the musical weeklies are nowadays a tissue of different selections from "northern soul" to "indie singles" to the chart of "hippy favourites" played by certain specialist discos.

It's important to remember that rock music, which may occasionally be a battleground of ideology and social class, is primarily an arena for play and for the exercise of free choice.

"Born in the virgin fifties from the dangerous mating of American slave rhythm-

and-blues and white country song structure, made manifest in proto-youth Presley, resurrected in Liverpool, prospered in Woodstock and 'underground', sank without trace in the seventies (except for Springsteen) then reappeared, raw and bleeding as Johnny Rotten swore his head off during a Bill Grundy television interview."

This is one writer's potted history of rock. As well as being a part of popular music, rock is a series of myths. Intellectuals (rather than record buyers) have fostered a mythic post-war history full of heroes (Bob Dylan, Jim Morrison) and villains (Elvis Presley selling out to Hollywood). The myth has itself become part of popular culture, the subject of song (as in Don Maclean's *American Pie*) and such films as *American Graffiti* and *American Hot Wax,* which tells the story of the New York disc jockey, Alan Freed, who allegedly gave rock 'n' roll its name and was hounded by the establishment.

The basis of the rock myth is demographic. Because child-bearing was delayed by the Second World War, both Britain and the United States had very large teenage populations in the later 1950s and 1960s. Economic growth in both countries led to an expansion of both leisure time and expenditure. The record industry was a prime beneficiary.

Rock music can be defined, in a neutral sense, as popular music produced specifically for a youth market. In this sense rock was born in the later 1950s when the major American record companies, seeing the success of smaller labels with black-influenced music, launched such regional performers as Elvis Presley and Buddy Holly nationally.

But during the 1960s, a decade of rapidly expanding higher education and (still) continuing economic growth, rock became, for some, the teenage group's means of collective self-expression. Bob Dylan, the Rolling Stones, the Beatles, The Who, semi-consciously produced music to stand as anthems for youth – expressing dissatisfaction (*I Can't Get No Satisfaction*); a vague sense of belonging (*My Generation*) and formless revolt (*Subterranean Homesick Blues*).

The function of popular music has not received much notice from sociologists, who perversely have spent more time assessing the impact of television, despite the fact that many people from the ages of ten to 25 are more heavily exposed to radio and records. For many people in this age group, popular music provides a sense of change, as records and styles replace each other in the instant history of the hit parades.

At any time in this history, each listener has a few records that enrich his feelings, extend his sense of love or despair, and feed his fantasies or fire some real relationship. He switches on the radio and waits for his music, or buys the records and plans his own programme of moods. – Charlie Gillett, *The Sound of the City,* Souvenir Press, 1983

Scholars of the history of rock, like the British writer Charlie Gillett, have concentrated on the way a white youth culture absorbed – some would say stole – the lyrical inflections of blacks. The high-gloss, "safe" music of Tamla Motown and the soul singers ran an interesting counterpoint to the dangerous music of the white "rebels" during the 1960s. Some writers, focusing on the shock value of such performers as Chuck Berry, Jerry Lee Lewis and Gene Vincent (perhaps also Tommy Steele and Cliff Richard in Britain) refer to "the few short years that composed original rock'n'roll."

The cross-fertilisation between the

BOOKS

Some useful additional reading:
Simon Frith, *Sound Effects: youth, leisure, and the politics of rock'n'roll,* Constable, 1983
Dick Hebdige, *Subculture: the meaning of style,* Methuen, 1979
Dave Marsh, *Before I Get Old: the story of The Who,* Plexus, 1983
David Pichaske, *A Generation in Motion; popular music and culture in the sixties,* Schirmer, 1979
Fred and Judy Vermorel, *The Sex Pistols: the inside story,* Star Books, 1978
Paul Willis, *Profane Culture,* Routledge & Kegan Paul, 1978

United States and Britain continued past 1970 but the rock mythologists tend to bracket the decade of the sixties off. As the American author, David Pichaske, wrote: "The legacy of the sixties – experimentation, vision, generosity, candour, and impatience with injustice – is still with us. What is gone is the sense of public emotion that made the generation act together, made them march and say decisively 'Now'." (Pichaske fosters the rock myth by using the word "generation". Demographically, the number of demonstrators, acid-takers or even Dylan album listeners was at no time large enough to be called a generation.)

Rock critics did not like the early and mid-1970s because much popular music was deemed to be insincere and superficial. Performers such as David Bowie were thought too personal or too glamorous; the Bay City Rollers were dismissed as "teeny-boppers". Such judgments, however much merited, reflect the fact that most of today's rock critics – the people who write books or contribute to *Rolling Stone* magazine – belong to the postwar baby boom era.

The diversity of rock music in the 1980s seems to have taken the critics by surprise. Punk impressed because its artlessness was thought sincere. New wave music and variants of reggae and Black British music have come and gone, the New Pop has harked back to old styles, while older artists, such as the Kinks or Van Morrison, have gone on producing. Yet, paradoxically, "rock" now seems to be a product of a past golden age. What once seemed shockingly new, now all too often appears to be comfortably nostalgic. Perhaps Elvis's biographer, Albert Goldman, was right when he said that rock music was simply institutionalised adolescence.

THE RULING CLASS

"Democracy is inconceivable without organisation, yet he who says organisation says oligarchy" – Robert Michels in *The Iron Law of Oligarchy* (1911)

"Opportunity means nothing unless it includes the right to be unequal" – Margaret Thatcher (1979)

The distribution of power, like the distribution of wealth, has fascinated writers for centuries, and the history of political thought is littered with ideas for the best form of government – Plato's Republic, Rousseau's Social Contract, Marx's communism. But how in the twentieth century is, or should, power be distributed?

Advanced industrialisation has given rise to massive concentrations of economic wealth, but it has also brought about huge concentrations of political power. Though both of today's superpowers – the Soviet Union and the United States – reckon to be democratic, can any modern government claim, in Abraham Lincoln's words, to be "government of the people, by the people, for the people?"

The dominant feature of advanced industrial societies appears to be an *elitist* distribution of power. Specialisation has given rise to a proliferation of elites in every walk of life – top politicians, businessmen, civil servants, trade unionists and so on. The question modern political sociologists have sought to answer is whether such elites are so organised, so integrated as to form a *power elite,* or even a *ruling class,* governing in their own interest. Or is the multitude of elites like a market place, with each one competing against and counterbalancing the others, so that no single group has dominant power?

This *elitist-pluralist* debate, as it has come to be called, is generally reckoned to have started in America with the publication in 1956 of C. Wright Mills's classic study, *The Power Elite.* At a time when the United States saw herself as the bulwark of freedom against communism, Mills's critique was devastating. The power of the US elite, Mills claimed, lay not in personal wealth but in three key institutions – the major corporations, the federal government and the military. These three elites were not separate but integrated through what he called "institutional proximity" – an extensive interchange of personnel and a common upper and upper middle class background and education.

Mills saw this elite as having not only "unprecedented power" – as it demonstrated at Hiroshima – but "unprecedented unaccountability". Far from being under popular control, it shaped and conditioned the masses through its hold on the media. Floyd Hunter's study in 1963 of *Regional City*, a town in the United States, supported many of Mills's conclusions, though Hunter identified only one elite, an economic one dominated by the business classes.

Inevitably such radical attacks on American democracy provoked a powerful counter-attack. Robert Dahl argued that the theorists of elitism had failed to show – with actual case studies – how many elite groups dominated decision-making. His famous study of decision-making in New Haven, Connecticut (*Who Governs?*, 1961), found the economic notables to be "only one of many groups", bargaining and competing against one another. The economist, J. K. Galbraith, put forward the concept of "countervailing power" – of the power of big business being checked by consumers and the unions (*American Capitalism*, 1952), while Suzanne Keller (*Beyond the Ruling Class*, 1963) talked of "strategic elites" – of different elites having influence over different issue areas.

These American studies have greatly influenced British sociologists in their analysis of the distribution of power in this country. On the face of it, we are a grossly unequal society. The Diamond commission, for instance, estimated that in 1976 the top 1 per cent of the population owned 25 per cent of total personal wealth, the top 10 per cent owned 60 per cent, leaving the bottom 90 per cent of the population to share out (unequally) the remaining 40 per cent. Other studies have shown that neither the welfare state nor progressive taxation has altered the fundamental distribution of wealth (as opposed to income). More than eight million people today live below the poverty line, and more than three million are unemployed.

Sociologists have tried to identify more of the sources of these inequalities:

SOCIAL AND EDUCATIONAL BACKGROUND: Our top institutions are dominated by people from privileged social backgrounds, educated in the main at public schools and Oxbridge. Only about 5 per cent of the population go to public schools, for example, but 40 per cent of all MPs did, as well as 60 per cent of permanent secretaries, 80 per cent of principal judges, 86 per cent of army officers and 85 per cent of Anglican bishops.

The higher up the institution you go, the more this is likely to be the case. In 1974 a survey by Philip Stanworth and Anthony Giddens found that 65 per cent of company chairmen went to public school. Recent Conservative cabinets have been dominated by ministers with public-school and Oxbridge backgrounds. Even Labour governments are unrepresentative of the population at large. Harold Wilson's 1969 cabinet was 80 per cent middle-class, with only three members in any sense of working-class origin. Such backgrounds and education help to reinforce an upper-class consciousness and, as John Rex argues, a belief in the right of certain people to rule.

THE ELITE NETWORK: Establishment connections are not only based on the "old school tie" – kinship is important as well. In a 1974 study of 27 financial firms in the City, Richard Whitley found that 26 of them had some links with another through kinship and marriage. T. Lupton and C. S. Wilson did a study in 1973 of the social backgrounds and connections of top decision-makers and found very close informal and kinship links between some of the leading figures involved in a "leak" of a change in the bank rate.

THE CIVIL SERVICE: The higher reaches of the civil service are dominated by the public schools and Oxbridge, and are able to "talk the same language" as those at the top of industry and other institutions. Indeed, many top civil servants retire onto the boards of top companies or banks (Sir William Armstrong,

the former head of the civil service, retired to a post at the Midland Bank). Two recent books (*The Secret Constitution* by Brian Sedgemore and *The Civil Servants* by Peter Kellner and Lord Crowther-Hunt, 1980) suggest that it is the civil service, rather than elected politicians, who run government today. The civil service serves the interests of the establishment, they say, by its use of secrecy, control of information, and manipulation.

THE MASS MEDIA: The Royal Commission on the Press (1977) showed how ownership of newspapers since the war has been concentrated in fewer and fewer hands. One man, Rupert Murdoch, owns four Fleet Street newspapers. In their studies, *Bad News* and *More Bad News* (1980), the Glasgow University Media Group have tried to show how, by a careful selection of information, the television news presents a pro-establishment point of view, while appearing to be both neutral and objective. Strikes, for example, are given a bad image, and controversial topics carefully vetted. A recent example of this was the dropping of the nuclear disarmer, E. P. Thompson, from the Dimbleby lectures.

But pluralist writers are not convinced by these arguments. This evidence might prove the existence of a British establishment, but it fails, they say, to prove that it is a ruling class – "that it rules" as Jean Blondel put it, "in the strongest sense of the word." It may, Blondel says, have a strong infuence over the Conservative Party, but can it really be said that it ran the postwar Labour governments, too – governments that brought in nationalisation and wealth taxes? In his view the British establishment is not a single unified elite but a cluster of elites, and its power is social and not political.

Similarly, a 1974 analysis by Christopher Hewitt of twenty-four policy issues over the period 1944–64 found no dominant elite at work, but a "wide diversity of conflicting interests." And only over the issue of capital punishment did Parliament go directly against public opinion. W. Grant and D. Marsh's examination of the CBI's relationship with governments (*The Confederation of British Industry*, 1977) found that "the CBI's ability to influence events is limited by the government's need to retain the support of other interest groups."

The reply of the elitists to this has been to broaden their definition of power. In a now-classic essay, "The Two Faces of Power" (1962), P. Bachrach and M. S. Baratz developed the concept of "non-decision-making" – the ability of the powerful to ignore or suppress all but the safest of issues, to control the political agenda and to mobilise the "bias" of the political system against those issues that might threaten the existing order. As the Labour MP, Frank Field, pointed out in a recent *Man Alive* programme on the "super-rich", Parliament has never debated such fundamental questions as the distribution of wealth or poverty.

Steven Lukes has sought to add another dimension to this concept – that real power is not only the ability to make decisions (or not to make them) but to control other people's wants and needs. "Is it not the supreme exercise of power to get another or others to have the desires you want them to have?" The problem for sociologists here is, how do you research such invisible power?

Marxists go well beyond analysing simple decision-making. Theirs is a critique of the whole capitalist system – what they see as its inherent inequalities and exploitation. For them, the prime source of power is economic, and so, almost by definition, the owners of the means of production constitute the ruling class. The power of this class, however, lies not only in its control of the state (the government, police, judiciary, army and so on) but through indoctrination – in getting the masses to accept capitalism as natural, inevitable, even just, and so legitimise its own rule. The media, the education system, the nuclear family, the Marxists say, are all means of promoting the values of materialism, individualism and inequality. However, modern Marxists are divided over the way the state actually operates. Is it actually run by the bourgeoisie, as Ralph Miliband argues in *The State of Capitalist Society* (1969): "The men who have manned all command positions in the state system have largely, and in many cases overwhelmingly, been drawn from the world of business and property or from the professional middle classes." Or is the state semi-independent, operating in the long-term interests of capital?

In the view of the French sociologist, Nicos Poulantzas, "The capitalist state best serves the interests of the capitalist class only when members of this class do not participate directly in the state apparatus, that is to say when the ruling class is not the politically governing class." Such relative autonomy is vital if the state is to unite the "diverse fraction" within the capitalist class (industry, finance, commerce), to present a limited front against organised labour, to grant such limited concessions as the welfare state, and yet maintain its image as representing the "national interest".

You might expect from this that in communist societies with "communal ownership" of the means of production, there would be less elitism, and certainly less exploitation. But so far western observers haven't been able to find much sign of it. The British sociologist, Tom Bottomore, says: "The political system of communist countries seems to me to approach the pure type of power elite" (*Elites and Society,* 1966). And another writer, Mervyn Matthews, has outlined the way in which privilege in the Soviet Union is not only accepted but promoted and institutionalised. In his book, *Privilege in the Soviet Union* (1976), he shows how people with influence in the Communist Party have access to better food, shops and restaurants, holiday homes, and so on. However, David Lane (in *The Socialist Industrial State,* 1976) argues that it's not as simple as this. Such power, he says, has been used not simply for elite self-enrichment, but also as a means to massive industrialisation, and thus the establishment of greater economic and educational equality.

So what conclusions can be drawn from this debate? Which theory presents a truer picture of the distribution of power in modern societies? Is elite rule inevitable? It is important to bear in mind here that the elitist and the pluralist models use different concepts of power (actual versus potential), and thus different methodologies. While pluralists concentrate on actual decision-making, elitists also seek to analyse the whole structure of power.

Further, they have contrasting views of non-elites – the mass of people. Elitists tend to see the apathy of the masses as part of elite control, and argue for greater popular participation, whereas pluralists see it as an important part of "representative democracy". A highly active populace, they say, leads to social instability, and the ordinary citizen is better leaving the complexities of government to those best fitted for it. As the sociologist, Karl Mannheim, put it in 1940: "It is sufficient for democracy that the individual citizens, though prevented from taking a direct part in government all the time, have at least the possibility of making their aspirations felt at certain intervals." Mannheim's view is strongly reflected in Britain's political tradition.

BOOKS

Some useful additional reading:

● Two excellent collections of articles on power are Stanworth and Giddens (eds.), *Elites and Power in British Society* (Cambridge University Press, 1974) and J. Urry and J. Wakeford's *Power in Britain* (Heinemann Educational Books, 1973).

● For fuller discussions of the political thought involved in the debate on elitism and democracy, Geraint Perry's *Political Elites* (Allen & Unwin, 1969) and Tom Bottomore's *Elites and Society* (Penguin, 1976) are very useful.

● M. Matthew's *Privilege in the Soviet Union* (Allen and Unwin, 1978) and D. Lane's *End of Inequality* (Penguin, 1971) give two detailed but readable outlines of elites in the Soviet Union.

● Highly recommended as a short and stimulating discussion on non-decision-making is Steven Luke's *Power – a Radical View* (Macmillan, 1974).

● The Marxist perspective on the subject is best dealt with in Ralph Miliband's *The State in Capitalist Society* (Quartet Books, 1973) and J. Westergaard and H. Resler's *Class in a Capitalist Society* (Penguin, 1976).

● Finally, as a general background to the topic, George Orwell's *Animal Farm* and *1984* are invaluable.

There is a danger, however, that such distancing can all too easily lead to alienation and even violent protest. This happened with the race riots in the United States in the 1960s (and could be said to have been a contributory cause of the recent urban rioting in British cities). The fact that only fifty per cent of the American electorate vote in presidential elections is hardly a great endorsement of representative democracy.

To a large extent, then, these two theories also represent contrasting ideological perspectives, with pluralists defending the existing system and elitists attacking it.

So any conclusion depends largely on your own view of democracy – is there too little or too much? It's certainly true that, as yet, the elitists have failed to prove that a power elite or ruling class rules "in the strongest sense of the word." This is due partly to weakness in their research methods and theories, but also to the secrecy of modern government – though episodes like the Blunt spy scandal, the Vestey tax avoidance affair and the recent discovery of a Freemason's circle in the midst of the Italian government, provide plenty of material for speculation.

In addition, elitist analyses, on the whole, haven't been able to put forward visible alternatives to the existing system. Certainly, standards of living and degrees of freedom in today's communist societies (notably Poland) are unlikely to inspire revolution amongst the western working class, and while pure democracy may have worked in the tiny ancient Greek city states (and then only for adult males), most attempts since have been less than successful. Even in Israeli Kibbutzim where wealth is communally shared, a study by Eva Rosenfield (*Social Stratification in a Classless Society,* 1974) has shown how there is a significant difference in status and authority among members.

Two modern solutions seem to be:

● To "open up" modern government by, say, a Freedom of Information Act or Bill of Rights and to increase membership and participation within the major political parties.

● To increase "grassroots" participation generally – at school, in the local community, and especially at work. Some people have seen the Yugoslavian workers' councils as a model of industrial participation. But there is still the problem of who is to control the large multinational companies.

One final consideration is worth bearing in mind. Perhaps all this conspiracy and secrecy is in fact non-decision-making of the worst kind. Perhaps no one is in control, and it may well be on this basis that man finally destroys himself. Anthony Sampson makes a powerful point when he says (in the *Anatomy of Britain,* 1962): "Radical people regard the idea of a small group of *them* operating under the cloak of a democracy as inherently sinister and threatening. But the alternative can often be much more alarming – that there is no 'they' at all and that those in positions of influence refuse to face up to their power."

SOCIAL CONTROL

In 1981 and 1985, there were major riots in several British cities. The distinguished judge, Lord Scarman, described the 1981 riots as involving "scenes of violence and disorder, the likes of which had not previously been seen this century."

It seemed that social control had broken down, and since then people have been arguing over the causes. Were the police to blame, or too much immigration? Was it the weather, or Mrs Thatcher's government? The fact that no one had been able to predict the trouble (despite their experience in 1981, the police were badly caught out in 1985) is a measure of how complex are the processes that make for order and control in society.

Not just British society. Most societies survive because people act in ways that conform to social norms and expectations. In fact, the very idea of "society" and "social life" implies order and predictability.

Social order exists at every level of behaviour, from conversation between individuals, right up to the way entire nations conduct their affairs. Everyday experience is orderly. Getting up, going to school, college or work, meeting friends, dealing with teachers – most of the time, such events happen smoothly and predictably, day after day. Similarly, whole societies remain more or less stable for generations – the reason the riots in Brixton, Toxteth, Handsworth and Tottenham seemed so shocking was because most people perceive Britain as a stable nation (though historically this has not always been the case).

But even in societies where social control breaks down completely, a form of order reasserts itself before long. For instance, the "westernisation" of Iran under the Shah led to instability and a bloody revolution. Yet it wasn't long before Iranian society settled down under a completely different system of control – Islamic law. The Soviet Union is one of the most "ordered" nations in the world, yet its present style of government emerged from a revolution in 1917.

So how is the social order achieved? What keeps us orderly? Social control is not just a matter of dealing with those who have stepped outside the rules. It refers also to the creation and the perpetuation of those rules, and to stopping rule-breaking before it happens.

At times, we are very aware of being controlled by others. Teachers tell us what to do, expect to be obeyed, and can punish us for failing to meet their expectations. Employers, too, are people to whom we have sold, for a fixed period of time, our right to direct our own activities. Parents control us from an early age, and growing up in a family involves a continuing negotiation of who has the right to decide how we dress, what time we come in at night and who we go out with. But most of the time we feel "free" and able to do what we want.

Even in these free times, though, we are still cooperating socially with other people, and life remains orderly. If you have ever been involved in a street riot, or beaten by a head teacher, or forcibly arrested, you will be only too aware of how physical force can be used in social control. In other situations – for instance, among the big crowds who turned out for the Queen's Silver Jubilee – it is often striking how order and control can be achieved voluntarily.

Generally, then, social order is a combination of two elements: force (or *coercion*), and voluntary agreement (or *consensus*). Both these elements are present in social control. We are kept in order by others, and we also create and sustain order willingly for our mutual benefit.

It is comparatively rare in modern society for control to be exercised through the threat of physical violence, as it is in a few South American states, or in South Africa. But even such severe threats *can* be defied by those being controlled. Throughout history, from before the Christian martyrs through to Lech Walesa in Poland, people have risked death or imprisonment rather than accept control from a source whose right to power they reject.

However, most of the rewards and punishments (the *sanctions*) that control us on a day-to-day basis involve no force. We fear being laughed at, or being excluded from groups. Most people are particularly keen to avoid being thought peculiar. (Adolescents, in their determination to be seen as unique individuals, are often an exception to this rule. This contradiction is at the root of teenage fashions such as punk, where uniformity and uniqueness are achieved simultaneously.)

The fear of being thought different results in people *choosing* to do what in practice they *have* to do to avoid ridicule or other sanctions. We consent to control and so create order. The *informal* control and sanctions, usually unspoken and unexercised, of family, friends and others who are important to us, are more significant in most people's lives than the *formal* ones vested in the police, the courts, and the armed forces.

But though informal controls are most effective, they don't always work. A student who finds a friend cheating in an exam, for example, may fail to do anything about it simply because he is a friend. On the other hand, many so-called formal controls are, in effect, really quite informal.

When seat-belt wearing was made compulsory in Britain in 1983, for instance, some police forces chose at first to let offenders off with a warning, rather than use their formal powers of prosecution. Similarly, the formal control of sending someone to prison is often superseded, once inside, by informal ones, operated in many cases by the inmates themselves.

The reason we readily accept informal controls is because of *socialisation*. As children, we learn what behaviour is expected of us. We learn actively to participate in social life, and to look for social acceptance. Other aspects of socialisation continue throughout life, as we learn new ways of behaving in each successive social context: school, work, parenthood, middle age, old age. Even an old person going into a home has to be socialised into that new environment.

But these rules and values, which seem to be external to our lives, only continue to exist because we follow them. And they are socially created in the first place. We may feel that "society" is somehow "out there", making us do things, but, in fact, "society" is nothing more than ourselves and others. This paradox is summed up in the epigram: "Man makes society; society makes man."

One writer has drawn an analogy with a public footpath across a field. We follow the route more or less closely, always conscious of the possible appearance of a farmer angry about trespass. We accept his right to keep us on the path, and so it guides us. But the path is a path only because of the thousands who have already walked across it and it remains so only because we continue to treat it as such. In other words, the way we behave is both the cause and the consequence of social behaviour in general.

The major schools of sociological thought agree that social order and control are central to social life. Where they differ is over exactly what this "order" is, how it is achieved, and in whose interests it is maintained. It is important to distinguish between two levels of order. On a basic level, there is the order and associated control of everyday social life – the orderliness that people need simply to communicate with each other. Then there is the order of society as a whole. This involves one of the most basic ideas in sociology, that of *social solidarity*.

The phrase was originally coined by the French sociologist, Emile Durkheim (1858–1917), to explain why societies stay together, even though their individual members are constantly changing. There are two kinds of solidarity, he said. One applies to pre-industrial, agrarian societies (*mechanical solidarity*) and the other to modern industrial societies (*organic solidarity*).

MECHANICAL SOLIDARITY means that most people are essentially *alike* – doing the same jobs, sharing the same beliefs, and probably knowing each other personally. This is only possible in small, simple communities – society has cohesion and unity because everybody is thinking the same way.

ORGANIC SOLIDARITY, on the other hand, stems from the fact that in modern society, everybody is *different*. Some are black; others are white; some work in factories; others on farms; some support Liverpool, others Everton. Solidarity is attained by a lot of people playing many different specialist roles, enmeshed with each other *organically* – like the organs of the body – and from which all may benefit.

Or do they? This idea that "everybody benefits" has been a profound source of disagreement between *functionalist* sociologists (who follow in the tradition of Durkheim) and *Marxists*.

Is the social order of, for example, modern capitalist societies in the interests of everybody in them ("the national interest"), or only of a powerful minority? If the economic system were to be changed, would the new order be in the interests of everybody, or simply of a different minority?

For functionalists, order is achieved through consensus, or general agreement, on certain core values, without which, they say, social life would be impossible. On the organic analogy, all parts of the organism contribute to the needs of the whole, whose continuity, stability and equilibrium are in the interests of all its elements. Socialisation is the crucial social process, and family, schools and religion are the key to the maintenance of social order and stability. Those who threaten order and the consensus must be punished and brought back into line in the interests of the whole society.

Marxists accept the same basic premise that order rests on agreement over values, but argue that this agreement is not achieved freely and voluntarily, nor is it in the interests of all concerned. The dominant class in society, which owns and controls the economic resources and thus exercises power in all other contexts, must, to maintain its dominance, control all those in whose interests it would be to change the power structure.

While this could be done through force (as it has been, ironically enough, in some "Marxist" societies like Czechoslovakia and Poland), it is far more effective through the control of ideas and of knowledge. If the people without power can be convinced of the justice, legitimacy, even the inevitability of the social system, the position of the dominant class will not be threatened. What a functionalist calls "culture" and "central value system", a Marxist calls "ideology" – a set of ideas that explains and makes sense of experience by distorting it in ways that justify the status quo.

Similarly, what functionalists call the "formal agencies of social control" become, for Marxists, the "repressive state apparatuses" – the police, prisons, and the armed forces. Why, it is asked, do the police spend so much time on working-class crime, when really substantial crime is taking place in offices and boardrooms?

A different dimension to the argument comes from *phenomenological* sociologists, such as Peter Berger and Thomas Luckmann. They are asking the same question as the functionalists and Marxists: "How is social order possible?" But, rather than stressing the way in which society influences people's behaviour, they concentrate on how order is constructed through the interaction of individuals in everyday situations.

The phenomenologists say that although most people are generally influenced by mutually accepted standards of behaviour, human conduct is highly variable, and, to a large extent, "order" only exists insofar as people actually give any meaning to it. A crime against society, for instance, has no objective meaning as such, but tends to be what a particular policeman, judge or jury thinks it is.

But what of those who do *not* behave as is expected of them? Who are they? Why do they behave in a deviant manner?

Confusing as it may seem, it is possible to regard deviance as something orderly, and even quite normal. It is not simply socially meaningless behaviour, but behaviour to which we give the meaning "deviant" if it occurs in a context where it contravenes the rules of a particular situation. For instance, public nakedness is normal in some contexts and deviant in others.

To go nude on the beach at Brighton does not contravene social rules because Brighton council permits nudity. But to streak at a rugby match is reckoned to be deviant. To be nude on stage is normal in a strip club but deviant at, say, the Royal

BOOKS

Some useful additional reading:
There are few studies of social control written for the beginner. Of these, the best is *Social Control* by C. Ken Watkins (Longman, 1975). Chapter 4 (by Mike O'Donnell) in *Fundamentals of Sociology,* edited by P. W. McNeill and C. Townley (Hutchinson, 1981), is an excellent and wide-ranging discussion, as is Chapter 16 of O'Donnell's *A New Introduction to Sociology* (Harrap, 1981). For a further discussion of social solidarity and of Weber's idea of legitimacy (not touched on here), try C. Brown, *Understanding Society* (John Murray, 1979).

Variety Performance. On the other hand, it could be said that streakers are predictable these days, that streaking is almost normal, and that strippers have an established role in our society.

In fact, if we consider all kinds of deviance, major and minor, public and private, it is actually pretty commonplace. If sexual deviance is so unusual, how do the many mail order firms dealing in "marital aids" flourish? What proportion of the population could say, in all honesty, that they had never stolen anything in their lives? We may even begin to wonder whether the "normal" really exists, other than as an idea.

However, there are some forms of deviance that are seen as anti-social by everybody – violent crime, especially, comes in this category. What explanations are there for the behaviour of muggers or terrorists?

Functionalist sociologists would argue that the problem is one of defective socialisation – a failure somewhere along the line to instil the values and norms that are necessary to a stable society. Resocialisation *may* be possible – and this is what prisons and borstals are theoretically for.

Marxists, on the other hand, would probably dispute this analysis. Their argument might run thus: "A capitalist society concentrates on certain acts, like terrorism, as deviant because they are a threat to those who hold power. Yet other acts which may be equally destructive of life, such as marketing a car known to be unsafe, are glossed over because they fit in with society's ideology." The idea of what makes a terrorist depends very much on ideological interpretation: in both Zimbabwe and Israel, terrorists have ended up as heads of government.

Again, the phenomenologists tend to disagree. They are most concerned with how certain acts come to be defined as deviant, rather than in their actual causes. But they also stress that people labelled as deviant may see their own behaviour as entirely rational and meaningful, even normal, in the context of a situation as they interpret it.

Social control is, then, a matter of competing definitions of order – and what counts as orderliness and normality is the outcome of relations of power. It is both complicated – and very basic. Together with social order, it is at the heart of the notion of society and of social life. To be social is to be controlled. The social is control.

SOCIAL MOBILITY

Margaret Thatcher, Samantha Fox and Bob Geldof all have one thing in common. They have all benefited from what sociologists call social mobility. It is a process by which individuals and groups move up and down the ladder of income and status that exists in most societies.

It is a concept which is familiar enough in everyday terms – the son of a manual worker who becomes the head of a big firm or a civil service department – but it is not easy to measure on a large scale. This is because it is hard to compare like with like.

Sociologists who try to measure the amount of social mobility that exists in a society need to be sure that they are catching children at the same point in the life cycle as their parents. Because the son of a solicitor, for instance, is merely an articled clerk at the age of 23, with relatively low earnings, it does not mean that he has slipped down from his father's class. He, too, will probably be a solicitor in due course. Again, in modern society where heavy industry is in decline and white-collar work, like computing, is expanding, the nature of jobs and their place in the social class structure is altering all the time. Hence mobility is related to the rate of change of the class and jobs pattern, as well as to the fluidity of the structure at any one moment.

To find out how much mobility there is, therefore, researchers cannot just rely on census or General Household Survey material, which lists heads of households according to their social grouping. The current position in Britain is that 5 per cent of male heads of household are professionals, 18 per cent are employers and managers, 17 per cent are intermediate and junior non-manual personnel, 40 per cent are skilled manual workers, 15 per cent are semi-skilled manual workers or involved in personal services, and 5 per cent are unskilled.

This is merely a snapshot picture. To calculate mobility rates one needs to compare class status over successive generations. Then one has to distinguish between "absolute mobility" – the total change in the number of jobs in all the various categories – and "relative mobility," which is the chance of an individual from each class going up or down.

The most thorough attempt to measure mobility in this country recently was made by a team from Nuffield College, Oxford. Their conclusions are based on a survey of 10 000 men in England and Wales in 1972, whom they divided into seven classes by occupation. (Social mobility studies have, so far, been mainly concerned with men rather than women.) Broadly, it was found that the proportion of people in the two top classes had risen steadily. Of men born between 1908 and 1917 only about 22 per cent belonged to this group, which John Goldthorpe, the Nuffield sociologist, describes as "the service class," but which others would call middle class. But nearly 30 per cent of those born between 1938 and 1947 were found to be in that group.

The less well-off classes have correspondingly declined. For instance, Goldthorpe's classes III to V – which include ordinary white collar workers, small shopkeepers and the supervisors of manual workers – amounted to 32 per cent of the men born in 1908-17, but to only 27 per cent of the 1938-47 batch. The same is true for industrial workers, Goldthorpe's classes VI and VII. The apparent rise in their proportions in the 1938-47 birth group almost certainly reflects the fact that a lot of youngsters who will eventually have jobs higher up the social hierarchy still do manual work to begin with.

All this suggests that absolute mobility upwards, to fill an expanded number of prestigious jobs, has been an important underlying trend in this country over the past fifty years. What this means is that the chance of a middle-class child staying in the same class has improved – for the amount of sliding-down which the Nuffield team discovered was small. In addition, a significant number of working-class children, at least a fifth, become middle-class in their own lifetime.

It appears that the bulk of the upward mobility has taken place since 1949, for it was in that year that David Glass and a team at the London School of Economics carried out the previous big study of social mobility. What they found was rather different: that the social structure was rather static and the number who rose was roughly equal to the number who fell. Goldthorpe and his colleagues conclude, therefore, that the marked expansion of

The social ladder

The Registrar General's classification of people by social class, which is the basis for many of the government's social statistics, goes back some forty years and nowadays seems rather arbitrary. Why should a chimney sweep be regarded as unskilled (class v) and a bus conductor as partly skilled (class IV)? Why is an architect in class I, but a sculptor in class II? The answers are that the Registrar General's view of class is based totally on occupation, and that the occupations were put into a hierarchy related to earnings, length and difficulty of training, and public esteem. Drastic alteration of this hierarchy is now rather difficult, in spite of changes of earnings and the job structure, because it would make it so hard to compare present social statistics with those collected in the past. Other systems of occupational classification you might come across are the Hall-Jones scale, which is less crude than the Registrar General's, and the market researcher's system of classification according to income groups ABCDE.

Social class I

professional

accountants	opticians
architects	scientists
chemists	university teachers
dentists	vets
engineers	vicars
lawyers	

Social class II

intermediate occupations

actors	hotel keepers
airline pilots	√journalists
artists	MPs
chiropodists	√nurses
company directors	police inspectors
diplomats	schoolmasters
farmers	sculptors

Social class III

skilled occupations:
non-manual and manual

athletes	policemen
bank clerks	printers
brewers	photographers
bus drivers	restaurateurs
butchers	secretaries
hairdressers	shop assistants
miners	undertakers
plumbers	upholsterers

Social class IV

partly-skilled

ambulancemen	hawkers
barmen	milkmen
bus conductors	postmen
farm labourers	telephonists
fishermen	waiters
gardeners	

Social class V

unskilled

builder's labourers	porters
charwomen	stevedores
chimney sweeps	ticket collectors
lorry drivers' mates	window cleaners
office cleaners	

white-collar jobs after 1949, particularly in service industries and backed by a growth in educational qualifications, explains most of the increased mobility this century.

However, if absolute mobility has expanded, the Nuffield team found that relative mobility – the chance of a working-class boy as against a middle-class boy ending up in the middle-class – may actually have worsened. This is partly a statistical consequence of the fact that the middle class has expanded considerably and, because virtually no middle-class people slip down into it, the manual working class is a diminishing and self-recruited group. But it also seems to reflect a tightening of the opportunities for class promotion of the younger working-class people in the sample.

Social mobility matters to students of society for a variety of reasons. It is important for itself, in that the prospect of upward mobility is pleasant for the individual, and helps to legitimise the social structure in his or her eyes. Alternatively, if an individual faces a real risk of sliding down the social scale, his attitudes may become desperately defensive. Social mobility is important also at a structural level, for it is related to class formation, the sense of class cohesion, and the possibility of class conflict.

Where social mobility is considerable, and expanding, there tends to be a blurring of the edges between classes. But where mobility, either upwards or downwards, is restricted, there is likely to be a greater class-awareness and a possibility of friction. In this sense, therefore, there is an interesting comparison to be made between social mobility and class in Britain and France. In Britain the enclosures movement (by which the owners took over the common land) broke the power of the peasantry in the eighteenth century, and by 1914 the proportion of agricultural workers was already quite small: the Brit-

Class origins and class destinations

John Goldthorpe and Keith Hope created a class hierarchy more up to date than the Registrar General's in their work in the late sixties and early seventies for the Social Mobility Group at Oxford. This was strictly based on occupations. On their classification, class I included people like senior civil servants, the managers of big firms and landowners; class II included higher grade technicians and managers of smaller firms; class III included salesmen and routine white collar workers; class IV (divided into a, b and c) included smaller shopkeepers and farmers; classes V and VI covered supervisors and skilled manual workers; class VII (divided into a and b) included semi and unskilled manual workers and farm labourers.

classes (Goldthorpe-Hope scale)	class origins (father's occupation)			class destinations (respondent's occupation)		
	England	France	Sweden	England	France	Sweden
	%	%	%	%	%	%
I	7	5	5	14	8	10
II	6	7	6	12	14	14
III	7	8	4	9	10	8
IVa	5	4	7	4	4	4
IVb	4	10	5	4	6	4
IVc	5	27	26	2	12	5
V/VI	39	18	24	33	23	30
VIIa	23	15	20	22	20	23
VIIb	4	7	5	2	4	2

Class distribution of John Goldthorpe's 1972 sample by birth dates

class	I-II	III-V	VI-VII
birth years	%	%	%
1908-17	22.2	32.0	45.7
1918-27	27.2	29.2	43.5
1928-37	29.3	30.5	40.2
1938-47	29.6	26.8	43.6

ish working class today is at least two generations away from the land.

In France, on the other hand, a significant proportion of urban workers today have rural origins. The migration of peasants' children from the land was occurring on a large scale as recently as the 1950s and 1960s. Hence there is something in common between the attitudes of the urban working class in Britain and what remains of the French peasantry – the somewhat defensive stance of a dwindling, almost totally self-recruited group.

Goldthorpe, who has recently been working with colleagues on comparative social mobility in England, France and Sweden, finds that all three have seen an increase in upward mobility this century. This is true of almost all western industrial countries. However, of the three, France has the most static structure. Sweden's is slightly more fluid than England's. Apart from differences which relate to the size of the rural workforce, Goldthorpe believes that the biggest reason for immobility in France is the comparatively large size of the petit bourgeois group, which is in a position to pass on a business, land or money to its children. In both Sweden and England education is more important, inherited wealth less.

One writer, Ralph Turner, draws a distinction between the prevalent system of mobility in Britain, which he calls sponsorship mobility, and that in the United States, which he calls contest mobility. The sponsorship system means that people tend to be chosen for positions of power by members of the existing elite because they have certain qualities that are deemed to be desirable. These could be the "right school" or family background or connections, or possessing the "right" attitudes. Contest mobility tends to be fairer – with the competitors striving on reasonably level terms, and with the highest status going to those with the highest quality.

Historically, of course, there have been many avenues of social mobility. The medieval church offered a route to power and riches for poor but clever children. Marriage, too, has been a traditional avenue of social mobility. Mrs Thatcher did not become wealthy on her prime minister's salary, but by marrying a wealthy man.

However, in Europe in the twentieth century, perhaps the most important means of upward mobility has been the education system, as the opportunities for children at school have been gradually divorced from their parents' ability to pay. What this has meant in England and Wales has been explored by A.H. Halsey and his colleagues in the Nuffield study, who have concentrated on the educational elements in mobility. They demonstrated that over a quarter (25.2 per cent) of the sample who had both parents at non-selective state schools were themselves educated at selective schools. They were being put on a route to a more favoured social status than their parents had enjoyed.

In fact, the width of this route varied over time – getting better for a working-class boy born between 1913 and 1942, but then getting narrower for children born between 1943 and 1952. Halsey and the team point out that this was contrary to the official policy of expanding opportunity set out in the Education Act of 1944. But what happened was that the steady increase in selective school places in 1943-52 was overwhelmed by two demographic changes which were more important. First, the relative size of the middle and lower middle classes was increasing; second, the birth rate jumped in the late 1940s. Extra places for working-class boys at grammar schools were balanced by the disappearance of places for them at selective technical schools.

Increased numbers of white collar jobs, tied to entry with specific educational qualifications, gave education particular importance in upward mobility from 1945 to 1972; the chances of a working-class boy who left school early working his way up into a higher social group in the course of his subsequent career were actually getting worse over that period.

However, there is no reason to suppose that education will always be so important in social mobility. For example, the Nuffield study showed that people from the highest class were actually the most varied in the secondary schools they had been to: more respondents from class I had been to elementary or secondary modern schools than went to the prestigious fee-paying schools of the Headmasters' Conference. Again, 21.1 per cent of the Nuffield sample who had one or both parents at private secondary schools themselves attended non-selective state schools. Yet, overwhelmingly, the children of the higher social classes retain the status irrespective of their school.

Social mobility, as sociologists define it, is about movement between jobs, classified according to income and status. These classifications are always subject to dispute, particularly when incomes vary rapidly at times of inflation, and new jobs emerge whose status is in doubt. Social mobility, in the wider sense, also involves lifestyles, possessions and, in Britain, even accents of speech.

BOOKS

Some useful additional reading:
P.M. Blau and O.D. Duncan: *The American Occupational Structure*, Wiley, 1962
D.V. Glass, ed: *Social Mobility in Modern Britain*, Routledge, 1954
John Goldthorpe, in collaboration with Catriona Llewellyn and Clive Payne: *Social Mobility and Class Structure in Modern Britain*, Clarendon Press, 1980
Christopher Jencks et al: *Inequality*, Allen Lane, 1973
A.H. Halsey, Anthony Heath and J.M. Ridge: *Origins and Destinations: Family, Class and Education in Modern Britain*, Clarendon Press, 1980
S.M. Lipset and R. Bendix: *Social Mobility in Industrial Society*, Heinemann, 1979

SOCIAL PROBLEMS

Sex'n'drugs'n'rock'n'roll. To these familiar "social problems" you could now add rioting black youth, football hooliganism, racial attack, battered wives, and half a dozen others. But what makes a social problem? And who decides that it is a problem, or what ought to be done about it?

Take an example. Victoria Gillick considered it a problem that girls aged under 16 would be encouraged to indulge in sexual activity if they could get contraceptive advice from their doctors without their parents knowing. She persuaded judges in the Court of Appeal that this should be illegal. Although this ruling was subsequently overturned by the Law Lords, it meant that for a long period of time doctors could no longer give such advice without the parents' consent.

But for others, it was Victoria Gillick's campaign that created the problem, by putting sexually active girls at risk of becoming pregnant. For Victoria Gillick, the problem to be dealt with is juvenile sex. For her critics, it is schoolgirl motherhood.

The competition between these two arguments illustrates an essential point about the sociology of social problems. This is that what counts as a problem is not as self-evident as it sometimes seems. Rather, it is the outcome of political debate and conflict.

The first distinction to make is between *social* problems and *sociological* problems. A sociological problem is any social event, action, or pattern of relationships that calls for sociological explanation. It is a problem in that it needs to be understood and explained sociologically.

Many people associate sociology with

the kind of "social problems" that we listed at the beginning of this article. But ordinary, everyday activities are just as much sociological problems, and just as interesting to sociologists. Thus, a rising divorce rate is a sociological problem, and may be seen by many as a social problem. But the fact that most marriages last until the death of one partner is just as great a sociological problem, for it is at least as hard to explain.

The fact that some children bunk off school is both a sociological and, arguably, a social problem. The fact that most do not is also a sociological problem. You could even say that there was another sociological problem in teachers seeing bunking off as undesirable, given that the absentees are often the troublemakers in an oversized class. Sociologists are concerned with explaining the ordinary and the normal as much as the deviant and the abnormal, and with explaining how something comes to be seen as a social problem, and by whom.

The definition of a social problem is much less straightforward. When sociology was dominated by a *functionalist* perspective, it was assumed that there was a consensus on central values. Social problems were defined in terms of actions or events that deviated from those values. In its earliest versions, at the beginning of this century, this view was linked to the organic analogy, in which society is compared with an organism where all the parts fit together (the comparison was often made with the human body), and in which there is a built-in tendency to balance and to equilibrium.

Social problems, on this view, occur where this equilibrium is disturbed, perhaps by rapid social change, and they must be explained and resolved if society is to remain stable and to function normally. The major cause of social problems, according to functionalist sociologists, is the behaviour of groups of people who are inadequately socialised, often because of some kind of moral breakdown. Thus, the rioters in Handsworth, Tottenham and Brixton would have to be "cured" of their problem. There would not be a need to search for a more general "cure" of society at large.

Among the early critics of this approach was the American sociologist, C. Wright Mills, who maintained (in 1943) that its supporters, most of whom came from small-town America, tended to see the social structure of such places as orderly and desirable, and anything else as disorganised and as cause for concern. Furthermore, their solutions to problems were partial and patchwork in scope, since they failed to locate social problems within the wider political and historical context of American society.

Mills's insight can be combined with that of *labelling theory,* which developed in America in the 1950s and 1960s. Labelling theory stressed that social problems only become problems when they are defined as such. Basing their arguments on studies of deviant groups such as drug takers, prostitutes and juvenile gangs, writers such as Howard Becker and Edwin Lemert stressed that deviant groups were those groups that were defined as deviant, rather than those who "broke the rules of society."

In the same way, social problems are those issues which are *defined* as problems. They vary from society to society and from time to time within any one society. It is the power to define something as a problem which matters, and the power to get that definition accepted. Circumstances may objectively exist, but a subjective awareness of them must also exist if they are to be regarded as problems, together with a sense that something ought to be done.

While Becker and his colleagues were praised for developing this approach, they were also criticised for failing to develop their ideas about power – about who the powerful are and about where they get their power from. It was also pointed out that their examples of social problems were of a limited type, usually involving subcultural minorities, and had little to say about things like poverty, war, unemployment and racism.

The problem is that there can never be complete agreement on what is or is not a social problem. Differences of interpretation may arise from differences between the *values* of different groups, or from differences in their *interests*, or from both.

Take poverty as an example. In value terms, we might think that everyone would regard poverty as an evil. But what of some religious orders, both western and eastern, who take vows of poverty as a means towards achieving grace and salvation? Renunciation of wealth is one of the central tenets of Christianity, which is still the key value system for most of western society.

In terms of interests, it can be readily shown that poverty is in the interests of the rich, for it is they who would be the losers if there were any major redistribution of wealth. Other groups, too, benefit from the existence of the poor, such as social workers and employees of the Department of Health and Social Security, who would be out of work if there were no claimants. This is not to say that these groups work to create the objective conditions of poverty, but they certainly have an interest in its continuance.

Crime, too, is something that we might assume all would agree, in terms of values, to be a social problem. But what of the professional criminal? Is it his problem? Whose interests would be threatened by a massive reduction in crime? The police are in a very ambivalent position here. It is in their interests that crime should be perceived as a growing problem since this will enhance their status. In recent years, it has certainly enhanced their income and power. At the same time, the police have to show that they are "winning the fight against crime" – it must at least *appear* that they are doing their job properly.

The way in which familiar "social problems" are seen and interpreted can also be affected by changes in values and interest. Male homosexuality was long regarded as a problem, and its solutions seen in terms of moral rehabilitation. Some people have defined it as a medical matter, requiring treatment. Recently, the "problem" has been redefined in terms of public attitudes to homosexuals, rather than the homosexuals themselves. According to groups like the Campaign for Homosexual Equality, who promote and protect the interests of homosexuals, the problem is prejudice, and the solution lies in changing the attitudes of prejudiced people, rather than the behaviour of homosexuals.

A similar redefinition has taken place in the context of race. For many years, the "problem" was seen as being the immigration of coloured people to this country, and the difficulty in integrating them into the "British way of life." More recently, it has been argued that the problem is not immigrants and their families, but whites and white racism. Equally it could be argued that the "heroin problem" has been created by the punitive reaction of the authorities, who have treated it as a criminal matter and thus driven it underground, making it harder for addicts to get help, and made it a more profitable activity for international gangsters.

Feminist approaches in sociology have also led to a reappraisal of problems such as mental illness, domestic violence, and attacks on women. The most common emotional disorder treated by doctors is depression, which is suffered particularly by young mothers at home with children. This was long regarded as an illness to which women were particularly prone by reason of their being female, sometimes associated with "postnatal depression" (another uniquely female "problem"), and treated with drugs. Recently, it has been argued that it is a problem rooted not so much in women themselves, but in their position in the social structure, especially in the context of young motherhood, when many women are left isolated and under-stimulated. The condition is objectively there, but its meaning and the response to it are subjectively reinterpreted.

With the recognition that social problems are *created* and *defined* rather than *given* and *self-evident* has come attempts to describe the process of their social creation. Many writers have developed this theme, paying particular attention to the role of pressure groups and of the mass media. The American sociologist, Howard Becker, has described some of the stages in the development of a "problem."

The first stage, he says, is when a person or a group defines a set of objective conditions as posing a danger or containing the seeds of future difficulties. Becker says that we must ask to whom it seems a problem, what draws it to their attention, and why other, objectively equally problematic issues are not so seen.

The next stage is that concern about the problem must become shared and widespread. It is possible to study how this happens, what kinds of people are persuaded and why, and what is the role of the media in the process. (Much recent sociology of the media has been concerned with what are called "moral panics," about such groups as drug-takers, skinheads, and muggers, and how and why these panics develop. A Marxist angle on this question, like the one taken by Stuart Hall in *Policing the Crisis* (1978), suggests that they are ideologically important in distracting us from the real issues of injustice in capitalist society.)

When widespread concern has been aroused, Becker says, a pressure group must take an interest, if the problem is to be maintained in the public eye. This may mean the adoption of the issue – by an already existing group, or the creation of a new group, such as Shelter in the 1960s, the Festival of Light in the 1970s or Women against Rape in the 1980s. It then becomes in the interests of that group that the problem should continue to be seen as important. Its disappearance would be a threat to their status. There may also be a matter of competing interest. Efforts by groups like ASH to redefine smoking as a social problem are opposed, very successfully, by those in whose interests it is

BOOKS

Some useful additional reading
Extracts from Howard Becker, C. Wright Mills and Peter Townsend are included in Michael O'Donnell's *New Introductory Reader in Sociology,* Harrap, 1983
Two other useful books are: Roger Gomm and Pat McNeill, *A Handbook for Sociology Teachers,* Heinemann, 1982
Peter Worsley (ed), *Problems of Modern Society,* Penguin, 1978

that cigarettes should be bought.

As well as studying the creation of social problems, sociologists must show how they are located in the social structure. As C. Wright Mills put it, private troubles that affect the individual are the outcome of structural arrangements, and are thus connected with wider public issues. The unemployment of one individual is a private trouble. The unemployment of between three and four million people is a public issue, transcending the individual and involving a crisis in economic arrangements. The British sociologist, Peter Worsley, puts it this way: "Social problems are personal in their impact, but patterned in both their causation and distribution."

Sociologists may also be concerned with social policy, the state's response to officially recognised social problems. Traditionally, social policy has been defined as covering state-provided services such as national insurance, social security, health and welfare services, housing, education and crime and its treatment.

All of these are supposedly designed to reduce suffering or disadvantage in specific areas of social life. This assumes that social problems can be alleviated or even removed through piecemeal social engineering by a benevolent government in a society where certain values are widely shared, and where, ultimately, everyone's interests are the same.

A more politicised standpoint argues that the problems of race, pollution, poverty, and the inner cities are the outcome of contests between groups for the control of scarce resources and of the application of political power. The idea of specific and separate social problems is itself ideological, concealing the fact that they are all part of political conflict, based on clashes of general interest groups in society. To treat them as social problems, as though something had gone wrong with an essentially sound system, is to suggest that they can be resolved without resort to politics, but through the non-political actions of experts.

In this way, measures can be taken which favour the interests of the powerful, as though they were non-political "solutions." A key contribution here has been made by the British researcher, Peter Townsend. Social policy, he says, involves more than just the administration of the welfare state, but must mean questioning the economic structure of society. Social policy must raise basic questions about how society *should* be, and about whether it should be fundamentally changed. Townsend's own view is that the problems of inequality cannot be resolved without a fundamental restructuring of society. Every time we read that there is a social problem, whether in Handsworth, South Africa or Liverpool, we should ask the following questions.

● Who says it's a problem?
● Why do they say it's a problem? Are their interests being threatened? Are their values being challenged? Do they gain from promoting the problem?
● How is the problem formulated, and whose version is to be believed?
● What theories are used to explain the problem, and how far do they explain it away by concealing that its origins lie in the social structure?

The last vital question of all is: "What is the source of the power that allows people to define a social problem in the first place?"

SOCIOLOGISTS: THE KEY THINKERS

Karl Marx (1818–1883)

LIFE

Marx was born the son of a lawyer in the Rhineland town of Trier. He grew up in an atmosphere of sympathy for the liberal ideas of the Enlightenment and the French Revolution. However, once he had become a student at Berlin University his political ideas began to move in a more radical direction. He was particularly influenced by a group of philosophers called the Young Hegelians, who were interested in using some of the ideas of the philosopher, G. W. F. Hegel, in order to criticise both religion and the politics of the Prussian state in which Berlin was situated.

After being frustrated in his hopes of becoming a university teacher, Marx turned to journalism. His articles on social and political problems for a radical Cologne newspaper between 1841 and 1843 earned him both respect and notoriety, leading to the closure of the paper by the authorities. A few months later Marx left for Paris, where he was introduced to the ideas of socialism and communism. There he met Frederick Engels, who was

to become his lifelong collaborator, and finally broke with Young Hegelianism because it did not want to look at the social and economic basis of politics.

During this period Marx was reading a great deal about economics, especially the theories of the classical economists, Smith and Ricardo. He began to believe that political domination follows directly from economic power, and as a result his political views came to be more and more entwined with his theories about developing capitalist society. After a brief spell in Germany, during the short-lived revolution of 1848, which Marx had predicted in his *Communist Manifesto,* he moved to London for what was to become a permanent exile.

For the rest of his life Marx devoted his time to two major tasks – the building of a revolutionary workers' party, and the detailed analysis of the capitalist socio-economic system. The two are connected intimately. Marx believed that a scientific theory of the inherent conflicts and contradictions of capitalism was a pre-requisite to its revolutionary overthrow.

Although his life in London was initially one of near-poverty and domestic tragedy (including the death of three of his children), things gradually improved – helped by financial assistance from Engels, journalism and small inheritances. However, Marx never finished the work of his later years – a massive study, called the *Economics,* which was to deal with almost all aspects of capitalist society. *Capital,* his most famous work, is only one small fragment of the great project – and even that was left unfinished. His health declined rapidly in his later years, and he died in 1883.

WORK

Engels once said that Marxism was made up of three vital parts: "German idealist philosophy, French socialism and English economic theory," and it is possible to see the development of Marx's thought moving through these three strands, in that order.

In 1844 Marx wrote the *Economic and Philosophical Manuscripts.* They were much influenced by the idealist philosophy of the Young Hegelians, and in them Marx examines the key concept of *alienation.* Marx looked at the theories of the classical economists and tried to show that the way in which they used concepts like *labour* and *property* tended to make real social relations between real men and women appear as if they were simply things, or *commodities.* In other words, classical economics presented economic relationships, which are only a historical form of social relationships, in an *alienated* or distorted way. Classical economics, Marx thought, tended to justify the division of capitalist society into owners and non-owners of property. It converted what men produced, using a part of themselves (their *labour*), into an alienated object which they could no longer feel to be part of them. Because human labour can be alienated, it follows directly that men themselves can be alienated, treated as "objects" in the production process.

This concern with alienation is a continuing theme in Marx's work. By 1848 Marx's involvement with revolutionary politics and communism led him to focus much greater attention on the political consequences of capitalism. In the *Communist Manifesto* he moves on from alienated man to a discussion of the class structure of capitalist society. Marx argued that the new form of society was simplifying all social relationships in such a way that "two great classes" were emerging: bourgeoisie and proletariat. The former owned the productive forces of capitalist society, while the latter owned only their labour power. The conflict of interests between these two groups was such that in their inevitable *class-struggle* over who should own the *means of production* (i.e. factories, farms, mines and so on) society would come to the point where a revolution would occur. The proletariat, or wage-workers, would inaugurate a new *classless* society, because their interests were those of society as a whole.

While Marx believed social revolution to be the driving force of history, and that the revolutionary overthrow of capitalism was inevitable, he also believed that for the proletariat to become a revolutionary force they would have to see themselves as a class with common interests. But that in itself would not be enough, for successful revolutions require the right economic, political and social conditions. Predicting when these conditions would appear thus became crucial, and made it essential that the proletariat had a reliable scientific theory about how capitalism worked.

Much of Marx's time was devoted to producing such a theory of capitalism. Although this project – the *Economics* – was unfinished, those parts that do exist give a good idea of the final theory. The key pieces are the *Grundrisse* ("Outlines"; 1857–58) and *Capital* (1865–87).

The key element of the mature theory of capitalism is Marx's explanation of how the capitalist *exploits* (and alienates) the labour power of his workers. Exploitation (which treats workers as machines instead of individuals) is the motor of capitalism, because it provides the profit on which the whole system is based, and defines the relationship between the two classes.

Marx said that the capitalist, because he controls the means of production and decides how long the labourer will work, is able to pay him less for the labour he has used in producing a commodity than the amount he is able to sell it for. This *surplus value* is exploited by the capitalist and becomes his profit. The creation of surplus value – which assumes that workers always produce *more* than their needs – leads, according to Marx, directly to the crisis of capitalism, and ultimately to its collapse.

Because he saw that economic forces were so important, Marx argued that all societies have to be seen as containing an economic *base* and an ideological *superstructure*. By this he meant things like the legal system, government, politics, religion, education, and even to a certain extent the arts. For Marx all forms of social life are ultimately determined by economic or *material* factors. So, Marxism is sometimes known as the "materialist conception of history."

There is a long debate within sociology about whether Marxism is a type of sociological theory, or something which stands on its own as a critique and theory of capitalist society linked to a political ideology. Whatever position one takes, it is clear that Marxism has been enormously influential, and much contemporary and past research, on topics like revolution, social class, ideology, alienation at work, the state, etc., has been directly influenced by Marxist theories and concepts.

Max Weber (1864–1920)

LIFE

Weber was born in Erfurt, Prussia (now part of East Germany), the son of a liberal politician and journalist. He lived throughout his life in a Germany which had only just achieved unification, and in which liberal political ideals were constantly under pressure from the dominant ruling class of Prussian landowners. Weber was at one stage all set to become a successful lawyer. But his wide-ranging academic interests took him away from law into the study of economics, history, philosophy, music, religion and sociology.

Although he began his university career teaching law at Berlin University in 1892, and moved rapidly to professorships in political economy at Freiburg and Heidelberg, Weber moved increasingly closer to sociology as a means of synthesising his vast range of intellectual interests.

Despite a severe nervous breakdown in 1899, which took him away from academic work until 1918, Weber continued to write, study and carry out research. He was one of the prime movers in the German Sociological Association, and tried hard to develop the discipline as a sort of midway scientific position between the "hard" natural sciences on the one hand,

and "cultural" studies – art, history, literature – on the other.

WORK

Weber's sociology attempted to make systematic statements about the social and historical context of social action. In contrast to both Marx and Durkheim, he was more interested in explaining *individual social action* and what motivates it than in detailed analysis of social structures. This followed from his belief in *causal pluralism* – the view that social and historical phenomena are infinitely complex, and that it is impossible to identify single or simple causes in the social sciences. What we can try to do is to *understand* how social actors make sense of the situations that they find themselves in, and try to see things through their eyes.

The principal method of sociology, for Weber, is what he called *Verstehen,* or interpretive understanding – trying to think oneself into the situations of the people one is interested in. Although this might seem difficult if one wanted to explain the action of an eleventh century Chinese mandarin, Weber argued that it was possible to form certain basic models of action as a guide to understanding. There are, he said, certain *ideal-typical* forms of action which can be applied to any situation. The *ideal-type* is a central and much-used component of Weber's thought: it is a means of classifying social reality in a very condensed way – for example, into four "pure" types of social action, as follows. (Action is different from behaviour: we use the term to describe the meanings which lie behind any particular, externally observable behaviour.)

(i) *technical-rational action,* where the actor rationally chooses both his objective and the means to achieve it, as a plane designer uses a stress theory to design a wing.

(ii) *value-rational action,* where the actor holds to an important moral value, and lives up to it in a rational way. A captain deciding to go down with his ship would be an example.

(iii) *affective action,* where the actor is guided by emotional motives – the lover embracing his beloved.

(iv) *traditional action,* where the actor is driven by custom, accepted uncritically as entirely "natural."

Weber thought that western society was becoming more and more dominated by *technical-rational action.* All sectors of society were affected by it, and it was driving out the other forms of action. The classic example of the development of modern *rational capitalism,* and his most famous study, *The Protestant Ethic and the Spirit of Capitalism* (1904–05), is devoted to understanding how a particular type of religious ethic came to influence economic behaviour, thereby making it more technically-rational. This cultural basis for capitalism, which saw the values of a particular social group – the Protestant middle-class – become dominant economic values, is exclusively to be found in western society. Weber carefully combed the cultures and religions of the non-western world in order to show that their failure to invent rational capitalism was rooted in cultural factors. In one sense, Weber was arguing against Marx, by saying that the rise of capitalism was due not simply to economic class factors, but to a multiplicity of social and cultural forces. His view that it is crucially important to consider status and power as sources of social division at least as important as economic class, has made Weber's work the starting point for all non-Marxist stratification theories.

One other key area of Weber's work is his concern with power and authority. Here again the ideal-type comes into play, in the distinction of the types of *legitimate authority.* Weber carefully separated *power* from *authority:* the former is the ability to get things done by threats of force or sanction, the latter the ability to get things done because the order is seen as justified or *legitimate.* In earlier types of society, authority was either:

(i) *traditional,* based on the belief that the ruler had a customary or natural right to rule, either god-given or because of his descent; or:

(ii) *charismatic,* based on the belief that the ruler had some special, unique virtue – religious or heroic.

In modern society, however, the rationalisation process has ensured that authority is increasingly of a third type – *rational-legal:* based in formal, written rules which have the force of law. Thus prime ministers, presidents, civil servants, managing directors can tell us what to do because we believe they have a legal right to do so. Weber's overriding fear at the end of his life was that there would inevitably arise a deadening and dictatorial bureaucracy – the ultimate consequence of the rationalisation which was chasing the magic from the world.

Emile Durkheim (1858–1917)

LIFE

The son of a rabbi, Durkheim was born at Epinal in Lorraine, eastern France. Originally he wanted to become a rabbi himself, but a conversion to Catholicism and then to agnosticism in his teens led him to seek an academic life. A brilliant student, he went to a Paris college frequented by the cream of French intellectual life – the Ecole Normale Supérieure. He didn't much like its rather literary style, however, and became increasingly interested in philosophy and the sciences.

After graduating in 1882 he taught in several Paris schools until 1885–86, when he made an important study visit to Germany. He was most impressed by German advances in social science and psychology, and his reports on academic developments there were so good that he was soon offered a teaching post at the University of Bordeaux. Because the young Third Republic in France saw education as a means of ensuring its stability against right-wing attacks by the church and the monarchists, men like Durkheim, who had progressive views, were encouraged. His job at Bordeaux was the first social sciences post in a French university, and during his period there Durkheim produced nearly all his most important and influential work, attracting a host of outstanding students who helped to spread the word about the new science of sociology. By 1902 he was so respected that he was called back to Paris to become, eventually, Professor of Education and Social Sciences at the Sorbonne.

Durkheim worked hard and successfully at the job of making sociology a respectable academic discipline. Although a socialist, he had little to do with politics, but he did make a minor intervention in the Dreyfus Affair – the scandal at the turn of the century involving the persecution of a Jewish army officer.

WORK

Durkheim's aim was to establish sociology as a distinct science with a specific subject-matter and clearcut methods. He always wanted this new science to have practical uses, so much of his work was devoted to looking at ways of making society operate more efficiently.

The overriding emphasis in Durkheim's sociological work is on the moral basis of social stability – what he called *social solidarity* (in other words, what holds society together).

His first major study, *The Division of Labour in Society* (1893), was overwhelmingly concerned with the problem of *individualism*. As modern society develops an increasingly complex division of labour, people are expected to be "their own masters," and to have *individual* rights and duties. Durkheim explains this by reference to the growing specialisation of roles in all spheres of social life.

Modern societies – especially those affected most by the democratic and industrial revolutions – need an ethic of social solidarity. In simpler and more traditional societies, solidarity is produced by the strong feelings people have of belonging to a group – in a tribe, for example, where the division of labour is so rudimentary that what everybody does is governed by the same set of moral rules. These rules are known to everybody, and enforced by strong repressive sanctions: solidarity is *mechanically* produced because no one has to wonder whether something is right or wrong, since everybody thinks the same way. (They have what Durkheim called a strong *collective consciousness.)*

The complex division of labour in modern society makes this mechanical solidarity impossible. The only way that such societies can maintain cohesion is through *organic solidarity*. Durkheim suggested that we might understand society better if we compared it to a human organism. As the human organism lives by the functional interdependence of its organs – heart, liver, lungs – so modern society survives through the relative interdependence of its constituent units; many different types and levels of social organisation. The interdependence of specialised tasks and roles holds the whole together. The role of the collective consciousness changes in the movement from mechanical to organic solidarity. No longer a system of strict moral rules governing all behaviour, it becomes increasingly concerned with establishing a set of basic values relating to individual rights and freedoms.

Durkheim's interest in the moral basis of social stability has been an important theme in the development of modern sociology. The theories put forward by the American sociologist, Talcott Parsons (1903–1979), on the ways in which societies can be thought of as systems of values governing social action, owe a great deal to Durkheim.

In the *Rules of Sociological Method* (1895) Durkheim set out a strong case for the distinctiveness of sociology as a science. Society, he said, must be looked at as an object of study in its own right, and not as something that can be reduced to either individual personalities or biological organisms. Society is something which we create as individuals, but it presents itself to us as something super-individual, because it makes us act in certain regular and patterned ways. To explain this, the sociologist deals with *social facts* – things which are both *external* to the individual and which control his behaviour in specific ways. Moral rules are a good example of this. These social facts must be dealt with in exactly the same way as the facts of other sciences, and opened up to both *causal* and *functional* explanation. By functional Durkheim meant the way in which social factors ensured the "health" of the social organism.

The clearest example of Durkheim's methods is to be found in *Suicide* (1897). Suicide is usually assumed to be an entirely *individual* act. But Durkheim set out to show that suicide rates in any country at any time, far from being merely the aggregate of a multitude of unrelated individual acts, could only be explained by collective *social* factors. Suicide is a social fact – there are clear and relatively stable differences between the rates for all European countries (England, for example, has twice the Italian rate). These imply that a specifically social causation is at work.

Durkheim argued that these differences were due to variations in the level of social solidarity found within societies – which meant that those which had a strongly integrated moral order had the lowest rates. Similarly those people who have a system of duties and responsibilities, like married people, tend to have lower rates of suicide than those who are relatively "free."

Durkheim distinguished three main types of suicide:
(i) *egoistic,* where the individual lacks integration in a social group – the young student, for example, living away from home for the first time, who has not made any friends at college, and belongs to no organisations or clubs.
(ii) *anomic,* where the individual loses faith in, or is unsure about, the moral values he should hold. A classic example is the successful businessman who becomes bankrupt through economic recession and feels that his economic values have been proved false.
(iii) *altruistic,* where the individual feels a strong commitment to a society or social group, and suicide may be an honourable duty – for example the Japanese *kamikaze* pilot.

After the study of suicide Durkheim turned increasingly to the study of religion as the foundation of social solidarity. In two important studies, *Primitive Classification* (1903) and *The Elementary Forms of the Religious Life* (1912), he looked in detail at traditional and primitive societies, using a great deal of anthropological evidence on the beliefs and ceremonies of their religions. He looked especially closely at the Australian aborigines. One aim of this work was to show how religion in the simplest societies is the basis of all categories of thought – like space, time, causality. Durkheim assumed that all societies evolve along the same lines, from primitive to complex. He argued that the division of the world into *sacred* and *profane* (or non-sacred) parts made by all primitive religions was the simplest pre-scientific level of classification. Similarly, the role of ceremonies and rituals in reaffirming the unity of the social group – the clan, kinship group, or tribe – he saw as the basis of moral values about social solidarity. As society became more complex, these simple religious beliefs and practices themselves became more detailed and complex, eventually moving away from their original functions to be transformed into more specialised ideas, values and behaviour. Later sociologists have called this a process of *structural differentiation*.

Durkheim has had a major influence on sociology in two ways: through his emphasis on the moral basis of social cohesion, and his outline of the scientific basis and methods of sociology.

George Herbert Mead (1863–1931)

Mead was a philosopher by training, and it is a curious fact that his contribution to sociology came not so much through books and articles as through his teaching at the University of Chicago. Strangely enough, he did not publish a single book on sociology, and what we know of his ideas has come to us through his students. After his death they put together their lecture notes, together with what fragments of writings they could find among his papers, and assembled the whole as a book called *Mind, Self and Society* (1934).

Mead's ideas formed one of the bases of *symbolic interactionism,* a sociological perspective which sees the basic unit of sociological analysis as people who are interacting – in other words, responding to one another and adjusting their behaviour accordingly. Symbolic interactionists believe that human societies should be viewed as people living together, sharing the same language, understanding each other and interacting in the light of shared meanings. They are particularly interested in such matters as:
● how children grow up to be thinking and problem-solving adults;
● how human language differs from communication systems used by other animals;
● how our language reflects our view of our environment;
● how various groups and organisations rely on language for their existence.

LIFE

Mead was the son of a New England church minister, and came from a family with a long line of Puritan forebears. His father was professor of homiletics (preaching) at a famous "progressive" theological college, and Mead grew up in a rather strange atmosphere of advanced social ideas (the college took black and women students at a time when this was frowned on elsewhere), but very narrow puritan ethics. Like many people brought up in such circumstances, Mead rebelled against the religious dogma but retained a strong social conscience.

His father died when Mead was 18, and after that he lived a rather insecure life involving part-time teaching and railway survey work. This lasted until he was 24, when he decided to take up full-time study again, going to Harvard University. There he became involved with the ideas of "pragmatist" philosophy, which interprets the meaning and justification of our beliefs in terms of their "practical" effects or content.

Mead went on to Germany to continue his philosophical studies, and was influenced by a number of psychologists (notably Wilhelm Wundt, one of the founders of scientific psychology). When the University of Chicago was opened in 1892, Mead was invited to teach there. He remained at Chicago until his death, always content to be a good teacher rather than a public personality.

WORK

Though Mead founded *symbolic interactionism* through his approach to philosophy and social pschology, the term was never used at Chicago during his lifetime. Despite this, almost all the elements of the perspective which came to be known by that name occur first in his work.

Mead's starting point was that individual consciousness can only be grasped in its social context: as he put it "the behaviour of an individual can be understood only in terms of the behaviour of the whole social group of which he is a member, since his individual acts are involved in larger, social acts which go beyond himself and which implicate the other members of that group."

Clearly, *communication* is central to this process – the conveying of meanings from one individual to another, through gesture or language. But how are these meanings learnt? One of Mead's greatest contributions was to describe the *socialisation* process – the development of consciousness and the idea of self in the child. Through socialisation the child comes to see his own behaviour from someone else's point of view.

There are three main stages of socialisation:

(i) The preparatory stage: From earliest infancy up to the age of about two and a half the child gradually acquires an awareness of other people, first through his contact with *"significant others"* such as his mother, and then through other people in his environment. As he learns language, he acquires a grasp of the objects it symbolises – he *internalises* a set of meanings, especially those relating to the identification of *significant others*. Once language is acquired, the child has the capacity to act on the world using a system of symbols he shares with others. Thus he develops a *reflexive* consciousness: he can reflect on actions he initiates as if they were the actions of another person.

(ii) The play stage: The child starts to "play" at being others – such as his father and his mother – whom Mead called the *significant others*. But he may also begin to dress up – as a cowboy, nurse, doctor or soldier, say. In doing so, he is beginning to *use* social roles in an exploratory way. He is learning not only through language, but also through the whole "presentation of self" involved in game-playing.

(iii) The game stage: By this time the child is ready to begin linking together what has been learnt in the play stage. This is most clearly evident in playing organised games with clearly defined rules, in which the child has to learn to use the concept of *"generalised other."* In playing the game the child must take on a series of roles – in cricket, for example, batsman, bowler, fielder, wicket-keeper – which all obey a set of "generalised" expectations of the other players.

Each child must, in playing the game, respond not to *particular others* – his friends with whom he is playing – but to their acting out of *general* rules, which remain the same whoever is playing. Once he is able to do this – to think of himself in terms of his functioning *within* a social group – he has acquired an *identity*, a "self."

When this "self" has developed it is not simply a collection of social attitudes, for it has, Mead said, two distinct elements: the "I" and the "me." The distinction between the two is subtle but important. The "I" is the immediate, momentary self – the instant reaction to events and situations. The "me" is really a data-bank of memories of how *others* act in particular situations, and it provides a sort of base on which the "I" is founded (i.e. how others perceive the individual).

Mead's theory about *roles* – as expectations others have about a particular person's action – forms a central aspect of current sociological thought. But there are some sociologists who reject this interactionist model altogether, arguing that it is too abstract and speculative and does not result in enough productive research.

Talcott Parsons (1902–1979)

Parsons is the only modern sociologist to have produced as influential a body of work as the founding fathers – Marx, Weber and Durkheim. His work stands in the same tradition: it is encyclopaedic in breadth, original in content and scope, and it represents a type of "total" or general theory of society.

At one time, Parsons's theory of *structural functionalism* – in which the various parts of society (family, government, economy and so on) contribute, as in a living organism, to the health of society as a whole – formed the basis of American and British sociology. But his ideas went out of fashion in the late 1960s, having been criticised for their conservatism and failure to explain social change.

LIFE

Parsons grew up in a home background similar to that of Mead – his father was an American midwest preacher and academic, and he was brought up in the same socially reformist and intellectually narrow atmosphere.

As a student, Parsons began in biology and philosophy, but went on to graduate work in sociology. Unlike most of his contemporaries he wanted to study in Europe, going first to the London School of Economics and then to Heidelberg – where he was strongly influenced by the sociology of Max Weber. Weber had only been dead five years when Parsons went there, and he used to attend a regular Sunday morning "salon" held by Weber's widow, where the dead master's ideas were discussed.

His period in Europe made an immense impression on Parsons. He examined the work of Weber, Marx and other German sociologists and economists at a time when American sociology was rather parochial. So impressive was his work that it gained him a job in Harvard University, where he remained for the rest of his life, eventually making it the centre of American sociology.

WORK

Parsons's most important work is his book, *The Social System* (1951), in which he saw human action as analogous in many ways to a biological system – the means by which an organism functions and maintains itself. He identified four "levels" or *systems* of action, which are interlinked but can be studied separately:
● the biological system
● the personality system
● the social system
● the cultural system

Each system is provided by the other systems with an "environment" within which it operates. For example, our personality system may want to remain awake and alert indefinitely in a period of anxiety, but the biological system may act against this, by sending us to sleep, for example.

Parsons was interested in how these systems maintained themselves and how they resolved the contradictions that threatened their survival. He looked most closely at the social system, in which individuals face a series of choices about how to respond to different situations. In any situation, he found, the choices are generally the same, and they provide a sort of

"pattern" to which the individual has to respond. Parsons called them *pattern variables,* and they provide a cornerstone of his sociological theories. There are four pattern variables:

(i) Universalism/particularism: the individual has to decide whether to treat a situation as a general one, or as a very special one. For instance, a teacher tends to treat his pupils with a *universal* approach; a father tends to treat his child with a *particularistic* approach.

(ii) Performance/quality: the individual treats a situation either in terms of what it does or achieves; or in terms of its own importance, independent of its benefit to him.

(iii) Affective neutrality/affinity: the individual either sets his feelings aside – as in many work situations – or involves his affections in the situation, as in his friendship with his family, friends, and so on.

(iv) Specificity/diffuseness: the individual may have very precise types of relationships with people, e.g. as doctor-patient, or he may have more of a total friendship, and be involved as a "whole" person, as in his family life.

Alongside these *pattern variables,* which determine the *pattern* of any given social relationship or *system* (a *social system* can be the interactions of two people or two million people – it depends upon the level of analysis: the *terms* of the analysis remain the same), Parsons identifies four *functional pre-requisites*. These have to do with the fact that any system of action (for example, a professional role, or a large-scale industrial organisation) has two types of needs: it must maintain itself within its *environment* (other professional roles, competing industrial firms) and it must maintain its own internal form (carrying out the duties of the professional role; ensuring that there is a proper balance of manual and clerical employees, etc.).

If these needs are to be met, the system of action must be carrying out four functions. These are:
● **Adaptation:** the system has to adapt to the other systems in its environment: it does this by exchanging things it produces for those it needs from the other systems –

a firm must buy raw materials to produce; a marriage involves an exchange of love and affection.

● **Goal-attainment:** the system has to have certain goals or objectives, which it must strive to achieve – the firm to sell its products; the marriage to ensure harmony between the couple, or children.

● **Pattern-maintenance:** all systems have to have an "energy base," or reservoir of *motivation,* which powers the system and channels it towards specific actions – a firm must have the energy to power its machines; a couple need the drive of sexual attraction or affection to keep them going.

● **Integration:** all systems have to guard against the imbalance which can occur in their constituent parts and avoid serious disturbances – the firm has to maintain a balance between the incomes of workers and executives; in a marriage the demands of one person must not overwhelm those of the other.

All Parsons's subsequent work was based on these ideas about systems of action. There is no space to cover them here, but his work touched on almost every aspect of social life. Because he was also influenced by the work of Freud, there is also much in his work of great relevance to social psychology as well as sociology. Indeed, his work makes a nonsense of the distinction between "macro" and "micro" sociology.

The main reason why Parsons's ideas have fallen from favour is that sociologists have argued that the functional model of society is by its nature conservative. The critics have said that the functionalist view (whether that of Parsons or anybody else) tends to explain and *justify* society as it is. Any characteristic of any society (however evil) can be described as "functional."

Erving Goffman (1922–1984)

The main thrust of Goffman's work has been to develop ways of describing how roles and identities are transacted and negotiated in "everyday" situations. In some ways he has taken *interactionism* to its limits by treating people like actors on a social stage.

LIFE

Goffman was brought up in Canada and was trained at Chicago University during the late 1940s, when symbolic interactionism was in its most important phase of development. He was greatly influenced by the ideas of G. H. Mead. It was during a study of crofters that he came to realise that the ways by which individuals "presented" their identities to others in everyday situations would be best analysed by using a *dramaturgical* approach. This theory first appeared in his book, *The Presentation of Self in Everyday Life* (1956). Later Goffman went very much his own way, splitting away from the rest of symbolic interactionism, and pursuing his own personal theories.

WORK

Goffman believed that, like stage actors, we are always presenting images of ourselves to the various "audiences" we come into contact with. We usually want to leave a "good" impression on others, so we "manage" our act to convey the best image of ourselves.

Like the experienced stage actor, we find it difficult to be our "true" selves, since there is always someone to impress – even if it is only our own narcissistic self. We play the role of dutiful or rebellious adolescent, of hard-working student, of ambitious young worker – the possibilities are infinite. We are always "presenting" ourselves to others, and we can never stop acting out the roles we have to play.

Goffman developed this idea in *Stigma* (1964), in which he looked at the way people with various sorts of disabilities "manage" them as identities in their interactions with others. He was interested in the way people thought of as socially "abnormal" respond to being treated as less than human by the rest of society – forced by society into the *stereotypes* of "cripple," "gay," "dwarf," "loony," and so on. Their problem, as Goffman sees it, is to redefine the situation that the stereotype puts them into – to assert that, despite their disability or *deviation* from particular social norms, they are intelligent, acceptable people. In one sense, Goffman was talking about how *labels* are applied to people, and then "stick" – affecting for ever afterwards how other members of society will treat them.

In *Asylums* (1968), Goffman took his approach a step further. He was concerned with how an enclosed "total institution" like a prison or mental hospital alters the identities of its inmates so as to be able to manage them better. For instance, a mental hospital patient can become so completely institutionalised that he cannot survive outside the total institution. Another example is the way armies spend the early weeks of a recruit's basic training in endless drill and discipline designed to "break him" and make him dependent on, and totally loyal to, the "total" institution of military service.

Latterly, Goffman's work turned to the closer examination of non-verbal communication by what he called *frame analysis*. In his book, *Gender Advertisements* (1979), he examines a range of photographs (mostly taken for advertising purposes) and describes how they symbolise in their choice of subject, poses and so on, a range of norms and values about social interactions and structures. Goffman says that the point of much of this image-making is to provide a condensed and idealised – almost *ritualistic* – image of what we *should* be, as consumers.

Over the past few years Goffman's idea of behaviour as a kind of dramatic role has passed into everyday usage. Thus, the TUC General Secretary is often described as playing a mediating role in industrial disputes. But this use of the word "role" also carries a cynical connotation – as though the person it refers to is not really sincere. Obviously, this need not be so, and some sociologists have attacked Goffman for overstating his case. The problem is, that "role" is a tearaway word that tends to carry all of human behaviour away with it.

Ferdinand Tönnies (1855–1936)

LIFE

Tönnies was born in the German province of Schleswig-Holstein to a family of Dutch settlers who had been farmers in the area for more than 200 years. He grew up on his parents' farm and got to know peasant culture at first hand.

When he was nine, he moved to the small town of Husum, where a young poet, Theodor Storm, had an important influence on him.

His brother, who was a merchant trading with the English, taught him about the industrialised world that he would later contrast with the peasant society that he already knew well.

When Tönnies was seventeen he went to the University of Jena to study philology and philosophy, and then went to Leipzig, Bonn, Berlin and Tübingen, where he received his doctorate of philosophy in 1877. In 1881 he became a lec-turer at the University of Kiel, where he remained until his dismissal by the Nazis in 1933.

His son-in-law described him a socialist who was more English than most German intellectuals, but more Marxist than the Fabians.

WORK

Tönnies was a contemporary of one of the founding fathers of sociology, Max Weber (1864–1920), though unlike his famous compatriot he survived into the Nazi era. Much of his work is, in fact, of little interest today, but he wrote one book which can be said to have had a very widespread influence on modern sociology. This book, *Gemeinschaft und Gesellschaft* (in English usually translated as either *Community and Society* or *Community and Association*), originally appeared as a doctoral thesis in 1881, but was reworked several times until a definitive version appeared in 1912.

In it, Tönnies dealt with a theme which

was of central importance to German sociology in his time – which, it should be remembered, was really only in the early stages of its growth as an academic discipline. This theme dwelt on the distinction between the *community* as a sort of "natural" or organic entity, on the one hand, and the *state* on the other.

The state was often presented as something changeable according to people's wishes (*rational choice*), whereas society was a less flexible entity – an organic whole expressed in the notion of a "people" who shared a certain collective psychology, expressed in customs, religious beliefs, folklore, and so on. The "people," in this sense, were part of a more or less rigid social order in which everyone had a "place" and accepted it. Indeed, both Marx and Weber employed this *state-society* division, though they used it in rather different ways.

Tönnies took this strong theme in German thought and used it for the basis of his distinction between two *types* of society – *Gemeinschaft* and *Gesellschaft*. He argued that the appearance of a new urban and industrialised society in Germany, Europe and North America during the nineteenth-century made a sharp break with past forms of society.

Gemeinschaft-type societies, which, for Tönnies, were ideally represented by the rural, pre-industrial society of the middle ages, were homogeneous entities. In them, people knew their place in the social order, and status was not likely to change for most of them – there was little or no *social mobility*. Social status was, as modern sociologists would say, *ascribed* rather than *achieved* – in other words, a peasant's son was and would always be a peasant, a noble's son would spend his life as a noble, and so on.

There was a clear and strong moral order founded on the church and the family, which enforced the rigid social order. Few people were prepared to question or challenge the belief-system that was deeply rooted in their consciousness. Social relationships were highly personalised, and linked closely to kinship and territorial ties, and because people did not move around much, either socially or geographically, they tended to have a great deal of *solidarity* within their families and villages.

This solidarity was made easier by the fact that most people knew most other people in their community. As a result, according to Tönnies, *Gemeinschaft* relationships displayed greater emotional cohesion, deeper sentiment, persisted longer and were thus more "meaningful" than those in modern industrial societies.

Gemeinschaft-type society was traditional but also at the same time more spontaneous and less "reflective" than modern industrial society.

In its translation as "community" Tönnies' idea of *Gemeinschaft* has come to encapsulate for us many aspects of life in traditional, non-industrial societies, and this idea has spilled over into our ways of thinking about small-scale settlement life in our own societies – especially in villages, hamlets, homogeneous (usually working-class) areas of cities, where "real communities" are thought to exist. Tönnies himself helped this "emotive" connotation of community to emerge: he suggested that it answers the "needs of real and organic life," by contrast with "society" which has an "artificial and mechanical" form. This contrast between "community" and "association" can be compared with Emile Durkheim's idea of *organic* and *mechanical* solidarity, with which it has some aspects in common.

It is easy to see why Tönnies thought that modern industrial societies were the polar opposite of *Gemeinschaft*-type communities, and in fact his characterisation of *Gesellschaft* is mostly composed of negations of the *ideal-type* of "real and organic" communities.

A *Gesellschaft*-type society is one in which everything is based on large-scale, impersonal, and especially *contractual* relationships. Industrialisation and urban development, Tönnies said, both lead to an increase in the scale of societies, which end up by becoming impersonal. This impersonality in society expresses itself in the institution of *contract*. Once social relationships are based upon impersonal contracts between individuals, groups and organisations, they can be made more calculative, restrictive, and *rational*. Status ceases to be *ascribed* and is increasingly *achieved* by individuals on the basis of their performance – in the education system, in the economy, in politics and so on.

It was the success of these new types of social relationships over those of *Gemeinschaft* which paved the way for capitalist industrial society to develop. By contrast with many other thinkers (notably Marx and Weber) Tönnies saw the loss of community as a cause rather than a result of capitalist industrialisation.

The power of Tönnies' idea of *Gemeinschaft-Gesellschaft* to express the many differences between pre-industrial and industrial societies, has made it of central importance in sociology and anthropology throughout the twentieth-century. If he were to be judged on his other work, Tönnies would be no more than an obscure German scholar. But this one book puts him at the centre of sociological thought, and it is no exaggeration to say that all attempts to devise typologies of different types of society owe something to the *Gemeinschaft-Gesellschaft* distinction.

Karl Mannheim (1893–1947)

LIFE

Mannheim was born and educated in Budapest, and grew up at a time when Hungary was torn by political conflict. He was twenty one when the First World War started, and between 1918 and 1919 Hungary was convulsed first by radical and Bolshevist revolutions, and then by a right-wing counter revolution.

Mannheim, who had been greatly influenced by the Marxist philosopher and literary critic Georg Lukacs (1885–1971) and served as a minister in the revolutionary government, left Hungary in 1920 to settle in Germany. There he held academic posts at Heidelberg and Frankfurt universities, and studied the problem that was to preoccupy him throughout his life: how to reassert the role of reason in modern society.

With the rise of the Nazis in 1933, Mannheim was again forced to flee – this time to England, where he taught at the London School of Economics and then at London University Institute of Education. Mannheim's personal experiences as a political refugee from right-wing regimes in Hungary and Germany are reckoned to have directly affected his sociological thinking.

WORK

Mannheim is important because he was the first sociologist to put forward a coherent *sociology of knowledge*. He argued that thought itself is socially *contingent* – in other words, the way we think is governed by sociological factors, like class, status, social organisation, and so on. Though he also produced important work on how sociology can influence social planning, his impact on the discipline has been mainly through his analysis of the social bases of knowledge, culture and ideology.

Mannheim's study of *Ideology and Utopia*, for which he is probably best known, first appeared in 1931 at a time when a subject such as the "sociology of knowledge" seemed to be badly needed. The competing intellectual and political claims of fascism, communism, socialism and liberalism had not yet come to a head in the Second World War, and the Germany in which Mannheim then lived was split by deep-seated ideological disputes. Part of the problem lay in the fragility of the Weimar Republic – the first German parliamentary democratic republic, established on the abdication of Kaiser Wilhelm in 1918.

Democracy was new to the Germans, and they did not take easily to it – there were many extremist political groups attempting to manipulate or overthrow the state. Even the more moderate parties found it difficult to generate public confidence in the political system. The effects of defeat in the First World War, high inflation and economic depression, were complicating factors which eventually paved the way for Hitler's rise to power.

Many intellectuals of that time believed, like Mannheim, that the solution of Germany's ills lay in finding a method to evaluate rationally the competing ideological claims of all the political groupings vying for power. Mannheim did not think it was possible to find the "essential" truth or falsity of any particular ideological or utopian position – but it was possible to show people that these positions were *related* to the social position of the group involved.

Karl Marx had effectively begun the sociology of knowledge by putting forward the proposition that those who controlled the material base of a society also controlled its "mental products." He considered *ideology* to be a form of thought which had been "invaded" by the vested interests of a ruling class, or the aspiring intentions of a subordinate class. Behind apparently objective, disinterested or selfless attitudes, Marx said, there was a hidden, though sometimes unconscious, class interest at work.

Mannheim built on this idea of Marx's, but with a crucial difference. Where Marx thought that ideology could be "unmasked" by penetrating to the "true" or "scientific" base of ideas, Mannheim believed that all thought, except mathematics and certain kinds of sciences, was related to its social context, and could not be freed from this relationship.

Ideology, Mannheim said, should not be regarded as a distortion of the truth, but as a complementary aspect of it. Every social position has its own perspective, and it was the sociologist's job to identify that perspective. It was up to the sociologists, he said, to locate the social origins of ideas, and to demonstrate the relationships between sociologists and social situations.

But why should sociologists be in such a special position to make these "independent" judgments? Mannheim's answer was that those who practised such a sociology of knowledge – the intellectuals – had a form of education which allowed them to avoid class standpoints and thus rise above ideology. The intelligentsia, he said, was socially unattached, and therefore uncommitted. Intellectuals could arrive at a "total perspective" by relating all the partial perspectives of various social positions.

Though Mannheim's sociology of knowledge contains some inconsistencies (and in the event failed to exert any influence in the Weimar Republic, which collapsed in 1933), it has been an influential base for studies of the social determination of thought. He was perhaps optimistic about the willingless of intellectuals to rise above class and political standpoints, but this discussion of ideologies and "world-views" has moulded research into political beliefs, cultural attitudes and the social organisation of science.

The Frankfurt School (founded 1923)

The Frankfurt Institute for Social Research was, like Mannheim's sociology of knowledge, a product of the intellectual torment of Weimar Republic Germany. It was founded in 1923 with funds from a socialist businessman, and its initial objectives were the study of "social life in its totality." As a result, it bought together sociologists, economists, philosophers, literary critics, historians, psychologists and others. The basic sympathies of its staff, despite the formal independence of party politics to which the institute was committed, were Marxist. This attachment to Marxism remained throughout the interwar period, during the institute's exile in France and the United States from 1933 to 1949, and has continued up to the present day.

It has produced what is known as *critical theory,* a fundamental approach to the analysis of society. Originally this was closely linked to Marx's own writings, but as the Frankfurt School developed, a number of more or less *revisionist* interpretations came to the fore. (Revisionism is an attempt to modify Marx's ideas in the light of experience.) The best-known modern exponent of critical theory – Jurgen Habermas, the director of the Frankfurt Institute – has even gone so far as to argue that Marx's categories of labour and material production are no longer really adequate for an effective analysis of modern capitalist society.

Over the years, the Frankfurt School has attracted a large number of important Marxist philosophers, sociologists and psychologists, of which the best known are Max Horkheimer, Theodor Adorno, Erich Fromm and Herbert Marcuse.

MAX HORKHEIMER (1895–1973)

Horkheimer coined the term *critical theory*. It was only after his appointment as director of the institute in 1930 that the main lines of the new theory were drawn, as he grouped around him a team of young intellectuals. Critical theory would, he said, be a way of replacing the "traditional" theory used by natural and social science. The idea was that it would provide the basis on which knowledge could be used to *transform* society. In other words, "traditional" theory simply allows society to be reproduced in its present form, whereas critical theory helps it to change.

Horkheimer took his opposition to its limits in suggesting that positivist science directly aided bourgeois domination of capitalist society. Positivist science was, he said, "traditional" theory *par excellence*, and could even be seen as preparing the way for fascism. In developing critical theory, Horkheimer infused Marxism with elements drawn from German *idealist* philosophy. (*Idealism* takes the view that the only things that really exist are minds or mental states, or both.) As a result, critical theory tended to take much more account of ideological and cultural factors in analysing capitalist society than other aspects of Marxism.

THEODOR ADORNO (1903–1969)

Adorno exemplified this concern with culture and ideology in the development of critical theory. His studies of music, the mass media and popular culture have been of central importance to the sociology of these fields. Adorno saw in the development of the culture industries and popular entertainment a form of cultural repression. Because it occurred under capitalist monopoly, mass culture was produced and distributed as if it were a commodity like any other.

Unlike many other researchers, Adorno was uninterested in topics like the measurement of audience-response to, say, television programmes. He was more concerned with pointing out the cultural conditions under which such broadcasts were produced. In doing so, he developed the idea that "giving the masses what they want" was only one aspect of the *manipulation* of the working classes. Their leisure pursuits involved them in the *consumption* of exactly the same standardised products as they created in their working hours.

ERIC FROMM (1900–1981)

The contribution of psychology to Frankfurt School theory was vital to its development. By and large, the critical theorists were concerned to explain the political docility of the working classes in capitalist and fascist societies. Why, they asked, did the masses not take revolutionary action?

Horkheimer's concern with culture and ideology was one attempt at an explanation. But there seemed to be a clear need for a *psychological* element in critical theory and Fromm did most to supply it, drawing particularly on Freudian psychoanalytical theory. Sigmund Freud (1856–1939) developed a psychological theory for the clinical treatment of nervous disorders and neuroses. Fromm found that its main elements fitted in well with Marxism. In particular, he suggested that what Freud called the *libido*, or sex-drive, could be modified by ideological factors. Both Freud and Marx seemed to be saying that, deep down, man has certain essential needs and drives which can be distorted by society.

Though a number of problems occurred with Fromm's use of Freud, psychoanalytic thought has come to play a large part in the development of critical theory. Until then, Marxist theory lacked a theory of individual personality, which Fromm supplied.

HERBERT MARCUSE (1898–1979)

Marcuse took the Freudian reconstruction of critical theory in different directions from Fromm. Frankfurt Institute members spent a lot of time in the 1930s and 1940s on research work relating to the psychic structure of the family and the authoritarian personality. Part of this interest came out of a concern to explain the rise of fascism in Germany. Marcuse, as with a number of other Frankfurt thinkers, saw fascism as the logical outcome of trends in capitalist society. He remained in the United States after the end of the Second World War and extended his critical analysis of capitalism's authoritarian tendencies.

Two important books, *Eros and Civilisation* (1955), and *One-Dimensional Man* (1964), greatly popularised the social philosophy of critical theory and made Marcuse one of the gurus of the 1960s student movement. The first book was a reworking of Freudian psychoanalytic theory. In it Marcuse proposed several crucial changes which would make Freud's ideas revolutionary, and which could lead to a non-repressive society. The second book returned to the earlier themes of critical theory, and analysed the repressive domination of people by the institutions of modern industrial society.

JURGEN HABERMAS (born 1923)

Habermas has provided an important break with the "past" of critical theory. He has set out to form a new type of theory which, he argues, "cannot be founded today on the critique of political economy." But as with that of his predecessors, Habermas's work has concentrated on the cultural and ideological *superstructure* of modern capitalist societies. His break with classical Marxism is explained in his recent book, *Legitimation Crisis* (1977). Here he argues that economic crisis can no longer produce the type of conditions under which revolution will occur in "late" capitalist societies. Because the state nowadays takes responsibility for economic crisis, a complete breakdown of the social order cannot occur unless the political-ideological apparatus, which legitimises it, were also to collapse.

SPORT

John McEnroe throws a tantrum on the tennis court. Harvey Smith gestures at the judges during a showjumping competition. Dennis Lillee kicks a batsman during a Test Match.

Incidents like these provoke mixed reactions. We may feel that such behaviour is "unsporting," and that it gives sport a bad name. At the same time, we may recognise that, in the highly competitive atmosphere of modern sport, it is inevitable; and that in these conditions, the superstars of modern sport are not bound by the rules of "sporting" behaviour.

Our attitude to sport generally is ambivalent. We expect it to be serious, but not too serious. We expect professional players to be paid, but not paid too much. (Hence the perennial debate about million-pound transfers of league footballers.) Winning is important, but so, too, is losing gracefully.

So what do we mean by "sport"? Serious play, or playful seriousness – war without weapons? UNESCO has provided one definition: "Any physical activity which has the character of play and which involves a struggle with oneself or with others, or a confrontation with the physical elements is a sport."

But does modern sport have "the character of play"? Play is spontaneous. As the older word "disport" suggests, it is a diversion, something done purely for pleasure. Sport today, particularly at national and international levels, is far from careless fun. It is an organised, competitive, *serious* business.

Some sociologists of sport believe that

sport today has almost lost its original sense of "disport" or play. In his pioneering book, *Homo Ludens* (1949), Johan Huizinga argued that "the play factor in sport has undergone almost complete atrophy" and that there has been a "fatal shift towards over-seriousness" in modern sport. Huizinga says that, in the past, western societies kept a balance between play and seriousness, but that in the nineteenth century, this balance was lost. People began to take themselves, and their sports, too seriously. The result, Huizinga says, was that "culture ceased to be played."

If the fun has gone out of modern sport, why does it have such a massive following? What has replaced the "play factor"? The American sociologist, Gregory Stone, suggests that "play" has been supplanted by "display." Sport has become a spectacle; something to watch rather than do. This, Stone says, has overturned the idea of "disport" – "the game (play), inherently moral and ennobling of its players, seems to be giving way to the spectacle, inherently immoral and debasing."

In this view, "spectator sports" are a debasement of an ideal; the ideal of contest for its own sake. Thomas Kando, in his book *Leisure and Popular Culture in Transition* (1980), draws a parallel between the way in which the United States has "debased" the European sports of the nineteenth century and the way in which Rome, with its "circuses", debased the sporting contest of the Greeks.

But whom does it debase – the spectator or the player? One view is that the players have suffered most – in the transition from amateur to professional. The amateur performs for love (of sport). The professional performs for hire. Play, to the professional, is work (just as the "work" of agrarian societies – hunting and shooting and fishing – has now become play).

This idea of "play as work" can be expanded to explain the nature of modern sport. The Marxist argues that sport *is* work in another guise. In his book, *Sport and Work* (1969), Bero Rigauer suggests that "the increasing dehumanisation of work has helped to determine the form,

the content and the organisation of sports activities." In this view, sport demonstrates the structures of the capitalist system. Teams illustrate the division of labour, for example. Measured time is as important on the running track as on the production line. Indeed the whole system of strenuous straining for ultimate success seems to mirror the protestant ethic – denial of immediate satisfaction for delayed rewards.

Is sport, then, merely a by-product of industrialisation? At first glance, this is a plausible explanation. As Eric Dunning and Kenneth Sheard point out in their book *Barbarians, Gentlemen and Players* (1979), "Britain was not simply the first industrial nation, but also the first sporting one." Cricket, horse racing, tennis, boxing, athletics, rugby and soccer all developed in Britain as modern sports and subsequently spread throughout the world.

What distinguished modern sport from anything that had gone before was the scale on which it was organised. James Walvin, in his book, *Leisure and Society 1830-1950* (1978), says that "organised games [in England] had been traditional since time out of mind, but hitherto on a local and informal basis. Within the space of fifty years, these pastimes had become almost unrecognisable, evolving into a collection of nationally organised recreations, each with its own sophisticated bureaucracy, finances, armies of players, officials and spectators."

What caused this transformation? Dunning and Sheard doubt whether it was simply economic determinism – the first industrial nation, therefore the first sporting nation. Instead, they suggest that the "social configuration" which provided the impetus for the industrial revolution – the way in which the "country" kept itself apart from the "court" in English society – also shaped the development of modern sports.

The "country" – the independent gentry – incorporated the new bourgeoisie. In an increasingly class-conscious age, this bourgeoisie needed new sports to mark itself off. Rugby was such a game. It emerged just as the public schools were assuming a new function: hothouses in which to grow the administrators of empire.

Dunning and Sheard also suggest that organised sports like rugby played an important part in what Norbert Elias called "the civilising process." In the case of sport, this meant a long-term change in the pattern of violence control. Organised sport emerged as an "acceptable" form of violence.

Folk games, like football – formerly a violent and uncontrolled game of the common people – were similarly refashioned. Games which were once considered disorderly, even subversive, were now thought to encourage manliness and gentlemanly virtues. Sport's purpose now became the formation of character – preparation for "the game of life." Sir Henry Newbolt's poem, *Vita Lampada,* which links the outposts of empire with the school playing fields, expresses a "games-dominated Tory imperialism."

The modern concept of amateurism can be traced back to Newbolt's refrain: "Play up and play the game." But when the schoolmasters and clergymen, who had been educated at public schools, introduced their games to the new populations of the industrial towns, something unexpected happened. The urban masses accepted the games, but rejected the amateur ideal. As local clubs began to compete for the best players, the idea of payment was introduced. Ultimately this led to the division of rugby and football into amateur and professional games. Today, with "shamateurism" rife amongst the Welsh rugby clubs, there is pressure to let even rugby union go professional.

Cricket developed differently, though the challenge to it was the same in the mid-nineteenth century; professionals threatened to "steal" the game from the amateurs. In his study, *English Cricket* (1978), Christopher Brookes points out that the

amateur-professional distinction became important just when cricket became a national game. The gentry, whose game it was, wanted to limit the impact of working-class teams and spectators. They did this by creating two roles *within* the game: master and servant, gentleman and player. In this way, says Brookes, cricket could become popular without reneguing on its elitist traditions.

The categories "gentleman and players" continued until 1962, and disappeared only because so few people could afford to play first-class cricket for nothing.

Overall, the picture at the turn of the century was of the sports of the *nouveau gentil* becoming appropriated by the working classes. For the bourgeoisie, sport might be character-forming. But for the poor, it was an escape from the mine and factory. A survey carried out by John Bale, of Leeds University's department of education, shows this is still true. Professional footballers and boxers are drawn in greatest numbers from areas of social and economic decline. The north-east produces two-and-a-half times as many professional footballers as the country as a whole. And South Wales provides three to four times the national average of professional boxers.

Today, professional sport may also give young blacks a chance to get out of the ghetto. Ten per cent of British professional boxers come from black families.

The advancement which professional sport can provide suggests that far from being "immoral and debasing," the spectacle or "display" has made sport more democratic and less exclusive – anyone, not simply the well-off, can excel.

Yet the conflict between amateur and professional still persists. The administration of sport, for example, is still largely in the hands of amateurs. In a major sport like football, this produces a tension between the Football Association, which is often seen as a vaguely patrician body, and the individual clubs, which are run like businesses. The FA has always been reluctant to allow the directors of clubs to be paid a salary, or to allow players to wear advertising on their strips. The clubs argue that the game has to be more businesslike if it is to survive.

The growth of commercial sponsorship is the latest challenge to amateur attitudes. Since the 1960s governments of both parties have encouraged industry to put money (and their name) into Britain's sports. With some success: money provided by Schweppes, for example, saved county cricket from extinction.

Yet there is a price to be paid. Sport gains new life, but possibly loses its soul. In his book, *The Name of the Game— Sport and Society* (1977), Fred Inglis suggests that "sponsorship may be said to be lethal in so far as it signals the penetration of sporting values, the non-productive, essentially human and creative virtues – by manipulative, merely commercial values."

In modern sport, "sporting values" are being displaced by "commercial values." To survive, sport must make money. To make money, it must attract spectators. And to attract spectators, it must entertain. And so sport acquires the characteristics of other forms of mass entertainment. The buying and selling of top players perhaps mirrors the old Hollywood star system. The game itself becomes an entertainment: a premium, in the form of bonuses and extra points, is paid for runs or goals.

Other forms of mass entertainment, which once appeared to threaten professional sport are now seen to be actively promoting it. In Britain, as in the United States, television has been a major cause of the decline in live attendances at sporting fixtures. Since the war, attendances at league football matches have fallen from over 44 million to 22 million. Meanwhile, an audience for televised sport has been created.

Television is not the bogey it was first supposed to be. Marshall McLuhan predicted that television would change the way we looked at sport. He believed that we would become dissatisfied with "linear" games like baseball and cricket in our search for *Gestalt* or total experience. But cricket and baseball survive.

Far from killing major sports, television has vastly expanded their total audience.

It has also popularised (or re-popularised) minor sports. Television has encouraged the rapid growth of professional snooker and darts competitions over the past five years. This, in turn, has encouraged people to take up these sports. The General Household Survey for 1980 shows that, next to going for a walk, snooker and darts are Britain's most popular participant sports; twice as popular as playing football.

The dividing line between spectator and participant is as blurred as the line separating amateur from professional. "Display" can lead to "play" and the spectator become a participant. Sociologists of sport like Gregory Stone may have panicked in their diagnosis of "spectatoritis" – their name for what they see as the creeping disease of modern sport.

The evidence in Britain suggests that recently there has been a move from passive to active enjoyment of sport. In the past ten years, league football has lost nearly seven million spectators. But in the same period, the number of amateur clubs has risen by more than 2000.

Even the number of women's football clubs has risen from 51 to 280. Increasingly, women are taking part in traditionally "male" sports, like rowing and judo. Yet in general women are under-represented among both participants and spectators of sport. Sport is still largely the preserve of young males; the more affluent they are the more likely they are to take part rather than simply watch.

The implicit male domination of organised sport is relatively recent, dating back from the Victorian concept of sport as a manly art. Even today, the idea of muscular women seems perverse and (to men) unattractive. The old dictum still seems to hold: that men should play seriously, but women should merely play.

Why do people take part in sports? And why do they watch sport? G.H. Mead and Jean Piaget have provided some answers. Both saw the function of sport as a "socialising" one. Through organised games children learn about role-taking (Mead) and rule following (Piaget). The world of sport is the world in miniature and taking part in games is a preparation for real life.

For adults, sport may be either an escape from work, or work in a different form. The need to win at games may mirror the need to succeed in one's job, for example.

People watch sport, however, for more complex reasons. Gregory Stone suggests that sports give spectators a sense of order and continuity which they cannot find in life outside. Others suggest that sport, like entertainment generally, has a cathartic function. It provides an outlet for pent-up feelings. Then again, sport may provide a sense of identity. The spectator at a football match is not simply one of 30 000 people. He is a Spurs or Arsenal fan.

A yet more plausible explanation is that organised sport in some way conveys the idea that "all's right with the world." It is one of the mechanisms which Talcott Parsons saw as maintaining society's normative pattern. Sport is a matrix of social justice and injustice. Harry Edwards suggests in his book, *The Sociology of Sport* (1973), that watching sport serves to "reaffirm the established values and beliefs defining acceptable means and solutions to central problems in the secular realm of everyday societal life."

This squares with the idea of sport as a quasi-religion, the opium of the people. Yet the growth of "football hooliganism" – particularly the tragic events in the Liverpool-Juventus match at Heysel in 1985 – suggest that this is no longer enough. That sport now merely provides an excuse, a trigger, for outbursts of the violence it was designed to control.

BOOKS

Some useful additional reading:
Rowland Bowen, *Cricket: A history of its growth and development throughout the world,* Eyre and Spottiswoode, 1970
Hunter Davis, *The Glory Game,* Weidenfeld & Nicholson, 1972
Eric Dunning (ed.), *The Sociology of Sport,* Frank Cass, 1970
Desmond Morris, *The Soccer Tribe,* Jonathan Cape, 1980
James Walvin, *The People's Game,* Allen Lane, 1975

However, the well-publicised "violence on the terraces" may show that sport matters more, not less, to today's spectators: Eric Dunning and Kenneth Sheard argue that "the increase in sports-related violence is primarily attributable, in our opinion, to the growing cultural centrality of sport." To cast football hooligans as "outsiders" who give the game a bad name, is to wilfully misunderstand them. Far from being outsiders, "not real fans," football hooligans, according to this view, are the nearest thing to a priesthood that the modern game has.

STATISTICS

"There are three kinds of lies – lies, damned lies and statistics," said Disraeli 100 years ago. Many people would still agree with him. Yet it is plain that we cannot do without statistics. It is vital for the organisation of society that we should know such things as how many people are unemployed, how many single parents there are or how many people are over retirement age.

Governments have collected statistics ever since chiefs and priests began exacting tributes and organising armies – the word itself derives from the German *Statistik* (or state-istic), the collection of facts and figures on population, trades, finance, and especially armed forces. However, social statistics as we know them today originated from the surveys of poverty by the social reformers, Seebohm Rowntree and Charles Booth, at the turn of the century.

The most important means we have of finding out about society is the census, which is held every ten years. According to initial reports from the last one, in 1981, Britain has a population of 54 285 422 – an increase of only 0.6 per cent in the last ten years. We have 10 per cent more pensioners and 12 per cent fewer children. Well over half the households in Britain are owner-occupied (56 per cent) and own a car (60 per cent). And contrary to popular belief it is the north-west not the south-east that is the most densely populated area in Britain.

Straightforward though such facts and figures may appear to be, do they really "speak for themselves" or are they, as Disraeli argued, a source of trickery – a means to dazzle, blind, or even manipulate, the uninitiated?

Much of this material is collected by questionnaires, which face certain inevitable problems – particularly involving clerical and sampling errors, ambiguous questions and the truthfulness of people's replies. For example, W.J. Reichman, in *The Uses and Abuses of Statistics* (1970), quotes the following example: "It has been suggested that a woman who is separated from her husband will still rightly declare herself as married, particularly if the interviewer is also wearing a wedding ring, whereas the husband is more likely to declare himself single again! How else, it is asked, may we explain that there are always more married women than there are married men?"

By concentrating on fairly factual information and threatening legal sanctions, official surveys, like the census, tend to overcome many of these problems, but not all government sources of information are so dependable. Strike statistics, for example, are collected through employers, and so the strike record of, say, the coal industry may depend to a considerable extent on the honesty of the National Coal Board. For sociologists, further problems arise because official definitions of such key concepts as class and household may differ from sociological ones; yet often there is no other source of data available.

Official statistics, therefore, need to be treated with considerable caution and subjected to two key questions:
● Are the figures presented reliable? Have all the strikes, crimes or suicides been accurately recorded, and what sources of error are involved?
● Are the figures presented valid? Did they really represent the social phe-

nomena they claim to be measuring, or something else?

Questions like these are part of an even more crucial debate within sociology as to the very nature of "social" knowledge. Is it the same as our knowledge of the natural world or fundamentally different? Does society, like the physical world, have an existence of its own or is it simply a mental concept arising out of the everyday interactions, interpretations and meanings given to particular acts, situations and routines by members of that society?

This is generally known as the positivist –phenomenological controversy. Insofar as this debate involves the interpretation of statistical information, official or otherwise, it can be summarised as follows:

From a positivist point of view, social phenomena like poverty, suicide and marriage can be considered as "real" as mountains or trees. So, by using "scientific method," social scientists hope to discover (and measure) the causes and effects of human behaviour in the way that a scientist might measure, say, barometric pressure.

From a phenomenologist's point of view there is no such thing as a social "fact." Things like strikes, divorce and suicide have no existence independent of the meaning given to them by the people involved. Poverty, for example, is an entirely relative concept that varies from society to society, situation to situation. What may be considered poverty in Britain would be luxury in India.

This perspective further rejects the grandiose claims of "scientific method" because it does not accept that social scientists studying other human beings can really be objective. Their own social concepts and values inevitably underpin every stage of the gathering of statistics. As Derek Phillips points out, in *Abandoning Method* (1972), "An investigator's values influence not only the problems he selects for study but also his methods for studying them and the sources of data he uses." Thus, far from the facts speaking for themselves, they inevitably reflect the sociologist – or official – who collects and interprets them. While positivists tend to

see human behaviour as determined by external social forces, phenomenologists see man as a self-conscious and purposeful being who acts on his environment rather than merely reacting to it.

Consider, for instance, the social

It depends on your school of thought . . .

Does this table show that:

a Direct grant schools are best?
b Secondary modern schools were better than grammar schools?
c Comprehensive schools are a failure?
d Such educational statistics are irrelevant because they are not comparing like with like?

School leavers' GCE results (England and Wales)

% of leavers who:	get 5 or more O-levels	get 2 or more A-levels
Maintained grammar	65.5	39.1
Secondary modern	1.9	0.2
Comprehensive	14.5	7.8
Direct grant	74.7	53.9
Independent	68.1	40.8
All schools	21.4	12.2

Answers: b and **d** may be the more correct. It is not surprising that most pupils at grammar, direct grant and independent schools passed GCE O and A-levels. These schools have "creamed" off the ablest of a particular age group by the 11-plus exam or through fee paying. What is surprising is that they didn't get more passes and that pupils from secondary moderns ever passed any GCEs at all. Statistics like this are not particularly helpful because they are not comparing like with like. It is equivalent to comparing, say, Prince Charles and a 16-year-old school-leaver – the result is already fixed. What is alarming is that only 21.4 per cent of our children passed GCE O level and 12.2 per cent A levels.

"problem" of suicide. Surely no one could claim that this highly individual – and usually isolated – act is in any way governed by external social forces, but this is exactly what Emile Durkheim tried to do in his classic study of 1897. His analysis of the official statistics of that time showed not only that some European countries had higher rates of suicide than others, but that these rates remained fairly stable over time. He therefore sought to prove that suicide is a social *fact*, with social causes above and beyond the motive of the individuals concerned.

His analysis further showed that the suicide rate was higher among Protestants than Catholics, in cities than in the countryside, among the unmarried than the married, among the childless than those with children, and so he concluded that the chief cause of suicide was the extent of integration into social groups. The more isolated individuals are, the more prone to suicide they are. "Suicide varies inversely with the degree of integration of the social groups of which the individual forms a part."

Phenomenologists not only reject this idea of suicide being a social fact, but argue that the idea of suicide says as much about the people who categorise it as it does about the behaviour of people who kill themselves.

The Oxford sociologist, J. Maxwell Atkinson, has asked: "How do deaths get categorised as suicide?" By definition, suicide involves intent, but with the victim dead who can know what his or her intentions were? Atkinson's study showed how coroners look for clues – a suicide note, the way the death occurred, the person's state of mind prior to death – in fact, any signs of unhappiness. Coroners' decisions are little more than common sense, yet they produce a sort of self-fulfilling cycle.

Their "official" decisions became official statistics, researchers studying suicide use the same statistics as the basis of their theories of suicide, and so tend to support the coroners' "commonsense ones," encouraging them to continue using such criteria. The suicide rate, according to Atkinson, is not "something out there" waiting to be discovered, but a reflection of the decisions of the officials involved.

As Jack Douglas has pointed out *(The Social Meaning of Suicide,* 1967), such decisions in turn rest on how a particular society defines suicide. Compare, for example, the Japanese view of self-death as a sign of honour with the Christian one of a sign of shame. A study of Danish coroners in 1975 showed that they were more likely to give a suicide verdict than their English counterparts, even when analysing the same type of case.

The study of crime is a classic example of the pitfalls of statistical analysis. According to official statistics, crime is rising, and most of it is committed by young, working-class males living in urban areas. The most common offences are theft and burglary; crimes of violence are still relatively rare. There are nearly 50 000 people in our prisons, yet the "clear-up rate" (the percentage of crimes solved) has fallen from 45 per cent to 40 per cent.

All this might seem fairly straightforward. But, unfortunately, it isn't. Many sociologists would challenge the reliability of such figures, arguing that official statistics represent only a small sample of the criminal population and an unrepresentative one at that – those who got caught. And what does the apparently rising crime rate mean? Does it mean an increase in criminal activity, or does it mean that more crimes are actually being discovered? Here are some of the additional things that need to be borne in mind when reading statistics that seem to say something about the crime rate, or the character of criminals.

● *The public.* Without people reporting crimes, few would be known, and though people still don't report everything – due to apathy or a lack of faith in the police – there has been a trend in recent years towards informing the authorities. People are more aware of violence – they are influenced by media campaigns like that over the Yorkshire Ripper – and they have more to lose: insurance claims require a police report. Crime is also easier to report, now that more than 70 per cent of households have telephones.

● *The police.* The current rise in crime could be due – ironically – to there being

How the police cooked the figures

"Black crime: the alarming figures"
This was the headline in the *Daily Mail* in March when Scotland Yard released its annual crime statistics. But the "alarming figures" about black crime were, in fact, highly selective. They related only to the category of "robbery and violent theft," which accounted for just 3 per cent of the serious offences recorded in London in 1981.

The breakdown by ethnic appearance was done only in the robbery and violent theft category, not for the 97 per cent of other crimes, and the figures dealt only with the victims' perceptions of their attacker, not with convicted offenders.

Critics of the police have suggested that the statistics were presented with a specific purpose in mind – to highlight the stereotype of the West Indian "mugger" in Brixton. If the police had bothered to record the race of the *victims*, for instance, they would have come up with a very different statistical picture. Home Office research has shown that blacks are 37 times more likely than whites to be the victims of racially motivated attacks, and Asians 50 times more likely.

more and better equipped police, who are discovering more crime (but solving proportionately less). Variations in the way the police record crimes also has an influence. As A. K. Bottomley noted in *Decisions in the Penal Process* (1973), "The crime of attempted housebreaking with intent to steal is regularly written down, when undetected, to the less serious malicious damage category. In some police areas this leads to an under-recording of 60 per cent in attempted housebreaking."

However, the really critical influence on the crime statistics is the decision of police on the beat whether to arrest or not. Such discretion is both inevitable and necessary if the courts and prisons are not to be overwhelmed. But a number of studies, particularly in the United States, of the basis upon which such decisions are made have caused some concern. Not only do policemen seem to be acting as

judge and jury in deciding on someone's likely guilt, but seem to make such decisions more according to some predetermined stereotype of a typical criminal than on the basis of the criminality of the act involved. According to an American study by S. Brian and I. Piliavin (1964), "compared to other youths, Negroes and boys whose appearance matched the delinquent stereotypes were more frequently stopped and interrogated by policemen – often even in the absence of evidence that an offence had been committed – and were usually given more severe dispositions for the same violations."

The key influence here seems to be not only the youths' appearance but their attitude, their demeanour, and whether or not they are respectful to the police. As the first gateway into the criminal system (and into the official statistics), such decisions are crucial, and represent a form of pre-trial.

Moreover, they have a self-fulfilling tendency, because those arrested and imprisoned mainly conform to the police stereotype and consequently, it is this stereotype that the courts and the prisons have to deal with, and sociologists base their theories on. Their views and theories then encourage the police's faith in the stereotype.

● *Politicians*. Governments obviously have a crucial influence, as it is they who decide what is or isn't criminal. The more laws that are passed the more crimes there will be. It has been argued, for instance, that by bringing the police up to full strength, introducing "short-sharp shocks" and making crime a public issue, Mrs Thatcher is "creating" a rise in crime.

Some criminologists, notably A. E. Bottoms, in *The Urban Criminal* (1976), have argued that sociologists have gone too far in their scepticism about crime statistics. In a study of crime in Sheffield, Bottoms suggests that "the man in the street may not be wrong after all." However, Marxist writers take the debate onto a different level, questioning the power of those who decide what is and isn't criminal and enforce such labels. Their analysis of capitalist society sees the state not as the impartial defender of the rule of law it claims to be, but as the agent of the "ruling class" – the bourgeoisie and the owners of the means of production. Laws are thus made to defend property rather than people, and the official portrayal of crime as a predominantly working class activity is simply a means of justifying the concentration of power in the hands of the ruling class.

Marxists point to the way official statistics more or less ignore the phenomenon of middle-class or white-collar crime, yet, as Frank Pearce argues in *Crimes of the Powerful* (1976), the criminal activities of the working class are a drop in the ocean compared with the illegal activities of the major American corporations. In Britain, the Inland Revenue estimates that £7 billion is lost each year in tax evasion. This compares with £50 million in social security fraud.

Such a critical perspective can be applied to the whole range of official statistics. In the Radical Statistics Group's volume, *Demystifying Social Statistics* (1979), the editors suggest that far from being objective facts based on expert analysis, official statistics are part of the ideological propaganda of the capitalist state – facts and figures produced to uphold the power structure of the capitalist system.

The sociologist, Theo Nichols, for example, rejects the Registrar General's definition of social class as failing totally to recognise the real basis of class in capital-

BOOKS

Some useful additional reading.
● Two good collections of examples of the misuse of statistics are : D. Huff, *How to Lie With Statistics*, Penguin, 1973 and W.J. Reichmann, *The Uses and Abuses of Statistics*, Penguin, 1970.
● The best and most stimulating specialised discussion of social statistics is J. Irvine *et al*, *Demystifying Social Statistics*, Pluto, 1979.
● Two excellent discussions of how sociological "knowledge" is produced are: C. Bell and H. Newby, *Doing Sociological Research*, Allen & Unwin, 1977; and M. Shipman, *The Limitations of Social Research*, Longman, 1972.

ist society – the ownership and non-ownership of the means of production. Why, he asks, does the official definition include the middle and working classes but not the upper classes? Such a limited definition allows those with real power in our society to avoid identification.

Similarly, poverty statistics depend entirely on how you measure poverty. So, while the Department of Health and Social Security estimates that there are two million people living in poverty, Professor Peter Townsend's more generous index puts the figure nearer 14 million. From a Marxist point of view, the state does not attempt to redefine poverty nor seek out non-claimants, since to do so would not only increase costs but threaten the official view that poverty is simply a "social problem" caused by people's inadequacies. To recognise fully the extent of the problem would necessitate recognition of the underlying structural inequalities of the capitalist system.

The Black report on inequalities in health (1980) showed, for example, that "for both men and women the risk of death before retirement is two and a half times as great in Class v (unskilled manual workers and their wives) as it is for class i (professional men and their wives)." Because the government didn't like the statistical picture presented, it only allowed a few hundred copies to be printed.

A radical perspective can be equally applied to any other area of official statistics – unemployment, strikes, race, and so on. So what can sociologists do to make official statistics more reliable, valid and critical? Are the questionnaires and statistical methods of sociologists any more penetrating, more likely to get truthful answers and accurate results than official ones? Aren't they replacing official assumptions with other equally challengeable ones?

Probably the most sensible course for anyone seeking to understand social statistics is to try to obtain them from as many sources as possible. Unfortunately, the government, in its pursuit of economies, has decided to cut back on the collection of statistics centrally. In addition, cuts in university research mean that fewer "independent" statistics are being collected. Useful sources of "alternative" statistics, however, are the reports by Counter Information Services, and Labour Research (which is independent of the Labour Party).

But whatever the source, the important thing to remember about all statistics is that they have been "touched" by human hand and should never be taken at face value. Derek Phillips compares them to Wolfgang Kohler's famous "goblet and faces" drawing, which to some people represents a goblet and to others, two men staring at each other. "The same person at different times, may see either the goblet or the two men – the drawing has not changed. What has changed is what I 'see'. Some might ask: But what is it 'really'? Such a question makes no sense here."

SUICIDE

Look at the latest international statistics on suicide, and you'll find that twelve times as many people on average kill themselves each year in East Germany than in Greece. Why? You might suppose that on the whole Greece is a pleasanter country to live in, and that the climate is better. That might be so, but how, then, do you account for the fact that the suicide rate in Northern Ireland is five times *lower* than it is in Switzerland?

Similar thoughts stuck a young Frenchman, Emile Durkheim (1858–1917), who was studying in Paris at the end of the last century. The fact that different groups of people have such widely differing suicide rates led him to believe that though suicide might appear to be a highly personal act, it was not a random or arbitrary occurrence, and you could not simply explain it in terms of the personality of individuals. So he set out to collect all the available statistics on suicide, and to identify the sorts of people who were likely to commit suicide and the circumstances in which it was most likely to happen.

He found that divorced people committed suicide more than married people, childless people more than people with children, Protestants more than Catholics, city dwellers more than rural people, army conscripts rather than those who volunteered, businessmen more than people in other jobs, and socially mobile people more than people who stayed in the same class. From these findings he published in 1897 his now famous work, *Suicide: A Study in Sociology,* in which he argued that suicide was not simply an individual act but a product of social forces external to the individual.

In suggesting that its causes were to be found in society, Durkheim was not just making an important finding about suicide, he was also laying down the basis of the new science of sociology. Suicide was the product, he said, of social facts, of "real, living, active, forces which, because of the way they determine the individual, prove their independence of him."

Equally important, in choosing the word "sociology" in the subtitle of his book, Durkheim was effectively saying that suicide was no longer just a matter for the moralists – as something that could be eradicated by condemning "sinning" individuals. If you wanted to do something about the suicide rate, you had to look at society as a whole.

Durkheim challenged the view, held throughout the history of Christian Europe, that people who committed suicide were the equivalent of the lowest criminals. In Elizabethan times, suicides would be buried on the highway, often at a crossroads. The idea was that the cross formed by the roads would dissolve the evil energy in the corpse. Sometimes a stake would be driven through the body or a stone placed over the dead person's face, to prevent them from rising as a ghost to haunt the living.

The last time this happened in England was in 1823, when a man called Griffiths was buried at the intersection of Grosvenor Place and the King's Road in London. But until the end of the last century, suicides could have their property confiscated by law – and the bodies of those who were destitute went to the schools of anatomy for dissection. Until as recently as 1961, an unsuccessful suicide could be sent to prison. In 1969 a court in the Isle of Man ordered a teenager to be birched for attempting suicide.

A lot of research has been done into suicide since Durkheim's day, but his main finding remains broadly true – that the greater a person's integration into social groups, the less likely he is to commit suicide. Suicide, Durkheim said, was morally condemned in all European societies, but the degree to which that condemnation had any effect on individuals was dependent on the level of social integration. The more integrated the social group, the greater the control over the behaviour of individuals, and the greater the moral pressure against suicide. Equally, where integration is low, the pressures against taking your own life are relatively weak.

More important than this, Durkheim said, man is essentially a social being – all his goals and values come from his position in society. If he doesn't participate as a social being, then his life lacks meaning or point. "The individual alone is not a sufficient end for his activity. He is too little." As a result he "yields to the slightest shock of circumstance, because the state of society has made him ready prey to suicide."

Durkheim reckoned that you could divide suicide up into three general types – *egoistic, altruistic* and *anomic* – and said that each type was a product of a specific social situation.

EGOISTIC suicide happened when a person was not properly integrated into society, and was, instead, thrown on to his own resources. Thus Protestant societies had a higher suicide rate than Catholic ones because, Durkheim argued, Catholicism, wih its emphasis on rituals and doctrines, involved people in a more collective religious life. Protestantism, on the other hand, placed greater importance on free will.

Egoistic suicide also happened when society was so unstable that people were unable to find meaningful guidance in times of moral uncertainty. So, the rise of science, which undercut people's belief in the way the world was created and the nature of God, brought with it a rise in the suicide rate.

ALTRUISTIC suicide is the opposite of egoistic suicide. It happened, Durkheim said, when an individual was so absorbed in the group that its goals and identity became his. Societies like this had such "massive cohesion" that the individual was prepared to sacrifice his own life for the "higher cause" of his peers. An example of this was the Japanese *kamikaze* pilots, who dive-bombed enemy shipping during the war, killing themselves in the process.

ANOMIC suicide, Durkheim said, was the result of a change in a man's social position that is so sudden that he cannot cope with his new situation. This could be great, unexpected wealth, or sudden poverty, the death of a close friend or even a divorce. The Wall Street crash in the United States in 1929 led to many rich Americans killing themselves. According to Durkheim's argument, they were driven to suicide not only by material loss, but also because of the stress involved in having to make the adjustment to a new life of poverty.

How right was Durkheim? If you follow his conclusions to their logical end, then you might expect that by somehow tinkering with society, you could reduce the suicide rate. Clearly, it's not as simple as that – Sweden, for instance, has one of the best social welfare systems in the world, but also one of the world's highest suicide rates. But looking at the suicide figures for England and Wales over this century, several of the trends fit in neatly with Durkheim's theories.

For instance, the suicide rate dropped dramatically during the two world wars – periods when, it could be argued, social integration was at its highest. For women the lowest rate this century so far was in 1915, and the male rate that year wasn't improved on until 1970.

Another of Durkheim's theories seems

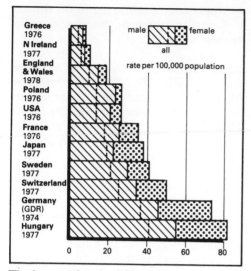

	male / female
	all
	rate per 100,000 population

The international suicide league

Greece 1976
N Ireland 1977
England & Wales 1978
Poland 1976
USA 1976
France 1976
Japan 1977
Sweden 1977
Switzerland 1977
Germany (GDR) 1974
Hungary 1977

0   20   40   60   80

to be borne out by the fact that the highest-ever suicide rate for men in England and Wales was in 1932, when 4045 men killed themselves. The following year, 1761 females took their lives – a figure only exceeded for a brief period in the late 1950s and early 1960s. The early 1930s were the worst period of economic depression in Britain: in 1932 2.8 million people were unemployed – 22 per cent of the insured workforce. The suicide peak during those years fits in neatly with the idea of anomic suicide during crises of prosperity.

Currently, the statistics show that roughly 4000 people take their lives each year in England and Wales. This is equal to about a fifth of all deaths other than from natural causes. The rate for males is now lower than it was in 1901, but for females it is higher. During the 1960s and much of the 1970s the rate dropped for both sexes, but since 1976 it has been going up again about three per cent a year.

However, suicide statistics are not easy to collect, and are frequently misleading in the way they are presented officially. In England and Wales, for instance, the job of deciding whether a person has committed suicide is done by a coroner, who must be satisfied that there was an intention of suicide. In Sweden and Denmark, on the other hand, suicide may be presumed if there is no evidence to the con-

trary. The difficulty of proving suicide in a legal sense means that many such deaths are recorded as accidental or undetermined. Some writers have suggested that the real figure for suicides could be half as much again as the official figures indicate.

The other complication in assessing whether the suicide rate is going up or down is measuring the number of *attempted* suicides (known in the official jargon as deliberate self-harm). This is obviously very difficult, as many people who have failed in a suicide attempt are reluctant to talk about it afterwards, or admit to their motives. But most researchers agree that hospital figures for poisoning by medicines or chemicals are a reasonably reliable proxy indicator of attempted suicide.

On this basis, it appears that recent trends in attempted suicide have been the opposite to completed suicides. The attempted suicide rate has gone up consistently since the war, from six or seven for every completed suicide to a figure of about twenty in 1979. On the other hand, just as the suicide rate is now showing signs of going up, the attempted suicide rate now appears to be going down.

This reinforces the view that attempted suicide is something more than just a suicide that has gone wrong. In their study, *Attempted Suicide* (1958), Erwin Stengel and N. Cook say that there is a clear, though to some degree overlapping, distinction between the two. Research since has shown that you are more likely to commit suicide successfully if you are:
● Old rather than young
● Male rather than female
● In the highest or lowest socio-economic groups
● Divorced
● Bereaved
● Living in a city
● Someone with a history of mental illness or chronic alcoholism

On the other hand, the characteristics of people who *attempt* suicide seem to be quite the opposite. Attempted suicides tend to be:
● Young
● Married
● Female

● Suffering from a temporary personality disorder, rather than from sustained mental illness.

In *Alive to Forty Five* (1967), Peter Sainsbury points out that suicides plan their actions carefully, taking care to avoid discovery and ensure death. The methods used are the ones most likely to be lethal – large doses of barbiturates, shooting and hanging. With attempted suicides, on the other hand, the action is usually unplanned, impulsive, and undertaken in a way that invites discovery.

Since we appear to know so much about the subject, can we get the suicide rate down? Britain as a whole has one of the lowest suicide rates in the world, but sociologists and medical researchers have spent a lot of time looking at ways in which it could be reduced still further. They have concentrated particularly on the period during the 1960s and 1970s when the suicide rate was dropping. Some clear factors seem to stand out:

Improved knowledge and treatment of mental illness: A Medical Research Council study of 100 suicides between 1966 and 1968 diagnosed mental illness in 93 cases. But during the 1960s, doctors were increasingly recognising that suicide-prone people could be successfully treated with drugs. Between 1963 and 1970 the number of prescriptions for anti-depressants rose from 2.4 million to 5.8 million, which ties in well with the drop in that period.

The growth of the Samaritans: Founded in 1953 by the Revd Chad Varah, the Samaritans now offer a 24-hour listening and befriending service for suicidal people. The organisation's growth during the 1960s – from 12 000 cases handled in 1964 to more than 156 000 in 1972 – exactly parallels the decline in the suicide rate.

Dramatic support for the case that the Samaritans can affect the suicide rate comes in a study by C. R. Bagley in 1968. Bagley chose fifteen pairs of similar towns in England and Wales – one of each pair having a branch of the Samaritans and the other not. The fifteen Samaritan towns showed a fall in their average suicide rate

of six per cent, while in the towns without a Samaritan branch, suicides rose by twenty per cent.

Reduction in the availability of barbiturates: Between 1964 and 1974 the number of suicides attributable to barbiturate (sleeping tablet) poisoning dropped from 1500 to less than 1000. Over the same period prescriptions for these drugs dropped by fifty per cent.

The switch to natural gas: Until the 1950s much of our heating and cooking was done with coal gas, which contains a high proportion of the poisonous chemical, carbon monoxide. During the 1950s, oil-based gas was introduced into the system, which has a much lower quantity of carbon monoxide. Then, in the 1960s came natural gas, which by now has almost entirely replaced coal gas. Natural gas is largely free from carbon monoxide. Studies have shown that there is an almost exact relationship between the fall in the suicide rate from 1960 to 1975 and the phasing out of carbon monoxide from the gas supply.

Publicity: A study of Beachy Head in Sussex showed that suicides there happened in clusters, implying that reports of a successful suicide there attracted other people intent on the same thing.

Aside from the personal tragedy and waste of life involved, suicide and attempted suicide have considerable economic costs. The cost of hospital facilities, for instance, is estimated at more than £20 million a year. Yet a fairly large proportion of "suicidal behaviour" may always be unavoidable. Some twenty per cent of attempted suicides give absolutely no warning beforehand of their condition or what they plan to do.

Is suicide a 'fact'?

The idea that an insight into suicide can be had through the collection of social statistics is rejected by *phenomenological* sociologists. The phenomenologists argue that the social sciences differ fundamentally from the natural sciences in that they deal with active, conscious human beings, rather than "unconscious" matter. Unlike chemicals or minerals, say, man's relation with the world is in terms of the meanings he puts on it – and those meanings do not have a separate existence from the people who perceive them.

So, it is argued, we are wrong to see suicide statistics as referring to events which have an objective reality of their own. The statistics are simply the meanings given by people to activities which they have perceived and interpreted as suicide. The British sociologist, J. Maxwell Atkinson, says that suicide is not an objective fact that can be distinguished from the perceptions of people like doctors, coroners and newspaper reporters – and that it is pointless for sociologists to try to explain its cause in this way.

Atkinson's research into coroners' courts led him to the conclusion that coroners have a "commonsense theory" of suicide. If information about the dead person fits into the particular theory, then the death is likely to be categorised as suicide. Coroners, Atkinson says, "are engaged in analysing features of the deaths and of the biographies of the deceased according to a variety of taken-for-granted assumptions about what constitutes a 'typical suicide,' a 'typical suicide biography,' and so on." This view is diametrically opposite to Durkheim's, and though perhaps an extreme one, does show that the "positivists" do not have all the answers.

BOOKS

Some useful additional reading:
A. Alvarez, *The Savage God*, Weidenfeld and Nicolson, 1971
R. Farmer and S. Hirsch (eds), *The Suicide Syndrome*, Croom Helm, 1980
P. Sainsbury, *Suicide in London*, Chapman and Hall, 1955
E. Stengel, *Suicide and Attempted Suicide*, 1964
N. Wells, *Suicide and Deliberate Self-Harm*, Office of Health Economics, 1981

TELEVISION

Who shot JR? Did Robin Day go over the top? Is *East Enders* too sexy? You can fairly reckon that where people get together socially, it won't be long before the conversation turns to television.

In a space of only thirty years, it has become the most pervasive mass medium in society and the principal leisure activity for adults and children. It is the main organiser of most people's social lives and the chief source of information about the lives of others. In 1981, a total of 750 million people watched the royal wedding on television across the world – an awesome landmark in the history of communication.

So it is easy to understand why social scientists have found television so fascinating. Many aspects have been studied. But in recent years two main areas of research have emerged. The first concerns the effects of television violence, especially on children. The second is the relationship between television and politics, in particular the pressures on news broadcasters to report events as politicians would like them to be reported.

This section concentrates on these two aspects. Both are very much "live" issues. Pressure groups such as Mary Whitehouse's National Viewers and Listeners' Association have kept up a constant barrage of criticism that there is too much violence shown on television. Recently the BBC felt it necessary to issue its producers with an updated booklet containing the official rules on how and when violence may be shown. The booklet says that the portrayal of violence must be related to programme context and never used simply for sensationalism or "to give excitement to a dull piece of writing."

BBC producers now have to keep a tally of all "moments of violence" in their programmes and report the total to the Board of Governors every six months. The rules extend not only to fictional programmes but cover news programmes, too. News producers are, for example, instructed not

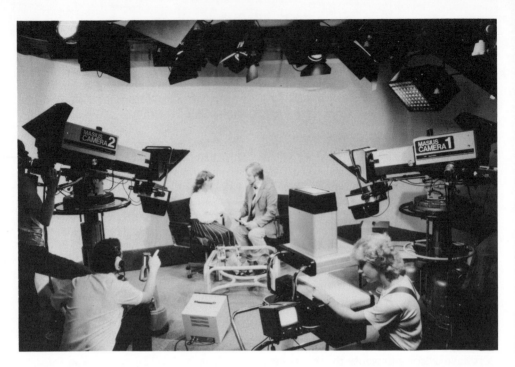

to show close-ups of dead bodies or to include details of the method when reporting suicides.

Television news has also come under scrutiny recently by researchers who have set out to examine the idea that broadcast news is "objective" – reported neutrally and not from any particular viewpoint. How far, for instance, does television live up to the pluralist ideal often talked about by its practitioners, as a free and open agency where all views can be reflected, whether of the powerful or the powerless?

Many sociologists have seen this notion of television as a neutral or "open" medium as misconceived. And not just sociologists. In its *Report on the Future of Broadcasting,* the Annan committee said: "Broadcasters must take account, not just of the whole range of views on an issue but also the weight of opinion that holds those views. Their duty to let the public hear various voices does not oblige them to give too much weight or coverage to opinions which are not widely held."

In other words, broadcasters operate according to a *consensus,* which they presume to be acceptable. Thus, we are taken to approve of, say, the royal family and the army's role in Northern Ireland, but not of "social security scroungers" or the Militant Tendency. This is probably a fair reflection of the way people think. But there are dangers.

One danger is described by Professor Stuart Hall: "This 'consensual' viewpoint has important political consequences. It carries the assumption that we all have roughly the same *interests* in society and that we all roughly have an equal share of power." The other danger is more subtle. Television is required to take note of public opinion, yet because it is such a powerful force in society, it is simultaneously creating that climate of public opinion. In other words, broadcasters are both using a consensual image of society and helping to reproduce it.

Some sociologists believe that this encourages broadcasters to come down insidiously on the side of the "ruling class." Foremost among these critics are the Glasgow University Media Group. In their series of *Bad News* books they argue that television news does not reflect a true consensus, but instead tends to reflect the views of the ruling power elite. For example, the group studied news bulletins in the early part of 1975. This was a period of high inflation, which the Labour government of the time blamed on high wage rises. The government was trying hard to get people to accept pay rises lower than the rate of inflation – in other words to accept a cut in living standards.

The group say that their study of how this story was treated by television news shows that the broadcasters accepted uncritically the government view that there was a direct link between high inflation and high wage rises. There were, say the group, other explanations for the rise in inflation. But these were largely ignored in news bulletins. The result was that, whether by design or not, the "objective" television news provided powerful backing for the government viewpoint.

A more recent criticism of the "consensus" values of broadcasters has come from the Labour politician, Tony Benn, who has written in the *Guardian*: "The Campaign for Nuclear Disarmament is probably the fastest-growing political organisation in the country. There are about 60 000 members of the Social Democratic Party and nearly 400 000 members of CND. Yet you compare the coverage of the SDP during the period of its birth with the coverage of the CND, and you will see that the coverage of CND has probably been 1 per cent of that of the coverage of the SDP."

Benn has also suggested that the views of people who were opposed to the Falklands war were similarly downgraded by the broadcast media. This is a theme that has been expanded by the Glasgow University Media Group in their book *War and Peace News* (1985). Were they? How far did the government put pressure on broadcasters to report the news in the way it wanted it reported? In this section we also look in detail at some of the stresses that developed during the war.

Is TV creating a violent society?

Social scientists have devised a number of experiments to study the effects of violence on the television screen.

Early experiments tried to discover how much children copied what they saw on TV. One such series of experiments was carried out by an American psychologist, Albert Bandura, in the early 1960s. These have become known as the "Bobo doll studies" because they involved a large inflatable doll with that name.

Children are shown one of three TV sequences. In one, the doll was subjected to various kinds of violence (punched, hit with a mallet, and so on) and then the person who had inflicted the violence was rewarded. In another version, the person inflicting the violence was punished. The third version ended with the aggressor being neither rewarded nor punished.

The children were then allowed to play with a Bobo doll themselves. Those who had seen the aggressor rewarded tended to imitate the behaviour they had seen on TV. So did the children who had seen the version in which the aggressor was neither rewarded nor punished. But the children who had seen the aggressor punished tended not to imitate the TV sequence.

At first sight, this might seem to show that children only copy violent TV behaviour which is shown as bringing rewards (or at least, shown as going unpunished). But further research showed that this was not the whole story. For when the children were asked to imitate what they had seen on TV, children in all three groups were able to copy the aggressive behaviour. There was little, if any, difference between the groups. This seemed to show that children in all three groups had absorbed the potential for aggressive behaviour.

Another experiment (by R. H. Walters and E. L. Thomas) tried to find out if people were more likely to give punishment after seeing a violent film. This used an "aggression machine": the subjects are told they can use the machine to give an electric shock to a person taking a learning test (in fact neither the shocks nor the test are real, but the subjects do not know this).

Walters and Thomas took three groups of people – hospital attendants, boys from a high school, and young women. They were shown either a film of a knife-fight, or a film of teenagers playing constructively. Before and after the viewing, each subject was allowed to use the aggression machine. The intensity of the shocks both before and after the viewing were measured. The results showed that in all three groups, those who had seen the aggressive film gave stronger shocks than those who had seen the other film.

Another version of the aggression machine was used in an experiment reported in 1972 by R. M. Liebert and R. A. Baron. This involved 136 boys and girls aged from five to nine. Half watched a violent TV sequence. The other half watched an exciting sports sequence. Then each child was taken to a room where there was a box with buttons marked HELP and HURT. They were told that in another room a child was playing a game involving turning a wheel. Each time the game started, a light would come on. At that point the subject would either aid the other child by pressing the HELP button (which made the wheel easier to turn), or hinder him by pressing the HURT button (which made the wheel hot).

In fact, there was no child playing, and the HELP/HURT buttons had no effect. But the subjects did not know this. The results showed that the children who watched the violent TV sequence were significantly more likely to hurt another child than were those who watched the sports sequence.

There have been many other studies. Their central finding is overwhelmingly clear. As one researcher, Michael Rothenberg, put it in 1975: "A total of 146 articles in behavioural science journals, representing 50 studies involving 10000 children and adolescents from every conceivable background, all showed that violence viewing produces increased aggressive behaviour in the young . . ."

But there have been dissenting views. Some psychologists have felt, for instance, that experiments on TV violence have been too artificial for their findings to be generalised to real life. After the riots in British cities, the British Film Institute commissioned a study to investigate allegations that saturation television coverage of the violence had caused a "copycat" effect (*Television and the Riots*, by Howard Tumber). Police, broadcasters and the rioters themselves were inter-

viewed, and the author found no one who subscribed to the copycat theory.

But what about the theory that TV violence makes people more tolerant of violent behaviour in others? In a 1974 experiment, R. S. Drabman and M. H. Thomas selected 44 boys and girls. Half were shown an aggressive cowboy film. The others saw no film. Then each child was asked to take charge of two other, younger, children playing in another room and seen on a TV screen. In fact, what the child in charge was seeing was a videotape, but as far as the child knew, it was real life.

What the child saw was two children come into a room and start to play. Then an argument began. Harsh words turned into a scuffle. The TV camera was knocked over and the screen went blank.

The experimenters timed how long it took each child left in charge to come and seek adult help. The results showed that those who had seen the aggressive film took longer to seek adult help and were much more likely to tolerate all but the violent scuffle before doing anything about it. These studies, and similar ones, have been taken as helping to prove claims that TV violence makes young viewers more apathetic over real-life violence.

One message that comes through all this is that TV is a powerful teaching medium. But that raises the question: if TV teaches anti-social behaviour, could it not also teach pro-social behaviour?

It was that desire which, in 1968, led to the Children's TV Workshop being set up in the United States. The first, and still the best-known, programme it produced was *Sesame Street,* now shown round the world. It set out to combine education and information in a way that would help pre-school children by fostering their intellectual and cultural development. In particular the series was aimed at poor children.

Early surveys showed that it did achieve its aims. For example, those who viewed regularly were better at reciting the alphabet than those who viewed less often. Regular viewers were judged by teachers to be better prepared for school. In addition, they scored higher in tests designed to measure attitudes to people of other

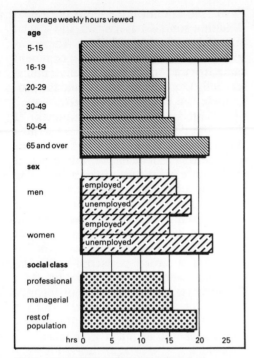

average weekly hours viewed

age
5-15
16-19
20-29
30-49
50-64
65 and over

sex
men: employed, unemployed
women: employed, unemployed

social class
professional
managerial
rest of population

hrs 0 5 10 15 20 25

A square-eyed nation: the television-watching habits of the British

races, and so on.

But *Sesame Street* has not escaped its share of criticism. Some studies showed that it tended to be watched more by children from richer homes than from poorer ones. So its final effect might be to widen the gap between deprived and advantaged children, rather than narrow it as the programme was designed to do.

Nothing is simple where TV is concerned. If it really does cause people to behave more violently, then what should be done? In Britain the broadcasters do a certain amount of self-censorship already. But should there be further censorship? If so, who should be the censor? The argument about violence on TV is only the prelude to a wider argument about the limits of free speech in a free society.

The other battle for the Falklands

Strains between broadcasters and politicians are inevitable. Broadcasters depend upon politicians for their licence to operate. Politicians depend upon broadcasters to put over their ideas and personalities to the electorate. Broadcasters always want more freedom. Politicians always want more control.

The Falklands war highlighted this conflict very sharply. The broadcasters saw the war as a marvellous story, guaranteed to win audiences, a chance to do in British terms what the American TV networks had achieved with their coverage of the Vietnam war.

But from the politicians' point of view that was exactly the problem. They shared the widespread view that one of the reasons the Americans lost the Vietnam war was the morale-sapping impact of TV.

The British authorities were much more wary during the Falklands conflict. They were helped by the fact that the Falklands are so remote. Without their permission and help no TV crew could get to the islands or, once there, send their pictures back. The authorities were less then eager to help. One result was that by the time the first pictures were shown in Britain, the war was very nearly over. In the islands themselves, all reporters had to submit to strict censorship. And the authorities were not above telling them lies in the hope that they would be broadcast and so confuse the Argentines.

The top Defence Ministry civil servant, Sir Frank Cooper, later defended this sort of behaviour before a House of Commons committee: "We did not produce the full truth and the full story and *you, as a politician, know that on many occasions the news is handled by everybody in politics in a way that rebounds to their advantage.*" (Italics added.)

Two particular incidents, both involving BBC TV programmes, showed up very sharply the conflict between the broadcasters' desire for more freedom and the politicians' desire to handle news to their own advantage.

The first came when *Newsnight* tried to piece together what was happening in the South Atlantic using reports not just from British sources, but from the United States and Argentina, too. The presenter concluded: "Until the British are demonstrated either to be deceiving us or to be concealing losses from us, we can only tend to give a lot more credence to their version of events."

This choice of words greatly upset some people. They felt that by raising the possibility that the British version might not be the truth, the programme was aiding the enemy. Among the critics was Mrs Thatcher. She told the House of Commons: "Many people are very concerned indeed that the case for our British forces is not being put over fully and effectively. I understand that there are times when it seems that we and the Argentines are being treated almost as equals and almost on a neutral basis. I can only say that if this is so it gives offence and causes great emotion among many people."

This statement struck at the heart of television tradition. The BBC is, after all, bound by Parliament to be neutral in its news coverage. Yet here was the most powerful figure in Parliament attacking the BBC for being neutral.

That night the then chairman of the BBC, Lord Howard, made a speech which, in part at least, accepted Mrs Thatcher's view. The BBC, he said, "is not and could not be, neutral as between our own country and the aggressor."

True, Howard did then go on to make the case for giving the fullest possible reports. But it was the first statement that Mrs Thatcher took note of – and used when another row broke out.

This happened a few days later when

Panorama examined the views of those – including some Conservative MPs – who opposed sending the task force. There was considerable uproar. A typical comment came from a former Conservative minister, Sally Oppenheim, who called the programme "an odious subversive travesty." Mrs Thatcher returned to the attack: "I share the deep concern . . . I know how strongly many people feel that the case for our country is not being put with sufficient vigour on certain BBC programmes. The chairman of the BBC has assured us . . . that the BBC is not neutral on this point and I hope his words will be heeded by the many who have responsibilities for standing up for our task force and our boys."

There is an ironic postscript. After the Falklands war was over and won, Mrs Thatcher visited the islands. For security reasons the trip was kept secret. But for political reasons, the Prime Minister's officials wanted as much TV publicity as possible.

As it happened, there was a TV crew on the Falklands. But they were planning to leave before Mrs Thatcher's arrival. Officials had to ensure they stayed, without giving away the secret of Mrs Thatcher's arrival. This they did by "finding it impossible" to supply an RAF plane to take them home.

The war had begun with the broadcasters unable to get pictures back – in part, at least, because it did not suit politicians that pictures should get back. It ended with politicians wanting very much that pictures should get back and therefore making sure that they did.

BOOKS

Some useful additional reading:
Campaign for Press and Broadcasting Freedom, *"Rejoice!" Media Freedom and the Falklands,* 1983
Defence committee minutes, *The Handling of Press and Public Information During the Falklands Conflict,* HMSO, 1982
R. Harris, *Gotcha! The Media, the Government, and the Falklands Crisis,* Faber, 1983
M. Howe, *Television and Children,* New University Education, 1977
Philip Schlesinger, Graham Murdock, Philip Elliot, *Televising Terrorism: political violence in popular culture,* Comedia, 1983

UNDERDEVELOPMENT

The 1980s have been bad news for the Third World. Recession has brought debt and falling living standards for the poor in most underdeveloped countries. There has been famine in Africa, the world's worst industrial accident in Bhopal, India, an earthquake in Mexico City and a volcano disaster in Colombia.

All this comes on top of the crude social facts that a quarter of the world's population consume four-fifths of the world's income, while some 800 million people live at the very edge of survival. The sociology of underdevelopment is concerned with why such global inequality exists, and how it might be changed.

One of the traditional explanations used by sociologists is *modernisation theory*. This is an amalgam of economics and American functionalist sociology. It views underdevelopment as a kind of backwardness or immaturity. The remedy is seen as progress towards the kind of society now found in the United States, northern Europe or Japan, with high living standards, large-scale industrialisation (mainly in private ownership), commercial agriculture, and political systems of the "western democratic" kind.

Modernisation theorists look to the history of the now-rich western nations for the clue as to how development might be fostered in the Third World. The economist, Walter Rostow (*The Stages of Economic Growth,* 1960), for instance, has placed the emphasis on capital investment, arguing that once capital investment reaches a certain point, industrial development will "take off" and be self-sustaining, as happened in nineteenth-century Britain.

Rostow's book has been a "bible" for modernisation theorists. It follows on from the ideas of the nineteenth-century German sociologist, Max Weber (*The Protestant Ethic and the Spirit of Capitalism*), who argued that the culture of northern Europe (especially its Protestant religion), provided the values necessary for capitalist development: values such as achievement, individualism, and the importance of investing rather than consuming wealth.

Weber's explanation of why capitalism developed initially in northern Europe has been widely used by modernisation theorists, who have scrutinised the cultures of Third World countries to find reasons for slow development.

Thus, the social organisation of the underdeveloped world tends to be seen in terms of what was once appropriate and functional for a pre-industrial society, but now stands in the way of development. High birth rates, for example, might be seen as appropriate to supply the labour needs of peasant farmers, but are now seen as an impediment to modern development, especially with increased rates of survival. Extensive kinship systems, once the organisational backbone of peasant societies, are seen now to damp down the individual achievement and motivation that a modern society requires, and to lead to nepotism, corruption and inefficiency.

As a recipe for development, modernisation sociologists place great emphasis on the importance of formal education, on the role of the media in spreading up-to-date knowledge and attitudes, and on the introduction of modern techniques of production and administration. The idea is that "technological transfer" can be effected both by aid programmes and by the establishment of subsidiaries of multinational corporations in the Third World countries.

However, within the modernisation camp, opinions are divided between those who subscribe to the liberal economics of the free market, and those who favour economic planning within nations, and some degree of international economic management through agencies such as the World Bank, the International Monetary Fund and the United Nations agencies.

Opinions differ, too, about why Third World countries have made such limited progress. Some modernisation theorists suggest that the time scale since the war has been too short – that it took Britain 150 years to develop into a modern industrial nation, and many very poor nations have actually shown an economic growth much more rapid than that shown by nineteenth-century Britain. On the other hand, free-marketeers like Milton Friedman (*Free to Choose*, 1979) blame government and international interference with the market for distorting and slowing down economic growth. This is Mrs Thatcher's and President Reagan's argument, too.

Those more inclined to Keynsian economics, such as the authors of the Brandt report (*North-South: a programme for survival*, 1979), argue that not enough has been done internationally to offset the trading disadvantages of nations attempting to industrialise. These writers point especially to the way in which the industrialised nations impose discriminatory import duties against the goods of poorer countries.

But the "modernisation" line has been rejected altogether by Marxist theorists, who have taken a very different approach to the explanation of underdevelopment. Marx's own theory of development, set out in his book, *Capital*, has all societies developing through a series of stages, of which capitalism is the penultimate, and communism the last. Each stage, bar the last, has the seeds of its own destruction built into it. For Marx one of the self-destructive features of capitalism is its tendency towards over-production or under-consumption. For capitalists to make a profit and re-invest it, they must pay their workers less than the market value of the goods they produce. According to Marx, the reaction of workers against attempts by employers to sustain their profits by cutting wages or employment would hasten the collapse of capitalist societies.

Lenin in his work, *Imperialism: the highest stage of capitalism*, argued that although the collapse of capitalism is inevitable in the long run, capitalists can stay one step ahead of the crisis by constantly expanding the capitalist economy into less developed areas of the world. The

development of empires by the European powers, on this view, extended the life of capitalism in the west. It provided capitalists with new markets, cheap raw materials and cheap labour, lowering their production costs. Because producers in the less developed world could be paid very low wages, workers in the developed countries were able to enjoy increasing living standards, and revolution was staved off. The harsh effects of the exploitation of workers by capitalists shifted out of the richer countries and into the poorer ones.

For Marxists and some other thinkers, this is of the essence. Rather than simply being the condition prior to development, underdevelopment is seen as a condition *created* by the exploitation of poor nations by rich ones. Over a long period of time, the economies and social systems of Third World nations were moulded as economic satellites to supply the needs of the imperial powers, rather than developed to serve the needs of the local population. Thus the West Indies were developed – or underdeveloped – to provide sugar for Europe. West Africa was underdeveloped to provide slaves for the West Indian sugar plantations, while in India traditional industries were actively destroyed by the British in favour of British manufacturers, and the subcontinent was milked for taxes for the British exchequer.

In each case, underdevelopment took the form of fostering the production of cheap mineral or agricultural raw materials, and discouraging the development of any industries which might compete with the industries of the colonial powers. Some writers argue that without the profits made from its colonies, capital investment in Europe would never have reached Rostow's "take-off" point.

Since the war, most colonies have obtained their political independence, but their economies continue to be distorted towards serving the needs of the developed countries for minerals and agricultural products. The world market for tropical agricultural products is especially unreliable, with prices fluctuating wildly from year to year. Moreover, since 1972 most commodities produced by Third

World countries have fallen in value: to buy the same tractor a Third World farmer has to produce three or four times as much today as in 1972. While a tonne of sugar in 1975 would buy forty-two barrels of oil, in 1985 it would buy only three.

Whether in copper or tea, vegetable oils or uranium, world trade in most of the commodities poor nations depend upon is controlled by a handful of giant multinational corporations, who are able to set poor nations in competition with each other and secure low prices. Dependent upon the export of a few unreliable basic commodities, the poorer countries find it difficult to raise the income for modern industrial development, health care or education.

In contrast to the modernisation theorists, Marxist writers view developing nations as containing different social groups with opposed interests. The development of a country to serve the interests of its ruling elite is not necessarily in the interests of the majority of the people. Third World elites are seen as sharing many of the interests of capitalists from the developed world. Thus, when multinational corporations establish subsidiaries in poorer countries, it is common

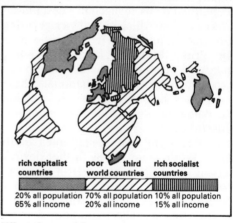

rich capitalist countries	poor third world countries	rich socialist countries
20% all population 65% all income	70% all population 20% all income	10% all population 15% all income

What the world earns

for them to offer directorships to members of the host government.

Modernisation theorists have laid great store by the development role of capital investment and technological transfer from multinational corporations. However, as "underdevelopmentalist" writers point out, the jobs provided by multinationals are usually for unskilled or semiskilled workers, who learn little of value on the job. Multinational corporations do not bring much capital into countries but raise it in the countries where they establish subsidiaries, and their high-technology production techniques may require the importation of expensive materials.

For instance, throughout the Third World, small soap-making industries using cheap locally-available raw materials have been replaced by the subsidiaries of the world detergent giants which use expensive imported oil as raw material, employ far fewer people, and make more expensive products.

Attempts by Third World countries to derive more benefit from the activities of multinationals have often been thwarted by alliances between multinational corporations, local right-wing opposition parties or the military, and the governments of richer countries. In Chile, where the socialist Allende regime nationalised the American-owned copper industry, the western banks cancelled their loans, the American government reduced its aid to almost nothing, and the CIA and a group of multinationals engaged in a destabilisation campaign which brought a right-wing government to power. In Jamaica, where the Prime Minister, Michael Manley, increased taxation on the aluminium ore exported by western multinationals, these companies helped finance the election campaign of his right-wing opponent, Edward Seaga.

Marxist sociologists see aid and loans to Third World countries as further devices serving the interests of powerful groups in both the rich "north" and the poor "south." A lot of aid, for instance, is given by governments only on condition that it is spent on the products of companies in the donor nations. Such "tied aid" represents nothing more than a transfer from the taxpayers of a rich country to the shareholders of companies in the same donor country. Often the projects built with such aid have been irrelevant to the needs of the majority of people: new roads in countries where most people cannot afford cars; prestige airports where most people do not fly.

Generally, Marxist writers take two views of all this. The orthodox Marxist position is that although the poor countries of the world are grievously exploited by international capital, this is a "progressive" movement, because it will lead eventually to the emergence of a world working-class revolution. Other Marxist writers, often called *dependency theorists,* see Third World countries as being in a state of permanently arrested development – always being sucked dry by the capitalists based in the rich north.

Both Marxists and modernisation theorists agree on one thing though – that industrialisation is beneficial to the Third World. However, there is a third school of thought that takes issue with this. Writers such as Ivan Illich (*Tools for Conviviality,* 1979), and many in the "green" movement, see further industrialisation and urbanisation as a disaster. They point out that the earth's resources are finite and unable to support a population of 5000 million two-car families in semi-detached houses with freezers and television. True development, they say, is not the pursuit of American styles and standards of living, but the cultivation of simpler, locally self-sufficient ways of life which do not destroy the earth's resources: stability, self-sufficiency and local control over local resources are the goals rather than economic growth.

For these thinkers, the development "problem" does not lie with the poor countries but with the rich ones who squander the earth's resources. As remedies they offer the propaganda of the green movement in the rich north, and small-scale development projects in the poorer countries, designed to assist rural communities to raise their living standards in ecologically sound ways. Though different in other respects, the "green" solution is similar to the rural socialism of countries such as Tanzania, with its

BOOKS

Some useful additional reading:
Annie Hoogvelt, *Third World in Global Development,* Macmillan, 1982
Hamza Alavi and Teodor Shanin, *Introduction to the Sociology of Developing Societies,* Macmillan, 1982
Andrew Webster, *Introduction to the Sociology of Development,* Macmillan, 1984

emphasis on the production of food for local consumption rather than cash crops or industrial goods for export.

Disasters and worse

The term "natural disaster" is misleading. Though droughts, floods, earthquakes and cyclones are natural phenomena, their effects on human populations depend upon the way in which a society is organised. Social, economic and political factors determine how vulnerable people are to disaster, and how effectively they can cope.

For example, in 1974 Cyclone Tracy devastated the town of Darwin on the north Australian coast causing 49 deaths. Within eighteen months the damage was repaired and Darwin was functioning much as before. In the same year a hurricane, Fifi, of approximately the same wind-speed hit the coast of Honduras, causing 8000 deaths. Ten years later, the damage has still not been fully repaired.

The difference in the severity of the impact has to be understood in social, political and economic terms. In Honduras peasant farmers had been dispossessed from the coastal plain by large American fruit companies and had begun to clear the forests from the mountain slopes. Once forest was removed, the soil became unstable and when the hurricane came there were landslips which caused flooding, deaths by drowning and rendered even larger areas uncultivable. Thus the impact of the hurricane was far greater than it need have been.

This process of *marginalisation*, whereby people are forced into ever more dangerous situations, is what makes disasters in the Third World even more disastrous. In the drought-stricken regions of Africa today, some 200 million people are on the brink of starvation. Poor rainfall has been a trigger for disaster, but vulnerability of the population has been increased by a host of other factors. Rising population has caused people to migrate into ever more drought-prone areas. Agricultural development has favoured crops such as cotton or groundnuts for export, taking the best land, and reducing local food production. Where multinational agribusiness companies are involved, local people have even been kept away from sources of water by troops.

Government policies have pegged food prices low to satisfy rebellious urban populations, which has meant that food-crop farmers have had little incentive to increase production. National boundaries across which people used to migrate when faced with drought have now been closed, and civil wars, which result from including unwilling partners within former colonial boundaries, have disrupted the distribution of food and materials.

In a similar way, Third World populations are usually much more vulnerable to industrial disasters, as the recent gas leak of the Union Carbide plant in Bhopal showed. Third World governments usually lack the technical expertise to appraise and monitor the risks of new industrial development, and in order to attract industrial plants to their countries accept lower standards of safety than would be accepted in developed countries.

UNIVERSITIES

The university, said the philosopher, Cardinal Newman, over a hundred years ago, is "the high protecting power of all knowledge and science, of fact and of principle, of inquiry and discovery, of experiment and speculation; it maps out the territory of the intellect, and sees that there is neither encroachment nor surrender on any side."

Universities were the product of Europe's high middle ages in the twelfth and thirteenth centuries. They were a response to the rediscovery of the ancient Greeks' knowledge of science and philosophy and of the intellectual tools of logic and rhetoric. To use modern jargon, the universities created "space" for the exploration of such ideas, free from direct state or church control.

When Oxford and Cambridge were founded in the late thirteenth century, that space hardly existed. For many years, their lecturers were priests, monks or friars and their students aspired to such positions. Their main business was to reconcile new thinking with Christian theology. But the germ of the idea that knowledge could be distinct from power – and thus free from political ends – was there from the beginning. This theme of independence from outside authority was to be of central importance in the universities' history, throughout the world.

But there is no single, universally accepted definition of what a university should be like. Despite Newman's stirring definition, universities have never had a monopoly on higher learning. In Britain, as the table shows, most full-time higher education takes place outside the universities.

In the United States, there is a hierarchy of universities, with different standards. But British universities have what David Riesman, the American sociologist, has called "a standard coinage." A degree from Oxford or Cambridge meets, theoretically at least, the same standards as one from Bradford or Exeter or, for that matter, from a polytechnic or college of higher education. At the same time, British universities are diverse. They have different strengths and weaknesses.

For example, the "technological universities" – such as Aston, Salford and Bradford – are noted for a heavy bias towards engineering and business studies; large proportions of students who take sandwich courses, involving a year of industrial training; and relatively little residential accommodation for students. Oxford and Cambridge are noted for a highly selective intake, about half of which comes from public schools; for high standards but some disdain towards industry and commerce; and for extensive provision of residential accommodation.

The "new," or "plateglass" universities (such as York, Sussex and Essex, all founded in the 1960s) are noted for parkland campuses sited away from major industrial and commercial centres; a bias towards arts and social studies; and for courses that allow students to combine several subjects.

British universities have several other important characteristics. Their lecturers are expected to engage in research as well as teaching. This is why they may teach students for only six to twelve hours a week for thirty or fewer weeks each year.

English universities are essentially elitist institutions. Though student numbers have increased substantially since the Robbins committee called for expansion of higher education in 1963, they are still well below numbers in other industrialised societies. In 1983, only 6.6 per cent of 18-year-olds entered university; the proportions in other western European countries are well over 10 per cent and, in Italy, close to 30 per cent. But the drop-out rate is lower than on the Continent and, therefore, the proportion of the population eventually emerging with degrees is not greatly different.

English universities have more intensive degree courses, too. Most students get a degree in three years, compared with at least four years on the Continent and often much longer. The staff-student ratio – around one to ten – is better than on the Continent. There is more emphasis on teaching through small tutorial groups, less use of mass lectures. ("English" is used deliberately; Scottish universities, in several respects, are closer to the Continental model. For example, the proportion of young people entering them is 26 per cent higher than in England, but drop-out rates are also higher.)

On the whole, universities have developed what Max Weber described as a "pedagogy of cultivation." Students are not taught specific skills, they are encouraged to develop certain habits of thinking, even certain moral and aesthetic approaches. The lifestyle of a university is just as important as the content of its courses. Oxford and Cambridge, for example, are composed of largely independent colleges, where students live and study in an intimate academic environment. Communal meals and sports traditionally play a central role in college life. Students are provided with "personal" or "moral" tutors who have general oversight of their welfare as well as their academic development. Jean Floud and A.H. Halsey have described this as "a process of cultural assimilation through the reconstruction of personalities previously conditioned by class or race."

Other universities have lacked the resources to imitate Oxford and Cambridge in every detail. But most English students leave home to attend a university. The system of non-repayable student maintenance grants – which has no real parallel anywhere else in the world – helps to make this possible.

Those who regard separation from home as an essential part of the student's educational experience tend to forget that it is a relatively small, localised and recent development. Though Oxford and Cambridge have always recruited nationally, most provincial universities began with a largely local recruitment. As recently as 1952, half the students at Sheffield University came from within a 30-mile radius. Local recruitment is still the rule rather than the exception in Scotland; at Glasgow, for example, 60 per cent

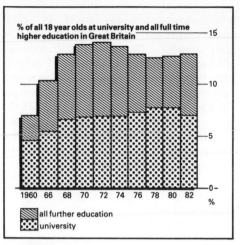

Britain's students

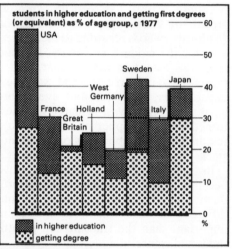

The world's students

of the students live in the parental home.

The "pedagogy of cultivation" is closely related to the idea of the "liberal university" of which Newman was the most eloquent prophet. He spoke of "raising the intellectual tone of society, cultivating the public mind, purifying the national taste." He described "useful knowledge" as a "deal of trash." The liberal university was traditionally independent of the values of industrial society, more concerned with "pure" rather than "applied" learning.

When the University of Buckingham was founded in the late 1970s – with the express intention of raising its money privately – many people talked of the "independent university." But, in theory, all universities are independent. Though the government provides most of their money, it is not supposed to dictate how they spend it. The money is channelled through the University Grants Committee, first established in 1919. Composed largely of university dons, the committee decides which universities should get the money and "recommends" how they should spend it. Within each university, the main academic decisions are taken by the Senate, which comprises the most senior dons. Universities are thus described as "self-governing academic communities" and this is central to the idea of the liberal university.

But the idea is under increasing challenge from several directions. First, the twentieth century has seen an explosive growth of knowledge. Clark Kerr, the Californian who is regarded as the spokesman for the modern university, has said that "this evolution has brought departments into universities, and still new departments; institutes and ever more institutes; created vast research libraries; turned the philosopher on his log into a researcher in his laboratory or the library stacks."

In other words, universities have become "cognitive" institutions: the production of knowledge, fragmented into different subjects, has become more important than the transmission of attitudes and values.

The second challenge is from governments which want to use universities for more overt social and economic ends. The current government wants them to produce more employable students in such subjects as business, computer studies and engineering. The University Grants Committee has been fairly compliant in carrying out these wishes and increasingly specific in saying how universities should spend their money. A Labour government might well endorse these trends, while also demanding that universities admit more students from working-class and ethnic minority backgrounds.

The third (and closely related) challenge is to the whole idea that universities should stand aside from industrial values. The extent to which they have always concentrated on "pure" learning has perhaps

A top-class education?

The elite nature of universities is dramatically underscored by the way the great expansion of education after the Education Act, 1944, failed to bring about an increase in the numbers of graduates from the working class.

The Oxford sociologist, A.H. Halsey, looked at the class origins of university graduates by dividing a sample of the male population into two groups – those born between 1913 and 1931 (who were educated before the act) and those born between 1932 and 1947 (who were educated after). His results showed that though the numbers of graduates from all social classes had greatly increased, the proportions from each social class had hardly changed.

The percentage of people from professional backgrounds who gained a university degree increased from 15 to 27 per cent, but the percentage of graduates from the skilled manual classes stayed low, rising from 1.3 per cent to just 2.3 per cent. As Halsey points out, "there has been no clear trend towards the elimination of class inequality in education."

been exaggerated. For centuries, Oxford and Cambridge provided what amounted to a vocational training in law, theology, medicine or public administration.

But, as one commentator wrote in 1764, "a proper course of studies is not provided for the principal stations of *active life*, distinct from the *learned professions*." The great civic universities were founded in the nineteenth and early twentieth centuries (Birmingham, Liverpool, Manchester, for example) largely by self-made

BOOKS

Some useful additional reading:
Michael Beloff, *The Plateglass Universities,* Secker & Warburg, 1968.
V. H. H. Green, *The Universities,* Penguin, 1969.
Maurice Kogan with David Kogan, *The Attack on Higher Education,* Kogan Page, 1983.
Peter Scott, *The Crisis of the University,* Croom Helm, 1984.

industrialists, to meet precisely that need. Thus, John Owen, cloth merchant and father of Manchester University, created a college to provide "such departments of knowledge as are most generally subservient to the purpose of commercial life."

Universities, however, have been vulnerable to what the educationist, Tyrrell Burgess, has called "academic drift." As several writers have pointed out, English culture is antipathetic to the spirit of manufacturing industry and commerce. In order to gain respectability, therefore, successive generations of universities have tended to imitate Oxford and Cambridge and to aspire to "pure," more theoretical learning. The civic and later the technological universities set out with the intention of supporting industrial values, but both have been accused of betraying them.

But there are signs that the tide is turning. In 1981, the government cut the universities' grant by an average of 15 per cent. Since then, those that were cut most heavily – notably Salford and Aston – have tried to raise more money through research or consultancy contracts with industry. Increasingly, too, industry helps to finance laboratories and even professorships.

So the university of the future is likely to be more responsive to the requirements of both industry and government. But it is not likely – unless a very radical administration comes to power – to be less elitist. As a result of the 1981 cuts, university admissions declined from 84 695 in 1980 to 77 431 in 1984. The proportion of students from working-class backgrounds has fallen from about 25 per cent in the 1970s (a figure that had remained unchanged for nearly half a century) to under 20 per cent in 1983.

Sir Keith Joseph, the Education Secretary, has asked the University Grants Committee to consider how more cuts might be implemented and how far universities could manage with fewer staff per student. In an equally important threat to university traditions, he is proposing new legislation which would remove the dons' job security (known as "tenure") which makes it almost impossible to sack them except for gross misconduct. Student loans, instead of grants, are another proposal that could greatly change the system.

In general, the government wants a leaner, cheaper, more utilitarian system of higher education. Though this could mean a reversal of "academic drift," there is also a danger that Britain could lose the universities' distinctive contribution to national life: the faith in rational, intellectual, disinterested solutions to social problems. And the space for independent knowledge, which the medieval universities created against such odds, could be threatened once more.

WAR & CONFLICT

I t is more than forty years since the end of the last world war. Yet it can hardly be said that the world has been at peace. In the past decade alone, there have been major conflicts involving the big world powers in almost every continent. If you add up all the people in the military forces of the world, they would amount to half of the population of the United Kingdom.

Yet despite the Falklands or Vietnam or Afghanistan or the Lebanon, we tend to think of peace as the natural state of human affairs. We also see it as an ideal state, something to be striven for. We talk of "peace, *perfect* peace." We believe that war, on the other hand, is unnatural and abnormal. There is a feeling that conflict of any sort represents a failure of human relations.

Yet there is plenty of evidence around us to suggest that conflict is the normal state of affairs. Every day, newspaper headlines draw on the vocabulary of violence. Leaders of political parties "attack" their opponents. Sporting teams "defeat" their rivals. Competing companies "fight" for a larger share of the market for their products. The Church of England even "fights the good fight."

Occasionally, this sort of conflict actually becomes violent. Police and pickets fight; Britain and Argentina fight; Catholics and Protestants fight in Northern Ireland. Most of the time, however, conflict is not allowed to become violent. Society controls conflict. Perhaps this restraint is the real meaning of peace. Keeping the lid on; keeping the peace.

To put it another way, the balance of war and peace in the popular imagination is, properly, the balance of violent and non-violent conflict.

How important is conflict? And what does it tell us about the future of *violent* conflict? If conflict is endemic, what about violent conflict? Can war be abolished? Or was the Chinese communist leader, Mao Tse-tung, right when he asserted that war was simply a continuation of politics?

The starting point is the nature of social conflict. There are two possible approaches: the quasi-biological and the sociological. The former attempts to explain conflict in evolutionary terms. Conflict is necessary for the survival and prosperity of societies. The most persuasive exponent of this view was the sociologist, Herbert Spencer (1820–1895).

Spencer thought that societies evolved in much the same way as species. Hence the labels for his theory – *social evolution* and *social Darwinism*. Spencer said that societies struggled constantly to become more stable, more coherent, and more complex. The process, he said, was roughly analogous to the growth of organisms. Societies were simply "super-organisms."

In the process of consolidation and integration, small units were absorbed by larger units, or tightly banded together to form larger units. This is how society evolves, says Spencer. Great nation states have evolved from wandering tribes.

In the early stages of a society's evolution, this process is "managed" by military force. Military force is a crude but effective aid to social integration. Later, as a society becomes more settled and sophisticated, coercion is replaced by cooperation. People and institutions band together because they want to rather than because they have to.

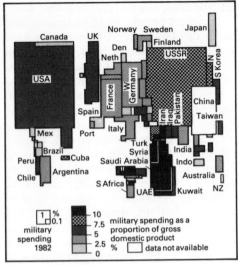

The world's armoury

This, Spencer says, is how societies evolve. They evolve from *military* (coercive) to *industrial* (cooperative) forms of social organisation. In his view, warfare is not a failure in social relations. It is an essential stage in a society's growing-up. It is the vice or clamp which provides the necessary social cohesion.

Even when the need for coercion, or violent conflict, is past, conflict is still necessary. Indeed, Spencer thinks it ought to be encouraged. Spencer's belief in "the survival of the fittest" (a phrase which has been wrongly ascribed to Darwin) persists in the injunction "may the best man win." Conflict is present, but under control, in the competitive process.

Like the political economist, Adam Smith (1723–90), Spencer suggests that competition is the socially acceptable form of social conflict.

It is easy to over-simplify the analogy between natural selection and social evolution. Natural selection does not mean that conflict matters more than cooperation. Nature operates in a perpetual state of conflict *and* harmony.

The second approach to the study of conflict – the sociological – recognises this dichotomy between conflict and harmony. Within this approach, there are two opposing ideas of how society works, plus a third one which – possibly – reconciles the first two.

The first perspective belongs to the *functionalists,* and owes much to the French sociologist, Emile Durkheim (1858–1917). The functionalists believe that society behaves much like the human body. Each part contributes to the health of the whole. The whole is greater than the sum of its parts.

In normal conditions, society is in a state of good health, or equilibrium. There is no conflict. The basis of this equilibrium is moral consensus; that is, people in that society share the same values. Shared values act as kind of glue which holds society together.

It follows the functionalists believe that *disequilibrium,* or conflict, is abnormal. Again the analogy with health is helpful. Commentators from Shakespeare to the present day have seen civil war as a kind of sickness of society.

The *conflict theorists* take a directly opposing view. This perspective owes much to the work of Karl Marx (1818–83), and conflict theory is now associated with Marxist sociology.

While functionalists stress shared cultural values like patriotism and religion, Marxists emphasise the importance of the economic system. They also emphasise the constant struggle between the two basic economic classes of people; those who own the means of production, and those who sell their labour.

Durkheim and Marx, therefore, represent two opposing views. The view of society as essentially stable and unchanging, and the view of society as essentially unstable and changing. Social order versus social change.

The two schools of thought might be characterised, very crudely, as *optimistic* (social order) and *pessimistic* (social change).

Ralf Dahrendorf, the German sociologist and former head of the London School of Economics, considers the "equilibrium and consensus" view of society is utopian. Society has an ugly face – conflict. But Dahrendorf sees this conflict not as a class conflict over economic resources but as a power struggle.

Dahrendorf argues that social organisa-

tions typically contain two groups whose interests are inherently opposed, those who rule and those who are ruled. They may not realise that their interests *are* opposed until something mobilises them. They then become "interest groups" and begin to organise.

Are the two models of society mutually exclusive, or two different facets of the same thing? Is there a bridge between the "consensus and equilibrium" model and the "conflict and change" model? One bridge that has been suggested is Max Weber's *social action theory.* Weber (1864–1920) was born half a century after Marx. As its name implies, this theory deals with how people relate to one another in society. Weber preferred not to generalise about social conflict. He considered that society was neither in equilibrium nor in conflict. Sometimes it was in one state, sometimes it was in another – it depended on the circumstances.

However, like Dahrendorf, he considered power was crucial. Power is unevenly distributed among groups and individuals, he said. Social order is a product of the rules and commands that the more powerful give to the less powerful. Therefore the social order normally operates in favour of the most powerful.

Any change in the social order will hurt the powerful rather than the powerless. Therefore the powerful tend to oppose change and support the status quo. The only hope of dramatic change comes from those individuals whom Weber calls "charismatic" leaders – Christ, Napoleon, Lenin, the Ayatollah Khomeini. These people stand to gain from change, and they accumulate the power which makes change possible.

The paradox of Weber's view of society is that it embraces both conflict and consensus. Although conflict is endemic in social life, it tends to operate in favour of the powerful; that is, those with a vested interest in the status quo. Thus Weber seems to say that although conflict is common, change is rare.

So far we have looked at conflict as it occurs within societies. What happens when we broaden the scope and look at nations rather than groups or individuals. The British sociologist, John Rex, suggests that when we are dealing with conflicting nations, conflict must take precedence over consensus. The reason is obvious. Any sovereign nation state can manage a consensus within its borders. But outside them, it has no such control. Instead it relies on a balance of power.

This turns the rules of social conflict upside down. Normal relations between individuals and groups within a nation depend on cooperation. When these break down, the result is a power struggle. International relations work differently.

The process is reversed. In the society of states, the normal relationship is a balance of power or power conflict. There is a possibility of modifying this conflict (that is, backing down from it) by engaging in economic or cultural exchanges.

Thus a series of favours are extended to other nations which can be withdrawn at will. This allows, Rex says, bargaining and negotiation well short of actual war. Even when nations need to take action publicly, there are plenty of unwarlike ways they can do it. John Rex distinguishes three levels of conflict:

● The imposition of *lesser sanctions*. Recent examples have been the withdrawal of the United States from the Moscow Olympic Games in 1980 and the withdrawal of the Soviet Union from the Los Angeles Games in 1984.

● The imposition of *economic sanctions*. Potentially, this is far more damaging. But in reality such damage can be sustained. The superpowers are self-sufficient and therefore not vulnerable to such sanctions. Even where sanctions may bite (as against South Africa) nations may find it politic to agree to sanctions in principle but to refuse to enforce them.

● The imposition of *military sanctions*. This is the third step, but not necessarily the final step – all-out nuclear war between the superpowers. A superpower can impose military sanctions without using its armed forces at all. It may simply plug itself into a conflict which is already in progress – typically a war of "liberation" in the Third World. By supplying arms or "advisers" to the insurgents it can exert pressure directly on the nation at war and indirectly on the superpower which offers it protection. Thus Soviet-backed guerillas are at work in southern Africa; American-supported insurgents are currently trying to undermine the left-wing regime in Nicaragua.

The top of this ascending scale of sanctions is the use of nuclear weapons. But, of course, such weapons cannot realistically be used for fear of retaliation and destruction. Hence, Rex says, the superpowers are forced to climb down the ladder a few rungs and negotiate arms-control agreements. This allows them to work out the rules for lesser forms of warfare.

So conventional wars are still possible. They need to be carefully managed, however. The balance of power between the two superpowers depends on neither having a clear advantage over the other. There is always a danger that one or other of the superpowers will escalate a conventional war to gain this advantage.

So what sort of war *can* the superpowers safely engage in? There is what Rex calls the proxy war. Vietnam is the classic example. It was a war in which the superpowers gave support to opposite sides. Playing upon divisions in a state is one of the ways of prosecuting a war against it. For conflict can take place within nations as well as between them.

But civil war is a different kind of conflict from international war. As Rex points out, sovereign nation states are compulsory associations. Conflict groups in civil wars are not. The sovereign nation state has, in Weber's words, a "monopoly of the legitimate use of physical force in the enforcement of its order." A "nation" without a state, like the Basques (or the Palestinians) has no such right to the use of force. This is why the state will describe collective violence by conflict groups as "terrorism," while the groups themselves will call it "war."

The popular explanation for civil war is the theory of "frustration and deprivation." This holds that a widely-shared sense of misery leads eventually to collective violence. But students of war who have collected data about actual outbreaks of civil war, have found no correlation between economic hardship (for example) and outbreaks of collective violence.

Nor does this theory hold good when it is applied to international wars. Generally, wars are more likely to have been started by wealthy nations rather than poor nations. The suggestion that the Second World War was a result of the reparations for the First World War looks shaky.

But there is a second broad explanation for wars, civil and international. It is that too-rapid social change disrupts the orderly functioning of society. But again, there is little evidence to support this. More plausible is a third explanation. As the social order changes, new groups attain access to greater resources. They seek to mobilise these resources to attain greater power. But in doing this they run up against the entrenched interests of an established social order.

Wars, in this theory, are a struggle for power, a struggle which may develop into violent conflict. But reliable patterns are hard to find. This makes life particularly difficult for the peace movement, which has had a huge renaissance in the past few years. E.P. Thompson, the historian and the current guru of British disarmers, has argued that the expectation of war has been habitual in our culture. The peace movement ought to be able to succeed, he says, by imbuing our culture and polity with similar expectations of peace.

The problem is that war and violent conflict may be habitual, but their causes are unpredictable. They are unpredictable because human beings still have the opportunity to change their behaviour. Perhaps we should be grateful at least for this.

BOOKS

Some useful additional reading:
Geoffrey Blainey, *The Causes of War*, Macmillan, 1973
Ralf Dahrendorf, *Class and Class Conflict in Industrial Societies*, Routledge & Kegan Paul, 1959
John Rex, *Social Conflict*, Longman, 1981
James Schellenberg, *The Science of Conflict*, Oxford University Press, 1982

WELFARE STATE

Until very recently most people in Britain have taken the welfare state for granted, with social services and benefits available literally from the womb to the tomb. Sociologists were even calling it a "structural tendency" in modern society.

Defined simply, the welfare state is government-protected minimum standards of income, health, housing and education assured as a political right, not as charity. But the recession has brought about a radical reappraisal of this concept – and not just in this country. High levels of social spending are being challenged by all governments in the developed capitalist world.

All these countries currently have a huge commitment to social well-being. On average they spend a quarter of their total income (gross domestic product) on education, health and payments to individuals and families in order to keep their incomes above official minimum levels.

Before the state became involved in welfare, it was left to voluntary groups to help the poor – and these were often poor themselves. Occasionally poverty led to violent social upheaval like the Peasants' Revolt, of 1381. But mostly, people who were afflicted by poverty and sickness simply suffered without any relief.

The responsibility for looking after the poor was taken over by the state with the Poor Law of 1601. Parishes looked after their own poor (though very meagrely), which was possible because Britain was still largely a rural society. It was the expansion of towns and cities in the Industrial Revolution that led to the breakdown of poor relief, and Victorian times were the worst period of English poverty. The Poor Law of 1834 effectively meant that the only relief was the workhouse.

But the squalor and deprivation in towns and cities in the nineteenth century prompted some important social surveys, whose findings helped develop the modern idea of a welfare state. Edwin Chadwick did his report into the "sanitary conditions of the labouring population" in 1842, and Charles Booth's report on the London poor in the 1880s showed that sickness, poverty, slums, bad working conditions and unemployment were all related. The principle was becoming clear that these could not be alleviated without positive state aid.

In the early part of this century, social reformers such as R. H. Tawney (1880–1962) talked about welfare rights conferred by the state as a means of achieving greater social justice. The concept of welfare was developed, too, with the growing strength of the trade unions. But it was the Second World War that brought the political momentum in Britain to establish a full system of social care. The core of the welfare state lies in the Education Act, 1944, the National Health Service Act, 1946, and the family allowance, national insurance and national assistance legislation of 1945–48.

Because most of these acts were passed by Labour, the welfare state is often considered to be essentially socialist. In fact, one of its founding fathers, William (Lord) Beveridge, was a Liberal. His famous report on social insurance, published in 1942, put great emphasis on people's freedom and their duty to help themselves by means of insurance schemes that would pay for themselves. Beveridge believed the need for direct state aid to poor people would diminish as they became enrolled in insurance schemes. His belief turned out to be cruelly wrong.

Certainly, measured by government spending, the expansion of welfare from 1945 to 1970 owes as much to Conservative governments as to Labour (and probably even more to twenty-five years of unparalleled worldwide economic prosperity). Conservative ministers in the 1950s and 1960s were as proud as their Labour counterparts to boast of record numbers of council homes built or new schools opened.

But since the mid-1970s broad political agreement on welfare has broken down. The election of Margaret Thatcher as Prime Minister in 1979 owed a lot to public anxiety over the rise of trade union and professional power within the public and welfare services. Her government's economic strategy has decreed a substantial reduction in local government spending on education and housing in order to "free" resources for private industry. The Conservatives have unhooked retirement and supplementary benefits from the retail price index, thus cutting their value in real terms. And other insurance-based items such as earnings-related unemployment benefit have been brought to an end. There has even been talk about scrapping the state pension scheme.

But the scale of welfare provision is being questioned in other countries, too. The American president, Ronald Reagan, has cut federal social programmes; in France there has been a

The Beveridge Plan – what went wrong?

William Beveridge's plan in the 1940s for a universal national insurance scheme, which would pay basic subsistence income in retirement and unemployment, was designed to be financed by a tax on employers and on employees, with limited help from central government funds.

The scheme soon fell through. Flat-rate benefits in exchange for flat-rate contributions turned out not to provide adequate security for pensioners or the long-term unemployed. The back-up national assistance programme did not wither away as was intended; instead means-tested assistance became more and more necessary to supplement the incomes of those whose insurance benefits did not cover their essential needs – especially old people. In 1966, national assistance was renamed supplementary benefit. By the beginning of the 1980s there were five million people on means-tested benefits. That is a measure of the failure of the welfare state.

The tangled web of benefits has, since the Conservative government took office, got even thicker. The lower paid are taxed excessively (the whole income tax system is out of line with the system of social security benefits); child support, especially for poor families where the breadwinner is in a job, is inadequate.

This led Norman Fowler, the Social Services Secretary, to set up a major review of the social security system. This has been hailed by some as a "new Beveridge," but others have seen it as a way for the government to make yet further cuts in welfare spending.

fierce debate about financing social security benefits by increasing employee and employer contributions to social insurance funds.

So what benefits have actually flowed from the huge commitment to welfare of the advanced nations? Looked at in the round, there is no doubt that the welfare state has improved the quality of life in Britain. Some of this improvement can even be measured. Take housing, for instance. Since 1950 successive governments have built an impressive number of council houses – 187000 a year in the 1950s and 144000 a year in the 1960s. In 1950, 63 per cent of dwellings in the United Kingdom had a fixed bath or shower. But in 1975, the proportion was 95 per cent – a quite dramatic improvement.

Education statistics, too, seem to be a clear indication of steadily rising standards. Whereas in the 1950s about 10 per cent of seventeen- and eighteen-year-olds were continuing their education, this had risen to 25 per cent by 1977. The attainment of school-leavers – as measured by their examination passes – and the quality of their teachers – as measured by their years of training – have both also risen. But some people would argue that such figures as these fail to get at the nub of education, which is subjective. They are probably right: this means conclusions about the welfare state's achievements will always be subject to political disagreement.

Improvement in health is also a contentious area. The most basic measure of health is how long people can expect to live – and this has improved dramatically since the Second World War. But other measures of health are more difficult to evaluate. For example, fewer people in Britain die from strokes than twenty years ago, but more now die from lung cancer and heart disease.

Assessing poverty and changes in social security benefits is as complex. By any absolute standard the people defined officially as poor now are better off than those so defined in 1948. But, as Professor Peter Townsend and others have forcefully argued, the numbers falling below official minimum levels have increased both absolutely and proportionately.

Some social security recipients are better off by any standard. The retirement pension paid to a married couple stood at around a third of average earnings in the 1950s, but has now risen closer to a half of average earnings. Some other benefits have also risen in real terms. But not benefits for children. A family with two children aged less than eleven years old receive less in benefit (the real value of family allowance or child benefit, plus tax allowance for a standard rate taxpayer) than they would have done in 1946.

Social security benefits are a jungle – the welfare state itself is responsible for trapping some people in poverty and reducing for others the incentive to enter the official economy to work. Thus the growth of the welfare state in Britain has had important "unintended" consequences. These include, for example, the encouragement given by the benefits jungle and high direct taxation to people to work unofficially in the so-called black economy (where work is done for "cash in hand," and no tax is paid).

The welfare state has been a large-scale job-creation agency itself. Between 1950 and 1982 the total of local government's full and part-time staff in England and Wales rose from 1.3 million to 2.5 million. Central government employment expanded at a slower but still impressive rate. Expansion on this scale has directly benefited one group above others. This includes the sons and daughters of working-class families given access to further and higher education by the reforms of the 1940s and 1950s.

Among other unintended consequences is the growth of non-wage costs of employment. In Britain, national insurance contributions are now a burden to employers and employees alike – in such countries as France these taxes on employment can add up to forty per cent of average wages to the cost of a job. This hits job creation and prejudices employers against new staff; they prefer existing staff to work overtime.

Some writers use examples like youth unemployment to suggest that the stage is set for growing conflict between basic economic "rights" (such as a job) and claims to social benefits. In Britain since 1945 there has grown up, along with welfare rights, a public sense that the state should guarantee full employment. But there is not always a direct connection between the two rights. Those in jobs often resent high levels of taxation or insurance contributions to pay for the social benefits of the unemployed or incapacitated.

Such disenchantment about transfers of income between those in work and those out of work could well grow. The idea of

people who claim welfare benefits as "scroungers" is certainly a popular one. And it is not just the sick and unemployed who are taking what seems to be a larger share of the cake. A recent study by the Policy Studies Institute estimated that the amount transferred to pensioners from the rest of the population could, by the middle of the next decade, cost as much as an additional £8000 million a year.

Conservatives tend to see other conflicts between economic and social rights. Members of Mrs Thatcher's government argue that there is a basic conflict between the pursuit of equality through the welfare state and economic success, which depends on competitiveness and hence on inequality. But this assertion is not backed up by available data.

First, the welfare state has only had a slight effect over the years on inequalities. A recent report by the president of the Royal College of Physicians, Sir Douglas Black, revealed striking differences in the access of working- and middle-class people to health care.

Nor does equality of incomes seem to have much apparent effect on economic performance. In a recent international study, Professor Lester C. Thurow concluded: "There is little or no correlation between these variables and economic performance."

Such evidence encourages those politicians on the left and in the centre, who argue that there need be no conflict between economic and social rights. In Britain in the 1970s there grew up the idea of uniting these rights in a "social contract." Under its terms, trade unions

BOOKS

Some useful additional reading:
E. Butterworth (ed.), *Social Welfare in Modern Britain,* Fontana, 1975
Frank Field, *Inequality in Britain,* Fontana, 1981
P. Morris and M. Rein, *Social Services in Britain,* HMSO, 1976
William A. Robson, *Welfare State and Welfare Society,* Allen & Unwin, 1976
Richard M. Titmuss, *Essays on "The Welfare State,"* Allen & Unwin, 1976
Peter Townsend, *Poverty,* Penguin, 1980

would give up their quest for higher economic rewards for their members in exchange for government policies favouring income redistribution and growth in the "social wage" (welfare rights).

When put into practice by the Labour governments of 1974–79, the social contract came unstuck. However, the notion retains much appeal, especially to sociologists, who have always insisted on a distinction between the welfare state and "welfare society" – meaning social attitudes and behaviour by private individuals, and by groups such as trade unions. To the late William A. Robson, a welfare society would accept various duties as complementing rights enjoyed in the welfare state. Robson's colleague, Richard Titmuss, gave a particularly telling example of such a duty from within the National Health Service – the gift of blood to strangers. At its best, said Titmuss, the welfare state promoted fraternity and the integration of society by encouraging such altruism as the blood donor system shows.

Sadly, few western countries, and certainly not Britain, look like being described as welfare societies in Titmuss's terms by the 1990s.

WOMEN & WORK

A woman has the top job in Britain. Yet Mrs Thatcher's tenure as Prime Minister has led to no great increase in the number of women at the top.

More women are spending more of their lives in paid employment outside the home. Yet most women still see their main job as looking after their families in the home.

Has the movement of women into work changed women's lives? There are two possible views. One is that paid work has changed little. Women are exploited at home. Paid work is merely another form of domestic enslavement.

The other is that work has changed women's lives drastically. It has given them a theoretical equality with men, financial independence and broader horizons. Paid work, in this view, is a form of emancipation.

As usual, the reality is probably somewhere in between. Much of the work women do is poorly paid, dull work, no more exciting than housework. At the same time, it does add money to the family income. And in some cases, it encourages a greater feeling of self-worth in women themselves.

Women now make up a sizeable chunk of the working population. Some ten million women, over forty per cent of the labour force, now do some sort of paid work outside the home.

Since the last war, the increase in the number of women at work has far outstripped the increase in the number of men. From 1951 to 1976, the number of women in paid work rose by three million. In the same period, the number of men in work rose by only 300000. By the late 1970s, nearly two in every three women of working age had a job.

This rapid increase in women's employment has reversed a trend of the past 150 years. From the early nineteenth century to the beginning of the First World War, women were progressively squeezed out of jobs in industry. This happened partly because of objections from men, who thought that women threatened their jobs, and partly because of the campaigning of philanthropic reformers, protesting about the effect on family life. The effect was dramatic. In 1851, one in four married women were employed. By 1911, this had fallen to one in ten.

The two wars brought women back, temporarily, into the labour force. But the real growth in women's jobs has happened recently, in the past twenty years. One of the chief reasons has been women's willingness to go back to work after the birth of their children. In itself, this decision is not new. In the late 1950s and early 1960s, the great majority – nine out of ten women who had had their first child – went back to work. What is new is the speed with which women are returning to work.

Over the past twenty-five years, returns to work have got steadily earlier. Half the women who had a first baby between 1950 and 1954 returned to work within ten years. Half the women who had a first baby between 1974 and 1979 went back to work within four years.

The earlier women return to work after the birth of a child, the more likely they are to seek part-time work. Fortunately, the increase in the number of early returners coincided with an increase in the number of part-time jobs. These grew by a million and a half from the mid-1960s to the end of the 1970s. Most of these jobs have been taken by women. The Office of Population Censuses and Surveys estimated in 1980 that all but six per cent of part-time workers were women.

The growth in part-time work was linked to structural changes in the economy. While jobs in manufacturing declined, jobs in the service sector increased. The service sector is one of what might be called the women's sectors of employment. Women are concentrated in a small number of occupational categories. The 1971 census showed that two-thirds of women in paid work belong to only 3 out of 27 occupational groupings. The 1981 census, which has reduced the groupings to 18, confirms this concentration. These are clerical jobs (33 per cent), service sector jobs (23 per cent) and professional jobs (14 per cent).

Generally, these are jobs with fairly low status. Service sector jobs include charwomen, office cleaners and canteen assistants. Even in the professional category, women's professions are more likely to be the minor ones, like librarianship and teaching, rather than the major ones, such as accountancy and law.

Women's position in teaching shows clearly how, generally, women are related to the lower levels of an occupational hierarchy. Half of Britain's teachers are women. Yet three-quarters of these women teachers work in primary schools. Women dominate the bottom and hardly figure at the top. A report in 1980 by the National Union of Teachers showed that although women provide 44 per cent of the teachers in secondary schools, they provide only 1 per cent of the heads.

The concentration of women in a few

Who does what

	Full time women	Part time women	All working women	Working men
	%	%	%	%
Managerial general	less than 1	less than 1	less than 1	1
Professionals supporting management	2	less than 1	1	6
Professionals in health, education and welfare	16	10	13	5
Literary, artistic and sports	1	1	1	1
Professionals in engineering and science	1	less than 1	1	5
Other managerial	5	1	4	12
Clerical	41	22	33	6
Selling	6	13	9	4
Security	0	less than 1	0	2
Catering, cleaning and hairdressing	10	41	23	3
Farming and fishing	1	2	1	2
Material processing (excluding metal)	1	1	1	3
Making and repairing (excluding metal)	6	4	5	6
Metal processing, making, repairing	3	1	2	20
Painting, assembling, packing	6	3	5	5
Construction and mining	less than 1	less than 1	less than 1	6
Transport	1	1	1	11
Miscellaneous	less than 1	less than 1	less than 1	1

source: Office of Population Censuses and Surveys

categories of occupation, and generally at a lower level, suggests that a sexual division of labour is at work. Women are getting the jobs that society thinks that women ought to do. (An exception is the National Health Service, where 30 per cent of doctors are women. But it is very much an exception.)

The sense of "women's work" – work which is more properly done by women – is reinforced by occupational segregation; that is, women working only with other women. In *Women and Employment: a lifetime perspective* – an Office of Population Censuses and Surveys and Department of Employment survey, carried out by Jean Martin and Ceridwen Roberts in 1980 – nearly two-thirds of a sample of 5500 women of working age worked only with other women, doing the same kind of work as them. Part-timers are even more likely to be segregated by sex. Some 70 per cent of part-timers, compared with 58 per cent of full-timers, worked only with other women.

Naturally, women who are segregated are more likely than those who are not to think of their work as "women's work." They see it as jobs that men either cannot do or would not want to do.

The sort of jobs women only do tend to mirror the unpaid jobs women do at home. They involve looking after children, looking after husbands, preparing and serving meals and clearing up after people generally.

Some studies of women's work have suggested that office work is the business equivalent of housework. They suggest that filing documents is as repetitious and tedious as washing dishes.

Seen in this way, the sexual division of labour at work is simply an extension of the division of labour at home. But it is unlikely to be this simple. Any sort of work outside the home, even if it is only "women's work," is bound to affect the married women's domestic role. Conversely, a woman's domestic role may limit the sort of paid work she can do. It may have to be part-time, for example, and is thus likely to be in the "women's sector" of employment; that is, in the service sector.

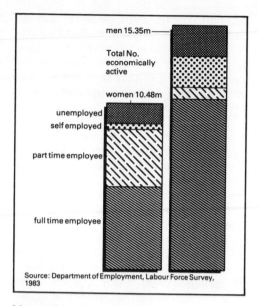

Source: Department of Employment, Labour Force Survey, 1983

Men and women at work

The entry of women into the labour market, therefore, has modified *both* sorts of women's work. The unpaid domestic work, and the paid outside work. In her book, *Redundant Women* (1984) Angela Coyle suggests that women have acquired a "dual role," in which they *combine* paid work and the unpaid domestic work of the family. This modification, rather than transformation of the sexual division of labour between men and women, is the crux of the matter.

The subordination of women in the family allows for a "specific exploitation of women at work." This distinguishes women's work from men's work. It cannot be seen in isolation. Married women with children who want or have to work, do whatever work their *primary* role as housewife and mother allows them to do.

The fact is that society still regards child care and housework as a woman's "real" job. Paid work is less important, and certainly less important than the paid work done by husbands. A majority of women still feel this to be true. The Martin and Roberts survey of women of working age found that "most married women still felt that work was less central to their lives and that a home and children were a woman's real aim and her main job."

Because women with young children

can only take on part-time work, they are unlikely to match their husband's earnings. Even women whose children have left home are unlikely to return to the same level of job that they left to have children. Downward occupational mobility is inevitable.

The Martin and Roberts survey found that only 15 per cent of women of working age earned as much or more than their husbands, and only 15 per cent worked longer hours. In this way, the role of the husband, as primary breadwinner, is perpetuated. A man's real job is outside the home.

This categorisation of husband and wife as "breadwinner" and "housewife and mother" is relatively recent. In her book, *Housewife* (1974), Ann Oakley shows how restrictions on the use of child labour in the nineteenth century began to tie women to the home.

Victorian belief that "a woman's place is in the home" strengthened these ties. Queen Victoria herself said, "Let a woman be what God intended, a help-mate for man, but with totally different duties and vocations." These duties and vocations were principally child care and house-work.

At the same time, men had less and less to do with the running of the home. The factory had replaced the household as the unit of production, and men took paid work outside. So the pattern was established. In theory, the man went out to work, while the woman kept the home (although, in practice, many women did continue working in unrecorded jobs).

Ann Oakley summarises the effects of industrialisation on work patterns thus. It separated men from the daily routine of domestic life. It isolated child care and housework from other work (it became a solitary rather than communal activity). And it made women economically dependent.

There have been other explanations, however, for this subordination of women within the family. Engels suggested that the economic dependence of women on their husbands was part of the control men exerted through monogamous marriage.

Monogamy, Engels said, was a device

by which men who had accumulated wealth could be sure of transferring it to their own children. Keeping one's wife at home was a way of keeping property in the family.

Engels and Marx believed that women would free themselves from this bondage when they took paid work outside the home. They would no longer be economically dependent on their husbands, and the roles of "breadwinner" and "housewife" would disappear.

This has not happened. Studies of married working women in the 1960s showed that paid work had not emancipated women in the way that Marx and Engels predicted. Women still retained the role of home-maker as their primary role. They did not want to take over, or even match, their husband's role as provider. In short, paid work outside was not a dash for freedom.

Modern Marxists have taken a more refined view of the situation. They suggest that women who work represent a "reserve army of labour," which the capitalist system can call on to keep profits up and costs down. Because of their continuing domestic subordination, women have to accept what work they are given and what wages they are paid. Employers can hire them in good times and fire them in bad times.

The "reserve army of labour" is used as

a regulator, Marxists say, to discipline other workers (by threatening them with replacement) and to keep wages low. Paid work, in this view, does not emancipate women. It simply makes them the agent of capitalism.

Yet, from women's point of view, entry into paid work *has* changed women's lives. Expectations about their roles have changed. Women now expect to be able to raise a family *and* continue in paid work. The Martin and Roberts survey suggests that this can be seen most clearly in the way young women without children talk about their future work plans.

Women's attitudes to their domestic role and their working role *are* changing, though slowly. Once, women left the labour market the moment they got married. Then, they left it when the first child arrived. Now, many younger women expect to stay in work, even when they have children.

In spite of the low status of much of women's work, it is assuming an increasing importance in women's lives. Sue Sharpe suggests why in her book, *Double Identity: the lives of working mothers* (1984): "Working today has assumed a more central and continuous place in most women's lives. It has become part of their identity and self-image, and an important component of their relationships with their families, and with the world outside the home."

Women who work, Sharpe says, have a "double identity." A working identity, as well as the identity of wives and mothers. It is no wonder, perhaps, that women are reluctant to give up work, however ill-paid or unrewarding such work appears.

There have been suggestions that, if women gave up work, there would be more jobs for Britain's unemployed. But women's work, as we have seen, is often work that only women can or will do.

There have also been suggestions, notably from Conservative ministers, that women belong in the home, not in the workplace. Patrick Jenkin once remarked that "If the good Lord had intended us all having equal rights to go out and work and to behave equally, you know he really wouldn't have created us man and woman."

In the end, it is the choice that women have, rather than the work itself, that matters. The women's movement argue that it is one of the few real choices women have. They will not give it up easily.

BOOKS

Some useful additional reading:
Ann Game and Rosemary Pringle, *Gender at Work,* Pluto Press, 1983
P. Moss and N. Fonda (eds), *Work and The Family,* Temple Smith, 1980
Anne Phillips, *Hidden Hands,* Pluto Press, 1983
Anna Pollert, *Girls, Wives, Factory Lives,* Macmillan, 1981
Sallie Westwood, *All Day, Every Day: factory and family in the making of women's lives,* Pluto Press, 1984

WORK: THE FUTURE

How much work?

Back in 1830, 70 per cent of the British workforce were employed in agriculture. Today, the figure is down to 3 per cent. Only fifty years ago, more than 50 per cent of the British workforce were employed in the manufacture of goods – now the figure is down to 25 per cent. Services will soon employ 70 per cent of the workforce – the same proportion who toiled on the land only a century and a half ago.

Now Britain is in the midst of further rapid change while unemployment remains stubbornly stuck at a record level. Some see this as merely a transitional problem, which will resolve itself as we move to a new type of economy. But many are beginning to ask such serious questions as: "Where will the jobs of the future come from?"; "What kind of work will be on offer?"; and "Should we forget about paid employment altogether?"

When the microchip gained prominence in the late 1970s, wild predictions were made about its supposedly devastating impact on employment. Books like Chris Evans's *The Mighty Micro* (1979) and Clive Jenkins's and Barrie Sherman's *The Collapse of Work* (1979) attracted much attention with their dire predictions of mass joblessness. Two major reports – one for the British government by Iann Barron and Ray Curnow (published as *The Future With Microelectronics*, 1979), the other for the French government by Simon Nora and Alain Mine (published as *The Computerisation of Society*, 1980) – argued that the microchip would soon become so pervasive that jobs would be replaced by computers on a huge scale. But, as it turned out, the economic recession destroyed many more jobs than the chip did.

In 1983, the Organisation for Economic Cooperation and Development, the rich countries' "club," reported that some 20 million new jobs would have to be created by the end of the 1980s just to hold unemployment stable at 35 million in its 24 member-countries. In the context of rapidly rising unemployment, it's not surprising that some of the more fanciful projections – for example, that only about 10 per cent of the current workforce would be required to do "all the work" by the turn of the century – gained credibility.

All this sparked off a new debate about the social impact of automation, the future of traditional employment and the role of the "work ethic" itself. There were wildly optimistic claims about the job-creating potential of high-tech. The only employment problems, some claimed, would be short, transitional ones.

New technology meant higher productivity, which in turn meant greater wealth and thus more jobs and prosperity for all in the long run. It was not automation itself but the *failure* to automate that risked jobs, said the optimists. Jobs had been created in the past and this would happen again. After all, hadn't the Luddites been proved wrong when overall employment in the British textile industry continued to grow during the nineteenth-century?

It is now clear that neither the pessimists nor the optimists have been proved correct. The onward march of the microchip has been fairly slow. But the shake-out in traditional manufacturing has been more severe than expected and unemployment remains high. According to Warwick University's Employment Institute, only 150 000 jobs will be created in Britain up to 1990. It estimates that the number of full-time employees will fall by 1.1 million while the number of part-timers will rise by 900 000; self-employment will also rise. Manufacturing industry is expected to shed a further 500 000 workers.

The growth in jobs will be less than the rise in the number seeking work, so there will be a slight rise in unemployment. The male unemployment rate is forecast to rise from 15 per cent to over 18 per cent in 1990, while the female rate will decline from 9 per cent to about 7 per cent.

Studies of the job-generating potential of high-tech suggest there is little warmth in the so-called "sunrise" industries. The majority of the jobs of the future will, in fact, be low-tech – in such occupations as cashier, caretaker and secretary. The United States is already pointing the way. High-tech industries in the US, for instance, will only generate between 750 000 and a million jobs in the next ten years – this is less than half the number of jobs lost from US manufacturing industry in the period 1980–83 alone.

The total number of high-tech jobs being created is fairly modest because the entire high-tech sector is relatively small.

Too old at 35?

Philips, the electronics firm, is following the example of Japanese firms like Hitachi by trying to get rid of its older employees. Scientists at its research labs at Redhill, Surrey, who are aged over fifty are being asked to go. Philips are also seeking volunteers among those over thirty five to go or to move to less demanding work since scientists of that age are felt to be past their prime.

Changes in employment 1951–1981 (thousands)

	inner cities	outer cities	smaller cities and larger towns	small towns and rural areas	Great Britain
Manufacturing					
1951–1961	−143	+84	−21	+453	+374
1961–1971	−428	−217	−93	+489	−255
1971–1981	−447	−480	−311	−717	−1929
Private services					
1951–1961	+192	+110	+128	+514	+944
1961–1971	−297	+92	−7	+535	+318
1971–1981	−105	+170	+91	+805	+958
Public services					
1951–1961	+13	+54	+38	+200	+302
1961–1971	+25	+170	+110	+502	+807
1971–1981	−78	+102	+53	+456	+488
Total employment					
1951–1961	+43	+231	+140	+1060	+1490
1961–1971	−643	+19	+54	+1022	+320
1971–1981	−538	−236	−150	+404	−590

source: Economic and Social Research Council

The high-tech industries employ a mere 3 per cent of America's non-agricultural workforce, and this will only climb to 4 per cent by 1995. Rapidly-rising productivity – outstripping that of other industries – will further depress the demand for labour as high-tech firms automate their own production lines.

Confirmation of the fragility of high-tech employment came with the "Great Silicon Valley Shakeout" in the summer of 1985. A series of plant closures, mass lay-offs and extended vacations reversed the California jobs boom.

And it has been the same story in Europe. ICL, Britian's only mainframe computer maker, has seen its payroll decline from 34 000 in 1980 to less than 15 000 in mid-1985. A recent report from Cambridge Econometrics concluded that employment in the British computers, electronics and telecommunications industries was likely to *decline* by about a fifth by 1990, despite a steady rise in output.

While high-tech is only creating a mod-est number of jobs, traditional "smoke-stack" industry – heavy engineering and manufacturing – continues to lose vast numbers of employees. British steel-making, shipbuilding and vehicle manufacturing have been decimated in past decades. There is a growing realisation that these jobs will never come back.

As with most employment patterns, the United States is leading the trend. According to US Labour Department figures, employment in the old "rust bowl" industries such as metals, rubber and chemicals will shrink from 20 per cent of the total American labour force to a mere 8 per cent by 1995. Meanwhile service sector employment will leap from today's 20 million to nearly 29 million.

To take one example, the car industry based around Detroit, Michigan. From 490 000 workers in 1958, employment in car supplier industries rose to a peak in 1978 of 941 000 (output tripled over the same twenty-year period). But fierce Japanese competition and the installation of 25 000 robots (which alone will displace

80–90 000 workers) will mean that employment will be down to early 1960s levels by 1990.

Birmingham, the British equivalent of America's "Motown," has also suffered appallingly. A report published in 1985 by the Economic and Social Research Council showed how the city's industrial base shrank by a third in the 1970s and the 26 largest companies cut their workforce by 40 per cent as the key sectors of manufacturing, engineering and cars declined. In British cities as a whole, employment has fallen 45 per cent in thirty years.

A study for the Manpower Services Commission in Britain, by researchers at the Universities of Aston and Sussex, found that over a million jobs were lost from British manufacturing in 1980–82 alone, compared with 1.5 million over the ten years from 1970 to 1980. Vehicles, mechanical engineering, textiles and clothing suffered declines in 1980–82 of nearly 20 per cent. Their more detailed study of the west midlands, Britain's industrial heartland, concluded that it will be many years before the employment

Mickey Mouse jobs?

According to consultants like the Henley Centre for Forecasting, we can expect to see many more jobs created in the so-called "leisure industries" – everything from McDonalds and video arcades to purpose-built sports and leisure centres. This is certainly the belief of the present Conservative government.

Critics claim these are only "Mickey Mouse jobs" which are usually part-time, low-skill, low-paid and insecure. But others say that skill levels are increasing and pay is improving. Fast food chains, in particular, have a good record of creating jobs for, and promoting, young black people in the big cities.

And *any* sort of job is not to be sniffed at: Alton Towers, the Staffordshire leisure park, has 400 permanent and 600 seasonal employees, while the new Disneyland-style development proposed for London's Battersea power station may be able to create 4500 jobs in the centre of London.

gains from new high-tech industries can begin to offset the enormous losses from the old heavy industries. In sectors as diverse as textiles, paper, rubber, food and drink, coal mining and consumer goods, labour-shedding is the order of the day.

As Peter Caudle of the British Chemical Industries Association put it in 1984, "The whole ethos now, I'm afraid, is to boost production without bringing back jobs which have been most expensively shed." Doug Hall of Hall Automation, Britain's only robot-maker, confirmed that "Many large companies are pursuing a policy of de-manning." The Austin Rover chairman, Harold Musgrove, recently said: "The day is not far off when entire areas of our plants will run automatically with minimal human supervision night and day, seven days a week."

In recent years, the way the Americans have been creating jobs has become the envy of the world. Unemployment in Europe has risen to record levels, but in America it has been falling. Between January 1983 and June 1984, the US economy generated four million new jobs. Over the period 1973–83, the US gained thirteen million jobs, while Europe suffered a net loss of three million. In the first two months of 1984, the US had created more jobs than the EEC has generated in the past fourteen years.

Of the total US workforce of around 105 million, roughly two-thirds are now in the service sector. The largest employment increases have been in business services (up 35 per cent), health (up 19 per cent), eating and drinking (up 14 per cent) and finance, insurance and real estate (up 12 per cent). The "eating and drinking" category includes the five-million-job fastfood sector. This is an area that the British government is eagerly trying to emulate. So much so that Mrs Thatcher's jobs minister, Lord Young, has been dubbed "the minister for fast food."

There are several reasons why America has been able to create so many jobs. A rising population has helped increase labour demand as well as supply, because each extra person has needs that take another to fill. Gross domestic product has been growing – thanks in part to greater productivity in farming and manufacturing – with the result that people have been consuming more services. But slow productivity growth in services has meant that service jobs have increased roughly in line with the increased demand for services. Foreign competition is also not so much of a problem in services – you can't import the services of a hairdresser – so increased demand again feeds directly into employment creation.

A high proportion of the new service jobs in the US have been generated by small business. The American genius for entrepreneurship – spotting business opportunities, figuring out new ways of making money – has come to the fore and stands in stark contrast to European complacency and pessimism. According to Professor David Birch of Massachusetts Institute of Technology, small companies in the US with fewer than 500 employees created no less than 2.7 million jobs between 1980 and 1983. In California, they account for 70 per cent of all new job growth.

Labour market flexibility – in contrast to European rigidity – has enabled America to adapt more rapidly to the new economy. Wage rates have gone down as well as up – real wages actually fell an average 11 per cent during the 1980–82 recession – with some industries, like airlines, recording massive cuts. This has enabled companies to retrain or recruit more labour after temporary lay-offs. In Europe, where wage-cuts and lay-offs are much less common, companies have preferred to substitute capital for labour wherever possible.

Labour mobility is also much greater in the US – no fewer than one in six Americans now move house every year. Most Europeans, on the other hand, are much less willing or able to move in search of work which might not be there anyway.

But in both Europe and America, there are growing doubts about the continuing capacity of the service sector to create so many jobs. In Britain, where manufacturing is down to 25 per cent of employment, there is evidence of a declining rate of job creation in the service sector.

In the US, both the General Accounting

The winners and losers

There has been no instant industrial revolution, no mass shut-out caused by automation alone. But the *pattern* of employment in Europe and America has been changing swiftly and significantly. In fact, the occupational structure has become a shifting mosaic of industrial winners and losers, the job market a mixture of dead ends and bright prospects.

Top gainers in Britain and the United States between now and 1995 are predicted to be computer systems analysts (whose numbers are expected to double). But in terms of total numbers, secretaries and shop workers are likely to do best.

Top losers are likely to be postal workers (down by a fifth – victims of technology) and college lecturers (down by an eighth – victims of government policy and falling rolls). Compositors and farmworkers are also likely to do particularly badly.

Office and the Bureau of Labour Statistics have questioned whether office and service sector employment will still expand once new technology begins to penetrate in a big way. In another study, Charles Jonscher of MIT predicted that jobs in the "information" sector will not increase as rapidly as they have done in the past. New capital investment in the service sector will lead inevitably to pressure on service sector jobs. "What we are seeing," wrote Irving F. Leveson of the Hudson Institute, "is the rapid industrialisation of the service sector." In particular, the growing practice of franchising – from Kentucky Fried Chicken to Dyno-Rod – is making possible the mass-production of services.

Economists can't seem to agree whether rising service-sector productivity will be good or bad for employment. Some say that average service-sector pay will remain at about 70 per cent of the manufacturing average and service-sector productivity will stay low, thus inhibiting economic growth. Others say that more productive, better-paid service-sector jobs are coming along.

Most seem to accept that the service sector can't go on expanding indefinitely without a strong, underlying industrial base. But where is that going to come from?

The new ways of working

For the first time in history, white-collar workers now outnumber blue-collar workers in Britain. Between 1973 and 1983, the shift from traditional manual to professional, managerial and clerical occupations meant that non-manual jobs grew from 43 per cent to 52 per cent of all jobs.

But this transition to a non-manual majority is not the only fundamental change that's taking place in the British pattern of employment:

● **SELF-EMPLOYMENT.** More of the British workforce are self-employed than at any time since 1921. In 1984, the total reached 2.5 million, a 32 per cent increase since 1979. The self-employed now account for roughly one in ten of the UK workforce and self-employment is becoming more common among men and women and young people – for obvious reasons!

● **PART-TIME WORKING.** No fewer than one in five of the UK workforce are part-time workers and the figure is expected to reach one in four by 1990. The number of part-timers has doubled in the past twenty years to 4.5 million. Two out of three part-timers are women.

● **FLEXI-WORKING.** Flexible working arrangements are on the increase, according to the Department of Employment. This is creating new patterns of working time – shorter working weeks, flexible working hours, even flexible working years.

● **HOMEWORKING.** One of the most interesting – and potentially most revolutionary – developments has been the big increase in homeworking or "telecommuting" by professionals like computer programmers. In Britain, there are 1.7 million homeworkers, who now account for 7 per cent of the workforce. In the US, where the figure is now more than 10 per cent, some 240 companies are running homework schemes.

It is said that the first industrial revolution destroyed the cottage industries and took people out of their homes and into the new factories. Now the information technology revolution is enabling people to return to their homes. But do they want to?

Severe doubts are being expressed about the *quality* of much of this new employment. Service sector jobs generally are lower-paid and offer few fringe benefits. Part-timers in particular are much less likely to get sickness benefit, paid holidays or occupational pensions. They have little job security and are more likely to be used as pools of temporary labour to be taken on and laid-off at the employer's whim or as demand dictates.

In the US, this trend to voluntary (and often involuntary) part-time work is creating a new stratum of second-class citizen, which now accounts for 20 per cent of the labour force. Some employers have welcomed the trend, seeing it as an easy way to cut labour costs in the face of foreign competition. But union leaders are fighting back against efforts to replace full-timers with part-timers.

Recent research in Britain, by Nick Bosanquet at City University and John Atkinson at the Institute of Manpower Studies, Sussex University, has identified a growing gulf between what are called "core" and "periphery" workers. Inner "core" workers are full-timers with secure jobs, who enjoy good terms and conditions of employment. The outer "periphery" workers are typically on temporary contracts or are working part-time, self-employed or are employed by sub-contractors.

Core workers are "functionally flexible" – in return for security and decent conditions, they are expected to do whatever work the company demands. The periphery, in contrast, is hired to do specific jobs and fired when not needed – they are "numerically flexible." The evidence from industry and commerce is that this two-tier job system is likely to become more common in the future.

A lot of work in the future – whether in factories or offices – will involve the use of

What is work anyway?

As the future of paid employment has become more problematical, sociologists have taken a new interest in what has been termed the "informal economy." The informal economy covers work done which is not traditional paid employment and consists of two main areas:

● The "grey" economy of work done for free at home (including housework) and voluntarily in the community. Do-it-yourself and the use of new home and garden gadgetry are part of the grey economy.

● The "black" economy, or hidden economy, of work which should be part of the formal economy but is done for cash on the side or "off the books" (that is, without the Inland Revenue knowing about it).

The black economy is small and illegal, while the grey economy of the household and the community is legal and large, involving almost all adults. Richard Rose estimated that the grey economy might account for 51 per cent of all labour hours, compared with 46 per cent in the formal economy and 3 per cent in the black economy.

Other estimates have put the size of the black economy as high as 7.5 per cent of GNP in Britain, 10 per cent in the United States and 20 per cent in Italy. But many now think that reports of the death of the formal economy have been very much exaggerated.

Some have argued that the black economy is bound to grow as the unemployed and the under-employed do more work on the side for others and do more DIY-type work for themselves round the house. But this theory has been knocked on the head by R. E. Pahl's recent study of households on the Isle of Sheppey in Kent (*Divisions of Labour*, 1984), which found that it was the already-employed rather than the unemployed who did more work around the house and more "self-provisioning" such as winemaking and beer brewing. The unemployed were, on the whole, apathetic, and lacked DIY equipment.

Not only is the grey economy of household and community work bigger, it may have a much longer-term significance for the future of paid employment. For example, in his book, *After Industrial Society? The emerging self-service economy* (1978), Jonathan Gershuny pointed out that capital goods in the home like washing machines, microwave ovens, hover-mowers and videos were being substituted for services purchased outside the home from laundries, cafes, gardeners and cinemas.

● A note on housework: recent research by Erik Arnold and Wendy Faulkner of the Science Policy Research Unit at Sussex University has found that the amount of time spent on housework has *not* declined in the past fifty years, despite the increased availability of modern "labour-saving" appliances.

Whatever the truth about the exact size and significance of the black economy and the grey economy, we should remember that there is more to work than paid employment. Jobs are important, but, as psychologists, perhaps, rather than sociologists, would point out, they are not the only way a person can contribute to society, make friends or find an identity.

---

computers. But sociologists disagree about whether computer-mediated work will be degraded and de-skilled or whether working with new technology will increase job satisfaction.

Harry Braverman, in his influential *Labour and Monopoly Capital: the degradation of work in the 20th century* (1974), argued that every effort by employers to introduce new technology and redesign jobs is merely an attempt to increase managerial control in order to squeeze more profit out of their employees.

More recently, in *Work Transformed: automation and labour in the computer age* (1985), Harley Shaiken argues that the new jobs being created in the "factories of the future" are often every bit as tedious, high-paced and stressful as the old assembly line jobs they are designed to replace. His studies for the US Office of Technology Assessment found that machine tool operators had been "de-skilled" by the removal of their decision-making power to office-based programmers. Employers, he says, are now looking for *less* skilled workers to mind machines.

Central, computerised monitoring systems keep an eye on work progress, further eroding the skilled machinist's autonomy. This, says Shaiken, has hidden costs because "degrading the work people do ultimately demeans their lives – a cost that is seldom figured in calculations as to which system is more efficient."

In a similar vein, David Noble, in *Forces of Production* (1985), argues that attempts to boost productivity are simply part of the ongoing power struggle between management and workers on the shop floor.

But these one-sided Marxist accounts rarely stand up to scrutiny. The main trouble is that they tend to see a conspiracy where there is none. Academic engineers have developed new systems in order to improve productivity, not necessarily to get one over on the workers. Surveys have shown that most engineers and draughtsmen *prefer* to work with computer-aided-design systems. Even Shaiken has to admit that machine tool operators in his study "generally preferred" the newer machines and that the new technology tends to make work "cleaner and physically lighter."

Likewise, the two prolific British critics of the new world of work, Professor Howard Rosenbrock of the University of Manchester Institute of Science and Technology and Mike Cooley, author of *Architect or Bee?* (1980), have similarly had their "de-skilling" arguments undermined somewhat by recent studies. For example, a study for the Engineering Industry Training Board found that computer-aided designs had not reduced the status of drawing office staff. Cooley's wild speculations about employers increasingly turning to "mentally handicapped" employees have not been borne out by events, nor are they likely to be.

Two British symposiums, *Information Technology in Manufacturing Processes,* edited by Graham Winch (1983), and *Job Redesign,* edited by David Knights, Hugh Willmott and David Collinson (1985), tend to steer a middle course between the "conspiracy theory" of the Marxist "labour process" arguments and the naive belief that all changes are being made with the interests of workers are heart.

Employers are not by any means simply motivated by a desire to "control" their workforce. The choice of new technology is dictated by competitive market pressures and traditional managerial ideologies as much as power relations in the workplace.

Some deskilling may occur, but this need not necessarily be so: "There is no single tendency towards deskilling or reskilling," writes Winch. There is a great deal of room for manoeuvre or "strategic choice" as to which type of technology to adopt and how work is organised.

Marxist critics have also had much to say about the "office of the future" scenario, which envisages today's paper-shuffling drudgery being replaced by relaxed, open-plan offices and banks of blinking computers and smooth-running word processors. The critics say that the office-of-the-future is more likely to be like the factory-of-the-past, with regimented ranks of operatives toiling in silent, soul-less information processing areas.

Certainly, the trend in offices since the turn of the century has been away from the formal to the informal, as Alan Degado made clear in his social history of the office, *The Enormous File* (1979). The introduction of office automation might herald a return to those "bad old days" of highly-regulated work. But this puts a

BOOKS

Some useful additional reading:

Tom Forester (ed.), *The Information Technology Revolution,* Basil Blackwell, 1985

Jonathan Gershuny and Ian Miles, *The New Service Economy,* Frances Pinter, 1983

Charles Handy, *The Future of Work,* Basil Blackwell, 1984

Kevin Hawkins, *Unemployment,* Pelican, 1984

Robert R. Reich, *The Next American Frontier,* Penguin, 1984

Diane Werneke, *Microelectronics and Office Jobs,* International Labour Office, 1983

Shirley Williams, *A Job to Live,* Penguin, 1985

halo around the contemporary "social office" which is not, in fact, particularly popular with office workers, according to most surveys. Badly-designed open-plan offices are particularly disliked because of the constant interruptions.

New office technology and the working environment that goes with it is also proving popular with at least some groups of workers. A survey last year by the recruitment agency, Manpower Ltd, found that three-quarters of qualified private secretaries thought that new technology relieved them of boring, repetitive tasks, enabling them to give more time to interesting, discretionary matters.

Far from leading to a decline of the "social office," high-tech systems might give the office a new lease of life. One American expert, Vincent Giuliano, says that the information-age office is people-centred rather than machine-centred. From their individual workstations, information-age office workers can generate and retrieve information at their own pace. Productivity is improved and so is job satisfaction. Instant access to information and happier staff mean greater customer satisfaction.

Whether the fans or critics of the office-of-the-future are proved right in the long run remains to be seen. The truth is there is no inevitability in either the rosy or the gloomy ways of looking at it. Technology itself doesn't *determine* anything: in a recent study of the introduction of word processing, David A. Buchanan and David Boddy found that changes in the overall pattern of jobs and skills were determined weakly and indirectly by technology, and strongly by management ideas about how work should be organised and controlled.

While the net employment effect of new office technology is to reduce the labour content of many office tasks, most studies emphasise the restructuring of office work: the proportion of jobs requiring technical training and higher skills is increased, while demand for clerks, typists and other workers in routine or semi-skilled jobs falls sharply.

A National Economic Development Office study in 1983 found that the jobs lost through new office technology were the boring ones, such as those of clerk, typist and machine or data processing operator. The jobs gained were more technical, demanding higher skills and training. They also offered greater responsibility, providing employees with a broader view of the company's entire operations.

The big problem is that there may not be enough of these high-skill, high-quality jobs to go round. In offices, we may see a growing polarisation between a high-tech elite of executives and technical specialists, and a diminishing band of old-style, semi-skilled office workers. But outside, there may be a growing army of unemployed knocking on the door.

The era of jobless growth?

In response to the growing doubts about the quantity and quality of the new service jobs, many economists, politicians and businessmen now argue that manufacturing will always play the key role in national economies. Every country needs a strong industrial base because manufactures are more "tradeable" than services.

In 1984, the British government launched a campaign to boost the use of technology in traditional industries, in recognition of the fact that the choice posed between "sunrise" industries on the one hand and "sunset" industries on the other was in reality a false one. The real task was to make manufacturing competitive once again, through the use of new technology, better design, better marketing and new working methods. After all, even the City of London only earns £1 for every £8 worth of exports by British manufacturing, despite everything that has been said about manufacturing's decline.

In the United States, a vigorous debate has developed between the proponents and opponents of a national industry policy. Harvard University's Robert Reich had argued in various books for new government agencies to help regenerate United States industry in the face of the Japanese assault. Critics say there is no point trying to "save" jobs in the old industries. This "prop-up-the-losers" approach has been dubbed by the Massachusetts Institute of Technology economist, Lester Thurow, "lemon socialism." But both sides agree that manufacturing is vitally important: the dispute is rather about how best its future might be secured.

Yet at the same time, in both Europe and the United States, it is also becoming obvious that any expansion of domestic manufacturing – through a general upturn in the economy or through greater competitiveness – is unlikely now to create many jobs. The weight of evidence suggests we are faced with a new phenomenon: *jobless growth*.

This paradox comes about because improved productivity and the installation of new technology reduces the demand for labour even as output increases. There is much spare capacity in industry, and firms are not about to take on a lot of new labour which had only recently – and expensively – been shed.

A comprehensive new study of the employment effects of new technology by Dan Finn, published by the Unemployment Unit, concluded that we are unlikely to see any significant growth in manufacturing employment because increases in demand stimulate the development of new production processes which require fewer workers. Professor John Constable, director-general of the British Institute of Management, was more blunt: he stated, "I do not believe manufacturing is going to create any new jobs in this country for a very long time – or possibly ever again."

The solution to unemployment does not therefore seem to lie in a general inflation. Policies which worked in the 1950s and 1960s now seem inadequate in the new era of jobless growth.

THE WORKING CLASS

Why bother to talk about the "working class?" In modern British society, few people own much in the way of wealth or property, and most of us have to sell what labour power we possess in return for wages. In this sense, aren't we all workers now?

Though some politicians like to see life in these classless terms, most sociologists would argue that things are not quite so simple, and that a distinct working class is still alive in Britain, with its own separate economic and cultural identity.

Writing over a century ago, Karl Marx (1818–83) made what has turned out to be the most influential study of class in modern society. He argued that a capitalist society like Britain was divided into two groups – the bourgeoisie, who owned the mines and factories and other means of production, and the working class (or proletariat), who sold their labour for wages and enabled the capitalists to make their profits.

Clearly, things have changed today – the man who runs the National Coal Board doesn't own it, he's on the wage bill like the miners. But there are still powerful divisions in society that Marx would probably recognise – the status, economic position and way of life of the people who do the actual work, producing the goods and services, is sufficiently different from those who do the organising to make them into a social group of their own.

A contemporary sociologist, Anthony Giddens, identifies three classes in British society:

● An upper-class based on "the ownership of property"

● A middle-class "based on the possession of educational and technical qualifications"

● A working-class "based on the possession of manual labour power"

Obviously, not everyone fits neatly into these categories – the fact that Princess

Margaret's son, Viscount Linley, is a carpenter does not make him working-class any more than a bus driver who wins the pools becomes upper-class. But there are important generalisations that can be made about the manual working classes.

For instance, though a schoolkeeper may earn as much as a schoolteacher, or a printer as much as a journalist, their *life chances,* as sociologists term it, will almost certainly be worse. In terms of job security and prospects, working conditions, health, housing, education and mortality, semi-skilled and unskilled manual workers (the Registrar General's classes IV and V) come off worst. Indeed, the working classes are the ones most likely to be *out* of work.

WORK is the place where most of the working class's disadvantages are apparent:

Career patterns: A young hospital doctor might earn the same as a man digging the road, but there the comparison ends. The doctor will become more skilled, will get promoted, and have a steadily rising income until he retires. If the road-digger is in his mid-twenties, he may already be on his peak earnings, with the prospect ahead of them only tailing off.

Job security: Though recession has made redundancy familiar to white-collar workers, it is still manual workers who are most hit by lay-offs, mass sackings and short-time working. Currently about a third of unemployed men are general labourers. Though legislation against arbitrary dismissal and the decasualisation of industries like dockwork have improved things since the war, manual workers can still expect to be made redundant several times in a lifetime.

Working conditions: Though the standard working week has been reduced since the war, the number of weekly hours put in by manual workers has hardly changed since the 1930s. This is because of the need for overtime to supplement low basic wages. In 1978, for instance, the average week for a manual worker was 46 hours, compared with 38 hours for his white-collar counterpart.

Manual workers are also worse off in respect of holiday allowances, sick pay, penalties for lateness, and so on. Though white-collar workers take it for granted that they will get sick pay from their firms, many manual workers still have to resort to state benefits (which are worth considerably less).

Job satisfaction: "It's the most boring job in the world. If I had a chance, I'd leave right away," a car assembly worker told Huw Beynon, when he was researching his book, *Working for Ford* (1973). Obviously, not all manual jobs are as unsatisfying as this, but most studies have found that, in general, manual workers are more powerless, bored and estranged than white-collar workers.

EDUCATION: When the Education Act, 1944, was introduced, bringing in free secondary education for everybody, it was hailed as a great opportunity for working-class children to "get on." Social class was deemed irrelevant to educational opportunity. Yet its effect has turned out, according to a major study by A. H. Halsey and his colleagues (*Origins and Destinations*, 1980), to have benefited the middle rather than the working class. Halsey looked at the educational opportunities of 8000 boys, and found that during the 1950s and 1960s, the chances of the son of a manual worker were little better than his father's had been, thirty years earlier.

HOUSING: The working classes live in the worst housing conditions. One manual household in seventeen, for instance, still has no bath, or has to share. Most, too, are excluded from the private housing market, since saving for and raising a mortgage is generally beyond most families' means. The fact that many have to live in council houses means that they have less choice about where they live, and are vulnerable to the mistakes of the planners – having to live in tower blocks, for example.

HEALTH: Working-class people are the least healthy. Nearly a third of unskilled male manual workers have suffered from long-term illness, compared with a fifth of professional men. The Black report on inequalities in health (1980) showed that a person at the bottom of the class scale is two-and-a-half times more likely to die before retirement age than one at the top.

But it's not just economic and social disadvantage that defines people as working-class. Take this example from Jilly Cooper's book, *Class:*

"Our archetypal working-class couple are Mr and Mrs Definitely-Disgusting. They have two children and live in a council house with walls so thin you can hear the budgie pecking its seed next door. He married young and lived for a while with his wife's parents. After a year or two he went back to going to the pub, football and dogs with the blokes. He detests his mother-in-law. But despite his propensity to foul language, he is extremely modest, always undressing with his back to Mrs DD and even peeing in a way different from other classes, splaying out his fingers in a fan, so they conceal his member."

Obviously, this is a caricature, but what Jilly Cooper is saying is that working-class people have their own culture, beliefs and lifestyle. This comes closer to the ideas of Max Weber (1864–1920) than to Marx. (Weber believed that society was divided up into *status groups* rather than social classes in a strict economic sense.)

There have been many accounts of working-class culture this century, ranging from the novels of D. H. Lawrence and Walter Greenwood and the essays of George Orwell to modern creations like *Coronation Street* and Andy Capp. But it wasn't until the 1950s that sociologists "discovered" what a rich cultural seam working-class life contained. Richard Hoggart's *The Uses of Literacy* (1957), describing his working-class upbringing in Leeds, was very influential in getting people to treat working-class culture seriously.

At the same time, Peter Willmott and Michael Young set up their Institute of Community Studies in London's Bethnal Green, and found that far from being isolated by big city life, the urban working classes had powerful traditional communities of their own. These "urban villages" were based on neighbourly values rooted in pubs, corner shops, darts leagues, brass bands, Sunday schools and working men's clubs.

But no sooner had the ink dried on this research than the planners of the 1960s started to change the picture. Swathes were cut through the old back-to-back terraces of the inner cities, and whole communities were decanted into new housing estates or tower blocks, often in disregard of community networks that had taken generations to create. Traditional industries like mining and shipbuilding went into decline. And television, fashion, advertising and pop music seemed to be creating a common, classless culture.

This has led some modern commentators to suggest that the working-class "way of life" is dead and that sociologists of the 1950s were merely taking a romantic snapshot of a doomed culture.

But, this is an oversimplification. For instance, the following account of working-class attitudes, from *The Uses of Literacy,* is as accurate today as it was then:

"*They* are the people at the top, the highers up, the people who give you your dole, call you up, tell you to go to work, fine you, get yer in the end, aren't really to be trusted, talk posh, are all twisters really, never tell yer owt (e.g. about a relative in hospital), clap yer in the clink, will do y'down if they can, summons yer, are all in a click together, treat y'like much."

As Jilly Cooper points out, "Jack may be getting nearer his master financially, but social stratification remains incredibly resistant to change. It takes more than jeans and pop music to make even the young all one class." A glance through the *General Household Survey* shows how different working-class tastes are, in the ways people spend their time and money, the newspapers they read and the sports they take part in.

For instance, manual workers are more likely to go in for football, billiards and darts; professionals for walking, table tennis and swimming. The working class are more likely to "go out for a drink"; professionals to "go out for a meal." Manual workers, true to the stereotype, are most likely to read the *Sun,* the *Mirror* or no

newspaper at all.

The classic inquiry showing the enduring nature of "working-classness" was John Goldthorpe and David Lockwood's study of Luton car workers, published in 1968 (*The Affluent Worker*). This came at a time when the *embourgeoisement thesis* was enjoying great popularity. The idea, put forward initially by Ferdinand Zweig, was that once working-class people became better off materially, they would throw up their old class values and join the middle class. It seemed particularly appealing during Harold Macmillan's "never-had-it-so-good" era, and was widely accepted as a reason why Labour lost in the 1959 general election.

Goldthorpe and Lockwood put the theory to the test by looking at the attitudes of 229 highly-paid manual workers in the prosperous town of Luton, in terms of their view of work, their relationships in the community, their social aspirations and their political views. If affluent workers *were* joining the middle-classes, then their attitudes should be similar to white-collar workers in all these areas.

In fact, Goldthorpe and Lockwood found the embourgeoisement thesis to be unproven on almost all counts. The Luton workers saw their jobs in *instrumental* terms – as a means of earning money to enjoy a higher standard of living outside work, rather than as a career. Few got any job satisfaction or had any commitment to the company in the way a white-collar worker might have.

Nor did they adopt a middle-class lifestyle when they left the factory gates. Though many of them owned their own houses and lived next to white-collar workers, they chose their friends from their own class. They saw "getting on," not in middle-class terms of occupational prestige, but in largely material terms of having more money and possessions. There was no sign of a shift to the Conservative Party: most had allegiance to Labour "as the party for which the manual worker would naturally vote."

Goldthorpe and Lockwood's conclusion was that rising affluence does not bring about any fundamental changes in the class structure. It may influence incomes, possessions and the type of area in which people live. But these changes do not necessarily alter the stratification system.

However, being seduced by affluence is hardly a major problem for the working class in the 1980s. The post-war process, noted by John Goldthorpe and others, whereby the middle class was growing at the expense of the working class, has come to an end. Recession has brought an unemployment level of more than three million, and recent technological changes in society – the so-called "microchip revolution" – mean that we might never go back to full employment again.

As for those who still have jobs, the repercussions of the new technology will be wide-reaching. In an influential study at the end of the 1950s (*Class and Class Conflict in an Industrial Society,* 1959), Ralf Dahrendorf predicted that it would no longer make much sense to talk about the working class, since it was becoming increasingly heterogeneous. He argued that "increasingly-complex machines require increasingly-qualified designers, builders, maintenance and repair men and even minders."

But the advent of micro-computers has brought technology a long way since Dahrendorf wrote this. Cars are now being built by robots which are themselves designed by computers. There have been major industrial disputes recently centring round the deskilling of "crafts" like printing and train-driving. In this sense, Marx may have been more correct, when he predicted that technical developments would mean the disappearance of craftsmen and tradesmen and that the bulk of the working class would become unskilled machine minders.

But Marx and his followers seem to have been wrong in their predictions about the future of the working class. According to the Marxist view, the working class eventually recognise the reality of their exploitation, and realise that only by collective class action will their opponents be overthrown. The working class becomes a "class for itself" and the result is a revolution.

Yet no revolution has happened in the advanced capitalist societies. Nor, despite record unemployment and a government that has cut welfare and legislated against the unions, is there any sign of one here.

Indeed, far from the working class becoming more class-conscious, the opposite seems to have been happening. Since 1966, the Labour vote in general elections has been declining. And in spite of an increase of six million voters between 1945 and 1979, Labour's highest total vote since the war was in 1951. One of the major factors in the party's defeats in 1979 and 1983 was the fact that only half the trade unionists who voted gave their vote to Labour.

The working class's response to the present crisis seems to have been less militancy, rather than more. And where there has been a stand – such as in the miners' strike or the stand by Liverpool councillors against a rate rise in 1985 – it has usually ended in disarray. Most unions have, in effect, acquiesced in wage cuts by agreeing to pay settlements below the rate of inflation.

Why, then, has the British working class failed to develop the sort of consciousness that would spark off revolutionary change? Sociologists have come up with several theories to explain its docility:

IMMEDIATE MILIEUX: The British sociologist, David Lockwood, argues that a unified class consciousness has failed to develop because workers have different images of society depending on their *immediate social milieux* – in other words the sort of social relationships they have at home and at work. "For the most part," Lockwood writes, "men visualise the class structure of their own society from the vantage points of their own particular milieux, and their perceptions of the larger society will vary according to their experience of social inequalities in the smaller societies in which they live out their daily lives."

INSTITUTIONALISATION OF CONFLICT: It has been argued, particularly during the 1950s, that a revolution was not necessary, because the working class had been enfranchised and had a power base of its own in a pluralist society. Trade unions were recognised by managements, and the Labour Party had become a party of government, able to further working-class interests without conflict. This view was put forward strongly by the Labour politician, Anthony Crosland, in *The Future of Socialism* (1956), but is not popular now, having given way to the idea of the *incorporation* of the working class.

INCORPORATION THEORY: Instead of the Labour Party and the unions promoting the interests of the working class, several sociologists have argued that their real role has been to contain working-class aspirations so as to avoid any serious challenge to vested interests. At the same time, the illusion is created that working-class interests are being served.

Today, examples of "incorporation" range from the miners' leader, Joe Gormley, accepting a peerage to the "social contract" of the mid-seventies, when the unions accepted a pay ceiling in order to serve what the Labour government of the time called "the national interest."

PRAGMATIC ACCOMMODATION: In *Class, Inequality and Political Order* (1971), Frank Parkin showed how we are exposed to the *dominant value* system of society: establishment ideas and values are successfully disseminated by the major ideological institutions – the mass media, schools and churches. But most people's response to this is neither whole-hearted moral approval nor a full-blooded rejection. They just accept the "system" as an everyday fact of life, because there seems to be no alternative.

Some of the reasons for this pragmatism are as much psychological as sociological – that human nature has a natural tendency to accept the status quo. Parkin even argues that voting Labour can be considered as "deviant."

Certainly, people's innate conservatism seems to be the most commonsense reason why the working class hasn't opted for revolution. "Anything for a quiet life" seems to have been the watchword, rather than "to the barricades." But Marx even has an answer to this: "It is not a question of what this or that proletarian, or even the whole proletariat *imagines* to be the aim. It is a question of what the proletariat is, and what it *consequently* is historically compelled to do." On that, we shall have to wait and see.

BOOKS

Some useful additional reading:
Martin Bulmer (ed.), *Working Class Images of Society,* Routledge & Kegan Paul, 1975
Anthony Giddens, *The Class Structure of the Advanced Societies,* Hutchinson, 1973
Kenneth Roberts, *The Working Class,* Longman, 1978

SUBJECT INDEX